Advance Praise for *Software Security*

"I have been involved with trying to solve security problems for over twenty years—starting with individual desktop systems and transitioning to network security as that became the prevalent issue. I have been an entrepreneur, executive in the industry, and am now an investor and company builder, all focused on trying to solve these important issues. What I have learned over these twenty years is that we have done an okay job at slowing down the problem, but we are no closer to solving the problem than we were when we started.

"Our twenty years of investment has been spent being reactive—trying to 'keep the bad guys out.' The idea has been to build a wall around our companies so high and so thick that no one with nefarious intentions could get in. In today's world this just does not work. We live in a wall-less economy where companies need to allow freedom of communication in and out of their enterprises. Freedom of information access and freedom of application usage are central drivers for staying competitive. In other words, the battlefield has changed. Thus the weapons and tactics we use to secure our assets must change as well.

"The only way I see the security conundrum getting solved is by confronting the problem and not the symptoms of the problem. We need to design and build security in from the beginning. No application, no operating system, no piece of middleware should ever be released that has not already been designed for security and reviewed for security vulnerabilities. Only then will we start to fight these new battles with the correct weapons and tactics that afford us the chance to win.

"I believe so fervently in these concepts that I founded a company called Fortify Software to develop, market, and sell solutions to attack and solve these issues directly. We need to get proactive not reactive, and fix the problems at the root cause.

"Gary McGraw is the father of software security. Much of what we did at Fortify was based on Gary's research. His new book should be the bible by which your company puts software security into action. You cannot afford to wait much longer."

—Ted Schlein
Managing Partner
Kleiner Perkins Caufield & Byers

"McGraw is leading the charge in software security. His advice is as straightforward as it is actionable. If your business relies on software (and whose doesn't), buy this book and post it up on the lunchroom wall. Transform the way you build software with the seven software security touchpoints. Then, finally, maybe I can get some sleep."

—Avi Rubin
Director of the NSF ACCURATE Center for Correct,
Usable, Reliable, Auditable, and Transparent Elections
Professor, Johns Hopkins University
Coauthor of *Firewalls and Internet Security*

"I'm sick of software that's full of stupid security holes. If you're going to write software that I may someday run, you need to read and understand this book.

"Gary's book shows us what we already should know: It's better to build security in when you develop your software. And he shows us how, step-by-step."

—Marcus J. Ranum
Inventor of the firewall
Chief Scientist, Tenable Security

"Gary McGraw's book shows how to combine development and testing to improve the quality of software. In doing so, he presents a framework that software developers, testers, and managers would do well to adopt. Dr. McGraw's knowledge and experience came through well in his earlier books, and this one continues his tradition of improving the state of the art of software security."

—Matt Bishop
Professor of computer science, UC Davis
Author of *Computer Security*

"Methodologies for assurance and assessment are fundamental ingredients of all modern engineering practice. While the development of secure software is an engineering discipline, rigorous assurance and assessment methodologies have been missing. Gary McGraw's *Software Security* is a landmark contribution to this area. Readers who follow its principles will not only get things done, they will get them done right."

—George Cybenko
Dorothy and Walter Gramm Professor of Engineering
Dartmouth College

"With this boon comes a curse: unintended interactions and security flaws. For almost everyone working on data security problems today, myself included, our main challenge is finding cost-effective ways to deliver the most functionality with the minimum risk. Excessive paranoia can paralyze a company or development team. At the same time, disasters are common; my company's customers have lost billions of dollars as a direct result of preventable software defects. Achieving the right balance is not easy.

"Cryptography (my area of specialty) is often hailed as a possible savior. On first blush, this seems plausible: Modern encryption algorithms offer mathematical strength that far exceeds what any attacker can today (or possibly ever) muster. Unfortunately, this is mostly an illusion—cryptographic systems are only as strong as the underlying implementations. My work designing SSL 3.0 highlights this fact all too well. Even though the protocol itself is believed to be solid, a 'lock' icon is hardly of much significance when displayed by a bug-riddled browser running on a spyware-infested computer talking to a compromised Web server. In other words, no matter what tools you use in building a system, your security will still be limited by your ability to build robust software.

"Clearly, some approaches do not work. The worst problems often arise when engineering techniques that work well for implementing features are misapplied to security. Traditional software development is an iterative cycle of writing code, then finding and correcting problems. The result is an evolutionary process that favors desirable functionality and removes the *visible* bugs. Unfortunately, most security flaws are invisible to conventional testing. As a result, many engineers' intuition will say that a system is sound when it is not.

"Ultimately, tackling the software security problem is easier said than done. You won't find any magic bullets (there aren't any), but this book provides one of the clearest strategies I've seen for coping with complexity."

—Paul Kocher
President and Chief Scientist
Cryptography Research, Inc.

"Software security is a continual process, requiring first an understanding of the issues. To be effective, this understanding and knowledge must then be incorporated into the software development lifecycle including design, coding, testing, and deployment. Several years ago I helped build a security analysis tool for Windows NT, called NtSpectre. We built the tool to analyze the security configuration of servers designed for an online game played for money. The game idea remained simply an idea, but our tool developed a nice cult following, and my understanding of the layers of security and their complexity grew considerably. This experience left me with one main philosophical and practical approach to software development, and software security specifically—test, neither assume nor guess.

"This book puts software security in its place, integral to your software development process. Whether you're agile, extreme, rational, or perhaps teetering at the top of a waterfall, this book will guide you in building security into your methodology. Theory and abstractions aside, Dr. McGraw concretely describes actual, and scarily common, security vulnerabilities he has encountered in the field. He goes on to show that security issues are inherently related to gaps in the development process, and expertly guides you to improvements in that process."

—Erik Hatcher
Developer, eHatcher Solutions, Inc.
Coauthor of *Lucene in Action*

"One of the most important ways we can solve information security problems for the long term is by making security part of the 'core DNA' of software development. McGraw's book tells you how to make the 'culture of security' part of your development lifecycle."

—Howard A. Schmidt
President and CEO, R & H Security Consulting LLC
Former White House cyber security advisor

Software Security

Addison-Wesley Software Security Series

Gary McGraw, Consulting Editor

Titles in the Series

Exploiting Software: How to Break Code, by Greg Hoglund and Gary McGraw
ISBN: 0-201-78695-8

Rootkits: Subverting the Windows Kernel, by Greg Hoglund and James Butler
ISBN: 0-321-29431-9

Software Security: Building Security In, by Gary McGraw
ISBN: 0-321-35670-5

 For more information about these titles, and to read sample chapters, please visit the series web site at www.awprofessional.com/softwaresecurityseries

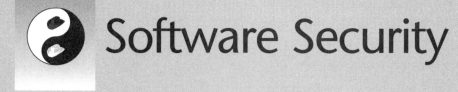

Software Security

Building Security In

Gary McGraw

✦Addison-Wesley

Upper Saddle River, NJ • Boston • Indianapolis • San Francisco
New York • Toronto • Montreal • London • Munich • Paris • Madrid
Capetown • Sydney • Tokyo • Singapore • Mexico City

Many of the designations used by manufacturers and sellers to distinguish their products are claimed as trademarks. Where those designations appear in this book, and the publisher was aware of a trademark claim, the designations have been printed with initial capital letters or in all capitals.

The author and publisher have taken care in the preparation of this book, but make no expressed or implied warranty of any kind and assume no responsibility for errors or omissions. No liability is assumed for incidental or consequential damages in connection with or arising out of the use of the information or programs contained herein.

The publisher offers excellent discounts on this book when ordered in quantity for bulk purchases or special sales, which may include electronic versions and/or custom covers and content particular to your business, training goals, marketing focus, and branding interests. For more information, please contact:

> U.S. Corporate and Government Sales
> (800) 382-3419
> corpsales@pearsontechgroup.com

For sales outside the U.S., please contact:

> International Sales
> international@pearsoned.com

This Book Is Safari Enabled

The Safari® Enabled icon on the cover of your favorite technology book means the book is available through Safari Bookshelf. When you buy this book, you get free access to the online edition for 45 days.

Safari Bookshelf is an electronic reference library that lets you easily search thousands of technical books, find code samples, download chapters, and access technical information whenever and wherever you need it.

To gain 45-day Safari Enabled access to this book:

- Go to http://www.awprofessional.com/safarienabled
- Complete the brief registration form
- Enter the coupon code M2FK-W8BG-APJ1-FQGQ-GMMY

If you have difficulty registering on Safari Bookshelf or accessing the online edition, please e-mail customer-service@safaribooksonline.com.

Visit us on the Web: www.awprofessional.com

Library of Congress Cataloging-in-Publication Data

McGraw, Gary, 1966–
   Software security : building security in / Gary McGraw.
      p.   cm.
   Includes bibliographical references and index.
   ISBN 0-321-35670-5 (pbk. : alk. paper)
   1. Computer security.   I. Title.
QA76.9.A25M4286 2006
005.8—dc22   2005031598

ISBN 0-321-35670-5
Text printed in the United States on recycled paper at R.R. Donnelley in Crawfordsville, Indiana.
First printing, January 2006

To my grandmother Ruth McGraw,
who lives life to the fullest.

Contents

Part III: Software Security Grows Up 237

Foreword

Software is easy to criticize and hard to do. The bigger the software, the more that is true. It is thus like speech—the more you say, the easier it is for the reader to find something to criticize, and the more likely the critic will get it wrong. Brevity may be the soul of wit, but it is wit that is the soul of brevity.

And, indeed, our software is nothing if not loquacious, slang-riven, ill-bred, bloated, and raw. Is it any wonder that software is as prone to misinterpretation as is our language, any wonder that our software, like our language, can be "twisted by knaves to make a trap for fools?" No, it is not, but, as with language, everything we collectively are now depends on software. Software is so very essential that it is unlikely that the world's population would be as great as it now is without software—software to transport, to transact, to transcribe, to translate, to transmit, to transform. In other words, the evidence is unarguable that we have to get software right, just as the evidence is unarguable that getting software right does not, and will not, come naturally.

As Dr. McGraw reminds us, breaking something is easier than designing something that cannot be broken, though I personally prefer Sam Rayburn's earthy formulation, *viz.*: "Any jackass can kick down a barn, but it takes a good carpenter to build one." And that is what makes secure software in particular the pinnacle of concern because the very definition of secure software is that it withstands sentient opponents. Parsing that definition in its contrapositive: If a product does not have sentient opponents, then it does not have security requirements. This is best examined by looking at why products fail—if your product fails because of a collection of clueless users ("Hey, watch this!"), alpha particles, or discharged batteries, security is not your issue. If your product fails because some gleeful clown discovers that he can be the super-user by typing 5000 lowercase As into some prompt, said clown may not be all that sentient, but nevertheless your product has security requirements.

This can't be a completely bright line, but it is an instructive distinction. Secure software is, by definition, designed with failure in mind. Secure software resists failure even when that failure is devoutly wished for by the opponent. Secure software is designed for the failure case as much as or more than the success case. Designers and implementers alike envision an opponent who can think.

As Dr. McGraw says throughout this book, baking in security only happens when there is intent to do so. My father used to scold me when my excuse for this or that was "I didn't mean to do it, Daddy." His stinging comeback, for which I am a better man, was always "But did you mean not to?" Given what I do for a living, I read vulnerability reports every day. Every one of them says, "I didn't mean to do it, Daddy." Sometimes they even try to say, "I didn't do it, but if I did I didn't mean to, and anyway you didn't notice, so all you have to do is install this tiny little fix unless you want what happens next to be your fault; aren't I a good boy?" I want to scream "Did you mean not to?" even though the honest answer will at best be "I thought I meant not to."

There is not enough security expertise to go around. Good people are hard to find, and the need for them rises faster than the supply of them. What do you do when some skill is rare but needful? You convert rare expertise into a process that others can follow, but the kind of process has to be one that reinforces disciplined thinking, avoids patronizing the people on whom it must be imposed, and can be measured sufficiently well to know if it works. Better still if the process is one where you don't have to take all or nothing, where you can get real value out of doing only some of it. Better to do it all, but at the limit any process will have diminishing return so partial value for partial effort is a good thing. Dr. McGraw, describing himself as not naturally a process person, does exactly what I asked for above.

A good idea is one where, once you've heard it, you say, "Well, that's obvious." Much of what you will find in this book has that quality—you will be tempted to say, "Well, that's obvious." For example, the idea that code review is the highest power weapon you can train on software security. For example, that you can't know how much of a fight your software will have to put up when challenged unless you study hard how it might come under intentional abuse. Of course, the process is only good if you use it. Buffer overflows remain the most common attack method, and we've known how to avoid them for years, so knowing what to do is provably insufficient.

You might say, "What makes Cigital's process better than XYZ's process?" For that there is one clear logical response: The question is moot. There is so little effective being done that there must be something wrong. That "something wrong" is either a shortage of skill or a shortage of discipline. If it is a shortage of skill, experts are duty bound to share what works in a way that others can use. There may be many workable processes, but this book shows there is at least one. With this book, the clock is ticking; any continuing failure must trace to a shortage of discipline. We'll know soon enough.

If the reader would prefer some numbers even in the Foreword, here are three: There's a new Windows virus every four hours. Perhaps 15% of all desktop machines are running malware of some sort. Embedded systems outnumber desktop machines by between one and two orders of magnitude, and they are almost never field upgradeable. The *raison d'être* for this book is thus shown useful.

My own research has satisfied me that the spread between the firms with the best software security practices and the worst is growing wider; my best guess is a disparity (measured by ratios of flaw density between best and worst) that is doubling every twelve months. If you believe, as I and Dr. McGraw do, that security is a subset of reliability, you have merely to borrow availability calculus: With five systems components in an e-commerce application, each of which has 98% uptime, you should expect to be down 2.5 hours per day.

Security is to software what mutation is to natural selection, but with the overwhelmingly important difference: With software security you are in control of your survival advantage. If that sounds attractive, adopt at least some of the McGraw/Cigital program. It won't be easy and it won't be fun, but as the U.S. Army Ranger Handbook says:

> *Two of the gravest general dangers to survival are the desire for comfort and a passive outlook.*

Ball's in your court.

Dan Geer
September 17, 2005
Cambridge, MA

Preface

Software security has come a long way in the last few years, but we've really only just begun. Software security is the practice of building software to be secure and to function properly under malicious attack. The underlying concepts behind *Software Security* have developed over almost a decade and were first described in *Building Secure Software* [Viega and McGraw 2001] and *Exploiting Software* [Hoglund and McGraw 2004]. This book begins where its predecessors left off, describing in detail how to put software security into practice.

After completing *Java Security* [McGraw and Felten 1996] and following it up with *Securing Java* [McGraw and Felten 1999], I began wondering how it was that such excellent designers, engineers, and architects went astray when it came to security. What was it about software that made security such a problem? If you wanted to build secure software, how would you do it? These questions and the perseverance of John Viega led to *Building Secure Software*.

Building Secure Software (BSS), the white hat book, seems to have touched off a revolution. Security people who once relied solely on firewalls, intrusion detection, and antivirus mechanisms came to understand and embrace the necessity of better software. *BSS* provides a coherent and sensible philosophical foundation for the blossoming field of software security.

Exploiting Software (ES), the black hat book, provides a much-needed balance, teaching how to break software and how malicious hackers write exploits. *ES* is meant as a reality check for software security, ensuring that the good guys address real attacks and invent and peddle solutions that actually work. The two books are in some sense mirror images.

Software Security unifies the two sides of software security—attack and defense, exploiting and designing, breaking and building—into a coherent whole. Like the yin and the yang, software security requires a careful balance.

Who This Book Is For

Software Security is a "how to" book for software security. In most organizations, software security is nobody's job, when software security really should be everyone's job. Hopefully this book will help explain both why this is so and what to do about it.

The number one audience for the book is *software security professionals*. If your job is to analyze software for security problems, you will find this book filled to the brim with ideas and processes that you can apply today. Software security professionals should seek to use each of the best practices (which I call *touchpoints*) throughout the software lifecycle, follow a risk management framework, and call on software security knowledge. If you're a software security person, I'm afraid you'll have to read the whole book.

As computer security evolves, the job of security analysis gets more complicated. *Computer security professionals* will benefit greatly from Chapters 1, 2, and 9. Chapter 1 provides a discussion of the software security problem and can help justify attention to software security. As philosophy in action, the risk management framework of Chapter 2 is directly applicable to computer security, regardless of software. Chapter 9 in particular was written for computer security professionals who may not necessarily know much about software. Turns out there is plenty for operational security people to do to enhance and support software security. We need your help.

Software developers and architects almost always enjoy learning new things. Hopefully, the lessons of *Software Security* will find their way into many development shops. Software people will probably benefit most from the description of code review and architectural risk analysis in Chapters 4 and 5, as well as the taxonomy of coding errors described in Chapter 12. Of course, all of the best practices described in this book are designed to be directly applicable by those at the rock face (Part II), so benefit should be derived from each chapter in Part II. If you're a coder and you've ever wondered what to *do* about software security other than wring your hands, this book will give you some concrete ideas. Also note that each chapter in Part II includes a Coder's Corner feature that was written with developers in mind.

Business people and technical managers may be surprised that we geeks don't have as much of a handle on the security problem as we should.

Business leadership will benefit from Part I of the book, though it may make you sleep a little less soundly. Risk management comes naturally to business executives, and putting a risk management framework, as described in Chapter 2, in place is very valuable (and can yield useful metrics to boot). Chapter 10 should also prove valuable, especially to upper-level managers worrying about how to transform an organization so that it produces good, solid, secure software.

Academics and researchers will probably appreciate Chapter 12 the most, though I am sure to be flamed to a crisp by some professor or other. The annotated bibliography in Chapter 13 will be useful to new scientists. I would hope that each of the touchpoints provides enough in the way of open questions to spark many a research program.

What This Book Is About

This book presents a coherent and detailed approach for putting software security into practice. Through the unification of proactive design and careful exploit-driven testing built on a foundation of risk management, *Software Security* explains in detail how to properly address software-induced security risk.

The book is divided into three parts. Part I, Software Security Fundamentals, is an updated introduction to the field of software security. Readers of *Building Secure Software* and *Exploiting Software* will find themselves in familiar territory here, though the treatment of the problem has been updated with new numbers.

Chapter 1, Defining a Discipline, begins with an in-depth description of the computer security problem and explains why broken software lies at its heart. This may be old news to some, but the trinity of trouble—connectivity, extensibility, and complexity—deeply impacts software as much as ever. Software is everywhere and is the lifeblood of business and society. Software security is relevant to the kind of software found in your phone, your car, and your washing machine (not to mention your computer and the Web-based applications it makes available to you). For this reason, a critical distinction is drawn between application security and software security. This book is about making *all* software behave, and how to do this in light of modern security demands. The most important material in Chapter 1 is the introduction of the three pillars of software security: applied risk management, software security best practices (touchpoints), and knowledge. Each of the three pillars is a necessity for software security.

Chapter 2, A Risk Management Framework, describes my philosophy of risk management and how to put it into practice. All too often in computer security, risk management is paid only lip service. We know we're supposed to be doing it, but nobody ever says how. Chapter 2 fixes that. A continuous risk management framework encompasses identifying, synthesizing, ranking, and keeping track of risks throughout software development. Only by practicing risk management and factoring in critical business information about impact will software security begin to enjoy the business relevance it deserves.

Part II of this book, Seven Touchpoints for Software Security, is devoted to software security best practices. The touchpoints are one of the three pillars of software security. Attaining software security may not be easy, but it doesn't have to be a burden. By describing a manageably small set of touchpoints based around the software artifacts you already produce, I avoid religious warfare over process and get on with the business of software security. You don't have to adopt all seven touchpoints to begin to build security in (though doing so is highly recommended). The figure on the inside front cover of the book shows the seven touchpoints ordered according to effectiveness and importance. The touchpoints are designed to fill the gap between the state of the art and the state of the practice—something that can be done only through the common adoption of best practices.

Touchpoints are a mix of destructive and constructive activities. *Destructive activities* are about attacks, exploits, and breaking software. These kinds of things are represented by the black hat (offense). *Constructive activities* are about design, defense, and functionality. These are represented by the white hat (defense). Both hats are necessary.

Chapter 3, Introduction to Software Security Touchpoints, provides a flyover of the touchpoints and discusses the critical idea of pushing security as early into the software lifecycle as possible (mostly to save money). I also discuss who should practice software security and how to build a software security group.

Chapter 4, Code Review with a Tool, is about one of the two most important software security best practices. Though not all software projects produce specifications, or even properly document requirements, they all produce code. Bugs (simple implementation errors in code) are responsible for 50% of all software security problems, so finding and fixing security-critical bugs at the code level is essential. Automated code review is a white hat (constructive) activity informed by a black hat history of known defects and exploits. The idea is to avoid implementation problems while we build software to be secure. Code review for security has come a long way in the last few years, and commercial tools are now mature enough to be put in use by all software practitioners. This chapter describes how.

The best practice described in Chapter 5, Architectural Risk Analysis, is just as important as code review. Flaws (architectural and design-level problems) are responsible for the other 50% of all software security problems. Unfortunately, identifying security flaws is more difficult than looking for bugs in code. This is partly because many software projects have only the most rudimentary handle on software architecture, and it's partly because finding software security flaws requires expertise and experience. Architectural risk analysis is a white hat (constructive) activity also informed by a black hat history of known defects and exploits. In this case, we work to avoid design flaws while we build software to be secure. Chapter 5 also describes a mature process for risk analysis developed over the last ten years at Cigital.

Chapter 6, Software Penetration Testing, covers a very common but often misapplied software security best practice. All too often, penetration testing devolves into a feel-good security activity: Security consultants are hired to "hack into" an application, and they almost always find a serious hole (usually in the configuration of the network or the commercial off-the-shelf products the application is built on). The hole gets fixed, and everyone declares security victory and goes home. Usually the developers don't learn anything profound (since the problems found tend to be operational in nature), and worst of all, no real understanding of wholesale software security risk is gained. Penetration testing is a black hat (destructive) activity. The best kind of penetration testing is informed by white hat knowledge of design and risk; but all the penetration testing in the world will not build you secure software. In Chapter 6, I describe an enhanced approach to penetration testing that takes an inside→out approach to testing as opposed to strictly outside→in. This makes penetration testing much more useful.

Chapter 7, Risk-Based Security Testing, is very similar in philosophy to Chapter 6. I discuss an approach to test planning and test execution that is directly aligned to risk analysis results coming out of an architectural risk analysis. I introduce a real-world case study. Risk-based security testing is a mix of constructive and destructive activities that requires a holistic black-and-white approach. Risk-based security testing is driven by abuse cases and risk analysis results.

Chapter 8, Abuse Cases, covers just that. Software security requires the ability to "think like an attacker." Abuse cases help to formalize this activity. Abuse case development is based on understanding and applying known attack patterns and also thinking about anti-requirements. A simple process is introduced to make adoption of abuse cases easier. Abuse cases are tricky. You might guess by the name that abuse cases involve only black hat (destructive) activities. That would be wrong. Abuse cases are themselves driven by the two threads. White hat thinking (constructive) drives security requirements, which are a necessary foundation for a goodly percentage of the abuse cases. Black hat thinking in the form of attack patterns drives the remaining portion. Although abuse cases clearly involve a mix of both black and white hats, the black hat is predominant.

Software security can benefit greatly from experience gained by practicing network security. Chapter 9, Software Security Meets Security Operations, describes how network security professionals can get involved in carrying out the touchpoints, providing experience and security wisdom that might otherwise be missing from the development team. Operations is a white hat activity, but it is only very weakly constructive. Operations is essential to security, of course, but in terms of building security in, the day-to-day tactics carried out by ops people are largely defensive.

Part III, Software Security Grows Up, contains a far-ranging treatment of essential software security knowledge and of large-scale software security programs.

Chapter 10, An Enterprise Software Security Program, describes an approach to the kind of cultural change required to adopt software security in a large organization. Because of this, Chapter 10 is the most business-oriented of the chapters in *Software Security*. There is little doubt that adopting software security touchpoints in a development organization that is running 100 miles an hour is like fixing your engine while your car is zooming down the highway, but it *is* possible. This chapter draws on years of experience at Cigital, helping large companies implement software security programs. A completely integrated Secure Development Lifecycle (SDL) is the result of combining your existing approach to software development with the software security touchpoints.

Chapter 11, Knowledge for Software Security, describes one of the three pillars. This chapter presents a taxonomy of seven knowledge catalogs useful to practitioners: principles, guidelines, rules, vulnerabilities, exploits, attack patterns, and historical risks. These knowledge catalogs are directly applicable throughout the software development lifecycle when you put the security touchpoints into action.

Chapter 12, A Taxonomy of Coding Errors, introduces a classification of common software security bugs. My goal is to make the taxonomy as simple as possible, but still fundamentally useful. Though there are literally hundreds of potential coding problems that can lead to security problems, I find that they fit very nicely into seven "kingdoms." This work hints at the coming maturity of software security, where science and technology begins to dominate over intuition and raw intelligence.

Finally, Chapter 13, Annotated Bibliography and References, has three parts: a list of the top five readings in software security, a complete list of references from this book, and a list of other important references. Each entry includes a sentence or two describing what I find valuable or useful about the reference.

Four appendices round out *Software Security*. Appendix A is a tutorial accompanying the CD that comes with this book. The CD introduces Fortify Software's Source Code Analysis Suite. Appendix B is a very basic list of coding rules from the early source code analysis tool, ITS4. This list serves two purposes. First, a glance through the list will expose you to the somewhat large pile of things that can go wrong in C (at the code level). Second, all source code analysis tools for security must make sure to cover this list. Publishing the list widely makes it more likely they will. Appendix C is an exercise in architectural risk analysis featuring the Smurfs. What more could you want? Finally, Appendix D is a very small glossary of terms.

Icons

The three icons used throughout this book are meant to help you navigate the waters of software security. The icons demarcate material in large sections of the book (chapters and parts).

Fundamental material is covered under this icon (which also adorns the cover of the book). The yin/yang design is the classic Eastern symbol used to describe the inextricable mixing of standard Western polemics (black/white, good/evil, heaven/hell, create/destroy, and so on). Eastern philosophies are described as holistic because they teach that reality combines polemics in such a way that one pole cannot be sundered from the other. In the case of software security, two distinct threads—black hat activities and white hat activities (offense/defense, construction/destruction)—intertwine to make up software security. A holistic approach, combining yin and yang (mixing black hat and white hat approaches), is required.

The three pillars of software security are applied risk management (Chapter 2), software security touchpoints (Part II), and knowledge (Chapter 11). Each of these major sections is marked with the pillar icon.

Seven best practices, the software security touchpoints, are introduced and discussed at length in the heart of *Software Security*. The touchpoints collectively make up one of the three pillars. Each touchpoint chapter is branded with the touchpoint icon.

The Series

This book is part of the Addison-Wesley Software Security Series of software security books for professional software developers. The series includes:

- *Building Secure Software: How to Avoid Security Problems the Right Way*
- *Exploiting Software: How to Break Code*
- *Software Security: Building Security In*
- *Rootkits*

More books in this series are planned for the future. Contact Addison-Wesley or Gary McGraw for more information (see also <http://www.buildingsecurityin.com>).

Contacting the Author

I welcome e-mail from anyone with comments, suggestions, bug fixes, and/or questions. Please contact me through the book's Web site: <http://www.swsec.com>.

Acknowledgments

A central and critical intellectual acknowledgment belongs to my friends and colleagues at *IEEE Security & Privacy* magazine. Many of the ideas in this book first saw the light of day as a collection of articles published over the course of almost two years in my "Building Security In" (BSI) department. A complete list of the BSI articles can be found in Table 0–1.

The now-infamous touchpoints picture, which you might think of as providing the skeleton of this book, originated at a National Science Foundation meeting convened by Carl Landwehr and run by Fred Schneider. Matt Bishop and I built the original picture instead of paying attention during the meeting. A copy of the resulting touchpoints for software security can be found on the inside front cover. The seed idea for this sort of life-cycle-based picture comes from the work of Mike Howard at Microsoft. I adapted the idea to be process-agnostic and based on software artifacts.

I owe a great deal of gratitude to the coauthors who helped me develop the *IEEE* BSI series, putting some flesh on the touchpoint bones. Each of them helped me to create, evolve, and expand the ideas at the very core of this book. I am also extremely thankful for the support of the *IEEE Security & Privacy* editorial board, Dick Price, and Jenny Ferrero. *IEEE Security & Privacy* lead editor Kathy Clark-Fisher went above and beyond the call of duty to help me.

I am grateful for the help of my original BSI coauthors: Annie Anton, Brad Arkin, Sean Barnum, Brian Chess, Paco Hope, Nancy Mead, Bruce Potter, Scott Stender, Dan Taylor, Katrina Tsipenyuk, Ken van Wyk, and Denis Verdon. Some of the chapters in *Software Security* evolved directly out of the *IEEE* BSI articles. Whenever this is the case, the chapter starts with an acknowledgment of the article and names its coauthors.

Table 0–1 List of Articles from the "Building Security In" department
of *IEEE Security & Privacy* magazine

Title	Author	*IEEE Security & Privacy* Citation
Software Security	Gary McGraw	2(2):80–83
Misuse and Abuse Cases: Getting Past the Positive	Paco Hope, Gary McGraw, and Annie Anton	2(3):32–34
Risk Analysis in Software Design	Denis Verdon and Gary McGraw	2(4):79–84
Software Security Testing	Bruce Potter and Gary McGraw	2(5):81–85
Static Analysis for Security	Brian Chess and Gary McGraw	2(6):76–79
Software Penetration Testing	Brad Arkin, Scott Stender, and Gary McGraw	3(1):84–87
Knowledge for Software Security	Sean Barnum and Gary McGraw	3(2):74–78
Adopting a Software Security Improvement Program	Dan Taylor and Gary McGraw	3(3):88–91
A Portal for Software Security	Nancy R. Mead and Gary McGraw	3(4):75–79
Bridging the Gap between Software Development and Information Security	Kenneth R. van Wyk and Gary McGraw	3(5);75–79

I encourage all of my readers to subscribe to *IEEE Security & Privacy* magazine. (Full disclosure: I am an unpaid volunteer on the magazine's editorial board.) For more information, see <http://computer.org/security>. Likewise deserving a tip of the hat and a friendly nod are my *IT Architect* magazine editors Drew Murray and Nancy Hung, who help me deal with the relentless monthly deadline associated with my column "[In]security." Some of the ideas in this book were first explored there. Also thanks to Alexa Weber-Morales and Nicole Garbolino for helping spread the software security gospel at SD East, SD West, and in *Software Development* magazine.

Even after taking into account the help of my *IEEE* BSI coauthors, there are many researchers and practitioners whose involvement was instrumental to this work. I'll take the blame for any errors and omissions, of course.

Brian Chess and Ken van Wyk were particularly helpful in making this book come to life. They both suffered through multiple drafts and always came up with excellent suggestions for improvement. The following people also provided helpful reviews of early drafts: Ivan Arce, Fabio Arciniegas, Richard Bejtlich, Matt Bishop, Kathy Clark-Fisher, Dan Geer, Michael Gegick, Erik Hatcher, Paco Hope, Brad Johnson, Rick Kingsland, Scott Matsumoto, Jim Muller, Gunnar Peterson, Greg Rose, Adam Shostack, Brian Sletten, Roger Thornton, Win Treese, and Stan Wisseman. Ellen Weiner helped me with the process models found in some of the touchpoints chapters. Michal Propieszalski developed the exercise in Appendix C. Brian Chess, Yekaterina Tsipenyuk, and Jacob West (all of Fortify) worked hard on the taxonomy of Chapter 12. Sean Barnum provided an interesting point of view on static analysis rules.

Finally, John Steven has been my right-hand idea person at Cigital for many years. A number of the concepts in this book sprang whole from his mind, and his suggestions for improvement were outstanding. In particular, John's approach to architectural risk analysis and his enterprise information architecture have both been incorporated into the book.

Addison-Wesley continues to be an excellent and necessary partner in the creation of my books (and the complete Addison-Wesley Software Security Series). Special thanks to my editor, Karen Gettman, whose support over the years has never wavered. Also thanks to her assistants, Elizabeth Zdunich and Ebony Haight, and to Chrysta Meadowbrooke, whose persistent copyediting banished many a hobgoblin.

Like my other books before it, *Software Security* has Cigital written all over it. Cigital <http://www.cigital.com> continues to be an exciting and vibrant place to work, where the never-ending effort of making software behave continues to be great fun. Hats off to the management team for putting up with my perpetual travel and writing: Jeff Payne, John Wyatt, Dede Haskins, and John Steven. Cigital's world-class Software Security Group (SSG), founded in 1999, continues to cut new ice in the software security field while helping customers identify and manage millions of dollars' worth of security risk. Paco Hope has been particularly outstanding during the last year. Ryan MacMichael builds and manages all of the Web sites for my books.

Like all of my books, this book is a collaborative effort of many. My friends in the security community who helped form my thinking in one way or another include Ross Anderson, Annie Anton, Steve Bellovin, Matt Bishop, Brian Chess, Bill Cheswick, Crispin Cowan, Drew Dean, Jeremy

Epstein, Dave Evans, Ed Felten, Dan Geer, Virgil Gligor, Li Gong, Greg Hoglund, Peter Honeyman, Mike Howard, Steve Kent, Paul Kocher, Carl Landwehr, Patrick McDaniel, Greg Morrisett, Peter Neumann, Jon Pincus, Marcus Ranum, Greg Rose, Avi Rubin, Fred Schneider, Bruce Schneier, Gene Spafford, Kevin Sullivan, Roger Thornton, Phil Venables, and Dan Wallach.

Thanks to DARPA, the National Science Foundation, and the Advanced Technology Program for supporting my research work over the years. Cigital customers I interact with on a weekly basis and who have influenced my view of security in the real world include Greg Rose, Ricardo Lopez, and Franklin Antonio (Qualcomm), Lance Johnson (Visa), Phil Venables (Goldman Sachs), and Mike Ackerman (Morgan Stanley).

Most important of all, I thank my family. Love to Amy Barley, Jack and Eli, beach moe, Uncle Chris, Walt, Nora and baby Simone, and grandma (who at 96 provides an excellent example for all of us). Shouts to the ever-expanding menagerie: the dog pack (walnut, ike, jocko [back to NH for him!], skillet, and honorary dog Eli), the cat herd (soupy, craig, soupy junes, winston J, struggle, and ghosty), sage and guthrie the sure-footed big guys, moustache the bunny, lewy and lucy the goats, and "the girls" who keep us in more eggs than we know what to do with. Also thanks to my dear friends Rhine, April, Cyn, Ant, Gina, and Aubrey (wherever he is).

About the Author

Gary McGraw, PhD, is the Chief Technology Officer and a Board member at Cigital <http://www.cigital.com>. Dr. McGraw is a world authority on software security and has coauthored five bestselling security books: *Exploiting Software* (Addison-Wesley, 2004) with Greg Hoglund of rootkit.com; *Building Secure Software* (Addison-Wesley, 2001) with John Viega; *Java Security: Hostile Applets, Holes, and Antidotes* (Wiley, 1996) and *Securing Java: Getting Down to Business with Mobile Code* (Wiley, 1999) with Prof. Ed Felten of Princeton; and *Software Fault Injection: Inoculating Programs against Errors* (Wiley, 1998) with Cigital cofounder Dr. Jeffrey Voas. Dr. McGraw regularly contributes to popular trade publications and is often quoted in national press articles. He writes a monthly column on security for *IT Architect* magazine and is a department editor for *IEEE Security & Privacy* magazine.

Working with Cigital Professional Services and Cigital Labs, Dr. McGraw sets software quality management technology strategy and oversees the Cigital technology transfer process. His aim is to bridge the gap between cutting-edge science and real-world applicability and to transfer advanced technologies for use in the field. In addition to consulting with major commercial software vendors and consumers, he founded Cigital's Software Security Group and chairs the Cigital Corporate Technology Council.

Dr. McGraw began his career as a research scientist, and he continues to pursue research in software security. He has written over ninety peer-reviewed technical publications and serves as principal investigator on grants from Air Force Research Labs, DARPA, National Science Foundation, and NIST's Advanced Technology Program. He holds a dual PhD in Cognitive Science and Computer Science from Indiana University, where he was a student of Doug Hofstadter, and a BA in Philosophy from the University of Virginia.

Dr. McGraw is a member of the Technical Advisory Boards of Authentica, Counterpane, and Fortify Software. He serves as an Advisor to the UC Davis Department of Computer Science and the University of Virginia Department of Computer Science, and he sits on the Dean's Advisory Council of the School of Informatics at Indiana University. He is a member of the IEEE Security and Privacy Task Force and was recently elected to the IEEE Computer Society Board of Governors.

PART I

Software Security
Fundamentals

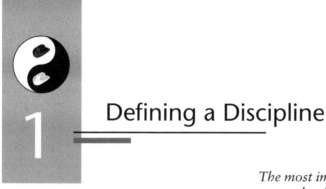

Defining a Discipline

1

The most important thing is to find out
what is the most important thing.

SHUNRYU SUZUKI

Software security—the idea of engineering software so that it continues to function correctly under malicious attack—is not really new, but it has received renewed interest over the last several years as reactive network-based security approaches such as firewalls have proven to be ineffective. Unfortunately, today's software is riddled with both design flaws and implementation bugs, resulting in unacceptable security risk. As Cheswick and Bellovin put it, "any program, no matter how innocuous it seems, can harbor security holes" [Cheswick and Bellovin 1994]. The notion of software security risk has become common knowledge, yet developers, architects, and computer scientists have only recently begun to systematically study how to build secure software.

The network security market weighs in at around $45 billion.[1] However, the 532% increase in CERT incidents reported (2000–2003)[2] and the fact that 43% of 500 companies responding to a popular e-crime survey reported an increase in cybercrime[3] show that whatever we're doing is clearly not working. Basically, the dollars spent on network security and other perimeter solutions are not solving the security problem. We must build better software.

A body of software security literature has begun to emerge in the research community, but in practical terms the practice of software security

---

[1]Network security total market value as reported by the analyst firm IDC in February 2003, Worldwide Security Market <http://www.idc.com/getdoc.jsp?containerId=32391>.
[2]According to data from Carnegie Mellon University's (CMU) Software Engineering Institute's (SEI) CERT Coordination Center (shown in Figure 1–1) <http://www.cert.org>.
[3]E-Crime Watch Survey, 2004. Sponsored by *CSO Magazine,* United States Secret Service, and CMU SEI CERT Coordination Center <http://www.csoonline.com/releases/ecrimewatch04.pdf>.

remains in its infancy.[4] The first books on software security and security engineering, for example, were published as recently as 2001 [Anderson 2001; Viega and McGraw 2001; Howard and LeBlanc 2002]. Today, a number of references do a good job of providing a philosophical underpinning for software security and discussion of particular technical issues, but much remains to be done to put software security into practice. This book is designed to help.

The Security Problem

A central and critical aspect of the computer security problem is a software problem. Software defects with security ramifications—including implementation *bugs* such as buffer overflows and design *flaws* such as inconsistent error handling—promise to be with us for years. All too often malicious intruders can hack into systems by exploiting software defects [Hoglund and McGraw 2004]. Moreover, Internet-enabled software applications are a commonly (and too easily) exploited target, with software's ever-increasing complexity and extensibility adding further fuel to the fire. By any measure, security holes in software are common, and the problem is growing.

The security of computer systems and networks has become increasingly limited by the quality and security of the software running on constituent machines. Internet-enabled software, especially custom applications that use the Web, are a sadly common target for attack. Security researchers and academics estimate that more than half of all vulnerabilities are due to buffer overruns, an embarrassingly elementary class of bugs [Wagner et al. 2000]. Of course, more complex problems, such as race conditions and design errors, wait in the wings for the demise of the buffer overflow. These more subtle (but equally dangerous) kinds of security problems appear to be just as prevalent as simple bugs.

Security holes in software are common. Over the last five years the problem has grown. Figure 1–1 shows the number of security-related software vulnerabilities reported to the CERT Coordination Center (CERT/CC) from 1995 through 2004. There is a clear and pressing need to change the way we approach computer security and to develop a disciplined approach to software security.

---

[4]See Chapter 13 for annotated pointers into the software security literature.

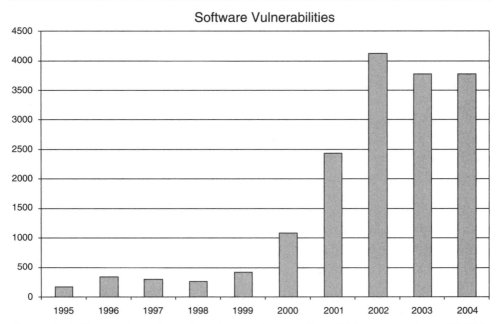

Figure 1–1 The number of security-related software vulnerabilities reported to CERT/CC over several years. Though the widespread adoption of network security technology continues, the problem persists.

Software security is about understanding software-induced security risks and how to manage them. Good software security practice leverages good software engineering practice and involves thinking about security early in the software lifecycle, knowing and understanding common problems (including language-based flaws and pitfalls), designing for security, and subjecting all software artifacts to thorough objective risk analyses and testing. As you can imagine, software security is a knowledge-intensive field.

Software is everywhere. It runs your car. It controls your cell phone. It keeps your dishwasher going. It is the lifeblood of your bank and the nation's power grid. And sometimes it even runs on your computer. What's important is realizing just how widespread software is. As businesses and society come to depend more heavily on software, we have to make it better. Now that software is networked by default, software security is no longer a luxury—it's a necessity.

The Trinity of Trouble: Why the Problem Is Growing

Most modern computing systems are susceptible to software security problems, so why is software security a bigger problem now than in the past?

Three trends—together making up the *trinity of trouble*—have a large influence on the growth and evolution of the problem.[5]

Connectivity. The growing connectivity of computers through the Internet has increased both the number of attack vectors and the ease with which an attack can be made. This puts software at greater risk. More and more computers, ranging from home PCs to systems that control critical infrastructure, such as the supervisory control and data acquisition (SCADA) systems that run the power grid, are being connected to enterprise networks and to the Internet. Furthermore, people, businesses, and governments are increasingly dependent on network-enabled communication such as e-mail or Web pages provided by information systems. Things that used to happen offline now happen online. Unfortunately, as these systems are connected to the Internet, they become vulnerable to software-based attacks from distant sources. An attacker no longer needs physical access to a system to exploit vulnerable software; and today, software security problems can shut down banking services and airlines (as shown by the SQL Slammer worm of January 2003).

Because access through a network does not require human intervention, launching automated attacks is easy. The ubiquity of networking means that there are more software systems to attack, more attacks, and greater risks from poor software security practices than in the past. We're really only now beginning to cope with the ten-year-old attack paradigm that results from poor coding and design. Ubiquitous networking and attacks directly related to distributed computation remain rare (though the network itself is the primary vector for getting to and exploiting poor coding and design problems). This will change for the worse over time. Because the Internet is everywhere, the attackers are now at your virtual doorstep.

To make matters worse, large enterprises have caught two bugs: Web Services and its closely aligned Service Oriented Architecture (SOA). Even though SOA is certainly a fad driven by clever marketing, it represents a succinct way to talk about what many security professionals have always known to be true: Legacy applications that were never intended to be inter-networked are becoming inter-networked and published as services.

Common platforms being integrated into megasolutions include SAP, PeopleSoft, Oracle, Informatica, Maestro, and so on (not to mention more

---

[5]Interestingly, these three general trends are also responsible for the alarming rise of malicious code [McGraw and Morrisett 2000].

modern J2EE and .NET apps), COBOL, and other ancient mainframe plat-forms. Many of these applications and legacy systems don't support common toolkits like SSL, standard plug-ins for authentication/authorization in a connected situation, or even simple cipher use. They don't have the built-in capability to hook into directory services, which most large shops use for authentication and authorization. Middleware vendors pledge they can completely carve out the complexity of integration and provide seamless connectivity, but even though they provide connectivity (through JCA, WBI, or whatever), the authentication and application-level protocols don't align.

Thus, middleware integration in reality reduces to something ad hoc like cross-enterprise FTP between applications. What's worse is that lines of business often fear tight integration with better tools (because they lack skills, project budget, or faith in their infrastructure team), so they end up using middleware to FTP and drop data globs that have to be mopped up and transmogrified into load files or other application input. Because of this issue, legacy product integrations often suffer from two huge security problems:

1. Exclusive reliance on host-to-host authentication with weak pass-words
2. Looming data compliance implications having to do with user privacy (because unencrypted transport of data over middleware and the middleware's implementation for failover and load balancing means that queue cache files get stashed all over the place in plain text)

Current trends in enterprise architecture make connectivity problems more problematic than ever before.

Extensibility. A second trend negatively affecting software security is the degree to which systems have become extensible. An extensible system accepts updates or extensions, sometimes referred to as *mobile code* so that the functionality of the system can be evolved in an incremental fashion [McGraw and Felten 1999]. For example, the plug-in architecture of Web browsers makes it easy to install viewer extensions for new document types as needed. Today's operating systems support extensibility through dynamically loadable device drivers and modules. Today's applications, such as word processors, e-mail clients, spreadsheets, and Web browsers, support extensibility through scripting, controls, components, and applets. The advent of Web Services and SOA, which are built entirely from extensible systems such as J2EE and .NET, brings explicit extensibility to the forefront.

From an economic standpoint, extensible systems are attractive because they provide flexible interfaces that can be adapted through new components. In today's marketplace, it is crucial that software be deployed as rapidly as possible in order to gain market share. Yet the marketplace also demands that applications provide new features with each release. An extensible architecture makes it easy to satisfy both demands by allowing the base application code to be shipped early, with later feature extensions shipped as needed.

Unfortunately, the very nature of extensible systems makes it hard to prevent software vulnerabilities from slipping in as unwanted extensions. Advanced languages and platforms including Sun Microsystems' Java and Microsoft's .NET Framework are making extensibility commonplace.

Complexity. A third trend impacting software security is the unbridled growth in the size and complexity of modern information systems, especially software systems. A desktop system running Windows XP and associated applications depends on the proper functioning of the kernel as well as the applications to ensure that vulnerabilities cannot compromise the system. However, Windows XP itself consists of at least forty million lines of code, and end-user applications are becoming equally, if not more, complex. When systems become this large, bugs cannot be avoided.

Figure 1–2 shows how the complexity of Windows (measured in lines of code) has grown over the years. The point of the graph is not to emphasize the numbers themselves, but rather the growth rate over time. In practice, the defect rate tends to go up as the square of code size.[6] Other factors that significantly affect complexity include whether the code is tightly integrated, the overlay of patches and other post-deployment fixes, and critical architectural issues.

The complexity problem is exacerbated by the use of unsafe programming languages (e.g., C and C++) that do not protect against simple kinds of attacks, such as buffer overflows. In theory, we could analyze and prove that a small program was free of problems, but this task is impossible for even the simplest desktop systems today, much less the enterprise-wide systems used by businesses or governments.

Of course, Windows is not alone. Almost all code bases tend to grow over time. During the last three years, I have made an informal survey of

---

[6]See the article "Encapsulation and Optimal Module Size" at <http://www.faqs.org/docs/artu/ch04s01.html#ftn.id2894437>.

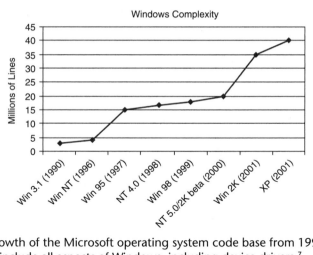

Figure 1–2 Growth of the Microsoft operating system code base from 1990 to 2001. These numbers include all aspects of Windows, including device drivers.[7]

thousands of developers. With few exceptions (on the order of 1% of sample size), developers overwhelmingly report that their groups intend to produce more code, not less, as time goes by. Ironically, these same developers also report that they intend to produce fewer bugs even as they produce more code. The unfortunate reality is that "more lines, more bugs" is the rule of thumb that tends to be borne out in practice (and in science, as the next section shows). Developers are an optimistic lot.

The propensity for software systems to grow very large quickly is just as apparent in open source systems as it is in Windows (see Table 1–1). The problem is, of course, that more code results in more defects and, in turn, more security risk.

Sometimes the code base grows (in executable space) even when the source code base appears to be small. Consider what happens when you target the .NET or J2EE platforms. In these situations, you adopt an unfathomably large base of code underneath your application. Things get even worse when you rely on the following:

- Data flattening: Castor, Java Data Objects (JDO), container-managed persistence
- Identity management and provisioning

---

[7]With regard to particular names for Microsoft operating systems, see <http://foldoc.doc.ic.ac.uk/foldoc/foldoc.cgi?NT5>.

Table 1–1 Source Lines of Code for Major Operating Systems and Kernels

19xx	SCOMP	20,000
1979	Multics	1,000,000
2000	Red Hat 6.2	17,000,000
2000	Debian.GNU/Linux 2.2	55,000,000
2000	Linux 2.2 kernel	1,780,000
2000	XFree86 3.3.6	1,270,000
2001	Red Hat 7.1	30,000,000
2002	Mac OS X Darwin kernel	790,000

Data on this chart gathered by Lee Badger, a DARPA program manager.[8]

- XML or other representational formats and associated parsers
- Model View Controller (MVC) frameworks: Struts deployment containers
- Application servers, Web containers
- Databases: Oracle, SQR, Informatica, and so on

To understand what I mean here, you should think about how much bytecode it takes to run "Hello World" in WebSphere or "Hello World" as a Microsoft ASP glob. What exactly is in that 2MB of stuff running on top of the operating system, anyway?

Basic Science

Everyone believes the mantra "more lines, more bugs" when it comes to software, but until recently the connection to security was understood only intuitively. Thanks to security guru Dan Geer, there are now some real numbers to back up this claim. On his never-ending quest to inject science into computer security, Geer has spoken widely about measurement and metrics. In the now famous monoculture paper, Geer and others decried the (national) security risk inherent in almost complete reliance on buggy

---

[8]Badger reports the Linux estimate from "Counting Potatoes: The Size of Debian 2.2" by Gonzalez-Barahona et al. <http://people.debian.org/~jgb/debian-counting>, and "More Than a Gigabuck: Estimating GNU/Linux's Size" by David Wheeler. The Multics estimate is from Tom Van Vleck and Charlie Clingen <http://www.multicians.org/mspp.html>.

Microsoft operating systems (see the acclaimed paper "Cyber*In*security: The Cost of Monopoly" [Geer et al. 2003]). Besides being fired from his job at @stake for the trouble, Geer raised some interesting questions about security bugs and the pile of software we're creating. One central question emerged: Is it true that more buggy code leads to more security problems in the field? What kind of predictive power do we get if we look into the data?

Partially spurred by an intense conversation we had, Geer did some work correlating CERT vulnerability numbers, number of hosts, and lines of code, which he has since presented in several talks. In an address at the Yale Law School,[9] Geer presented some correlations that bear repeating here. If you begin with the CERT data and the lines of code data presented in Figure 1–2 you can then normalize the curves.

Geer describes "opportunity" as the normalized product of the number of hosts (gleaned from publicly available Internet Society data) and the number of vulnerabilities (shown in Figure 1–1). See Figure 1–3. One question to ask is whether there is "untapped opportunity" in the system as understood in this form. Geer argues that there is, by comparing actual incidents curves against opportunity (not shown here). Put simply, there are fewer incidents than there could be. Geer believes that this indicates a growing reservoir of trouble.

By normalizing the lines-of-code curve shown in Figure 1–2 against its own median and then performing the same normalization technique on the data in Figure 1–3 as well as data about particular incidents (also from CERT), Geer is able to overlay the three curves to begin to look for correlation (Figure 1–4). The curves fit best when the lines-of-code data are shifted right by two years, something that can be explained with reference to diffusion delay. This means that new operating system versions do not "plonk" into the world all at once in a massive coordinated switchover. Instead, there is a steady diffusion into the operating system population. A two-year diffusion delay seems logical.

The next step is a bit more complex and involves some rolling average calculation. A code volume curve, which Geer calls MLOCs3 (millions of lines of code smoothed), is computed as the three-year moving average

---

[9]Dan Geer, "The Physics of Digital Law," keynote address, CyberCrime and Digital Law Enforcement Conference, Information Society Project, Yale Law School, March 26, 2004. (Unpublished slides.)

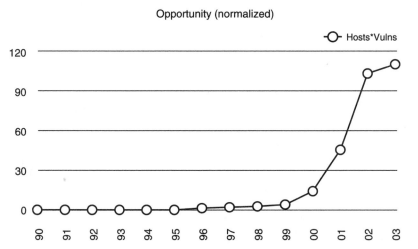

Figure 1–3 Total number of open holes, or "opportunity," as a normalized product of the number of hosts and the number of vulnerabilities (vulns). (After Geer.)

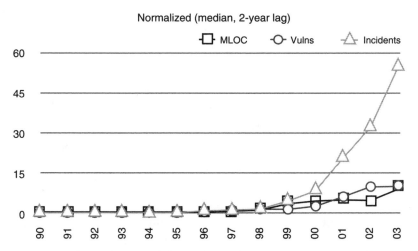

Figure 1–4 Normalized versions of the millions of lines of code, vulnerabilities, and incidents data. Now that we have put these curves together, we can begin to compute curves for correlation and prediction. (After Geer.)

of code volume. A second such curve, called MLOCs3^2+1, is the square of the three-year moving average of code volume shifted right one year. Justification for the squaring operation comes from the commonly accepted rule of thumb that program complexity grows with the square of the number of lines of code. Given the resulting curves (shown in Figure 1–5), Geer argues:

> *Security faults are a subset of quality faults and the literature says that quality faults will tend to be a function of code complexity, itself proportional to the square of code volume. As such, the average complexity in the field should be a predictor of the attack-ability in an a priori sense. Shifting it right one year is to permit the attack community time to acquire access and skill to that growing code base complexity. This is not a statement of proven causality—it is exploratory data analysis.*[10]

Geer's analysis shows that intuitive claims about how growth in simple lines of code metrics correlates with growth in security problems actually hold analytical water.

To boil this all down to one line—more code, more bugs, more security problems.

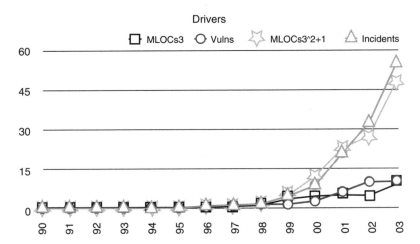

Figure 1–5 Computation of two kinds of code volume curves (MLOCs3 and MLOCs3^2+1; see text for definition) results in curves with some predictive power. (After Geer.)

---

[10]Dan Geer, "The Physics of Digital Law," keynote address, CyberCrime and Digital Law Enforcement Conference, Information Society Project, Yale Law School, March 26, 2004. (Unpublished slides.)

Security Problems in Software

Software security, that is, the process of designing, building, and testing software for security, gets to the heart of computer security by identifying and expunging problems in the software itself. In this way, software security attempts to build software that can withstand attack proactively.

Bugs and Flaws and Defects, Oh My!

Though Figure 1–1 clearly shows that the software problem is large, scientists have done little work in classifying and categorizing software security problems.

Perhaps the reintroduction of basic terminology—defect, bug, flaw, and risk—with a security emphasis can help clarify the categorization problem. I propose the following usage.

Defect: Both implementation vulnerabilities and design vulnerabilities are defects. A defect is a problem that may lie dormant in software for years only to surface in a fielded system with major consequences.

Bug: A bug is an implementation-level software problem. Bugs may exist in code but never be executed. Though the term *bug* is applied quite generally by many software practitioners, I reserve use of the term to encompass fairly simple implementation errors. Bugs are implementation-level problems that can be easily discovered and remedied. An example of a bug is described in the following box—The (Much Ballyhoo'd) Buffer Overflow: An Implementation Bug.

Researchers have made significant progress in detecting security vulnerabilities stemming from low-level and mid-level implementation bugs. Early research tools include FIST [Ghosh, O'Connor, and McGraw 1998], ITS4 [Viega et al. 2000a], Jscan [Viega et al. 2000b], Splint [Evans et al. 1994], Metal [Engler et al. 2000], and Prefix/Prefast [Bush, Pincus, and Sielaff 2000]. Commercial tools (e.g., Fortify Software's Source Code Analyzer) were introduced to the market in 2005, and development of these tools continues apace. The tools are effective in detecting a wide range of implementation bugs, including buffer overflow vulnerabilities, format string bugs, resource leaks, and simple race conditions—all of which depend on only limited code analysis and knowledge of the external environment. (See Chapter 4 for more on code review and static analysis tool use.)

The (Much Ballyhoo'd) Buffer Overflow: An Implementation Bug

The most pervasive security problem today in terms of reported bugs is the buffer overflow. A now classic paper by Dave Wagner in 2000 looked over CERT data and determined that almost 45% of all software security problems reported to CERT were caused by buffer overflows. Figure 1–6 shows a copy of Wagner's data.

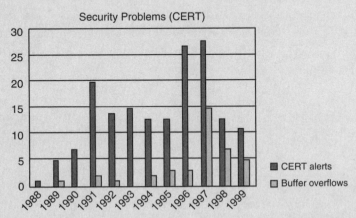

Figure 1–6 Dave Wagner's study determined the prevalence of buffer overflows as causes of CERT alerts (around 45%), showing how large a problem such buffer overflows are [Wagner et al. 2000].

The buffer overflow problem exists because it is so easy to write beyond the bounds of data objects in languages like C and C++. Type-safe languages like Java and C#, do not suffer from this issue, since the definition of exactly what constitutes a data object is much more tightly controlled.

In C, it is also extremely easy to allocate some bytes and then try to use more. The language does not care. For example, consider the two lines below:

```
char x[12];
x[12] = '\0';
```

In the code snippet, an array of 12 chars is declared. Then the *thirteenth* element is set to 0. Everyone in "the club" knows that for hazy historical reasons (offsets), array references in C start with 0! What a silly language.

Continued

There are two main flavors of buffer overflows: those associated with stack-allocated buffers and those associated with heap-allocated buffers. Overflowing a stack-allocated buffer is the most common attack. This is known as "smashing the stack." *The C Programming Language* (the C "bible") shows C programmers how they should never get input (without saying "never") [Kernighan and Ritchie 1988, p. 164]. Since we teach people to program in C as an introduction to programming, we should not be surprised at how common buffer overflow vulnerabilities are.

Many, many C library functions and arithmetic issues can lead to buffer overflows. Consider the snippet below. This is a dangerous piece of vulnerable code. Not only are we using `gets()` to get (unbounded) input, but we're using it to load a local variable on the stack. By providing just the right kind of input to this program, an attacker can obtain complete control over program control flow.

```
void main() {
  char buf[1024];
  gets(buf);
}
```

For more on buffer overflows, see *Building Secure Software* (where you are taught in excruciating detail how buffer overflows work) and *Exploiting Software* (which describes trampolining and other more advanced buffer overflow attacks, as well as plenty of real-world examples) [Viega and McGraw 2001; Hoglund and McGraw 2004].

If you are concerned about buffer overflow problems and other basic software security bugs, don't use C. If you must use C, use a source code security scanner as described in Chapter 4.

By the way, C++ is even worse than C from a security perspective. C++ is C with an object model crammed halfway down its throat.

Flaw: A flaw is a problem at a deeper level. Flaws are often much more subtle than simply an off-by-one error in an array reference or use of an incorrect system call. A flaw is certainly instantiated in software code, but it is also present (or absent!) at the design level. For example, a number of classic flaws exist in error-handling and recovery systems that fail in an insecure or inefficient fashion. Another example can be found in the box, Microsoft Bob: A Design Flaw, that follows. Automated technologies to detect design-level flaws do not yet exist, though manual risk-analysis processes can identify flaws (see Chapter 5).

Table 1–2 provides some simple examples of bugs and flaws. In practice, we find that software security problems are divided 50/50 between bugs

Microsoft Bob: A Design Flaw

This is an oft-repeated story that may be apocryphal, but it is amusing and teaches an interesting lesson.

Microsoft's Bob program was meant as a helper for Windows ME and Windows 98. Though the security posture of these early PC operating systems is known to be very poor, Windows ME did include a facility for setting a system password.

Microsoft Bob would pipe up (like Clippie the Paperclip in Word) when the program determined that the user was stuck doing something. Bob's most insecure function occurred when a user attempted three times (unsuccessfully) to type in his or her password. Bob would pop up and proclaim: "I see you have forgotten your password, please enter a new password." Then the user was allowed to change the password even though the user apparently had no idea of the old one.

Microsoft Bob, hacker's friend.

Table 1-2 Examples of Bugs and Flaws

Bugs	Flaws
Buffer overflow: stack smashing	Method over-riding problems (subclass issues)
Buffer overflow: one-stage attacks	
Buffer overflow: string format attacks	Compartmentalization problems in design
Race conditions: TOCTOU	Privileged block protection failure (`DoPrivilege()`)
Unsafe environment variables	
Unsafe system calls (`fork()`, `exec()`, `system()`)	Error-handling problems (fails open)
	Type safety confusion error
Incorrect input validation (black list vs. white list)	Insecure audit log design
	Broken or illogical access control (role-based access control [RBAC] over tiers)
	Signing too much code

Software security defects come in two basic flavors, each of which accounts for approximately 50% of software security problems.

and flaws. This means that eradicating bugs through code review will solve only about half of the problem. This may come as a big surprise to those people who believe that software security is exclusively about coding issues. Clearly, it isn't. Microsoft reports that more than 50% of the problems the company has uncovered during its ongoing security push are architectural in

nature [Mike Howard, personal communication]. Cigital data show a
60/40 split in favor of flaws, reflecting Cigital's specialization in architectural risk analysis.

Risk: Flaws and bugs lead to risk. Risks are not failures. Risks capture
the probability that a flaw or a bug will impact the purpose of the software
(that is, risk = probability × impact). Risk measures must also take into
account the potential damage that can occur. A very high risk is not only
likely to happen but also likely to cause great harm. Risks can be managed
by technical and non-technical means.

Building secure software is like building a house. I liken correct low-
level coding (such as using functions likely to cause buffer overflows) to the
use of solid bricks as opposed to bricks made of sawdust. The kinds of
bricks used are important to the integrity of the house, but even more
important (if the goal is to keep bad things out) is having four walls and a
roof in the design. The same thing goes for software: Which system calls and
libraries are used and how they are used is important, but overall design
properties often count for more. In general, software security to date has
paid much more attention to bricks than to walls.

The Range of Defects

Drawing a hard-and-fast distinction between bugs and flaws is nice, but
in practice things are much messier. Sometimes determining whether a
defect is a flaw or a bug is difficult. That's because flaws and bugs exist
along a continuum of defects. Security defects in software systems range
from local implementation errors (e.g., use of the `gets()` function call in
C/C++) to interprocedural interface errors (e.g., a race condition between
an access control check and a file operation) to much higher design-level
mistakes (e.g., error-handling and recovery systems that fail in an insecure
fashion or object-sharing systems that mistakenly include transitive trust
issues).

We can consider these defects as defining a large range based on how
much program code must be considered to understand the vulnerability,
how much detail regarding the execution environment must be known to
understand the vulnerability, and whether a design-level description is
best for determining whether or not a given vulnerability is present. For
example, we can determine that a call to `gets()` in a C/C++ program can
be exploited in a buffer overflow attack without knowing anything about
the rest of the code, its design, or the execution environment other than

assuming that the user entering text on standard input may be malicious. Hence, a `gets()` vulnerability can be detected with good precision using a very simple lexical analysis. This kind of approach is the subject of Chapter 4. A taxonomy of low-level coding defects can be found in Chapter 12.

Midrange vulnerabilities involve interactions among more than one location in code. Precisely detecting race conditions, for example, depends on more than simply analyzing an isolated line of code—it may depend on knowing about the behavior of several functions, understanding sharing among global variables, and being familiar with the operating system providing the execution environment.

Design-level vulnerabilities carry this trend further. Unfortunately, ascertaining whether or not a program has design-level vulnerabilities requires great expertise (and is the subject of Chapter 5). This makes finding design-level flaws not only hard to do but particularly hard to automate as well. The problem is that design-level problems appear to be prevalent and are at the very least a critical category of security risk in code.

Consider an error-handling and recovery system. Failure recovery is an essential aspect of security engineering. But it is complicated because it interacts with failure models, redundant design, and defense against denial-of-service attacks. Understanding whether or not an error-handling and recovery system in an object-oriented program is secure, for example, involves figuring out a global property spread throughout many classes in typical design. Error detection code is usually present in each object and method, and error-handling code is usually separate and distinct from the detection code. Sometimes exceptions propagate up to the system level and are handled by the machine running the code (e.g., Java 2 Virtual Machine exception handling). This makes determining whether or not a given error-handling and recovery design is secure quite difficult. The problem is exacerbated in transaction-based systems commonly used in commercial e-commerce solutions where functionality is distributed among many different components running on several servers.

Other examples of design-level problems include object-sharing and trust issues, unprotected data channels (both internal and external), incorrect or missing access control mechanisms, lack of auditing/logging or incorrect logging, ordering and timing errors (especially in multithreaded systems), and many others. In order to make progress as a scientific discipline, software security professionals must understand and categorize these sorts of problems in a rigorous way.

The Problem with Application Security

Because the idea that software is a major problem in computer security is fairly new, many diverse sets of people are working on the problem. One set of network security practitioners, led by a number of security tools vendors, has worked hard and spent lots of marketing money to coin "application security" as the moniker of choice to describe the software security space. There are a number of reasons to be wary when confronted with application security. Personally, I am a proponent of the term *software security* over the term *application security,* especially when discussing the idea of building security in. Here's why.

One problem is that the term *application security* means different things to different people. In many circles, it has come to mean the protection of software *after it's already built.* Although the notion of protecting software is an important one, it's just plain easier to protect something that is defect-free than something riddled with vulnerabilities.

Pondering the question, "What is the most effective way to protect software?" can help untangle software security and application security. On one hand, software security is about building secure software: designing software to be secure; making sure that software is secure; and educating software developers, architects, and users about how to build security in. On the other hand, application security is about protecting software and the systems that software runs in a post facto way, only after development is complete. Issues critical to this subfield include sandboxing code (as the Java Virtual Machine does), protecting against malicious code, obfuscating code, locking down executables, monitoring programs as they run (especially their input), enforcing the software-use policy with technology, and dealing with extensible systems.

Application security follows naturally from a network-centric approach to security by embracing standard approaches, such as "penetrate and patch" and input filtering (trying to block malicious input), and by generally providing value in a reactive way. (See the next box—Application Security Testing Tools: Good or Bad?) Put succinctly, application security is based primarily on finding and fixing known security problems after they've been exploited in fielded systems, usually by filtering dangerous input on its way to broken software. Software security—the process of designing, building, and testing software for security—identifies and expunges problems in the software itself. In this way, software security practitioners attempt to build software that can withstand attack proactively. Let me give you a specific example:

Although there is some real value in stopping buffer overflow attacks by observing HTTP traffic as it arrives over port 80, a superior approach is to fix the broken code in order to avoid the buffer overflow completely.

Another problem I have with the term *application security* is that it unnecessarily limits the purview of software security. Sure, applications have security problems, with Web-based applications leading the pack. But if you step back a moment, you'll see that we have a much bigger problem at hand than simply errant Web applications. Ask yourself, what do wireless devices, cell phones, PDAs, browsers, operating systems, routers, servers, personal computers, public key infrastructure systems, and firewalls have in common? The answer is "software." What an interesting and wide-ranging list. It encompasses everything from consumer devices to infrastructure items to security apparatus itself. We should not be surprised that real attackers go after bad software—no matter where it lives. A myopic focus on "application" code ignores the bigger picture. That's why I like to call the field *software security*.

It is important to think about the impact of simple vocabulary choices in large enterprises. When a large organization sets an application development project in motion, it involves lots of diverse groups: systems people, network people, the architecture group, and a whole bevy of application developers. If the security group buys into application security thinking, they'll likely end up pushing some vendor or product at their applications people (the VB.NET implementers at the bottom of the software food chain). By contrast, software security thinking focuses its scrutiny on both the applications people and those middleware architects responsible for all of the hard-core "services" code that is extremely susceptible to design flaws. (Of course, both application code and the middleware services it relies on can possess bugs.)

Suborganizations like application development and the architecture group are very territorial, and even if the vendor or product chosen as an application security solution does end up finding defects in the application, the people in the cross hairs are likely to pass the buck: "Oh, you need to talk to the architects." The security ball has a big chance of being dropped in this situation—especially since the architecture and "real" code is usually set in stone and the architects redispatched to other projects before the VB.NET application implementers are even contracted.

Application Security Testing Tools: Good or Bad?*

Application security testing products are being sold as a solution to the problem of insecure software. Unfortunately, these first-generation solutions are not all they are cracked up to be. They may help us diagnose, describe, and demonstrate the problem, but they do little to help us fix it.

Today's application security products treat software applications as "black boxes" that are prone to misbehave and must be probed and prodded to prevent security disaster. Unfortunately, this approach is too simple.

Software testing requires planning and should be based on software requirements and the architecture of the code under test. You can't "test quality in" by painstakingly finding and removing bugs once the code is done. The same goes for security; running a handful of canned tests that "simulate malicious hackers" by sending malformed input streams to a program will not work. Real attackers don't simply "fuzz" a program with input to find problems. Attackers take software apart, determine how it works, and make it misbehave by doing what users are not supposed to do. The essence of the disconnect is that black box testing approaches, including application security testing tools, only scratch the surface of software in an outside→in fashion instead of digging into the guts of software and securing things from the inside.

Badness-ometers

That said, application security testing tools can tell you something about security—namely, that you're in very deep trouble. That is, if your software fails any of the canned tests, you have some serious security work to do. The tools can help uncover known issues. But if you pass all the tests with flying colors, you know nothing more than that you passed a handful of tests with flying colors.

Put in more basic terms, application security testing tools are "badness-ometers," as shown in Figure 1–7. They provide a reading in a range from "deep trouble" to "who knows," but they do not provide a reading into the "security" range at all. Most vulnerabilities that exist in the architecture and the code are beyond the reach of simple canned tests, so passing all the tests is not that reassuring. (Of course, knowing you're in deep trouble can be helpful!)

The other major weakness with application security testing tools is that they focus only on input to an application provided over port 80. Understanding and testing a complex program by relying only on the protocol it uses to communicate provides a

---

*A version of this example first appeared in my "[In]security" column in *Network* magazine, November 2004. *Network* magazine is now called *IT Architect.*

Figure 1–7 A badness-ometer can be useful in some cases but is not the same thing as a security-ometer.

shallow analysis. Though many attacks do arrive via HTTP, this is only one category of security problem. First of all, input arrives to modern applications in many forms other than HTTP: consider SSL, environment variables, outside libraries, distributed components that communicate using other protocols, and so on. Beyond program input, software security must consider architectural soundness, data security, access control, software environment, and any number of other aspects, all of which are dependent on the application itself. There is no set of prefab tests that will probe every possible application in a meaningful way.

The only good use for application security tools is testing commercial off-the-shelf software. Simple dynamic checks set a reasonably low bar to hold vendors to. If software that is delivered to you fails to pass simple tests, you can either reject it out of hand or take steps to monitor its behavior.

In the final analysis, application security testing tools do provide a modicum of value. Organizations that are just beginning to think through software security issues can use them as badness-ometers to help determine how much trouble they are in. Results can alert all the interested parties to the presence of the problem and motivate some mitigation activity. However, you won't get anything more than a rudimentary analysis with these tools. Fixing the problems they expose requires building better software to begin with—whether you created the software or not.

Software Security and Operations

One reason that application security technologies, such as application firewalls, have evolved the way they have is because operations people dreamed them up. In most corporations and large organizations, security is the domain of the infrastructure people who set up and maintain firewalls, intrusion detection systems, and antivirus engines (all of which are reactive technologies).

However, these people are operators, not builders. Given the fact that they don't build the software they have to operate, it's no surprise that their approach is to move standard security techniques "down" to the desktop and application levels. The gist of the idea is to protect vulnerable things (in this case, software) from attack, but the problem is that vulnerabilities in the software let malicious hackers skirt standard security technologies with impunity. If this were not the case, the security vulnerability problem would not be expanding the way it is. Clearly, this emphasizes the need to get builders to do a better job on the software in the first place. (See the Security versus Software box.)

Protecting a network full of evolving software is difficult, even if the software is not patched every five minutes. If software were in some sense self-protecting (by being designed defensively and more properly tested from a security perspective) or at least less riddled with vulnerabilities, running a secure network could become easier and more cost effective.

In the short run, we clearly—desperately—must make progress on both fronts. But in the long run, we must figure out ways to build easier-to-defend code. Software security is about helping builders do a better job so that operators end up with an easier job.

Security versus Software

Security Has Come a Long Way

Security was the exclusive domain of guns, dogs, and concrete not too many years ago. Since the worldwide deluge that is the Information Age, all things security have changed radically. In tandem with the stunning growth of the Internet, the new field of computer security has taken root and grown like a weed. Computer security quickly became everyone's business as commerce, entertainment, and personal communications were swept up in the Internet flood. Yet computer security remains a relative newcomer.

In the early days, computer security was about protecting the expensive machine from people (remember when computers took up entire rooms?). There were no networks, and there were not really that many users. Operations people ruled the roost.

Once things shrank to a more reasonable size and the network was invented, computer security confronted its first major shift. The trusted machine was connected to untrusted machines not necessarily under the control of operations people. And the dang things could be anywhere. The need for network security was paramount, so a host of reactive technologies came into being, including the firewall, antivirus programs, and intrusion detection systems. Computer security on the Internet relies on these technologies to this day. Operations people continue to rule the roost.

The problem is that, though certainly necessary, the kinds of common computer security technologies we are counting on today simply don't work well enough. Take a look at any study, from the annual CSI/FBI report to CERT findings to reports commissioned by NIST—by every measure the computer security problem is growing even though adoption of network security technologies continues unabated. Why?

Security Has Not Come Very Far

Defending any human artifact against malicious adversaries is difficult. This is a lesson from way back in the days of physical security. The notion of "defending the perimeter," adapted from the physical security of castles and fortresses, requires the existence of a perimeter. Some castles and fortresses were better designed than others, and as a result they were easier to defend.

The perimeter defense paradigm has its issues, though. Consider the Maginot Line, built as a perimeter defense in France against German aggression after World War I. The problem was that the defense failed when the attackers changed their traditional invasion routes and came through Ardennes Forest and once-neutral Belgium.

Computer security has come to rely too heavily on a perimeter defense mentality, and the attackers have already changed their invasion routes. The perimeter metaphor makes sense if you take the view that the trusted inside machines need to be protected from the untrusted machines outside. The problem is that the notion of a perimeter is quaint, outdated, and too simple to work. Today's Web-based systems are highly distributed and involve explicit connection with machines that merit varying degrees of trust. Reactive technologies, such as firewalls that attempt to protect "the system" from the "outside," don't work when the very design of the system involves tunneling through the firewall with impunity.

Solving the Problem: The Three Pillars of Software Security

Software security is an ongoing activity that requires a cultural shift. There is unfortunately no magic tool or just-add-water process that will result in secure software. Software security takes work. That's the bad news. The

Figure 1–8 The three pillars of software security are risk management, software security touchpoints, and knowledge.

good news is that any organization that is developing software, no matter what software development methodology it is following (if any!), can make straightforward, positive progress by following the plan laid out in this book.

Software security naturally borrows heavily from software engineering, programming languages, and security engineering. The three pillars of software security are applied risk management, software security touchpoints, and knowledge (see Figure 1–8). By applying the three pillars in a gradual, evolutionary manner and in equal measure, a reasonable, cost-effective software security program can result. Throughout the rest of this book, I discuss the three pillars and their constituent parts at length.

 Pillar I: Applied Risk Management

No discussion about security is complete without considering risk management, and the same holds true for software security. To make risk management coherent, it is useful to draw a distinction between the application of risk analysis at the architectural level (sometimes called *threat modeling* or *security design analysis*) and the notion of tracking and mitigating risk as a full lifecycle activity. Architectural risk analysis is a best practice and is one of the central touchpoints (see Chapter 5). However, security risks crop up throughout the software development lifecycle (SDLC); thus, an overall approach to risk management as a philosophy is also important. I will call this underlying approach the *risk management framework* (RMF).

Risk management is often viewed as a "black art"—that is, part fortune-telling, part mathematics. Successful risk management, however, is nothing more than a business-level decision-support tool: a way to gather the requisite data to make a good judgment call, based on knowledge of vulnerabilities, threats, impacts, and probabilities. Risk management has a storied history. Dan Geer wrote an excellent overview [Geer 1998]. What makes a good software risk assessment is the ability to apply classic risk definitions to software designs in order to generate accurate mitigation requirements.

Chapter 2 discusses an RMF and considers applied risk management as a high-level approach to iterative risk identification and mitigation that is deeply integrated throughout the SDLC. Carrying out a full lifecycle risk management approach for software security is at its heart a philosophy underpinning all software security work. The basic idea is to identify, rank, track, and understand software security risk as the touchpoints are applied throughout the SDLC.

Chapter 5 provides a discussion of architectural risk analysis. In that chapter I briefly introduce some practical methods for applying risk analysis techniques while software is being designed and built. There are many different, established methodologies, each possessing distinct advantages and disadvantages.

 Pillar II: Software Security Touchpoints

On the road to implementing a fundamental change in the way we build software, we must first agree that software security is not security software. This is a subtle point often lost on development people, who tend to focus on functionality. Obviously, there are security functions in the world, and most modern software includes security features; but adding features such as SSL to your program (to cryptographically protect communications) does not present a complete solution to the security problem. Software security is a system-wide issue that takes into account both security mechanisms (such as access control) and design for security (such as robust design that makes software attacks difficult). Sometimes these overlap, but often they don't.

Put another way, security is an emergent property of a software system. A security problem is more likely to arise because of a problem in a system's standard-issue part (say, the interface to the database module) than in some given security feature. This is an important reason why software security must be part of a full lifecycle approach. Just as you can't test quality into a piece of software, you can't spray paint security features onto a design and expect it to become secure. There's no such thing as magic crypto fairy dust—we need to focus on software security from the ground up. We need to build security in.

As practitioners become aware of software security's importance, they are increasingly adopting and evolving a set of best practices to address the problem. Microsoft has carried out a noteworthy effort under its Trustworthy Computing Initiative [Walsh 2003; Howard and Lipner 2003]. (See the next box, Microsoft's Trustworthy Computing Initiative.) Most approaches in practice today encompass training for developers, testers, and architects; analysis and auditing of software artifacts; and security engineering. In the fight for better software, treating the disease itself (poorly designed and implemented software) is better than taking an aspirin to stop the symptoms. There's no substitute for working software security as deeply into the development process as possible and taking advantage of the engineering lessons software practitioners have learned over the years.

Figure 1–9 specifies the *software security touchpoints* (a set of best practices) that I cover in this book and shows how software practitioners can apply the touchpoints to the various software artifacts produced during software development. These best practices first appeared as a set in 2004 in *IEEE Security & Privacy* magazine [McGraw 2004]. Since then, they have been adopted (and in some cases adapted) by the U.S. government in the National Cyber Security Task Force report [Davis et al. 2004], by Cigital, by the U.S. Department of Homeland Security, and by Ernst and Young. In various chapters ahead, I'll detail these best practices (see Part II).

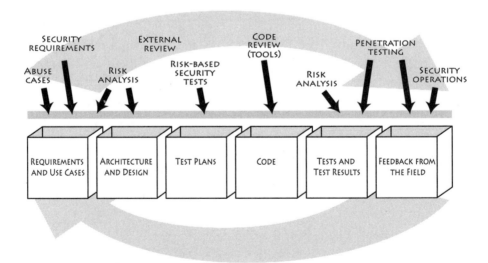

Figure 1–9 Software security best practices applied to various software artifacts. Although in this picture the artifacts are laid out according to a traditional waterfall model, most organizations follow an iterative approach today, which means that best practices will be cycled through more than once as the software evolves.

Microsoft's Trustworthy Computing Initiative

The Gates memo of January 2002 reproduced here highlights the importance of building secure software to the future of Microsoft. Microsoft's Trustworthy Computing Initiative, kicked off by the memo, has changed the way Microsoft builds software. Microsoft has spent more than $300 million (and more than 2000 worker days) on its software security push.

Microsoft is focusing on people, process, and technology to tackle the software security problem. On the people front, Microsoft is training every developer, tester, and program manager in basic techniques of building secure products. Microsoft's development process has been enhanced to make security a critical factor in design, coding, and testing of every product. Risk analysis, code review, and security testing all have their place in the new process. External review and testing also play a key role. Microsoft is pursuing software security technology by building tools to automate as many process steps as possible. Tools include Prefix and Prefast for defect detection [Bush, Pincus, and Sielaff 2000] and changes to the Visual C++ compiler to detect certain kinds of buffer overruns at runtime. Microsoft has also recently begun thinking about measurement and metrics for security.

Microsoft has experimented with different ways to integrate software security practices into the development lifecycle. The company's initial approach is shown in Figure 1–10. This picture, originally created by Mike Howard, helped to inspire the process-agnostic touchpoints approach described in this book. Howard's original approach is very much Microsoft-centric (in that it is tied to the Microsoft product lifecycle and is not process agnostic), but it does emphasize the importance of a full-lifecycle approach.

Figure 1–11 shows a more up-to-date version of Microsoft's process for software security. A detailed paper describing the current version of Microsoft's Trustworthy Computing Secure Development Lifecycle is available on the Web through MSDN.*

The Gates Memo[†]

The refocusing of Microsoft to pay more attention to security was sparked by Bill Gates himself. In an e-mail sent to all Microsoft employees in January 2002 and widely

---

*Steve Lipner and Michael Howard "The Trustworthy Computing Security Development Lifecycle," MSDN, March 2005, Security Engineering and Communications, Security Business and Technology Unit, Microsoft Corporation <http://msdn.microsoft.com/library/default.asp?url=/library/en-us/dnsecure/html/sdl.asp>.

[†]The complete Gates memo is included with permission from Microsoft.

Continued

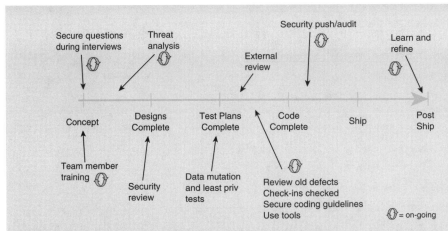

Figure 1–10 Early on, Microsoft put into place the (Microsoft-centric) software security process shown here. Notice that security does not happen at one lifecycle stage; nor are constituent activities "fire and forget."

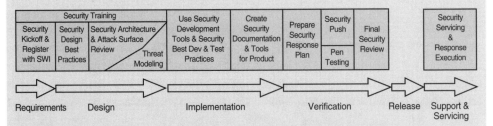

Figure 1–11 An updated view of Microsoft's software security process.*

distributed on the Internet (see <http://news.com.com/2009-1001-817210.html>), Microsoft Chairman Bill Gates started a major shift at Microsoft away from a focus on features to building more secure and trustworthy software. The e-mail is reproduced in its entirety here.

---

*Steve Lipner and Michael Howard "The Trustworthy Computing Security Development Lifecycle", MSDN, March 2005, Security Engineering and Communications, Security Business and Technology Unit, Microsoft Corporation <http://msdn.microsoft.com/library/default.asp?url=/library/en-us/dnsecure/html/sdl.asp>.

From: Bill Gates
Sent: Tuesday, January 15, 2002 2:22 PM
To: Microsoft and Subsidiaries: All FTE
Subject: Trustworthy computing

Every few years I have sent out a memo talking about the highest priority for Microsoft. Two years ago, it was the kickoff of our .NET strategy. Before that, it was several memos about the importance of the Internet to our future and the ways we could make the Internet truly useful for people. Over the last year it has become clear that ensuring .NET as a platform for Trustworthy Computing is more important than any other part of our work. If we don't do this, people simply won't be willing—or able—to take advantage of all the other great work we do. Trustworthy Computing is the highest priority for all the work we are doing. We must lead the industry to a whole new level of Trustworthiness in computing.

When we started work on Microsoft .NET more than two years ago, we set a new direction for the company—and articulated a new way to think about our software. Rather than developing standalone applications and Web sites, today we're moving towards smart clients with rich user interfaces interacting with Web services. We're driving the XML Web services standards so that systems from all vendors can share information, while working to make Windows the best client and server for this new era.

There is a lot of excitement about what this architecture makes possible. It allows the dreams about e-business that have been hyped over the last few years to become a reality. It enables people to collaborate in new ways, including how they read, communicate, share annotations, analyze information and meet.

However, even more important than any of these new capabilities is the fact that it is designed from the ground up to deliver Trustworthy Computing. What I mean by this is that customers will always be able to rely on these systems to be available and to secure their information. Trustworthy Computing is computing that is as available, reliable and secure as electricity, water services and telephony.

Today, in the developed world, we do not worry about electricity and water services being available. With telephony, we rely both on its availability and its security for conducting highly confidential business transactions without worrying that information about who we call or what we say will be compromised. Computing falls well short of this, ranging from the individual user who isn't willing to add a new application because it might destabilize their system, to a corporation that moves slowly to embrace e-business because today's platforms don't make the grade.

Continued

The events of last year—from September's terrorist attacks to a number of malicious and highly publicized computer viruses—reminded every one of us how important it is to ensure the integrity and security of our critical infrastructure, whether it's the airlines or computer systems.

Computing is already an important part of many people's lives. Within ten years, it will be an integral and indispensable part of almost everything we do. Microsoft and the computer industry will only succeed in that world if CIOs, consumers and everyone else see that Microsoft has created a platform for Trustworthy Computing.

Every week there are reports of newly discovered security problems in all kinds of software, from individual applications and services to Windows, Linux, Unix and other platforms. We have done a great job of having teams work around the clock to deliver security fixes for any problems that arise. Our responsiveness has been unmatched—but as an industry leader we can and must do better. Our new design approaches need to dramatically reduce the number of such issues that come up in the software that Microsoft, its partners and its customers create. We need to make it automatic for customers to get the benefits of these fixes. Eventually, our software should be so fundamentally secure that customers never even worry about it.

No Trustworthy Computing platform exists today. It is only in the context of the basic redesign we have done around .NET that we can achieve this. The key design decisions we made around .NET include the advances we need to deliver on this vision. Visual Studio .NET is the first multi-language tool that is optimized for the creation of secure code, so it is a key foundation element.

I've spent the past few months working with Craig Mundie's group and others across the company to define what achieving Trustworthy Computing will entail, and to focus our efforts on building trust into every one of our products and services. Key aspects include:

Availability: Our products should always be available when our customers need them. System outages should become a thing of the past because of a software architecture that supports redundancy and automatic recovery. Self-management should allow for service resumption without user intervention in almost every case.

Security: The data our software and services store on behalf of our customers should be protected from harm and used or modified only in appropriate ways. Security models should be easy for developers to understand and build into their applications.

Privacy: Users should be in control of how their data is used. Policies for information use should be clear to the user. Users should be in control of when and if they receive information to make best use of their time. It should be easy for users to specify appropriate use of their information including controlling the use of email they send.

Trustworthiness is a much broader concept than security, and winning our customers' trust involves more than just fixing bugs and achieving "five-nines" availability. It's a fundamental challenge that spans the entire computing ecosystem, from individual chips all the way to global Internet services. It's about smart software, services and industry-wide cooperation.

There are many changes Microsoft needs to make as a company to ensure and keep our customers' trust at every level—from the way we develop software, to our support efforts, to our operational and business practices. As software has become ever more complex, interdependent and interconnected, our reputation as a company has in turn become more vulnerable. Flaws in a single Microsoft product, service or policy not only affect the quality of our platform and services overall, but also our customers' view of us as a company.

In recent months, we've stepped up programs and services that help us create better software and increase security for our customers. Last fall, we launched the Strategic Technology Protection Program, making software like IIS and Windows .NET Server secure by default, and educating our customers on how to get—and stay—secure. The error-reporting features built into Office XP and Windows XP are giving us a clear view of how to raise the level of reliability. The Office team is focused on training and processes that will anticipate and prevent security problems. In December, the Visual Studio .NET team conducted a comprehensive review of every aspect of their product for potential security issues. We will be conducting similarly intensive reviews in the Windows division and throughout the company in the coming months.

At the same time, we're in the process of training all our developers in the latest secure coding techniques. We've also published books like *Writing Secure Code*, by Michael Howard and David LeBlanc, which gives all developers the tools they need to build secure software from the ground up. In addition, we must have even more highly trained sales, service and support people, along with offerings such as security assessments and broad security solutions. I encourage everyone at Microsoft to look at what we've done so far and think about how they can contribute.

But we need to go much further.

In the past, we've made our software and services more compelling for users by adding new features and functionality, and by making our platform richly extensible. We've done a terrific job at that, but all those great features won't matter unless

Continued

customers trust our software. So now, when we face a choice between adding features and resolving security issues, we need to choose security. Our products should emphasize security right out of the box, and we must constantly refine and improve that security as threats evolve. A good example of this is the changes we made in Outlook to avoid email borne viruses. If we discover a risk that a feature could compromise someone's privacy, that problem gets solved first. If there is any way we can better protect important data and minimize downtime, we should focus on this. These principles should apply at every stage of the development cycle of every kind of software we create, from operating systems and desktop applications to global Web services.

Going forward, we must develop technologies and policies that help businesses better manage ever larger networks of PCs, servers and other intelligent devices, knowing that their critical business systems are safe from harm. Systems will have to become self-managing and inherently resilient. We need to prepare now for the kind of software that will make this happen, and we must be the kind of company that people can rely on to deliver it.

This priority touches on all the software work we do. By delivering on Trustworthy Computing, customers will get dramatically more value out of our advances than they have in the past. The challenge here is one that Microsoft is uniquely suited to solve.

Bill

Note that software security touchpoints can be applied regardless of the base software process being followed. Software development processes as diverse as the waterfall model, Rational Unified Process (RUP), eXtreme Programming (XP), Agile, spiral development, Capability Maturity Model integration (CMMi), and any number of other processes involve the creation of a common set of *software artifacts* (the most common artifact being code). In the end, this means you can create your own Secure Development Lifecycle (SDL) by adapting your existing SDLC to include the touchpoints. You already know how to build software; what you may need to learn is how to build *secure* software.

The artifacts I will focus on (and describe best practices for) include requirements and use cases, architecture, design documents, test plans, code, test results, and feedback from the field. Most software processes describe the creation of these kinds of artifacts. In order to avoid the "religious warfare" surrounding which particular software development process is best, I introduce this notion of artifact and artifact analysis. The basic idea is to describe a number of *microprocesses* (touchpoints or best practices) that can be applied inline regardless of your core software process.[11]

This process-agnostic approach to the problem makes the software security material explained in this book as easy as possible to adopt. This is particularly critical given the fractional state of software process adoption in the world. Requiring that an organization give up, say, XP and adopt RUP in order to think about software security is ludicrous. The good news is that my move toward process agnosticism seems to work out. I consider the problem of how to adopt these best practices for any particular software methodology beyond the scope of this book (but work that definitely needs to be done).

 ### Pillar III: Knowledge

One of the critical challenges facing software security is the dearth of experienced practitioners. Early approaches that rely solely on apprenticeship as a method of propagation will not scale quickly enough to address the burgeoning problem. As the field evolves and best practices are established, knowledge management and training play a central role in encapsulating and spreading the emerging discipline more efficiently. Pillar III involves gathering, encapsulating, and sharing security knowledge that can be used to provide a solid foundation for software security practices.

Knowledge is more than simply a list of things we know or a collection of facts. Information and knowledge aren't the same thing, and it is important to understand the difference. Knowledge is information in context—information put to work using processes and procedures. A checklist of potential security bugs in C and C++ is information; the same information built into a static analysis tool is knowledge.

Software security knowledge can be organized into seven knowledge catalogs (principles, guidelines, rules, vulnerabilities, exploits, attack patterns, and historical risks) that are in turn grouped into three knowledge categories (prescriptive knowledge, diagnostic knowledge, and historical knowledge).

Two of these seven catalogs—vulnerabilities and exploits—are likely to be familiar to software developers possessing only a passing familiarity with software security. These catalogs have been in common use for quite some time and have even resulted in collection and cataloging efforts serving the security community. Similarly, principles (stemming from the seminal work

---

[11]Worth noting is the fact that I am not a process wonk by any stretch of the imagination. If you don't believe me, check out Chapter 1 of my software engineering book *Software Fault Injection* [Voas and McGraw 1998].

of Saltzer and Schroeder [1975]) and rules (identified and captured in static analysis tools such as ITS4 [Viega et al. 2000a]) are fairly well understood. Knowledge catalogs only more recently identified include guidelines (often built into prescriptive frameworks for technologies such as .NET and J2EE), attack patterns [Hoglund and McGraw 2004], and historical risks. Together, these various knowledge catalogs provide a basic foundation for a unified knowledge architecture supporting software security.

Software security knowledge can be successfully applied at various stages throughout the entire SDLC. One effective way to apply such knowledge is through the use of software security touchpoints. For example, rules are extremely useful for static analysis and code review activities.

Figure 1–12 shows an enhanced version of the software security touchpoints diagram introduced in Figure 1–9. In Figure 1–12, I identify those activities and artifacts most clearly impacted by the knowledge catalogs briefly mentioned above. More information about these catalogs can be found in Chapter 11.

Awareness of the software security problem is growing among researchers and some security practitioners. However, the most important audience has in some sense experienced the least exposure—for the most part, software architects, developers, and testers remain blithely unaware of the problem. One obvious way to spread software security knowledge is to train software development staff on critical software security issues.

The most effective form of training begins with a description of the problem and demonstrates its impact and importance. During the Windows security push in February and March 2002, Microsoft provided basic awareness training to all of its developers. Many other organizations have ongoing software security awareness training programs. Beyond awareness, more advanced software security training should offer coverage of security engineering, design principles and guidelines, implementation risks, design flaws, analysis techniques, and security testing. Special tracks should be made available to quality assurance personnel, especially those who carry out testing.

Of course, the best training programs will offer extensive and detailed coverage of the touchpoints covered in this book. Putting the touchpoints into practice requires cultural change, and that means training. Assembling a complete software security program at the enterprise level is the subject of Chapter 10.

The good news is that the three pillars of software security—risk management, touchpoints, and knowledge—can be applied in a sensible, evolutionary manner no matter what your existing software development approach is.

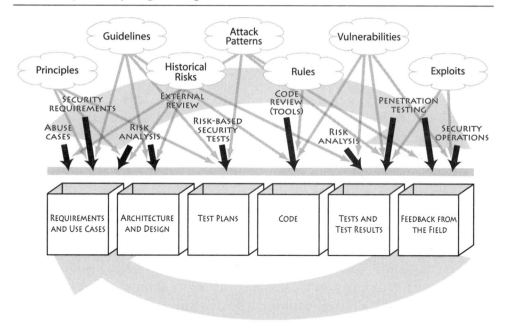

Figure 1–12 Mapping of software security knowledge catalogs to various software artifacts and software security best practices.

The Rise of Security Engineering

Designers of modern systems must take security into account proactively. This is especially true when it comes to software because bad software lies at the heart of a majority of computer security problems. Software defects come in two flavors—design-level flaws and implementation bugs. To address both kinds of defects, we must build better software and design more secure systems from the ground up.

Most computer security practitioners today are operations people. They are adept at designing reasonable network architectures, provisioning firewalls, and keeping networks up. Unfortunately, many operations people have only the most rudimentary understanding of software. This leads to the adoption of weak reactive technologies (think "application security testing" tools). Tools like those target the right problem (software) with the wrong solution (outside→in testing).

Fortunately, things are beginning to change in security. Practitioners understand that software security is something we need to work hard on. The notion that it is much cheaper to prevent than to repair helps to justify investment up front. In the end, prevention technology and assurance best practices may be the only way to go. Microsoft's Trustworthy Computing Initiative is no accident.

If we are to build systems that can be properly operated, we must involve the *builders* of systems in security. This starts with education, where security remains an often-unmentioned specialty, especially in the software arena. Every modern security department needs to think seriously about security engineering. The best departments already have staff devoted to software security. Others are beginning to look at the problem of security engineering. At the very least, close collaboration with the "builders" in your organization is a necessity.

Don't forget that software security is not just about building security functionality and integrating security features! Coders are likely to ask, "If I use [this API], is it good enough?" when doing their building thing. The question to ask in response is, "What attacks would have serious impact and are worth avoiding for this module?" This line of questioning works to elicit a better understanding of design and its security implications.

Software Security Is Everyone's Job

Connectivity and distributed computation is so pervasive that the only way to begin to secure our computing infrastructure is to enlist everyone.

- Builders must practice security engineering, ensuring that the systems we build are defensible and not riddled with holes (especially when it comes to the software).
- Operations people must continue to architect reasonable networks, defend them, and keep them up.
- Administrators must understand the distributed nature of modern systems and begin to practice the principle of least privilege.
- Users must understand that software *can* be secure so that they can take their business to software providers who share their values. (Witness the rise of Firefox.) Users must also understand that they are the last bastion of defense in any security design and that they need to make tradeoffs for better security.
- Executives must understand how early investment in security design and security analysis affects the degree to which users will trust their products.

The most important people to enlist for near-term progress in computer security are the builders. Only by pushing past the standard-issue operations view of security will we begin to make systems that can stand up under attack.

2 A Risk Management Framework[1]

> *No noble thing can be done without risks.*
> MICHEL DE MONTAIGNE

We've all said it—security is risk management. However, nomenclature remains a persistent problem in the security community. The idea of risk management as a key tenet of security, though pervasive and oft repeated, is presented under a number of different rubrics in software security, attached to particular processes, such as "threat modeling" and "risk analysis," as well as to larger-scale activities such as "security analysis." As I describe in Chapter 1, a continuous risk management process is a necessity. By teasing apart architectural risk analysis (one of the critical software security touchpoints described later in the book) and an overall risk management framework (RMF, described here), we can begin to make more sense of software security risk.

An RMF is at its heart a philosophy for software security. Following the RMF is by definition a full lifecycle activity, no matter whether you're working on a little project or a huge corporate application strategy. The key to reasonable risk management is to identify and keep track of risks over time as a software project unfolds. As touchpoints are applied and risks are uncovered, for example, an RMF allows us to track them and display information about status. For the purposes of this chapter, consider risk management as a high-level approach to iterative risk management that is deeply integrated throughout the software development lifecycle (SDLC) and unfolds over time. The basic idea is simple: identify, rank, track, and understand software security risk as it changes over time.

What follows in this chapter is a detailed explanation of a mature RMF used at Cigital. This chapter may be a bit heavy for some. If you're more

---

[1]Parts of this chapter appeared in original (more detailed) form as an internal Cigital document authored by Andrew Lefko, Stan Wisseman, Gil Matta, Paco Hope, and myself. The RMF was the brainchild of Karl Lewis and Hugo Sanchez.

interested in specific best practices for software security, you should skip ahead to Part II. If you do skip ahead, make sure you cycle back around later in order to understand how the framework described here supports all of the best practices.

Putting Risk Management into Practice

The software security touchpoints exist to drive out technical risk. Critical to proper application of the touchpoints is the notion of keeping track of security risks as they are uncovered and making sure they are properly dealt with. The RMF is about identifying, tracking, and mitigating software risk over time.

Central to the notion of risk management is the idea of describing impact. Recall from Chapter 1 that risk is defined as probability × impact. Without a clear and compelling tie to either business or mission consequences, technical risks, software defects, and the like are not often compelling enough on their own to spur action. Though the risks I focus on in this book are all tied directly to software and all have clear security ramifications, unless they are described in terms that business people and decision makers understand, they will not likely be addressed. There is nothing more frustrating to a technical person than identifying a serious problem that never gets fixed. We can avoid that frustration by properly describing impact.

Put more succinctly, a major hurdle to the proper handling of technical risk has been the inability to tie risk clearly to business impact. This leads to the techno-gibberish problem. Software is a fairly geeky domain. It's about arcane technology that business people don't understand. The question needs to be: How do you get business people to care whether their software works or not? The answer has to be that software risk must be discussed, understood, and related in terms of business impact. As a technical person, you need to say something like, "If the flimflobble in sector four has a floos-blozzle failure, that means we will miss the first quarter number by $2 million" (as opposed to just saying the first part). Business people can relate to the last part of the statement.

The RMF described here is a condensed version of the Cigital RMF, which has been applied in the field for almost ten years. An RMF is designed to manage software-induced business risks. For purposes of clarity, the RMF is described here in the context of a particular project; however, many of the activities can be applied at different levels. Through the application of these activities, analysts bring to bear their own technical expertise, relevant tools, and technologies.

The purpose of an RMF like this is to allow a consistent and repeatable expertise-driven approach to risk management. By converging on and describing software risk management activities in a consistent manner, the basis for measurement and common metrics emerges. Such metrics are sorely needed and will prove to be extremely valuable, allowing organizations to better manage business and technical risks given particular quality goals; make more informed, objective business decisions regarding software (e.g., whether an application is ready to release); and improve internal software development processes so that they in turn better manage software risks.

How to Use This Chapter[2]

An RMF like the one described here should be applied by anyone charged with software risk management. This goes for reliability, performance, and safety risk managers just as well as it does for security personnel. Whether software risk management is being imposed from above in a top-down exercise of corporate governance or bubbling up from the technical trenches, a clear and consistent approach to risk is a necessity. For that reason, the RMF is designed to fit a tiny little summer internship project just as well as it fits a large-scale enterprise risk management regimen.

Application of the RMF occurs in parallel with standard SDLC activities. Applying the RMF as a parallel thread is not a particularly time-consuming undertaking (especially if parts of the framework have been automated). In our experience at Cigital, a small risk management team of two to four people can track and manage risks for even the largest project. For a small project, the RMF can be applied as the part-time activity of an existing team member.

The RMF is not specific to security risks. In fact, the RMF is general enough that it is likely to apply even in non-software situations. We do know from experience that the RMF works well for tracking reliability risks, project management and governance risks, and a host of other

---

[2]Or "Danger, Will Robinson, tortuous reading ahead."

software-induced business risks just as well as it tracks security risks. To remind you of this applicability, the example used in this chapter to step you through the RMF does not concentrate solely on security risks.

Don't forget that the main purpose of the RMF is to consistently track and handle risks. By grounding the touchpoints described in Part II in the RMF philosophy, you can develop a powerful risk management capability.

The Five Stages of Activity

The RMF is described in a pyramid fashion. Because this material is difficult, it may help to understand the presentation order. I begin with a picture (Figure 2–1) and then present a bird's-eye view of the five fundamental activities, which I refer to as *stages*. Next, a detailed walkthrough features the mythical company KillerAppCo, whose product, iWare 1.0 Server, is under analysis. The example is rigorous and provides a number of "work product" tables and other guides to help make each of the five stages concrete and applicable. As you step through the example, don't forget that the skeleton of the process is available for your reference in Figure 2–1.

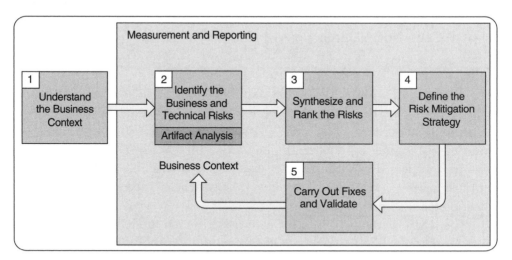

Figure 2–1 The risk management framework (RMF). In this picture, the RMF is a closed-loop process with five basic activity stages, each of which is numbered. Throughout the application of the RMF, tracking, reporting, measurement, and display activities that focus on understanding progress regarding software risk can occur. The touchpoints described in this book feed the RMF with risks and other data. The RMF displayed here is a condensed version of the Cigital RMF, which has been used for almost ten years in the field.

The RMF consists of the five fundamental activity stages shown in Figure 2–1:

1. Understand the business context
2. Identify the business and technical risks
3. Synthesize and prioritize the risks, producing a ranked set
4. Define the risk mitigation strategy
5. Carry out required fixes and validate that they are correct

Each of the stages is briefly summarized next. Particular tasks, processes, measurements, work products, and templates are described in detail later in the chapter. Critical business decisions, including release readiness, can be made in a more straightforward and informed manner by identifying, tracking, and managing software risk explicitly as described in the RMF.

Stage 1: Understand the Business Context

Software risk management occurs in a business context. Risks are unavoidable and are a necessary part of software development. Management of risks, including the notion of risk aversion and technical tradeoffs, is deeply impacted by business motivation. Thus the first stage of software risk management involves getting a handle on the business situation. Commonly, business goals are neither obvious nor explicitly stated. In some cases, you may even have difficulty expressing these goals clearly and consistently. During this stage, the analyst must extract and describe business goals, priorities, and circumstances in order to understand what kinds of software risks to care about and which business goals are paramount. Business goals include but are not limited to increasing revenue, meeting service-level agreements (SLAs), reducing development costs, and generating high return on investment (ROI). The purpose of this stage is to gather data to answer the all-important "Who cares?" question.

Stage 2: Identify the Business and Technical Risks

Business risks directly threaten one or more business goals. The identification of such risks helps to clarify and quantify the possibility that certain events will directly impact business goals. Business risks have impacts that include direct financial loss, damage to brand or reputation, violation of customer or regulatory constraints, exposure to liability, and increase in development costs. The severity of a business risk should be expressed in financial or project management terms. These include but are not limited to market share (percentage), direct cost, level of productivity, and cost of rework.

Business risk identification helps to define and steer use of particular technical methods for extracting, measuring, and mitigating software risk given various software artifacts. The identification of business risks provides a necessary foundation that allows software risk (especially impact) to be quantified and described in business terms. This makes impact statements tangible and spurs action on risk mitigation.

The key to making risk management work for any business lies in tying technical risks to the business context in a meaningful way. The ability to thoroughly identify and understand risks is thus essential. Uncovering and recognizing technical risks is a high-expertise undertaking that usually requires years of experience. But on their own, out of the business context, technical risks are often not actionable.

Central to this stage of the RMF is the ability to discover and describe technical risks and map them (through business risks) to business goals. A technical risk is a situation that runs counter to the planned design or implementation of the system under consideration. For example, a technical risk may give rise to the system behaving in an unexpected way, violating its own design strictures, or failing to perform as required. If the builders do not make proper use of touchpoints, these kinds of risks may slip by unnoticed. Technical risks can also be related to the process of building software. The process an organization follows may offer too many opportunities for mistakes in design or implementation. Technical risks involve impacts such as unexpected system crashes, avoidance of controls (audit or otherwise), unauthorized data modification or disclosure, and needless rework of artifacts during development.

Technical risk identification is supported by the software security touchpoints described throughout this book.

Stage 3: Synthesize and Rank the Risks

Large numbers of risks will be apparent in almost any given system. Identifying these risks is important, but it is the prioritization of them that leads directly to creation of value. Through the activities of synthesizing and prioritizing risks, the critical "Who cares?" question can (and must) be answered. Synthesis and prioritization should be driven to answer questions such as: "What shall we do first given the current risk situation?" and "What is the best allocation of resources, especially in terms of risk mitigation activities?" Clearly, the prioritization process must take into account which business goals are the most important to the organization, which goals are immediately threatened, and how likely technical risks are to manifest themselves in a way that impacts the business. This stage creates as its output lists of all the risks and their appropriate weighting for resolution.

Typical risk metrics include but are not limited to risk likelihood, risk impact, risk severity, and number of risks emerging and mitigated over time. Collection and display of these metrics can be automated. The Cigital Workbench, which automates parts of the RMF, including collection and display of metrics over time, is described later in the chapter.

Stage 4: Define the Risk Mitigation Strategy

One of the big problems in software security is that technical analysts are pretty good at finding technical problems and pointing them out, but not so good at determining what to do about them.[3] Nobody wants to hear about their problems without hearing some suggested fixes. A risk analysis is only as good as the mitigation strategy it contains.

Given a set of risks and their priorities from stage 3, the next stage is to create a coherent strategy for mitigating the risks in a cost-effective manner. Any suggested mitigation activities must take into account cost, implementation time, likelihood of success, completeness, and impact over the entire corpus of risks. A risk mitigation strategy must be constrained by the business context and should consider what the organization can afford, integrate, and understand. The strategy must also directly identify validation techniques that can be used to demonstrate that risks are properly mitigated.

Typical metrics to consider during this stage are financial in nature and include estimated cost takeout, ROI, method effectiveness in terms of dollar impact, and percentage of risk coverage (related in terms of removing costly impact).

Stage 5: Carry Out Fixes and Validate

Once a mitigation strategy has been defined, it must be executed. Those artifacts where problems have been identified (e.g., architectural flaws in a design, requirements collisions, coding errors, or problems in testing) should be rectified. Risk mitigation is carried out according to the strategy defined in stage 4. Progress at this stage should be measured in terms of completeness against the risk mitigation strategy. Good status metrics include but are

---

[3]This inability to determine how to fix the problems holds true for a majority of security consultants. It is always easier to break something than to design something that can't be broken. (See Dan Geer's Foreword.)

not limited to progress against risks, open risks remaining, and any artifact quality metrics previously identified.

This stage also involves carrying out the validation techniques previously identified. The validation stage provides some confidence that risks have been properly mitigated through artifact improvement and that the risk mitigation strategy is working. Testing can be used to demonstrate and measure the effectiveness of risk mitigation activities. The central concern at this stage is to validate that software artifacts and processes no longer bear unacceptable risk. This stage should define and leave in place a repeatable, measurable, verifiable validation process that can be run from time to time to continually verify artifact quality.

Typical metrics employed during this stage include artifact quality metrics as well as levels of risk mitigation effectiveness.

Measuring and Reporting on Risk

The importance of the central activity of identifying, tracking, storing, measuring, and reporting software risk information cannot be overemphasized. Successful use of the RMF depends on continuous and consistent identification and storage of risk information as it changes over time. A master list of risks should be maintained during all stages of RMF execution and continually revisited. At Cigital, we use a tool called the Workbench to track risk information. Before the Workbench existed, we used Excel spreadsheets.

Measurements regarding this master list make excellent reporting fodder. For example, the number of risks identified in various software artifacts and/or software lifecycle phases can be used to identify problem areas in the software process. This makes topnotch driving data for defect phase containment activities, the gist being to figure out where in the software lifecycle problems are born. Likewise, the number of risks mitigated over time can be used to show concrete progress as risk mitigation activities unfold.

The RMF Is a Multilevel Loop

The RMF shown in Figure 2–1 has an obvious loop. This loop is meant to graphically represent the idea that risk management is a continuous process. That is, identifying risks only once during a software project is insufficient. The idea of "crossing off a particular stage" once it has been executed and never doing those activities again is incorrect. Though the five stages are shown in a particular serial order in Figure 2–1, they may need to be applied over and over again throughout a project, and their particular ordering may be interleaved in many different ways.

There are two main reasons for this complication. First, risks can crop up at any time during the software lifecycle. One natural way to apply a cycle of the loop is during each particular software lifecycle phase. For example, software risks should be identified, ranked, and mitigated (one loop) during requirements and again during design (another loop). Second, risks can crop up between stages, regardless of where in the process a project finds itself.[4]

In addition to the issue of continuous looping is a further complication regarding level of application. Put simply, the RMF is fractal. In other words, the entire process can be applied at several different levels. The primary level is the project level. Each stage of the loop clearly must have some representation during a complete project in order for risk management to be effective. Another level is the software lifecycle phase level. The loop will most likely have a representation at the requirements phase, the design phase, the architecture phase, the test planning phase, and so on. A third level is the artifact level. The loop will have a representation during both requirements analysis and use case analysis, for example. Fortunately, a generic description of the validation loop as a serial looping process is sufficient to capture critical aspects at all of these levels at once.

In order to facilitate the learning process, this chapter presents the RMF as a series of stages, tasks, and methods that can be performed in succession, each stage following a particular process and producing a new set of work products and metrics that enhances and clarifies previously created data sets. In reality I describe how the RMF encompasses a particular cycle of the loop that is repeatedly executed on more than one level. The RMF loop restarts continuously so that newly arising business and technical risks can be identified and the status of existing risks currently undergoing mitigation can be kept up.

Understanding that the risk management process is by nature cumulative, and at times arbitrary and difficult to predict (depending on project circumstances), is an important insight. Given this insight, I acknowledge that the practice of specific RMF stages, tasks, and methods (as described serially

---

[4]Note that the process-agnostic view described in Chapter 1 still holds here. I am not suggesting the utility of any one software process over any other. Just like the touchpoints, the RMF is process agnostic as well.

here, for pedagogical reasons) may occur independently of one another, in parallel, repeatedly, and unsystematically.

Analysts may "skip through" an analytical process, as information gained from the performance of one activity may require the analyst to perform an activity located earlier, or several steps later, in the process cycle. For instance, after finding a rare technical risk, an analyst may need to conduct additional research prior to reprioritizing the risk tables and updating the risk mitigation strategy. In light of our discussion, users of the RMF should focus more on the basic concepts and activities presented here than on the particular order they are presented in.

In practice, less experienced analysts should rely on following these processes as closely as possible, preserving order, and proceeding in continuous loops. Expert analysts are likely to devise work patterns that use the concepts and processes described here, but in a less ordered way.

Applying the RMF: KillerAppCo's iWare 1.0 Server

Now that we have a basic understanding of the RMF and its five stages, we can push down a level or two into the details of its application. I use the fictional company KillerAppCo's iWare 1.0 Server product as an example. Don't forget that we're still following the five stages as described earlier. It may be useful to refer back to Figure 2–1 from time to time to track where we are.

Although the RMF is a multilevel loop, the remainder of this chapter describes the RMF as a series of stages, tasks, and methods to be performed in succession. The idea is to step through an imaginary example (in this case, KillerAppCo is producing iWare 1.0 Server) and show the kinds of tasks and work products that the RMF suggests. I've already given you a bird's-eye view of the five stages; now it's time to roll up our sleeves and get our hands dirty. In the following treatment, each of the five stages previously introduced follows a process to produce various tables and metrics that build on each other.

This example is overly simple. In a normal application of the RMF, it is not unusual for 30 to 50 risks to be identified and tracked. Thus the sizes and makeup of the tables shown in this section would vary.

An enhanced version of the RMF has been automated in order to make following the various processes described here more intuitive and less tedious (see the description of the Cigital Workbench near the end of this chapter).

Understanding the Business Context

During the first stage of RMF execution, an analyst must extract and describe business goals, priorities, and circumstances in order to understand what kinds of software risks to care about and which business goals are paramount.

Gathering the Artifacts

The first step is to obtain documentation about target system resources and artifacts. This is a good time to identify any missing resources necessary for the analysis but not in hand. Typical resources include system architecture (especially with regard to software), accounts, permissions, environments, documents, software artifacts, automated documents, data, and supporting materials.

After collecting the artifacts and resources, it is important to validate that they are the correct versions and that the set is complete. Note that an analyst may discover the need to obtain additional system resources and/or to collect additional software artifacts at any point in applying the RMF.

Conducting Project Research

An analyst should research the business, program, processes, systems, products, and technologies to the extent dictated by the project's scope. This work should be done independently. In particular, an analyst characterizes the system and may author draft documents and illustrations that summarize the system. One example that almost always comes in handy is a one-page overview of the system's software architecture (see Chapter 5). If a forest-level view is not available, it should be created as early as possible in the RMF process. At this point the analyst should also determine any technical, management, and operational controls that the project currently has in place to detect or prevent software risk.

The scope of the RMF project and the size and complexity of the system under review may not allow a uniform approach to analysis across the entire system. To resolve this problem, the analyst should examine the overall system and make an effort to decompose it into a reasonably small set of manageable components. These components comprise the system's software architecture (and should thus be represented in the one-page architectural overview).

Each component and the interfaces between them can be analyzed separately by applying a different level of rigor. Depending on function and importance, a subsystem may reside in one component or may be made up of multiple components. The importance of each subsystem is assessed in terms of the identified business goals. All subsystems are subsequently prioritized based on the identified business goals, and a decision is made based on the scope of the RMF project about the depth of the analysis that will be conducted against each subsystem. This approach goes hand-in-hand with the concept of risk management, as the depth of the analysis of any subsystem depends on the importance of the subsystem, and the analyses of different subsystems is likely to shed light on the quality and security of the software system in general.

At the end of the research activities, the risk posture of the entire system is examined based on the results obtained for each of the subsystems and their interactions. Knowledge and experience with analysis of similar systems is extremely helpful in this process.[5] During performance of this research, analysts generate research notes and gain a general understanding of the business context, how the target products work, and the role that software plays in the final product.

Identifying the Business and Technical Risks

The identification of business risks provides a necessary foundation that allows software risk (especially its impact component) to be quantified and described in business terms. Business risk identification helps to define and steer use of particular technical methods for extracting, measuring, and mitigating software risk given various software artifacts.

Developing Risk Questionnaires

Preliminary research results should be organized so that an initial set of business risks is identified. At this point, developing a set of risk questions to ask about the project is an important step. These questions should address *business risks* (e.g., motivation, market, resource, schedule, people, facilities, budget, contracts, program interfaces), *project risks* (e.g., development process, development system, management methods, work environment), and *product risks* (e.g., technical defects, design flaws, bugs, issues with languages and platforms).

Particular effort should be made to address questions regarding risk indicators, the likelihood that risks may occur, and business impact

---

[5]See Chapter 11 for a discussion of the kinds of knowledge useful to software security.

estimates in case risks materialize. Questions should directly address the project's concerns, how the target technologies work, the fundamental assumptions built into the target, and expected quality and security requirements.

After developing a set of risk questionnaires, the analyst must identify the RMF project's key information sources and schedule *independent* interviews with each of the following types of personnel:

- Upper management
- Project management
- Architects
- Developers
- Testers

Other technical personnel, such as configuration managers, as well as subject matter experts and end users may also be interviewed. An independent interview approach permits the interviewee to openly disclose and discuss sensitive, critical information without bias or constraints that may be imposed by the presence of others. In most cases, two analysts—a facilitator who asks the questions and a recorder who scribes the responses—interview the principals to ensure efficiency and accuracy.

Interviewing the Target Project Team

During an interview, the analyst:

- Collaborates with the interviewee to validate the comprehensiveness and accuracy of the draft summary documentation
- Employs the risk questionnaire as a reference to question the interviewee (not a script)
- Records the interviewee's answers to the questionnaire as well as other pertinent information discussed during the interview
- Identifies content presented by the interviewee that is inconsistent with the analyst's present knowledge set, resolves any inconsistencies, and documents the necessary changes

Based on an analysis of the quality of the interview results, and the number and type of new questions that may have resulted from the interview, the analyst may elect to conduct additional research and perform additional risk discovery interviews with newly identified stakeholders to gain a better understanding of the project's software risks and possible solutions.

Analyzing the Research and Interview Data

After completing the first set of interviews with the project team, the analyst reviews the interview data to identify, list, and prioritize the business goals and business risks.

As an example, Table 2–1 indicates that KillerAppCo's most important business goal, represented by the high (H) ranking, is to release the initial version of their software, iWare Server version 1.0, on January 1, 2008, so that the company can be first-to-market and secure an estimated 25% market share prior to its competitor's entry. KillerAppCo's next most important business goal, ranked as moderate (M), is for the iWare 1.0 Server to meet its Fortune 500 end-user availability requirements: 99.999% uptime, not including normal maintenance and upgrade activities.

Another of KillerAppCo's moderate business goals is for the product to perform all transactions with 100% accuracy, as required by federal financial regulations and standards. Table 2–2 provides very rough guidelines for ranking business goals.

After listing and prioritizing the business goals, the analyst analyzes the data gathered to identify and list the business risks.

Table 2–1 KillerAppCo's Prioritized Business Goals

Rank	Business Goal	Description
H	TIME TO MARKET iWare 1.0 Server must be released on January 1, 2008.	KillerAppCo desires to release iWare 1.0 on January 1, 2008, to achieve first-to-market status, which will enable KillerAppCo to secure 25% of the market prior to competitor entry.
M	AVAILABILITY iWare 1.0 Server must provide 99.999% uptime.	A large share of the iWare 1.0 Server market consists of Fortune 500 companies with whom KillerAppCo will have SLAs. The server's availability is a critical factor in enabling KillerAppCo to meet the SLA requirements.
M	ACCURACY Transactions must be recorded with 100% accuracy, with no invalid, duplicate, or missing transactions.	Federal regulations stipulate that iWare 1.0 Server must perform all financial transactions with 100% accuracy.

Table 2–2 Guidelines for Business Goal Rankings (from NIST)

Rank	Definition
High (H)	These goals are critical to the existence of the project (and possibly the company). If these goals are not met, there is a real risk that the project will cease to exist and the company will be directly impacted.
Medium (M)	These goals are very important for the existence of the project (and possibly the company). A large number of employees may be affected if these goals are not met. A failure to achieve a medium-rank business goal (e.g., to successfully release an important project) may result in a negative affect to high-rank goals (e.g., damage to the company's brand and reputation).
Low (L)	These goals affect only a small portion of the company's revenue. A small number of employees may be affected if these goals are not met.

Note: New analysts should use the business goal ranking definitions in this table as guidelines only. Ideally, analysts should attempt to define these rankings early in the RMF project process in terms of the project's unique business context. More senior analysts can draw on prior experience to help define these rankings against previous performance and comparable industry benchmarks.

As indicated in Table 2–3, in our example, the analyst identifies and records four business risks. A similar table should be created as a work product in each application of the RMF.

After fully populating business risk tables with data (the tables shown here present a very small amount of example data), the analyst identifies the risk indicators associated with each identified business risk, as well as the likelihood that each of the identified risks will occur. A *risk indictor* is a sign that the risk is materializing, an objective, measurable event that can be monitored and measured by the analyst to determine the status of a risk over time.

As an example, Table 2–4 identifies the principle risk indicators for the four business risks shown in Table 2–3. For example, one indicator for the risk of failing to meet the acceptance criteria is the number of missed project milestones. Based on experience, professional consultation, and research, the analyst assigns the likelihood that the server will not meet the final acceptance criteria as high (H) (as defined in Table 2–5 on page 56). The analyst also defines indicators for the remaining business risks and assigns the probability of their occurrence as moderate (M). The impact of business risks on business goals should be evaluated. The level of impact and the likelihood of occurrence will allow the analyst to evaluate the impact of a business risk on different business goals.

Table 2–3 KillerAppCo's Business Risks

Business Risk	Description
The software fails to meet the acceptance criteria required for release.	The software may fail user acceptance testing criteria. Such failure will affect the release date, negatively affecting the time to market and possibly the company's brand and reputation. The share price of a publicly owned company may be negatively impacted.
System failures cause unplanned downtime.	Any unplanned downtime caused by system failures negatively affects the revenue from the project. In case of the existence of an SLA, this may cause direct monetary loss for the company. Unplanned downtime requires additional resources to execute disaster recovery plans and, possibly, to manually process the data usually processed by the system. News about the unplanned downtime may damage users' perceptions about the system and negatively affect users' demand for the system's services. The share price of a publicly owned company may be negatively impacted.
Security weaknesses cause system failures.	A successful attack against a system negatively affects many business goals at once. First, a successful attack demonstrates that the system is not robust, something that negatively affects the public's perception of the system. This, in turn, causes a decrease in the demand for system services and a decline in revenue. Every successful attack requires investigation and disaster recovery efforts. These efforts consume additional resources, negatively affecting the bottom line. The share price of a publicly owned company may be negatively impacted.
The software fails to perform critical operational functions correctly.	The failure of the system to perform critical operational functions negatively affects users' interest in the system. The use of the system may decline, thus negatively affecting revenue. Large efforts may be needed to apply fixes to shore up system functionality. These efforts may be resource-intensive and will negatively affect the bottom line of the product. News about the failure of the system may damage the company's brand and reputation, and the share price of a publicly owned company may be negatively impacted if the information about the failures makes it to the media.

Table 2–4 KillerAppCo's Business Risk Indicators and Likelihood of Occurrence

Business Risk	Description	Business Risk Indicators	Likelihood of Occurrence
The software fails to meet the acceptance criteria required for release.	The acceptance criteria normally include formal parameters describing the conditions under which the system will be accepted by users and the software development contract will be considered successfully completed.	• Number of missed project milestones • Number of critical-level errors • Effort required to fix critical and important errors • Decrease in the price of the company's shares	H
System failures cause unplanned downtime.	The impact of system failures on the business can be evaluated by studying the costs associated with each failure and the number of these failures.	• Number of reported errors related to system failure • Effort required to execute disaster recovery procedures • Effort required to fix the errors that caused the failures • Number of clients lost • Decline in revenue • Decrease in the price of the company's shares	M
Security weaknesses cause system failures.	The impact of system failures on the business can be evaluated by studying the costs associated with each failure and the number of these failures.	• Number of security vulnerabilities reported • Effort required to execute patching or other remediation • Effort required to fix the errors that caused the failures • Number of clients lost • Decline in revenue • Decrease in the price of the company's shares	M

Continued

Table 2–4 *Continued*

Business Risk	Description	Business Risk Indicators	Likelihood of Occurrence
The software fails to perform critical operational functions correctly.	The failure of the system to perform critical operational functions is better assessed with the decline of use of that system and direct costs associated with system maintenance and upgrade.	• Number of incorrect critical operations performed • Effort required to perform the same business functions using alternative routes • Effort required to fix the errors that caused the failures • Number of clients lost • Decline in revenue • Decrease in the price of the company's shares	M

Table 2–5 Risk Likelihood Scale (from NIST)

Likelihood Value	Definition
High (H)	The threat is highly motivated and sufficiently capable, and controls to prevent the risk from occurring are ineffective.
Medium (M)	The threat is motivated and capable, but controls are in place that may impede successful materialization of the risk.
Low (L)	The threat lacks motivation or capability, or controls are in place to prevent or at least significantly impede the risk from occurring.

Note: New analysts should use the risk likelihood definitions in this table as guidelines only. Ideally, analysts should attempt to define these rankings early in the RMF project process in terms of the project's unique business context. More senior analysts should draw on prior experience to help define these rankings against historical performance or comparable industry benchmarks. The analyst should in all cases document the reasons for selecting the likelihood value of an event.

Table 2–5 shows likelihood values and definitions that analysts can use to determine the likelihood that a risk will occur.

After identifying the risk indicators and likelihood probabilities of each business risk, the analyst determines the business impact of each business

Table 2–6 Business Impacts of KillerAppCo's Business Risks

Business Risk	Business Risk Indicators	Likeli-hood	Impact	Estimated Cost	Impact
The software fails to meet the acceptance criteria required for release.	Number of missed project milestones	H	KillerAppCo will be unable to release the product to the market.	Revenue loss: $10 million Market share loss: 15% Brand and reputation damage: limited	H
System failures cause unplanned downtime.	Clients reporting downtime due to system failures Need to execute disaster recovery plans	M	KillerAppCo will be unable to meet its clients' SLA availability requirements.	Revenue loss: $3 million Market share loss: 5% Brand and reputation damage: extreme	M
Security weaknesses cause system failures.	Clients reporting system failures due to security breaches Need to create software patches	M	KillerAppCo will be unable to meet its clients' SLA availability requirements.	Revenue loss: $3 million Market share loss: 5% Brand and reputation damage: extreme Regulatory violation Legal risk	M
The software fails to perform critical operational functions correctly.	Clients reporting inaccurate transaction data processing Liability case filed	M	KillerAppCo will be noncompli-ant with federal regulations. Lawsuits will ensue.	Revenue loss: $2 million Market share loss: 2% Brand and reputation damage: extreme Regulatory violation Legal risk	M

risk in case the risk materializes. This determination is made by qualitatively describing each risk's impact, including an estimation of the total cost of a materialized risk.

For example, in Table 2–6, the analyst specifies that if the iWare 1.0 Server is unable to meet its final acceptance criteria, KillerAppCo will be unable to release the product to the general public on January 1, 2008, and will experience significant business loss due to schedule slippage. The analyst also notes that forecasts currently estimate a product release date of April 1, 2008. Based on initial market analyses, the analyst concludes that the estimated revenue loss due to the protracted schedule is $10 million. Market share loss is also estimated to be 15% and limited brand damage may occur. Given the significance of these drawbacks, a high (H) business impact rating is used (as defined in Table 2–7). The impacts and costs of the remaining three business risks are also defined by the analyst, and the business impact rating for them is determined to be medium (M).

Table 2–7 shows values that can be used to rate the business impact caused by specific business risks. After assessing the business impact of each business risk, the analyst determines each risk's severity, which is a function of the *likelihood* that the risk will occur (Table 2–5) and the risk's *business impact* (Table 2–7).

Table 2–7 Business Impact Scale (from NIST)

Business Impact Value	Definition
High (H)	(1) Very costly loss of major tangible assets or resources; (2) significant violation of, or harm or impediment to, an organization's mission, reputation, or interest; or (3) human death or serious injury.
Medium (M)	(1) Costly loss of tangible assets or resources; (2) violation of, or harm or impediment to, an organization's mission, reputation, or interest; or (3) human injury.
Low (L)	(1) Loss of some tangible assets or resources; or (2) a noticeable effect on an organization's mission, reputation, or interest.

Note: New analysts should use the business impact definitions in this table as guidelines only. Ideally, analysts should attempt to define these rankings early in the RMF project process in terms of the project's unique business context. More senior analysts can draw from prior experience to help define these rankings against historical performance or comparable industry benchmarks. In the final analysis, analysts should define business impact in terms of financial impact: revenue and market share loss. Other primary determinants are liability exposure, brand and reputation damage, and productivity loss.

Table 2–8 Risk Severity Key (from NIST)

Likelihood	Impact		
	Low	**Medium**	**High**
High (H)	L	M	H
Medium (M)	L	M	M
Low (L)	L	L	L

The following severity value descriptions are used to rate business risks:

- **High**—Indicates a strong need for corrective measures. An existing system may continue to operate, but a corrective action plan must be put in place as soon as possible.

- **Medium**—Indicates that corrective actions are needed and a plan must be developed to incorporate these actions within a reasonable period of time (possibly in a future release).

- **Low**—Indicates that the system's decision authorities must determine whether corrective actions are still required or decide to accept the risk.

Note: New analysts should use the risk severity key definitions defined in this table as guidelines only. Ideally, analysts should attempt to define custom business impact levels (similar to what the International Electrotechnical Commission [IEC] refers to as Safety Integrity Levels, or SILs). The idea is to create a set of target quality metrics for each type of software subsystem or system component to be implemented. That is, the analyst should develop relative target failure and success metrics for each system or system component related to stated quality goal(s). (See IEC 61508; Parts 3, 6 and 7; Version 12.0 05/12/97 [IEC 61508].) The integrity levels may be expressed in terms of low, medium, and high as defined by underlying "cut levels" or target metrics dictated by quality goals. Experienced analysts can draw on prior experience to help define these rankings against historical performance or comparable industry benchmarks.

In our example, the likelihood that iWare 1.0 Server will be unable to meet its final acceptance criteria is high, and the business impact rating of the risk is also high. By referencing Table 2–8, the analyst deduces that high likelihood and high impact produce a high (H) severity score. The severity scores of the three remaining business risks are determined by the analyst to be medium (M).

After determining the severity score of each business risk, the analyst compiles the full set of business risk data. An example of the resulting table is presented in Table 2–9.

Uncovering Technical Risks

This stage of the RMF also involves discovering and describing technical risks and mapping them to business goals. A technical risk is a situation that

Table 2-9 KillerAppCo's Full Set of Business Risk Data

Business Risk	Business Risk Indicators	Likeli-hood	Impact	Estimated Cost	Impact	Severity
The software fails to meet the acceptance criteria required for release.	Series of major project milestones missed	H	KillerAppCo will be unable to release the product to the market.	Revenue loss: $10 million Market share loss: 15% Brand and reputation damage: limited	H	H
System failures cause unplanned downtime.	Clients reporting downtime due to system failures Need to execute disaster recovery plans	M	KillerAppCo will be unable to meet its clients' SLA availability requirements.	Revenue loss: $3 million Market share loss: 5% Brand and reputation damage: extreme	M	M
Security weak-nesses cause system failures.	Clients reporting system failures due to security breeches Need to create software patches	M	KillerAppCo will be unable to meet its clients' SLA availability requirements.	Revenue loss: $3 million Market share loss: 5% Brand and reputation damage: extreme Regulatory violation Legal risk	M	M
The software fails to perform critical operational functions correctly.	Clients reporting inaccurate transaction data processing Liability case filed	M	KillerAppCo will be noncompliant with federal regulations. Lawsuits will ensue.	Revenue loss: $2 million Market share loss: 2% Brand and reputation damage: extreme Regulatory violation Legal risk	M	M

runs counter to the planned design or implementation of the system under consideration.

Analyzing Software Artifacts

The analyst begins to evaluate software artifacts by performing selected analytical best practices (including the software security touchpoints), some of which require the execution of tools, to help identify technical risks.

Table 2–10 presents technical risks resulting from the application of software security touchpoints. In our example, the analyst discovers technical risks that may threaten KillerAppCo's time-to-market, availability, and accuracy business goals. Note that a technical risk may yield multiple business impacts (see TR3 and TR5 in Table 2–10).

Now it's time to determine the indicator(s) associated with each identified technical risk and specify the probability that each risk will materialize. In Table 2–11, the analyst specifies two indicators for the TR4 denial-of-service (DoS) susceptibility risk: a post-deployment increase in unauthorized logins and a post-deployment decrease in mean server availability. Based on independent research, professional experience, and expert collaboration, the

Table 2–10 KillerAppCo's Technical Risks

ID #	Technical Risk
TR1	Developers do not have access to quality assurance (QA) tools for unit testing.
TR2	QA tests do not fully evaluate requirements.
TR3	A. Testing does not cover fault tolerance. System failures are likely.
	B. Testing does not cover fault tolerance. Hardware failures can create incorrect transactions.
TR4	System is susceptible to denial-of-service attacks.
TR5	A. Poor random number generation (RNG) makes crypto weak. Unauthorized access may cause system crashes or unexplained behavior.
	B. Poor RNG makes crypto weak. Attackers can influence transactions or create illegitimate transactions.
TR6	Poor enforcement of access control rules allows misuse by insiders and outsiders.
TR7	Poor password choices make system attacks easier. Unauthorized access can create invalid transactions.
TR8	System does not require good passwords. Attackers can get in more easily and cause unpredictable behavior.

Table 2–11 KillerAppCo's Categorized Technical Risks and Likelihood of Occurrence

ID #	Technical Risk	Technical Risk Indicators	Likelihood
TR1	Developers do not have access to QA tools for unit testing.	Number of development-phase bugs reported	H
TR2	QA tests do not fully evaluate requirements.	Number of requirements-phase bugs reported post-implementation	H
TR3	A. Testing does not cover fault tolerance. System failures are likely. B. Testing does not cover fault tolerance. Hardware failures can create incorrect trans actions.	Number of faults reported Number of inaccurate transactions	H
TR4	System is susceptible to denial-of-service attacks.	Number of unauthorized logins Mean server availability	H
/TR5	A. Poor RNG makes crypto weak. Unauthorized access may cause system crashes or unexplained behavior. B. Poor RNG makes crypto weak. Attackers can influence transactions or create illegitimate transactions.	Number of unauthorized logins Number of unauthorized accesses Number of inaccurate trans-actions	H
TR6	Poor enforcement of access control rules allows misuse by insiders and outsiders.	Number of unauthorized accesses Number of IDS anomalies	H
TR7	Poor password choices make system attacks easier. Unauthorized access can create invalid transactions.	Number of unauthorized accesses Number of inaccurate trans-actions	H
TR8	System does not require good passwords. Attackers can get in more easily and cause unpredictable behavior.	Number of unauthorized logins and accesses Number of IDS anomalies	H

Note: When determining the likelihood that a technical risk will materialize and ascertaining its business impact, analysts should consider controls (e.g., management, operational, and technical) and characteristics (e.g., type of attack, capability of the attacker, intent of the attacker, and resources of the attacker) associated with the risk.

Sometimes functionality gets into a product that none of the product managers or higher-level executives know about or think about strategically. You may find these kinds of things by looking into the code and asking questions (which usually get answered like this: "Oh, yeah. Without that, the system doesn't work for our clients who use Oracle."). At this point it is worth a pause to think. Perhaps you found a business goal that the stakeholders don't focus enough attention on. Business goal omissions are problematic because these omissions lead to requirements omissions, and in turn to design decisions that ripple back and forth along the interface with implementation and support of the real production environments.

For an example, see NIST Special Publication 800-53, "Recommended Security Controls for Federal Information Systems" [NIST 800-53].

analyst also determines the likelihood that the DoS susceptibility risk will occur is high (H). Each remaining technical risk's indicator and likelihood are also defined.

After determining the likelihood that an identified technical risk will occur, the analyst estimates the business impact of each technical risk should it materialize. This link back to business impact is *essential*.

In the example, the analyst documents that poor RNG implementation may lead to system failures, unexplained behavior, and inaccurate transactions (see Table 2–12). Because of this technical vulnerability, unauthorized users can gain access to the system, cause system crashes or unexplained behavior, influence transactions, or create illegitimate transactions. Business impacts are defined by the analyst for each remaining technical risk. If different subsystems are analyzed separately, a cumulative analysis of risks associated with different subsystems is performed. At this time, inter-subsystem risks should also be identified.

Only after the RMF project team is fully satisfied with the initial set of collected business and technical risk data can the analyst proceed to the risk synthesis and prioritization stage. Peer review is an excellent idea.

Synthesizing and Ranking the Risks

To better understand and manage risk, analysts establish relationships between the business goals, business risks, and technical risks and subsequently prioritize them in meaningful business terms. The initial objective may be achieved from the bottom up by first determining the technical risks that lead to each business risk(s) and then determining the business risks associated with each business goal. Analysts can also work from the top

Table 2-12 Impacts of KillerAppCo's Technical Risks

ID #	Technical Risk	Technical Risk Indicators	Likelihood	Impact
TR1	Developers do not have access to QA tools for unit testing.	Number of development-phase bugs reported	H	The inaccessibility of QA tools for developers to use in unit testing may lead to QA problems and acceptance criteria failures.
TR2	QA tests do not fully evaluate requirements.	Number of requirements-phase bugs reported post-implementation	H	The partial evaluation of requirements by QA tests may lead to QA problems and acceptance criteria failures.
TR3	A. Testing does not cover fault tolerance. System failures are likely. B. Testing does not cover fault tolerance. Hardware failures can create incorrect transactions.	Number of faults reported Number of inaccurate transactions	H	Lack of fault tolerance test coverage may lead to unplanned downtime and inaccurate critical operations.
TR4	System is susceptible to denial-of-service attacks.	Number of unauthorized logins Mean server availability	H	DoS susceptibility may lead to unplanned downtime.

TR5	A. Poor RNG makes crypto weak. Unauthorized access may cause system crashes or unexplained behavior. B. Poor RNG makes crypto weak. Attackers can influence transactions or create illegitimate transactions.	Number of unauthorized logins Number of unauthorized accesses Number of inaccurate transactions	H	Poor RNG implementation may lead to system failures, unexplained behavior, and inaccurate transactions.
TR6	Poor enforcement of access control rules allows misuse by insiders and outsiders.	Number of unauthorized accesses Number of IDS anomalies	H	Poor access rule enforcement may lead to unexplained behavior and system failures.
TR7	Poor password choices make system attacks easier. Unauthorized access can create invalid transactions.	Number of unauthorized accesses Number of inaccurate transactions	H	Poor password choices may lead to unauthorized logons and inaccurate transactions.
TR8	System does not require good passwords. Attackers can get in more easily and cause failures. unpredictable behavior.	Number of unauthorized logins and accesses Number of IDS anomalies	H	The system's failure to require good passwords may lead to unexplained behavior and system

down, starting with business goals. In either case, to visualize the problem, analysts create the goal-to-risk relationship table, which displays the relationships between:

- Business goals
- Business risks
- Technical risks (by identification number)

Note that no attempt is made at this point to set priorities in the goal-to-risk relationship table because this action is performed during the following synthesis activity.

As an example, in Table 2–13 the analyst concludes, based on research, professional experience, and expertise, that KillerAppCo's unplanned downtime and system failure business risks directly correspond with the availability goal. The analyst also notes how inadequate fault tolerance testing and DoS susceptibility feed the business risk of unplanned downtime. A similar linkage is created between poor password requirements, inadequate RNG implementation, and limited enforcement of access rules and their collective contribution to the business risk of system failure. Similar relationships are drawn by the analyst for the project's time-to-market and accuracy business goals.

There may be a one-to-many relationship among an identified technical risk and the multiple business risks to which it is related. Note, for example, that the inadequate fault tolerance testing risk (TR3) contributes to both the unplanned downtime *and* inaccurate operational functions business risks.

After developing the goal-to-risk relationship table, the analyst is ready to create a table showing the technical risk severity by business goals. This table depicts how severely an identified technical risk impacts each of the business goals. To determine the severity level, the analyst assesses the likelihood that the technical risk will materialize and builds an estimate of the realized risk's business impacts in terms of each identified business goal.

As an example, in Table 2–14 the analyst deduces that inadequate fault tolerance testing (TR1) and DoS susceptibility (TR2) will negatively impact the project's most important business goal—time to market—since the likelihood of the risks are high and continued acceptance criteria failures (the business risk to which the technical risks are tied) will inevitably prevent the project team from releasing the product on time. No impact (N/A) is discerned between TR1 and TR2 and the other business goals. Note that a single technical risk, such as poor RNG implementation (TR5), may impact *multiple* business goals—availability and accuracy. A single technical risk may also impact multiple business goals at different severity levels.

Table 2–13 KillerAppCo's Goal-to-Risk Relationship Table

Business Goal	Business Risk	ID #	Technical Risk
TIME TO MARKET iWare 1.0 Server must be released on January 1, 2008.	The software fails to meet the acceptance criteria required for release.	TR1	Developers do not have access to QA tools for unit testing.
		TR2	QA tests do not fully evaluate requirements.
AVAILABILITY iWare 1.0 Server must provide 99.999% uptime.	System failures cause unplanned downtime.	TR3	A. Testing does not cover fault tolerance. System failures are likely.
		TR4	System is susceptible to denial-of-service attacks.
	Security weaknesses cause system failures.	TR8	System does not require good passwords. Attackers can get in more easily and cause unpredictable behavior.
		TR5	A. Poor RNG makes crypto weak. Unauthorized access may cause system crashes or unexplained behavior.
		TR6	Poor enforcement of access control rules allows misuse by insiders and outsiders.
ACCURACY Transactions must be recorded with 100% accuracy, with no invalid, duplicate, or missing transactions.	The software fails to perform critical operational functions correctly.	TR7	Poor password choices make system attacks easier. Unauthorized access can create invalid transactions.
		TR5	B. Poor RNG makes crypto weak. Attackers can influence transactions or create illegitimate transactions.
		TR3	B. Testing does not cover fault tolerance. Hardware failures can create incorrect transactions.

By completing the table linking technical risk severity with business goals, analysts indicate the most severe technical risks that the project should address in order to meet prioritized business goals. In the end, the chart presents the critical risk management information necessary to make informed decisions, such as those involving release management, production, and process improvement. This marriage of business and technical

Table 2–14 KillerAppCo's Technical Risk Severity by Business Goals

		Business Goal		
ID #	Technical Risk	Time to Market (H)	Availability (M)	Accuracy (M)
TR1	Developers do not have access to QA tools for unit testing.	**H**	N/A	N/A
TR2	QA tests do not fully evaluate requirements.	**H**	N/A	N/A
TR3	A. Testing does not cover fault tolerance. System failures are likely. B. Testing does not cover fault tolerance. Hardware failures can create incorrect transactions.	N/A	**H**	**H**
TR4	System is susceptible to denial-of-service attacks.	N/A	**H**	N/A
TR5	A. Poor RNG makes crypto weak. Unauthorized access may cause system crashes or unexplained behavior. B. Poor RNG makes crypto weak. Attackers can influence transactions or create illegitimate transactions.	N/A	**H**	**H**
TR6	Poor enforcement of access control rules allows misuse by insiders and outsiders	N/A	**H**	N/A
TR7	Poor password choices make system attacks easier. Unauthorized access can create invalid transactions.	N/A	N/A	**H**
TR8	System does not require good passwords. Attackers can get in more easily and cause unpredictable behavior.	N/A	**H**	N/A

concerns is a central driver to the RMF. These are the sort of data that can be used to answer the all-important "Who cares?" question.

Reviewing the Risk Data

Next, the analyst schedules a meeting with the RMF project team to brainstorm about the accumulated risk data. During the brainstorming session, the meeting attendees:

- Confirm the accuracy and comprehensiveness of the business and technical risks
- Confirm the risk likelihood, impact, and severity rankings

- Confirm the relationships between business goals, business risks, and technical risks
- Create a preliminary outline of the risk analysis report, which includes strategic risk mitigation content

The brainstorming activity typically produces notes as well as updated risk tables. It may also reveal the need for the RMF project team to perform additional analytical activities.

Conducting the Business and Technical Peer Review

After completing all research, risk identification, and synthesis activities, the analyst creates an interim report or presentation summarizing the risk findings and outlines a preliminary risk mitigation strategy. The completed summary is submitted to the RMF project team for business and technical peer review. Note that peer review can sometimes be a time-consuming process; make sure that time is allocated both for necessary peer reviews and for the incorporation of feedback.

Defining the Risk Mitigation Strategy

During this stage, the analyst builds and finalizes a risk mitigation strategy. An outline of this strategy will have been created during the risk synthesis activity. To develop a coherent strategy, the RMF project team meets to brainstorm on possible risk mitigation methods, their effectiveness, and control over the project's software-induced business risks. Results of this work are reported in a comprehensive *risk analysis report* document.

Brainstorming on Risk Mitigation

During the risk mitigation brainstorming session, the RMF project team should answer the question, "How can the software risks that have been identified be managed?" Using this question as a guidepost, the RMF project team members list potential mitigation methods on a whiteboard. Next, they associate the proposed methods with identified technical risks. The group then estimates the effectiveness of the proposed mitigation methods and the level of rigor at which each method must be performed. The resulting approach is a technical strategy motivated by business concerns. Methods must make sense economically, and in the best of all cases they will have a clear ROI that can be demonstrated.

All costs of mitigation must be weighed against each method's predicted effectiveness and compared against potential downside costs (in case a risk materializes). The RMF project team should ensure that the proposed miti-gation methods cover as many of the risks as possible. Those methods that provide large risk coverage at low cost are more valuable. The team also assesses the impact of legislation, regulation, and organizational policy on the ability to perform specific mitigation methods, as well as the impact of method implementation on operations.

After strategizing activities are complete, the team creates a mapping between specific methods and the mitigation of identified business risks. The mapping is given a level of confidence (high, medium, or low). The fully populated table of recommended risk mitigation methods presents the

Table 2–15 KillerAppCo's Recommended Risk Mitigation Methods

Business Risk	Supporting Technical Risk	Improve QA in Early SDLC Phases	Add Fault Tolerance to QA Tests	Add Security Requirements and Security Requirements Testing to SDLC	. . .
The software fails to meet the acceptance criteria required for release. **(H)**	TR1	H			
	TR2	H		M	
System failures cause unplanned downtime. **(M)**	TR3	M	H		
	TR4		M		
Security weaknesses cause system failures. **(M)**	TR5			H	
	TR6			H	
	TR8			H	
The software fails to perform critical operational functions correctly. **(M)**	TR3	M	H		
	TR5			H	
	TR7			H	

information needed to help make risk mitigation decisions crucial to the success of the business. Using these data, stakeholders can clearly think through costs, benefits, and return for various technical activities. This table provides the basis for a description of the risk mitigation strategy.

As an example, in Table 2–15 the analyst highly recommends that the project impose additional QA activities in early SDLC phases to improve the company's chances of meeting its number one business goal—timely release of the product to the market. Although the coverage of this mitigation method is limited to only two of the four business risks, it is estimated that the practice of the method will result in the highest possible ROI in terms of (1) avoided loss of revenue and market share and (2) bypassed brand and reputation damage (see Table 2–9). Specific QA mitigation activities may include having developers use best-of-breed QA tools for early lifecycle unit testing and evaluating requirements during QA test-planning activities.

Authoring the Risk Analysis Report

After completing the table of recommended risk mitigation methods, the analyst authors a risk analysis report.[6] Much of the RMF project's analytical plan content and summary risk data can be used to build the final document. The report contains the following information in this order:

1. An executive summary that establishes purpose, poses a clear problem statement, and motivates future action
2. A summary of the analytical results, which includes the following tables:
   - Goal-to-risk relationship
   - Technical risk severity by business goals
   - Recommended risk mitigation methods
3. A list of the actual risks discovered. Each risk is described in detail with:
   - Context
   - Impact description
   - Mitigation recommendation
   - Validation steps

---

[6]This is not meant to imply that looping through the RMF process is complete. In this case, I am sticking with my "serial order" presentation for reasons of clarity. Also, a report is oriented toward consulting, but you get the idea.

    4. A complete validation plan that includes the following:
- A monitoring and measurement strategy
- A measurement plan that lists and describes the measurements and metrics necessary to quantify the status of each risk undergoing mitigation
- Procedures for collecting risk mitigation data
- A list of the risk indicators to be employed during mitigation
- Risk exit criteria

    5. Conclusions that directly discuss next steps and overall themes in the risks

    6. Appendices that include information such as:
- A list of participants
- A list and description of the analyzed artifacts
- A list and description of the materials used
- A list and description of the key metrics employed
- A list and description of the analytical methods employed

By addressing the preceding information, the risk analysis report:

- Identifies and prioritizes software-induced business risks
- Ensures risk management becomes an integral part of the ongoing SDLC
- Lists and describes the methods and technologies used to mitigate software risks
- Sets up the monitors and measures that can be used to demonstrate risk mitigation progress
- Defines acceptable levels of quality to attain through the practice of custom software risk management strategies and software security touchpoints
- Establishes critical exit criteria linked to business goals

Producing Final Deliverables

After completing the draft risk analysis report, the analyst presents the document to the RMF project team for peer review and subsequent editing. The analyst then uses the document as the basis for creating a draft risk mitigation project plan. The interim risk analysis report is also used to develop a risk analysis presentation to be delivered by the team. The presentation should contain a cost-based summary of the critical content included in the risk analysis report and focus on post-risk mitigation ROI. The analyst should incorporate feedback resulting from the risk analysis presentation into the final draft of the risk analysis report as well as the accompanying project plan.

Carrying Out Fixes and Validating

This stage involves execution of the risk mitigation strategy. Each strategic approach to risk mitigation will differ according to what sorts of risks were identified, what the business context is, and what methods were chosen to manage risk.

Progress at this stage should be measured against the risk mitigation strategy. Good metrics include but are not limited to progress against risks, open risks remaining, and any artifact quality metrics previously identified.

This stage involves application of those validation techniques identified earlier in order to give some confidence that risks have been properly mitigated through artifact improvement. In many respects, the validation plan is a test plan for risk mitigation assurance. Each project will have a unique validation plan that directly depends on the risks identified and the methods chosen to address them.

Testing can be used to demonstrate and measure the effectiveness of various software assurance activities. The central concern at this stage is to validate that the artifacts and processes no longer carry unacceptable risks. This stage should define and leave in place a repeatable, measurable, verifiable validation process that the project can run from time to time to continually verify artifact quality.

The Importance of Measurement

One foundational approach that is critical to any science is measurement. As Lord Kelvin put it:

> *When you can measure what you are speaking about, and express it in numbers, you know something about it; but when you cannot measure it, when you cannot express it in numbers, your knowledge is of a meager and unsatisfactory kind: it may be the beginning of knowledge, but you have scarcely, in your thoughts, advanced to the stage of science.*

Measurement is critical to the future of software security. Only by quantizing our approach and its impact can we answer questions such as: How secure is my software? Am I better off now than I was before? Am I making an impact on the problem? How can I estimate and transfer risk?

We can begin to approach the measurement problem by recycling numbers from the software literature. For example, we know that fixing software problems at the design stage is much cheaper than fixing them later in the lifecycle.[7] An IBM study reports relative cost weightings as: design, 1; implementation, 6.5; testing, 15; maintenance, 100. We also know relative cost expenditures for lifecycle stages: design, 15%; implementation, 60%; testing, 25%. These and similar numbers can provide a foundation for measuring the impact of software security.

Measuring Return

A preliminary study reported by @stake (now part of Symantec) demonstrates the importance of concentrating security analysis efforts at the design stage relative to the implementation and testing phases (see Figure 2–2).

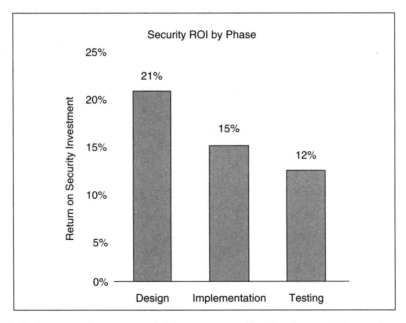

Figure 2–2 Return on investment (ROI) as measured by @stake over 23 security engagements.[8]

---

[7]See Chapter 3, Figure 3–2.
[8]See the trade magazine article by Kevin Soo Hoo, Andrew Sudbury, and Andrew Jaquith, "Tangible ROI through Secure Software Engineering," *Secure Business Quarterly*, Q4 2001 <http://www.sbq.com/sbq/rosi/sbq_rosi_software_engineering.pdf>.

Microsoft reports that more than 50% of the software security problems it finds are design flaws.

Risk management calls for quantitative decision support. Work remains to be done on measuring software security and software security risk, but some metrics are obvious. The most effective metrics involve tracking risk over time.

Measurement and Metrics in the RMF

The most natural and easiest form of measurement in the RMF involves measuring and tracking information about risks and risk status at various times throughout application of the RMF. The Cigital Workbench (explained in the next section) helps to automate this activity. The fact that software development unfolds over time is a boon for measurement because a relative quantity (such as number of risks) measured at two different times can be used to indicate progress.

Risk measurements include but are not limited to:

- Outstanding risks by priority
- Identified risks by priority
- Outstanding risks by type
- Identified risks by type
- Outstanding risks by subtype
- Identified risks by subtype
- Overall risk mitigation status percentage
- Risk mitigation by priority: percentage resolved and percentage outstanding
- Risk mitigation by priority: number resolved and number outstanding
- Number of outstanding risks by financial impact
- Number of identified risks by financial impact
- Number of risks identified without defined mitigation by priority
- Number of risks identified without defined mitigation by type
- Risk discovery rate by priority
- Risk discovery rate by type
- Risk mitigation rate by priority
- Risk mitigation rate by type
- Number of outstanding risks by schedule impact

These kinds of measurements should be made as early as possible and as continuously as possible during the SDLC.

The Cigital Workbench

A key requirement for putting the RMF into practice is automating aspects of the process. Without automation, the elaborate steps of the RMF can become tedious. Those aspects best suited for automation include tracking, storing, and manipulating data about risks; displaying and measuring data about risks; and providing critical information and automation regarding processes. Note that automation like this supports the notion of ongoing, continual updating and refinement of risk data over time.

Cigital provides professional services based on applying the RMF philosophy. We created and use a toolset called the Workbench to make our jobs as consultants more efficient, effective, and consistent. The Workbench, in some sense, is an automated RMF. It is a combination of simple tools and automated processes used to help consultants assess software quality.

The Workbench has three major components:

1. Quality workflows and knowledge
   - Automated RMF[9]
   - Process models and detailed descriptions of software assurance methods (called "the Matrix" internally)
   - Deliverable templates, reporting, and metrics
2. Project communication and collaboration tools
   - A risk management dashboard, used to communicate risk mitigation status and progress (Figure 2–3)
   - A complete knowledge management and document management system (which in version 1 leverages the Livelink knowledge management software)
   - Decision criteria and guidance
3. Process evolution and knowledge capture
   - Process models built to be instantiated and adjusted in particular projects
   - History and knowledge catalogs

---

[9]The Workbench automates a more detailed RMF than the one presented in this chapter.

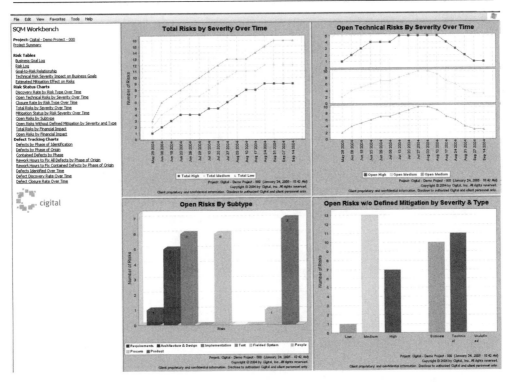

Figure 2–3 The Cigital Workbench risk management dashboard displays information about software risk and business impact over time.

These components capture fundamental aspects of the RMF.

Central to the idea of the Workbench is the notion of tracking information about risks. The Workbench allows for the automatic creation of technical risk ↔ business risk associations, impact analysis, and ranking. Basic risk information is available in a risk log (Figure 2–4). Information about the relationship between business goals and technical risks is displayed in one of many available tables (Figure 2–5).

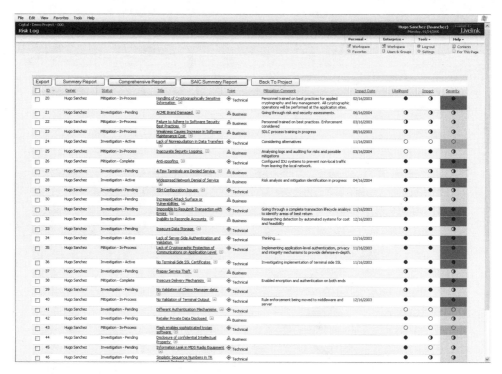

Figure 2–4 The Cigital Workbench allows technical risks and business risks to be tracked over time. The risk log here provides a snapshot of risk status. Tracking risk status is central to the success of the RMF process.

Technical Risk Severity Impact on Business Goals

Project: Cigital - Demo Project - 000

ID#	Business Goals / Technical Risks	Increase ticket sales	Maintain ACME Brand	Maintain Confidentiality of ACME Intellectual Property	Maintain Retailer Privacy	Meet deployed environment SLA	Minimize Fraud and Liability	Minimize Maintenance Costs	Support Decisions with Accurate Incidence Data	Verifiable Audit Trail
20	Handling of Cryptographically Sensitive Information		●					●		
24	Lack of Nonrepudiation in Data Transfers		◑					◑	◑	
26	Anti-spoofing	●	●				●	●		
29	SSH Configuration Issues	●	●				●	●		
31	Impossible to Resubmit Transaction with Errors						●	●		●
33	Insecure Data Storage							◑		
34	Lack of Server-Side Authentication and Validation							●		
35	Lack of Cryptographic Protection of Communications on Application Level							●		
36	No Terminal-Side SSL Certificates		●				●			
38	Insecure Delivery Mechanism		●				●			
39	No Validation of Claims Manager data						●	●		●
40	No Validation of Terminal Output		●				●	●		●
41	Different Authentication Mechanisms				◑			◑		
43	Flash enables sophisticated trojan software		◑	◑	◑					
45	Information Leak in MDS Radio Equipment							◑	●	
46	Simplistic Sequence Numbers in TR Connect Protocol		●			◑		◑		
47	Continued use of plaintext SNMP	●	●					●		

January 24, 2005 - 10:47 AM

Figure 2–5 Technical risks must be tied to business goals or wither under the glare of the ultimate question: "Who cares?"

Risk Management Is a Framework for Software Security

Whether you apply the RMF with the help of an automated tool, such as the Workbench, or simply track risks in an Excel spreadsheet, there is no question that identifying, synthesizing, ranking, and keeping track of risks throughout the SDLC is a central software security practice. The touchpoints described in Part II of this book are best applied in concert with this kind of RMF. That way, risks are properly handled once they are highlighted by particular software security best practices.

There is no such thing as 100% security. Only by practicing risk management and factoring in critical business information about impacts will software security escape the realm of the geeks and have an impact on business.

PART II

Seven Touchpoints
for Software Security

3

Introduction to Software Security Touchpoints[1]

Touchpoints, which are universal, are those predictable
times that occur just before a surge of rapid growth in any
line of development—motor, cognitive, or emotional. . . .

T. BERRY BRAZELTON

A key aim of this book is to explore and describe a set of software security best practices that I call *touchpoints*. Putting software security into practice requires making some changes to the way organizations build software. The good news is that these changes do not need to be fundamental, earth shattering, or cost prohibitive. In fact, adopting a straightforward set of engineering best practices, designed in such a way that security can be interleaved into existing development processes, is often all it takes. Integrating software security best practices into the software development lifecycle is the center of the three pillars of software security.

The software security best practices that I prescribe have their basis in good software engineering and involve explicitly pondering the security situation throughout the software lifecycle. This means knowing and understanding common risks, designing for security, and subjecting all software artifacts to thorough, objective risk analyses and testing. During these activities, software risk should be explicitly tracked and monitored according to the RMF presented in Chapter 2. This chapter presents a quick introduction to the software security touchpoints (a 50,000-foot view, really) and suggests an ordering for their adoption.

Figure 3–1, which also adorns the inside front cover of this book, specifies the software security touchpoints and shows how software practitioners can apply them to the various software artifacts produced during software development. This means understanding how to work security engineering

---

[1]Small portions of this chapter appeared in original form in *Software Development* magazine in September 2005 under the title "The 7 Touchpoints of Secure Software" [McGraw 2005].

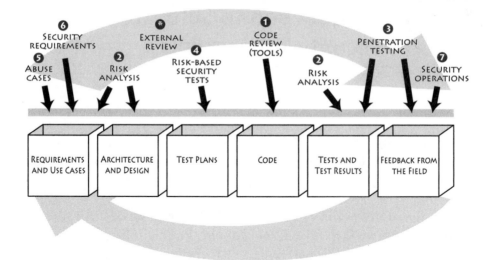

Figure 3–1 Lightweight software security best practices called *touchpoints* are applied to various software artifacts. The best practices are numbered according to effectiveness and importance. Note that by referring only to software artifacts, we can avoid battles over any particular process.

into requirements, architecture, design, coding, testing, validation, measurement, and maintenance.

Although the artifacts are laid out according to something that looks like a traditional waterfall model in the picture, most organizations follow an iterative approach today, which means that touchpoints will be cycled through more than once as the software evolves. In any event, by focusing on the artifacts we can avoid broader process issues (including the ever-present warfare surrounding which software process is the one true way and the light).

As I discuss in Chapter 1, the software security touchpoints are designed to be process agnostic. That is, the touchpoints can be applied no matter which software process you use to build your software. As long as you are producing some minimal set of software artifacts (and every project should at least be producing code!), you can apply the touchpoints.

I used to present the software security touchpoints in order from left to right. Although that works OK, a better pedagogical approach is to order the touchpoints by their natural utility and present them in some sort of ranking. Some touchpoints are by their very nature more powerful than others, and you should adopt the most powerful ones first.

Here are the touchpoints, in order of effectiveness:

1. Code review
2. Architectural risk analysis
3. Penetration testing
4. Risk-based security tests
5. Abuse cases
6. Security requirements
7. Security operations

The ordering I describe will not be a perfect fit for every organization. In fact, the ordering reflects a bias developed over many years of applying these practices in code-o-centric organizations. For that reason, code review comes before architectural risk analysis. However, the fact is that both of the top two touchpoints are critical. If you do code review and skip architectural risk analysis, you will not properly address the software security problem. Harking back to my definitions in Chapter 1, software defects that lead to security problems come in two varieties: bugs and flaws.

Code review aims at finding the bugs. Architectural risk analysis aims at finding the flaws. If you skip one or the other, you're most likely to solve only half the problem. (Remember the 50/50 bug/flaw split.) In any event, the top two touchpoints can be swapped around without any loss of generality.

As for the rest of the touchpoints, the ranking I present is based on years of experience applying the touchpoints at many different kinds of organizations, ranging from large independent software vendors to huge credit card consortiums. The ordering is not absolute. However, any attempt to change the order, say, by doing penetration testing before you do code review, is likely to be not as successful as the way I suggest. Ironically, the "penetration testing first" ordering is the ordering found in most organizations dealing with software security today, especially those shops where the security division is pushing software and application security. This ordering reflects the reactive approach to security that I am trying to counter by talking about building security in and by involving actual builders in the process.

Big organizations can adopt several touchpoints simultaneously in some cases. For more on adopting touchpoints in a large enterprise, see Chapter 10.

Flyover: Seven Terrific Touchpoints

1. Code Review (Tools)

Artifact: Code

Example of risks found: Buffer overflow on line 42

All software projects produce at least one artifact—code. This fact moves code review to the number one slot on our list. At the code level, the focus is on implementation bugs, especially those that *static analysis tools* that scan source code for common vulnerabilities can discover. A taxonomy of these bugs can be found in Chapter 12. Several tools vendors now address this space. Code review is a necessary but not sufficient practice for achieving secure software. Security bugs (especially in C and C++) are a real problem, but architectural flaws are just as big a problem. In Chapter 4 you'll learn how to review code with static analysis tools.

Doing code review alone is an extremely useful activity, but given that this kind of review can only identify bugs, the best a code review can uncover is around 50% of the security problems. Architectural problems are very difficult (and mostly impossible) to find by staring at code. This is especially true for modern systems made of hundreds of thousands of lines of code. A comprehensive approach to software security involves holistically combining both code review and architectural analysis.

2. Architectural Risk Analysis

Artifact: Design and specification

Examples of risks found: Poor compartmentalization and protection of critical data; failure of a Web Service to authenticate calling code and its user and to make access control decisions based on proper context

At the design and architecture level, a system must be coherent and present a unified security front. Designers, architects, and analysts should clearly document assumptions and identify possible attacks. At both the specifications-based architecture stage and at the class-hierarchy design stage, architectural risk analysis is a necessity. At this point, security analysts uncover and rank architectural flaws so that mitigation can begin. Disregarding risk analysis at this level will lead to costly problems down the road.

Note that risks crop up during all stages of the software lifecycle, so a constant *risk management* thread, with recurring risk-tracking and monitoring activities, is highly recommended. Chapter 2 describes the RMF process and how to apply it. Chapter 5 teaches about architectural risk analysis and will help you ferret out flaws in software architecture.

3. Penetration Testing

Artifact: System in its environment

Example of risks found: Poor handling of program state in Web interface

Penetration testing is extremely useful, especially if an architectural risk analysis informs the tests. The advantage of penetration testing is that it gives a good understanding of fielded software in its real environment. However, any such testing that doesn't take the software architecture into account probably won't uncover anything interesting about software risk. Software that fails during the kind of canned black box testing practiced by prefab application security testing tools is truly bad. Thus, passing a low-octane penetration test reveals little about your actual security posture, but failing a canned penetration test indicates that you're in very deep trouble indeed (see Chapter 1).

One pitfall with penetration testing involves who does it. Be very wary of "reformed hackers" whose only claim to being reformed is some kind of self-description.[2] Also be aware that network penetration tests are not the same as application or software-faced penetration tests. If you want to do penetration testing properly, see Chapter 6.

4. Risk-Based Security Testing

Artifact: Units and system

Example of risks found: Extent of data leakage possible by leveraging data protection risk

Security testing must encompass two strategies: (1) testing of security functionality with standard functional testing techniques and (2) risk-based security testing based on attack patterns, risk analysis results, and abuse cases. A good *security test plan* embraces both strategies. Security problems aren't always apparent, even when you probe a system directly, so standard-issue quality assurance is unlikely to uncover all critical security issues. QA is about making sure good things happen. Security testing is about making sure bad things don't happen. Thinking like an attacker is essential. Guiding security testing with knowledge of software architecture, common attacks, and the attacker's mindset is thus extremely important. Chapter 7 shows you how to carry out security testing given some insight into the system's construction.

---

[2] How do we know they're reformed? Because they told us they were reformed.

5. Abuse Cases

Artifact: Requirements and use cases
Example of risks found: Susceptibility to well-known tampering attack

Building abuse cases is a great way to get into the mind of the attacker. Similar to use cases, abuse cases describe the system's behavior under attack; building abuse cases requires explicit coverage of what should be protected, from whom, and for how long. Underused but important, abuse and misuse cases are the subject of Chapter 8. Practitioners wondering how abuse cases might work for them will get lots of mileage out of that chapter.

6. Security Requirements

Artifact: Requirements
Example of risks found: No explicit description of data protection needs

Security must be explicitly worked into the requirements level. Good security requirements cover both overt functional security (say, the use of applied cryptography) and emergent characteristics (best captured by abuse cases and attack patterns). The art of identifying and maintaining security requirements is a complex undertaking that deserves broad treatment. Interested readers are encouraged to check out the references in the Security Requirements box on the next page for pointers. A brief treatment of the subject can be found spread throughout Chapters 7 and 8.

7. Security Operations

Artifact: Fielded system
Example of risks found: Insufficient logging to prosecute a known attacker

Software security can benefit greatly from network security. Well-integrated security operations allow and encourage network security professionals to get involved in applying the touchpoints, providing experience and security wisdom that might otherwise be missing from the development team. Battle-scarred operations people carefully set up and monitor fielded systems during use to enhance the security posture. Attacks do happen, regardless of the strength of design and implementation, so understanding software behavior that leads to successful attack is an essential defensive technique. Knowledge gained by understanding attacks and exploits should be cycled back into software development.

*. External Analysis

This is not really a touchpoint, but it's important enough to emphasize so I've put it in the touchpoints picture anyway. External analysis (i.e., analysis by somebody outside the design team) is often a necessity when it comes to security. *All* software security touchpoints are best applied by people not involved in the original design and implementation of the system.

Every programmer has been stuck for hours working on a bug only to have a buddy (coming to drag you off for pizza) show up and point out the error: "How come you did that?!" This always warrants a huge groan. Argh! This phenomenon can happen in all stages of the software lifecycle— one reason why external analysis is a necessity.

Security Requirements

Study of security requirements is fairly new, and the literature is spotty. Here are two pointers to recommended reading:

Jonathan D. Moffett, Charles B. Haley, and Bashar Nuseibeh, "Core Security Requirements Artifacts," Technical Report 2004/23. Department of Computing, The Open University, Milton Keynes, UK, June 2004.

Nancy Mead, "Requirements Engineering for Survivable Systems," Technical Report CMU/SEI-2003-TN-013. Pittsburgh, PA: Software Engineering Institute, Carnegie Mellon University, 2003.

Why Only Seven?

Some approaches to software security are way too bulky for most organizations to swallow. By limiting the touchpoints to seven best practices, I hope to make effective best practices easier to adopt while still making a huge impact on software security. The touchpoints are not only amenable to whatever process you already follow to make software (you do ship software already, right?) but also lightweight and easy to use. If you apply the seven terrific touchpoints outlined here, your software will be much more secure.

Black and White: Two Threads Inextricably Intertwined

As I note in the Preface, the two threads of black hat and white hat activities intertwine to make up software security. This idea serves as inspiration for the cover of this book. The yin/yang design is the classic Eastern symbol related to the inextricable mixing of standard Western polemics. Eastern philosophies are for this reason called holistic. A holistic approach, mixing yin and yang—that is, mixing the black hat and white hat approaches—is just what the doctor ordered.

I define *destructive activities* as those about attacks, exploits, and breaking software. These kinds of things are represented by the black hat. I define *constructive activities* as those about design, defense, and functionality. These are represented by the white hat. Perhaps a less judgmental way to think about the dichotomy is in terms of defense and offense. Neither defense nor offense is intrinsically bad or good, and both are necessary to play almost any sport well. In any case, based on destroying and constructing, we can look back over the touchpoints and describe how the black and white threads intertwine.

Code review is a white hat (constructive) activity informed by a black hat history. The idea is to avoid implementation problems while we build software to be secure.

Architectural risk analysis is a white hat (constructive) activity also informed by a black hat history. In this case, we work to avoid design flaws while we build software to be secure.

Penetration testing is a black hat (destructive) activity. The best kind of penetration testing is informed by white hat knowledge of design and risk. But all the penetration testing in the world will not build you secure software.

Risk-based security testing is a mix of constructive and destructive activities that requires a holistic two-hat approach. Because risk-based security testing is driven by abuse cases and risk analysis results as well as functional security requirements, a mix of black hat and white hat is unavoidable.

Abuse cases are tricky. You might guess by the name that abuse cases involve only a black hat (destructive) activity. That would be wrong. Abuse cases are themselves driven by the two threads. White hat (constructive) thinking drives security requirements, which are a necessary foundation for a goodly percentage of the abuse cases. Black hat thinking in the form of attack patterns drives the remaining portion. Though abuse cases clearly involve a mix of both hats, the predominant hat is black.

Security requirements and the resulting security functionality are squarely constructive, white hat activities. These are defined and built as an explicit defense against the black hat world. In fact, the notion of security requirements is in some sense the ultimate white hat activity.

Security operations is a white hat activity, but it is only very weakly constructive. Operations is essential to security, of course, but in terms of building security in, the tactics carried out by network-faced ops people are largely defensive.

Many of the touchpoints amount to assurance activities focused on assessing the security situation by looking at the state of various artifacts. Others, like abuse case development and security test planning, involve creating security-related artifacts from scratch. In general, those activities that involve creating new artifacts are in the business of attack creation, design, and simulation.[3] They are, in a sense, the kinds of activities best carried out with your black hat on. The others are more about constructing software properly. They are best performed while wearing your white hat.

Software security requires a matching set of both black hats and white hats, inextricably bound together.

Moving Left

Software people know that it is much more economical to find software defects early in the lifecycle than it is to find them later. Academia provided some data about this during the 1970s but has been remiss in its duty to drive the point home with even more data.[4] Nevertheless, the fact is that fixing a problem at the requirements stage (before design, architecture, and code exist) is bound to be much cheaper than fixing even a simple bug once thousands or millions of copies of the fielded software are installed.

Simply put, early is better (Figure 3–2). This fact may seem to run at cross-purposes with the "effectiveness" ordering of the touchpoints that I suggest. However, effectiveness for me takes into account much more than simply cost. I also thought about which software artifacts are likely to be available, what kinds of tools exist (and how good they are), and the challenge presented by cultural change. When you factor in those things, I stand by my ordering.

If early is better, it seems somewhat crazy to focus all of our attention in software security at the end of the lifecycle. But that's what we seem to be doing. Hiring reformed hackers to carry out a penetration test against your fielded software or running some kind of penetration testing tool is

---

[3]It's peculiar that these "constructive" activities—building new artifacts—are really destructive in nature! Such are the vagaries of software security.

[4]The most oft-cited data in this regard are those gathered by TRW and IBM under the guidance of Barry Boehm <http://sunset.usc.edu/people/barry.html>. See Figure 3–2.

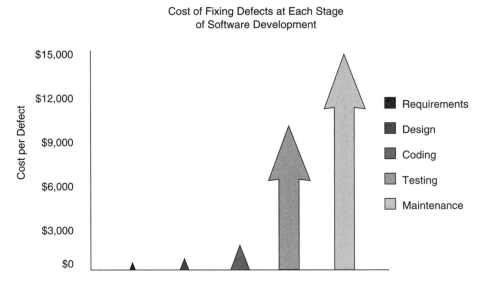

Figure 3–2 Data from Barry Boehm's work showing how much cheaper it is to fix a defect early in the lifecycle. Use this chart to convince management of the importance of starting early. Source:TRW

probably better than doing nothing. But when these late lifecycle methods find problems in your software, what are you going to do? This reactive strategy (which is really a kind of penetrate-and-patch approach) may well work OK when the fix involves something operational or environmental in nature such as installing a better operating system version, changing firewall rules, or otherwise tweaking an operational environment. But a reactive approach doesn't work so well when the problems are deep in the software itself (which is, frankly, where most of the core problems are). The state of the practice, "penetration testing first," is not very clever. One caveat is in order. Penetration testing can be very effective in lighting the security fire. That is, in a skeptical organization that thinks it is doing everything right from a security perspective, there is nothing quite as powerful as a working, demo-able remote exploit to scare the heck out of people. Use this approach with great care.

Actually, there is one strategy worse than "penetration testing first," and that is the "panic when attacked" approach. Large numbers of organizations are so far behind in computer security that they don't even realize what trouble they're in until it's way too late. If you're reading this book, you're not likely in that boat.

The answer to both of these lame strategies is to "push left" in the touchpoints diagram (Figure 3–1). In fact, the top two touchpoints—code review (with a tool) and architectural risk analysis—exist just to the left of penetration testing. In terms of economic return, those touchpoints further to the left are going to perform better. (Of course, return alone is not the best measurement for the efficacy of a touchpoint.) In a nice coincidence, the "push left" rule gets us to the top two touchpoints very early in the game.

I predict that the software security world will soon move left into code review and that this will result in great benefit. Much more sophisticated tools exist now than were around only a few short years ago. Of course, code review with an advanced tool is no panacea for software security. We know that even the best tool in the world will find only about half the problems. Of course, finding half of the problems sure beats finding none of them.

Evidence of the move to the left already exists. A number of traditional IT firms that offered network security testing and very basic application security testing with black box tools are beginning to offer security code review (using tools, of course). This is an encouraging development.

Next will come a wave of architectural risk analysis. This is a much trickier undertaking, best performed by experts today. With better knowledge and better process models, risk analysis will be adopted by a much larger target market. In absence of in-house experts, start with your existing requirements managers and other savvy stakeholders and enhance them with outside consultants until they get on their feet. If your stakeholders know the domain well enough to hand-build a capacity plan (the performance analog of a risk analysis), they can hold the architects' feet to the fire during a more rigorous pencil-and-paper security review process.

Ultimately, pushing all the way left into requirements is our goal. By taking on security at the very beginning of the software lifecycle, we can really do the best job of building security in.

This natural evolution of adoption can easily be mirrored in any organization, from the largest to the smallest. Begin moving left as soon as possible (see Chapter 10). And by all means, get "inside" as quickly as you can. External penetration tests can help you determine how severe the problem is, but they do little to fix it.

In some cases, especially when outside consultants are involved, it is possible to combine best practices into a more holistic assessment. For example, my company, Cigital, ensures complete coverage of the software defect space by combining code review and architectural risk assessment into one service offering. Other potent combinations of touchpoints involve risk-based security testing married with penetration testing, security requirements analysis with abuse case development, code review with penetration testing, and architectural risk analysis with risk-based testing. Don't be afraid to experiment with combinations. The touchpoints are teased apart and presented separately mostly for pedagogical reasons.

Touchpoints as Best Practices

As noted earlier, the software security field is a relatively new one. The first books and academic classes on the topic appeared in 2001, demonstrating how recently developers, architects, and computer scientists have started systematically studying how to build secure software. The field's recent appearance is one reason why best practices are neither widely adopted nor in some cases obvious.

The good news is that technologists and commercial vendors all acknowledge that the software security problem exists. The bad news is that we have barely begun to instantiate solutions; moreover, many proposed solutions are impotent. Not surprisingly, early commercial solutions to the software security problem tend to take an operational stance—that is, they focus on solving the software security problem through late lifecycle activities such as firewalling (at the application level), penetration testing, and patch management. Because security has tended to be operational in nature (especially in the corporate world, where IT security revolves around the proper placement and monitoring of network security apparatus), this operational tack is only natural. This leads to a bifurcation of approaches when it comes to software, into application security and software security.

The core of the problem is that building systems to be secure cannot be accomplished by using an operations mindset. Instead, we must revisit all phases of system development and make sure that security engineering is present in each of them. When it comes to software, this means taking a close look over all software artifacts. This is a far cry from black box testing.

Best practices are usually described as those practices expounded by experts and adopted by practitioners. As a group, the touchpoints vary in terms of adoption. While almost every organization worried about security makes use of penetration testing, very few venture into the murky area of abuse case development. Though I understand that the utility and rate of adoption varies among the touchpoints in this book, I am comfortable calling them all best practices.

Coder's Corner*

Count the problems in the following chunk of code. Use your knowledge of the touchpoints to think about what kinds of best practices might help you identify the different "levels" of problems here.

```
1 read(fd, userEntry, sizeof(userEntry));
2 comparison = memcmp(userEntry, correctPasswd, strlen(userEntry));
3 if (comparison != 0)
4     return (BAD_PASSWORD);
```

Line 1: Return value from read() ignored. Always a bad sign but not directly resulting in an attack. This is the sort of bug that a fairly simple source code analyzer can alert you to. Manual code inspection for quality issues can find these kinds of bugs as well.

Line 2: Comparing a user entry directly with the correct password. Hmm. The implication is that the system stores passwords in such a manner that they can be directly recovered in plaintext (as opposed to storing a hash). This is an architectural flaw best found during architectural risk analysis.

Line 2: strlen() relies on the read() plopping a null terminator down at the end of the buffer. No guarantee of that. A fancier source code analyzer can see the connection between the read() and the strlen(). Code review with a tool is helpful for finding bugs like this.

Line 3: The comparison succeeds if the entered password exactly matches the correct password *or* if the entered password is of length zero. Oops. Bye-bye password security. This kind of problem can be uncovered with good testing based on reasonable requirements and solid test planning.

There's a slightly more subtle truth at play here beyond the point problems discussed above. Although the example is contrived to pack lots of badness into a small number of lines, it's really not that unusual to find security problems clustered like this. The clueless are often gifted with the ability to be clueless in multiple dimensions simultaneously. The seven touchpoints help find all manner of cluelessness and stamp it out.

---

*This example is adapted from an interview in *Slashdot* by Paul Kocher. See <http://interviews.slashdot.org/interviews/03/03/27/1357236.shtml?tid=172>.

Fortunately, an organization is not required to put all touchpoints into practice to see progress on software security. Chapter 10 explains how to put together an enterprise-wide software security program and describes why adopting even only one or two of the software security touchpoints can help. Think of the touchpoints as a maturity map for your organization. The more you adopt and the more deeply you adopt, the better . . . but every little bit helps.

As you adopt touchpoints in your organization, do not overlook the importance of a consistent approach to risk management. The RMF (see Chapter 2) provides a potent foundation for all touchpoints. There is little use in identifying security risks unless you intend to do something about them. Use the RMF to track progress against identified risks over time.

Who Should Do Software Security?

As it stands in many organizations, software security is nobody's job. Developers, architects, and other builders are often unaware of security and possess little in the way of software security knowledge. When their software suffers from security failure, they don't often feel responsible, arguing that security is up to the people in operations who install and operate the software they create.

A very common reaction among developers and software teams when confronted with a security problem in their system (say, during the presentation of risk analysis results) is "You can't do that! Nobody would ever do that! And even if they did, you're not supposed to do that!" Those software people who say things like that usually believe that security is IT's job and an infrastructure issue. By now you should know why that is incorrect. One key goal of the software security touchpoints is to arm software teams with enough information that these excuses never crop up. By understanding and thinking about security throughout the software development lifecycle, developers can avoid nasty surprises.

Operations people become upset when their pristine, mostly secure network is sullied by insecure software. They don't understand why software people produce such "crap," and they don't feel responsible for the ensuing security mess. They decry the pathetic state of software and wish that software developers knew more about security. In desperation, operations people grasp at security straws such as application firewalls and intrusion detection systems.

Obviously, this is not a healthy situation. When a security problem happens because of bad software, there really is nobody to hold responsible. The standard security people in operations are not really at fault (it's not their broken software), and neither are the software people (they're not security people). Organizationally, this is a textbook management problem.

In the best possible world, software security would be everybody's job. In a more realistic world, assigning responsibility and accountability to a particular group can help solve the problem.

One suggestion worth thinking about involves finding the person with the best handle on the way your whole software system works and tapping that person for software security. Ask who you turn to when something goes drastically wrong, but you don't have a clue about what is causing the problem. The jack-of-all-trades whom you turn to is your new software security person.[5]

Building a Software Security Group

The world has not yet produced many software security people. That's a shame because the world certainly needs more. Fortunately, academia appears to be slowly rising to the occasion, and a number of schools are beginning to teach software security and/or security engineering courses (see the next box, Software Security in the Academy).

There is not enough time to wait for academia to produce the solution. Instead, software security people need to be developed inside existing organizations (like yours). If you want to invent some software security people in your organization, consider the following advice.

Don't start with security people. Though software security is certainly essential to addressing the computer security fiasco we find ourselves in, a standard reactive approach will fail. Network security people often don't know enough about software to make good software security people. They may know loads of stuff about how software operations work (even more in many cases than developers and architects know), but this is not what we need to solve the software security problem. Normal security practitioners

---

[5]This is way too glib, of course (though it will appeal to those "builders" who are accustomed to the hero approach—"we threw a guy at that"). More mature organizations need a better-fleshed-out "who," "what," "where" framework. Different people accept different portions of the responsibility as you divide, conquer, and collaborate. See Chapter 10.

Software Security in the Academy

A number of academic institutions now offer security courses very much relevant to *Building Security In*. The best include the following:

- University of California at Davis
- University of Virginia
- Johns Hopkins University
- Princeton University
- Purdue University (especially the CERIAS center)
- Rice University
- University of California at Berkeley
- Stanford University
- Naval Postgraduate School (a military school for graduates)
- University of Idaho
- Iowa State University
- George Washington University
- United States Military Academy at West Point

Just to highlight a couple of examples, here are some of the courses offered by these schools:

- Introduction to Computer Security (practice): UC Davis
- Computer and Information Security (theory): UC Davis
- Computer Security: An Intrusion Detection Approach: UC Davis
- Foundations of Computer and Information Security: UC Davis
- Computer Incident Detection and Response: Purdue
- Cryptography and Data Security: Purdue
- Penetration Analysis: Purdue
- Advanced Topics in Security (information assurance): Purdue

Instrumental groundbreaking work in security education has been spearheaded by Matt Bishop of UC Davis and Cynthia Irvine of the Naval Postgraduate School. Eugene Spafford of Purdue has also been extremely active in calling for better security education. For more on this important topic, see the "Education" department in *IEEE Security & Privacy* magazine <http://www.computer.org/security>.

almost never know anything about compilers, language frameworks, software architecture, testing, and the myriad other things necessary to be a solid software person.

Arming a normal infosec guy with a silly first-generation code scanner like ITS4 or a black box testing tool like Sanctum's Appscan rarely helps. Tools do not have enough smarts to turn network professionals into software people over night. Beware of security consultants who claim to be application security specialists when all they really know how to do is run ITS4 or Appscan and print out an incomprehensible report.

Start with software people. Security is much easier to learn about and grok than software development is. Good software people are very valuable, but software security is so important that these highly valuable people need to be repositioned. Also note that software people pay attention only to other software people, especially those with impressive scars. Don't make the mistake of putting lamers or newbies in front of a group of seasoned developers. The ensuing feeding frenzy is downright scary (if not hugely entertaining).

Identifying a responsible person or two is critical to a successful software security program (see Chapter 10). Not only is this important from an accountability perspective, but the sheer momentum that comes from a dedicated person can't be matched. If you want to adopt a new way to do code review (using a tool like Fortify), identify a champion and empower that person to get things done.

Often the most useful first person in a software security group is a risk management specialist charged with addressing software security risks that have been uncovered by outside consultants. Appointing a risk management person makes it much less likely that important results will be swept under the rug or otherwise forgotten by very busy organizations (and who is not busy these days?). The risk management specialist can be put in charge of the RMF.

Mentoring or otherwise training a new software security person may be impossible if there are no existing software security types in your organization. If that's the case, hire outside consultants to come and help you boot up a group. The extensive experience and knowledge that software security consultants have today are as valuable as they are rare, but it is well worth investing in mentoring your people in order to build that capability.

Ultimately, you want two types of people to populate your software security group: black hat thinkers and white hat thinkers. If you're lucky, you'll find people who can switch hats at, um, the drop of a hat. But more likely, you'll have some good constructive types (who naturally swing toward the white hat side) and some devious destructive types (who naturally swing toward the black hat side). In some sense, this matches the distinction between builders and auditors. You need both, of course, because the touchpoints demand both. Know that the builders are much more important than the auditors, though.

Software Security Is a Multidisciplinary Effort

Software security as a discipline is a new undertaking. On the plus side, new disciplines benefit from a creative mix of seemingly unrelated disciplines (see the box Creativity in a New Discipline). On the negative side, software security is so new that sometimes it is not clear exactly how it should be practiced.

Software security can and should borrow from other disciplines in computer science and software engineering when developing and evolving best practices. A quick shout out to related fields is important, as the literature defining software security remains fairly sparse. The following topics are of particular relevance and well worth diving into:

- Security requirements engineering
- Design for security, software architecture, and architectural analysis
- Security analysis, security testing, and use of the Common Criteria
- Guiding principles for software security and case studies in design and analysis
- Auditing software for implementation risks, architectural risks, automated tools, and technology developments (code scanning, information flow, and so on)
- Common implementation risks (buffer overflows, race conditions, randomness, authentication systems, access control, applied cryptography, and trust management)

A number of these topics have some coverage in the annotated bibliography found in Chapter 13. Much work remains to be done in each of the best practice areas defined by the touchpoints, but other basic practical solutions should be adapted from areas of more mature practice as well.

Creativity in a New Discipline*

We are experiencing a time of great creativity in computer security and must seize the opportunity presented by our current situation while we can. The diversity of backgrounds represented by today's security practitioners may be a high-water mark. Consider that today's security thought leaders were trained in fields as diverse as biostatistics, divinity, economics, and cognitive science, and thus bring with them interesting new perspectives on the security challenge. This leads to creative interplay in the field and has resulted in interesting progress, including the emergence of economic theories of security, an embrace of risk management, an emphasis on process-driven approaches (versus product sets), a shift toward software security, the rise of security engineering, and so on. As the worldwide security paradigm shift from guns, dogs, and concrete to networks, information systems, and computers continues unabated, we must leverage this time of creative diversity for all it's worth.

A number of young researchers joined the computer security field in the mid-1990s, changing the focus of security research from spookware and national defense (think crypto, multilevel security, communications monitoring, and the like) to commercial systems and commerce. This movement away from military-oriented research was driven in part by the widespread public adoption of the Internet and the growing trend of e-commerce. With money at stake, security quickly became as relevant to business as it was to national defense. This influx of "new blood" shook up the scientific security research community and continues to have far-reaching effects that are only now affecting commercial security—the commercialization of firewalls, the rise of antivirus technology, and the adoption of modern security platforms, such as Java and .NET, were all predicted and spearheaded by new thinkers in the security research community.

Where Today's Security People Come From

Only a handful of people working in computer security today started their careers in the field. In fact, academic programs expressly designed to train security practitioners are a recent phenomenon and remain rare.

Interestingly, it may be in this dearth of "qualified" people trained in security that a critical opportunity can be found. Though few practitioners have academic security

---

* Portions of this text box originally appeared in my *Network* magazine "[In]security" column from February 2005 entitled "Are We in a Computer Security Renaissance?" The seed idea came from a conversation with Dan Geer. *Network* magazine is now *IT Architect*.

Continued

training, they most assuredly do have academic training in some field of study. That means that as a collective, the computer security field is filled with diverse and interesting points of view. This is exactly the sort of Petri dish of ideas that led to the Renaissance at the end of the Dark Ages.

Diversity of ideas is healthy, and it lends a creativity and drive to the security field that we must take advantage of. A great example of this can be found in the new subfield of software security. Only five years ago the notion that bad software might be a major root cause of security issues was not common. Today, software security is the subject of keynote talks at the RSA security conference <http://rsaconference.com/>, and we all seem to agree that we have a software problem to solve. This change was partially due to the involvement of programming languages people (once found only at obscure academic conferences like OOPSLA) in the security field. Such involvement resulted in the creation of modern languages like Java and .NET that include security models in their very design. When languages are declared "secure," things get interesting! The evolutionary arms race between attackers and defenders jumps a level, new avenues for security design emerge, and dusty but thorny problems (think "buffer overflow") become less relevant to the next generation of systems.

Where Tomorrow's Security People Will Come From

These days, academic and professional training programs are being put in place to train the next generation of security professionals. Soon, standard curricula will be developed, and students will be required to understand the same core set of concepts. This will certainly help to solidify the field of computer security, but at the same time, there is a danger that generalization may lead to a homogenization of security. Instead of the creative soup afforded by a multiplicity of points of view spanning many fields, security runs the risk of becoming staid and static. If we are careful to avoid complete homogenization of the field, we can retain the benefits of diversity while building a solid academic discipline. One way to do this might be to encourage those students seeking computer security degrees to study widely in other supposedly unrelated disciplines as well. Another is to ensure that outside perspectives remain welcome in the field and are not dismissed out of hand. Computer security must remain an inclusive discipline in order to retain its creativity.

In any case, we must take advantage of the situation we find ourselves in now. Computer security is, in fact, experiencing an important rebirth, and now is the time to make great progress. We must pay close attention to different ideas, embrace change, and help security continue to evolve even as it begins to crystallize.

Touchpoints to Success

As I have said before, software security is not security software. Security functionality alone will not make software secure. The touchpoints outlined here reinforce and flesh out that perspective by emphasizing the kinds of assurance activities necessary to build security in. To attain software security, software projects must apply the touchpoints throughout the software lifecycle, practicing security assurance as they go. The touchpoints I have identified take into account both security mechanisms (such as access control) and design for security (such as robust design that makes software attacks difficult). These encompass both black hat and white hat activities. Sometimes the areas overlap, but often they don't. They are, however, closely aligned.

One central goal of this book is to describe the best practices overviewed in this chapter in more detail. Touchpoints are one of the three pillars of software security. As the connectedness, complexity, and extensibility of modern software continue to impact software security in a negative way, we must begin to grapple with the problem in a more reasonable fashion than simply spray painting cryptography on our code. Integrating a decent set of best practices into the software development lifecycle is an excellent way to do this. Playing the game of software security requires both good offense and good defense (in other words, two hats), and for that reason the touchpoints use both constructive and destructive approaches. Although software security as a field has much maturing to do, it already has a lot to offer to those practitioners interested in striking at the heart of security problems.

Code Review with a Tool[1]

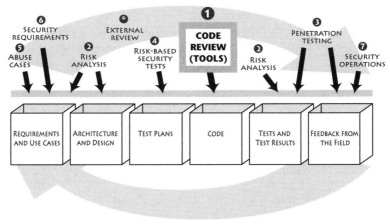

*Debugging is at least twice as hard as programming. If
your code is as clever as you can possibly make it,
then by definition you're not smart enough to debug it.*

BRIAN KERNIGHAN

All software projects are guaranteed to have one artifact in common—
source code. Because of this basic guarantee, it makes sense to center
a software assurance activity around code itself. Plus, a large number of security problems are caused by simple bugs that can be spotted in code (e.g.,
a buffer overflow vulnerability is the common result of misusing various
string functions including `strcpy()` in C). In terms of bugs and flaws, code
review is about finding and fixing bugs. Together with architectural risk
analysis (see Chapter 5), code review for security tops the list of software
security touchpoints. In this chapter, I describe how to automate source
code security analysis with static analysis tools.

---

[1]Parts of this chapter appeared in original form in *IEEE Security & Privacy* magazine co-
authored with Brian Chess [Chess and McGraw 2004].

Using a tool makes sense because code review is boring, difficult, and tedious. Analysts who practice code review often are very familiar with the "get done, go home" phenomenon described in *Building Secure Software* [Viega and McGraw 2001]. It is all too easy to start a review full of diligence and care, cross-referencing definitions and variable declarations, and end it by giving function definitions (and sometimes even entire pages of code) only a cursory glance.

Instead of focusing on descriptions and discussions of processes for generic code review or code inspection in this chapter, I refer the reader to the classic texts on the subject [Fagan 1976; Gilb and Graham 1993]. This chapter assumes that you know something about manual code review. If you don't, take a quick look at Tom Gilb's Web site <http://www.gilb.com/> before you continue.

Catching Implementation Bugs Early (with a Tool)

Programmers make little mistakes all the time—a missing semicolon here, an extra parenthesis there. Most of the time, such gaffes are inconsequential; the compiler notes the error, the programmer fixes the code, and the development process continues. This quick cycle of feedback and response stands in sharp contrast to what happens with most security vulnerabilities, which can lie dormant (sometimes for years) before discovery. The longer a vulnerability lies dormant, the more expensive it can be to fix. Adding insult to injury, the programming community has a long history of repeating the same security-related mistakes.

One of the big problems is that security is not yet a standard part of the programming curriculum. You can't really blame programmers who introduce security problems into their software if nobody ever told them what to avoid or how to build secure software. Another big problem is that most programming languages were not designed with security in mind. Unintentional (mis)use of various functions built into these languages leads to very common and often exploited vulnerabilities.

Creating simple tools to help look for these problems is an obvious way forward. The promise of static analysis is to identify many common coding problems automatically, before a program is released.

Static analysis tools (also called source code analyzers) examine the text of a program statically, without attempting to execute it. Theoretically, they can examine either a program's source code or a compiled form of the program to equal benefit, although the problem of decoding the latter can be difficult. We'll focus on source code analysis in this chapter because that's where the most mature technology exists (though see the box Binary Analysis?!).

Manual auditing of the kind covered in Tom Gilb's work is a form of static analysis. Manual auditing is very time consuming, and to do it effectively, human code auditors must first know how security vulnerabilities look before they can rigorously examine the code. Static analysis tools compare favorably to manual audits because they're faster, which means they

Binary Analysis?!

Source code analyzers are particularly useful when you're building software, but what about those times when you don't have source code? One common situation arises when you buy commercial software that is delivered only in executable form. As *Exploiting Software* explains, attackers really don't need source code to find vulnerabilities and develop exploits [Hoglund and McGraw 2004]. In fact, disassemblers and decompilers are tools that feature prominently in the attacker's toolkit. If the attackers can do this, why can't the good guys?

The answer is not so simple. Finding one or two vulnerabilities in a binary is very easy. In fact, grep-like engines that look for simple patterns in binaries in much the same way that ITS4 looks for them in source code already exist. One of the first was Hoglund's BugScan. The complexity of the problem has its roots deep in the basic asymmetry of computer security. Since attackers need to find only *one* problem (and build an exploit for it) and defenders need to find *all* problems (and fix them or otherwise defend against attack), attackers' tools can lack precision and still be useful.

Building a binary scanner is an uphill battle, but it is not impossible. The main problem is creating the same kind of abstract internal representation of a binary that is created when a sophisticated source code analyzer does its thing. Once that is done, standard sorts of analysis engines can be applied to this representation just as in the (easier) source code approach.

Of course, once you find a problem in a binary, what are you to do about it? If you don't have the source code, it seems you are left with either building and applying a binary patch or creating a rule for an external filter. Not pretty.

In the end, it should be clear why source code analysis is superior if you are concerned about the software security big picture and you are creating code. If you are consuming more code than you produce, a binary scanner may be helpful for keeping your software vendors in line.

can evaluate programs much more frequently, and they encapsulate security knowledge in a way that doesn't require the tool operator to have the same level of security expertise as a human auditor. Just as a programmer can rely on a compiler to enforce the finer points of language syntax consistently, the operator of a good static analysis tool can successfully apply that tool without being aware of the finer points of security bugs.

Testing for security vulnerabilities is complicated by the fact that they often exist in hard-to-reach states or crop up in unusual circumstances. Static analysis tools can peer into more of a program's dark corners with less fuss than dynamic analysis, which requires actually running the code. Static analysis also has the potential to be applied before a program reaches a level of completion at which testing can be meaningfully performed. The earlier security risks are identified and managed in the software lifecycle, the better.

Aim for Good, Not Perfect

No individual touchpoint or tool can solve all of your software security problems. Static analysis tools are no different. For starters, static analysis tools look for a fixed set of patterns, or rules, in the code. Although more advanced tools allow new rules to be added over time, if a rule hasn't been written yet to find a particular problem, the tool will never find that problem. When it comes to security, what you don't know is pretty darn likely to hurt you, so beware of any tool that says something like, "Zero defects found, your program is now secure." The appropriate output is, "Sorry, couldn't find any more bugs."

A static analysis tool's output still requires human evaluation. There's no way for any tool to know automatically which problems are more or less important to you, so there's no way to avoid trawling through the output and making a judgment call about which issues should be fixed and which ones carry an acceptable level of risk. Plus, knowledgeable people still need to get a program's design right to avoid any flaws. Static analysis tools can find bugs in the nitty-gritty details, but they can't even begin to critique design. Don't expect any tool to tell you, "I see you're implementing a funds transfer application. You should tighten up the user password requirements."

Finally, there's computer science theory to contend with. Rice's theorem,[2] which says (in essence) that any nontrivial question you care to ask

---

[2] See <http://en.wikipedia.org/wiki/Rice's_theorem> if you need to understand more about Rice's theorem.

about a program can be reduced to the halting problem,[3] applies in spades to static analysis tools. In scientific terms, static analysis problems are undecidable in the worst case. The practical ramifications of Rice's theorem are that all static analysis tools are forced to make approximations and that these approximations lead to less-than-perfect output.

Static analysis tools suffer from *false negatives* (in which the program contains bugs that the tool doesn't report) and *false positives* (in which the tool reports bugs that the program doesn't really contain). False positives cause immediate grief to any analyst who has to sift through them, but false negatives are much more dangerous because they lead to a false sense of security.

A tool is *sound* if, for a given set of assumptions, it produces no false negatives. Unfortunately, the downside to always erring on the side of caution is a potentially debilitating number of false positives. The static analysis crowd jokes that too high a percentage of false positives leads to 100% false negatives because that's what you get when people stop using a tool. A tool is *unsound* if it tries to reduce false positives at the cost of sometimes letting a false negative slip by. Most commercial tools these days are unsound.

Ancient History

The first code scanner built to look for security problems in code was Cigital's ITS4 <http://www.cigital.com/its4/>.[4] Since ITS4's release in early 2000, the idea of detecting security problems by looking over source code with a tool has come of age. Much better approaches exist and are being rapidly commercialized.

ITS4 and its counterparts RATS <http://www.securesoftware.com> and Flawfinder <http://www.dwheeler.com/flawfinder/> are extremely simple—the tools scan through a file (lexically), looking for syntactic matches based on a number of simple "rules" that might indicate possible security vulnerabilities. One such rule might be "use of `strcpy()` should be avoided," which can be applied by looking through the software for the pattern "`strcpy`" and alerting the user when and where it is found. This is

---

[3]See <http://en.wikipedia.org/wiki/Halting_problem> if you're not a computer science theory junkie.

[4]ITS4 is actually an acronym for "It's The Software Stupid Security Scanner," a name we invented much to the dismay of our poor marketing people. That was back in the day when Cigital was called Reliable Software Technologies.

obviously a simple-minded approach that is often referred to with the derogatory label "glorified `grep`."[5]

The best thing about ITS4 and company was that creating them involved gathering and publishing a preliminary set of software security rules all in one place. When we released the tool (as open source), our hope was that the world would participate in helping to gather and improve the ruleset. Though over 15,000 people downloaded ITS4 in the first year it was out, we never received even one rule to add to its knowledge base. The world did not end, however, and a number of prominent commercial efforts to build up and evolve rulesets were undertaken. Appendix B describes a very basic set of software security rules (those included in ITS4) to serve as part of a *minimum set of security rules* that every static analysis tool should cover.

Worth mentioning is the fact that ITS4 and friends were never intended to be "push the button, see the bug" kinds of tools. The basic idea was instead to turn an impossible problem (remembering all those rules while doing manual code review) into a really hard one (figuring out whether the things flagged by the tool matter or not). Simple tools like ITS4 help you carry out a source code security review, but they certainly don't do it for you. The same can be said for modern tools, though they definitely make things much easier than the first-generation tools did.

Approaches to Static Analysis

Probably the simplest and most straightforward approach to static analysis is the UNIX utility `grep`—the same functionality you find implemented in the earliest tools such as ITS4. Armed with a list of good search strings, `grep` can reveal a lot about a code base. The downside is that `grep` is rather lo-fi because it doesn't understand anything about the files it scans. Comments, string literals, declarations, and function calls are all just part of a stream of characters to be matched against.

You might be amused to note that using `grep` to search code for words like "bug," "XXX," "fix," "here," and best of all "assume" often reveals interesting and relevant tidbits. Any good security source code review should start with that.

---

[5]For the non-UNIX geeks in the audience, `grep` is a command-line UNIX utility for finding lexical patterns.

Better fidelity requires taking into account the lexical rules that govern the programming language being analyzed. By doing this, a tool can distinguish between a vulnerable function call:

```
gets(&buf);
```

a comment:

```
/* never ever call gets */
```

and an innocent and unrelated identifier:

```
int begetsNextChild = 0;
```

As mentioned earlier, basic lexical analysis is the approach taken by early static analysis tools, including ITS4, Flawfinder, and RATS—all of which preprocess and tokenize source files (the same first steps a compiler would take) and then match the resulting token stream against a library of vulnerable constructs. Earlier, Matt Bishop and Mike Dilger built a special-purpose lexical analysis tool specifically to identify time-of-check–time-of-use (TOCTOU) flaws [Bishop and Dilger 1996].

While lexical analysis tools are certainly a step up from `grep`, they produce a hefty number of false positives because they make no effort to account for the target code's semantics. A stream of tokens is better than a stream of characters, but it's still a long way from understanding how a program will behave when it executes. Although some security defect signatures are so strong that they don't require semantic interpretation to be identified accurately, most are not so straightforward.

To increase precision, a static analysis tool must leverage more compiler technology. By building an abstract syntax tree (AST) from source code, such a tool could take into account the basic semantics of the program being evaluated.

Armed with an AST, the next decision to make involves the scope of the analysis. *Local analysis* examines the program one function at a time and doesn't consider relationships between functions. *Module-level analysis* considers one class or compilation unit at a time, so it takes into account relationships between functions in the same module and considers properties that apply to classes, but it doesn't analyze calls between modules. *Global analysis* involves analyzing the entire program, so it takes into account all relationships between functions.

The scope of the analysis also determines the amount of context the tool considers. More context is better when it comes to reducing false positives, but it can lead to a huge amount of computation to perform.

A History of Rule Coverage

Coding rules in explicit form have evolved rapidly in their coverage of potential vulnerabilities. Before Bishop and Dilger's work [1996] on race conditions in file access, explicit coding rulesets (if they existed at all) were only checklist documents of ad hoc information authored, managed, and typically not widely shared by experienced software security practitioners. Bishop and Dilger's tool was one of the first recognized attempts to capture a ruleset and automate its application through lexical scanning of code.[6] For the next four years, plenty of research was done in the area, but no other tools and accompanying rulesets emerged to push things forward.

This changed in early 2000 with the release of ITS4, a tool whose ruleset also targeted C/C++ code but went beyond the single-dimensional approaches of the past to cover a broad range of potential vulnerabilities in 144 different APIs or functions. This was followed the next year by the release of two more tools, Flawfinder and RATS. Flawfinder, written by David Wheeler, is an "interestingly" implemented C/C++ scanning tool with a somewhat larger set of rules than ITS4. RATS, authored by John Viega, not only offers a broader ruleset covering 310 C/C++ APIs or functions but also includes rulesets for the Perl, PHP, Python, and OpenSSL domains. In parallel with this public development, Cigital (the company that originally created ITS4) began commercially using SourceScope, a follow-on to ITS4 with a new standard of coverage—653 C/C++ APIs or functions. Figure 4–1 shows how the rulesets from early tools intersect.

Today a handful of first-tier options are available in the static code analysis tools space. These tools include but are not limited to:

- Coverity: Prevent <http://www.coverity.com/products/products_security.html>
- Fortify: Source Code Analysis <http://www.fortifysoftware.com/products/sca/>
- Ounce Labs: Prexis/Engine <http://www.ouncelabs.com/prexis_engine.html>

---

[6]Bishop and Dilger's tool was built around a limited set of rules covering potential race conditions in file accesses using C on UNIX systems [Bishop and Dilger 1996].

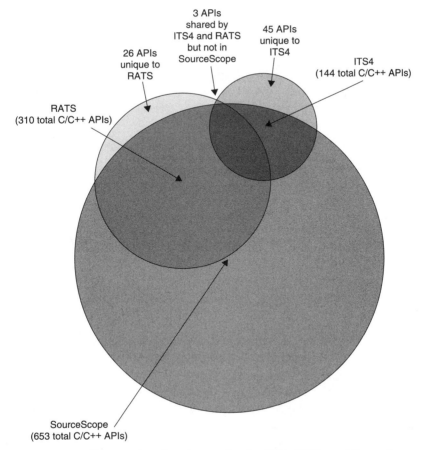

3 APIs
shared by
ITS4 and RATS
but not in
SourceScope

45 APIs
unique to
ITS4

26 APIs
unique to
RATS

ITS4
(144 total C/C++ APIs)

RATS
(310 total C/C++ APIs)

SourceScope
(653 total C/C++ APIs)

Figure 4–1 A Venn diagram showing the overlap for ITS4, RATS, and SourceScope rules. Together, these rules define a reasonable minimum set of C and C++ rules for static analysis tools. (Thanks to Sean Barnum, who created this diagram.)

- Secure Software: CodeAssure Workbench <http://www. securesoftware.com/products/source.html>

Each of the tools offers a comprehensive and growing ruleset varying in both size and area of focus. As you investigate and evaluate which tool is most appropriate for your needs, the coverage of the accompanying ruleset should be one of your primary factors of comparison.

Together with the Software Engineering Institute, Cigital has created a searchable catalog of rules published on the Department of Homeland

Security's Building Security In portal <http://buildsecurityin.us-cert.gov/portal/>. This catalog contains full coverage of the C/C++ rulesets from ITS4, RATS, and SourceScope and is intended to represent the foundational set of security rules for C/C++ development. Though some currently available tools have rulesets much more comprehensive than this catalog, we consider this the *minimum standard* for any modern tool scanning C/C++ code for security vulnerabilities.

Modern Rules

Since the early days of ITS4, the idea of security rules and security vulnerability categories has progressed. Today, a number of distinct efforts to categorize, describe, and "tool-ify" software security knowledge are under way. My approach is covered in Chapter 12, where I present a simple taxonomy of coding errors that lead to security problems. The first box, Modern Security Rules Schema, describes the schema developed at Cigital for organizing security rule information and gives an example.[7] The second box, A Complete Modern Rule on pages 119 through 122, provides an example of one of the many rules compiled in the extensive Cigital knowledge base.

Tools from Researchland

Researchers have explored many methods for making sense of program semantics. Some are sound, some aren't; some are built to detect specific classes of bugs, while others are flexible enough to read definitions for what they're supposed to detect. Some of the more recent tools are worth pondering. You really won't be able to download most of these research prototypes and merrily start finding bugs in your own code. Rather, the ideas from these tools are driving the current crop of commercial tools (not to mention the next round of research tools).

- **BOON** applies integer range analysis to determine whether a C program can index an array outside its bounds [Wagner et al. 2000]. While capable of finding many errors that lexical analysis tools would miss,

[7]Also of note is the new book *The 19 Deadly Sins of Software Security,* which provides treatment of the rules space as well [Howard, LeBlanc, and Viega 2005]. Chapter 12 includes a mapping of my taxonomy against the 19 sins and the OWASP top ten <http://www.owasp.org/documentation/topten.html>.

Modern Security Rules Schema

The schema shown in this table associates several distinct fields with each rule. This schema was developed at Cigital and is the skeleton of one of many knowledge catalogs. Though not all of the fields are relevant to static analysis per se, they do help in organizing and categorizing rules, which can then be consumed by a tool.

Fieldname	Field Description	Selection Choices
Number	Unique rule descriptor.	
ID	Shorthand label for the rule.	
Title	Short rule descriptor.	
Identification Difficulty	How hard is it to apply this rule? Do we need simple text scanning? A complete type tree in an AST? Data flow analysis?	Scan—*Text scanning* AST—*AST parse tree analysis* Data flow analysis
Accuracy	How likely is this rule to be accurate? Will there be a large number of false positives?	False negatives High false positives False positives Low false positives
Priority	How important is this rule?	Low—*Look at instances of the rule if there is time* Medium—*All instances should be examined, but not always fixed* High—*All instances should be fixed* Info—*Simply flagged for info*
Attack Category	What typical types of attacks does this rule help expose and/or mitigate?	Denial of service Spoofing Impersonation Log forging None Path spoofing or confusion problem Resource injection Setting manipulation SQL injection

Continued

Modern Security Rules Schema

Fieldname	Field Description	Selection Choices	
Vulnerability Kingdom	What types of vulnerabilities are exposed by this rule? (See Chapter 12.)	Input validation and representation API abuse Security features Time and state Error handling Code quality Encapsulation Environment	
Software Context	In what area of software implementation does the rule have likely impact?		
Context	Software implementation context of impact for this rule.	Authorization Critical sections Cryptography Debug API File creation File I/O File management Filename management File path management Handle duplication Impersonation Inheritance Internet ISAPI Memory management OLE registration National language support	Process management Security Shell functions String conversion macros String formatting String management String parsing Sundry platform pitfalls Temporary file management Threads and processes Using named kernel objects in services Other
Other Context	New software development contexts that are not in the Context list.		

Fieldname	Field Description	Selection Choices
Location	Header file, class, or module where this rule's APIs live.	
Description	Full explanation of the rule, things to search for, and (potentially) context of what can reduce the level of false positive hits on this rule.	
APIs	Which APIs does this rule apply to?	
Function Name	API name.	
Comments	Comments describing any special conditions of how this rule applies to the API.	
Method of Attack	Context/motivation of how this rule is important to an attacker. How would the attacker leverage this weakness to exploit the software?	
Exception Criteria	Under what conditions is it okay to ignore the triggering of this rule?	
Solution	What needs to be done to fix the code to avoid this rule and therefore improve the security of the code? What should be changed?	
Solution Applicability	A natural language explanation of when it is appropriate to consider this solution.	
Solution Description	Description of the proposed actions or steps for this solution.	
Solution Efficacy	A natural language explanation of the efficacy of this particular solution.	

Continued

Modern Security Rules Schema

Fieldname	Field Description	Selection Choices
Signature Details	What specific code signature will indicate that this rule is relevant for the code being analyzed?	
Code Examples Negative	Specific code examples that exhibit this rule in failure mode.	
Code Examples Positive	Specific code examples that exhibit this rule in solution mode.	
Source References	Any supporting bibliography entries (sources) for this rule.	
Recommended Resources	Recommended resources for better understanding the context, nature, and implications of this rule.	
Resource Name	Name of the resource being recommended.	
Resource Link	URL link to the resource (if applicable).	
Maturity	What is the state of maturity of the definition of this rule?	Draft, low, medium, high

the checker is still imprecise: It ignores statement order, it can't model interprocedural dependencies, and it ignores pointer aliasing.

- Inspired by Perl's taint mode, **CQual** uses type qualifiers to perform a taint analysis, which detects format string vulnerabilities in C programs [Foster, Terauchi, and Aiken 2002]. CQual requires a programmer to annotate a few variables as either tainted or untainted and then uses type inference rules (along with pre-annotated system libraries) to propagate the qualifiers. Once the qualifiers are propagated, the system can detect format string vulnerabilities by type checking.

- The **xg++** tool uses a template-driven compiler extension to attack the problem of finding kernel vulnerabilities in Linux and OpenBSD [Ashcraft and Engler 2002]. It looks for locations where the kernel uses data from an untrusted source without checking it first, methods by

A Complete Modern Rule

Given the schema shown in the previous table, Cigital has collected, categorized, and fleshed out many rules. The table here is an example of a complete rule for `catgets()`. Reading an entire set of rules, even if they are presented with this advanced schema, is difficult and no fun. (Try it for yourself by perusing Appendix B.) A static analysis tool can enforce rules like these without forcing every developer in the world to internalize all possible potential vulnerabilities. In fact, by applying these rules with a tool during development (especially when the tool is completely integrated into an IDE), developers can more naturally internalize the rules.

Title	catgets
Attack Category	Path spoofing or confusion problem
Vulnerability Kingdom	Input validation and representation • Format string • Buffer overflow
Software Context	National language support
Location	`nl_types.h`
Description	Text obtained from message catalogs may not be trustworthy, and care must be exercised in how it is used.
	The function `catopen()` opens a message catalog file located either according to a supplied path (containing a / character) or by searching for a named catalog (with no /) by referencing the values of the NLSPATH, LANG, and LC_MESSAGES environment variables. Subsequently, the `catgets()` function may be used to obtain message text from the catalog. If an attacker can influence the environment in which the program runs, he or she can cause a program to load strings from arbitrary files.
	Careless use of text returned by `catgets()` can create vulnerabilities that can be exploited by an attacker who manages to substitute text. Depending on how the text is used, buffer overflow or format vulnerabilities may be present, which, if exploited, could result in the execution of arbitrary code.

Continued

A Complete Modern Rule

APIs	Function Name	Comments
	`catopen`	Opens message catalog based on environment
	`catgets`	Returns arbitrary length string
Method of Attack	Attacker can manipulate `NLSPATH` and related environment variables to control what gets returned by `catopen()` and `catgets()`. Alternatively, the standard catalog file could be overwritten if catalog directories are not secure. By installing a custom catalog of messages, the attacker can cause arbitrarily long strings to be returned and/or can include format string information (e.g., %s) into the string, which may be interpreted if the text is used as a format string. In many cases, setuid programs access locale-specific message catalogs to print messages. If this is not done with due care, an attacker can use this to cause arbitrary code execution.	
Exception Criteria	`catgets()` is safe if the standard catalog directory is secure and the catalog descriptor received from `catopen()` was opened using a fully specified path containing a / character, or `NLSPATH` and other environment variables are validated before being used. `catgets()` is also safe if the returned message text is used in a safe fashion.	

	Solution Applicability	Solution Description	Solution Efficacy
Solutions	Particularly applicable to setuid programs for which the user can control the environment.	Validate that `catopen()` will return an authentic message catalog. This requires that the the message database (i.e., set of directories containing message catalog files) be in a secure, trusted directory. This requires either certainty that an attacker could not manipulate the program environment (not necessarily an option for a setuid program) or that the information used to locate the particular message catalog file was validated before `catopen()` was called. Specifying a fully qualified catalog path containing a / character would work, but	Effective, but hard to implement correctly. Best used in combination with the solution of using text safely.

Solutions	Solution Applicability	Solution Description	Solution Efficacy
		it largely defeats the purpose of using a message catalog. The alternative is to examine NLSPATH and related environment variables to confirm that they correspond only to the expected secure directories. This also requires that the message catalog locations be constrained, with those constraints known to the program at compilation time.	
	Particularly applicable to setuid programs for which the user can control the environment.	Use text obtained from `catgets()` safely, in a way that reflects its untrustworthy nature. Text obtained from `catgets()` is typically used in printed or displayed messages. This should not be used as a format string, as in `printf(text)`, but should instead be used as a data string, as in `printf "%s", text`). If the text must be used as a format string, it should be parsed and validated as being safe before it is used. If text obtained from `catgets()` is placed in a buffer, care must be exercised to ensure that buffer overflows cannot occur.	Effective. Validating text to be used as a format string could be tricky unless rigid constraints are enforced.
Signature Details	Any use of `catopen()` or `catgets()` should be examined. If no checks are done on NLSPATH and usage of `catgets()` result matches the signature for a potential format string problem or buffer overflow problem, a problem exists. Most relevant for setuid programs, for which the user can control the execution environment.		

Continued

A Complete Modern Rule

| Code Examples Negative | ```nl_catd catd = catopen("MyCatalog", 0);
char *text = catgets(catd, 2, 10, "Default text.");
printf(text); // vulnerable to format string attack
strcpy(buffer, text); // vulnerable to BO attack``` |
|---|---|
| Code Examples Positive | ```// Verify an expected secure path will be searched
if (!nlsPathIsSafe()) exit(EXIT_FAILURE);
nl_catd catd = catopen("MyCatalog", 0);

// Ensure safe usage of retrieved text
char *text = catgets(catd, 2, 10, "Default text.");
printf("%s", text);
strncpy(buffer, text, bufferSize);``` |
| Source References | N/A |

Recommended Resources	**Resource Name**	**Resource Link**
	catgets(3) man page	<http://www.freebsd.org/cgi/man.cgi?query=catgets&sektion=3>
	catopen(3) man page	<http://www.freebsd.org/cgi/man.cgi?query=catopen&sektion=3>
Discriminant Set	**Operating System**	• UNIX (all) • Windows (all)
	Language	• C • C++

which a user can cause the kernel to allocate memory and not free it, and situations in which a user could cause the kernel to deadlock.

- The **Eau Claire** tool uses a theorem prover to create a general specification-checking framework for C programs [Chess 2002]. It can help find common security problems like buffer overflows, file access race conditions, and format string bugs. Developers can use specifications to ensure that function implementations behave as expected.

- **MOPS** takes a model-checking approach to look for violations of temporal safety properties [Chen and Wagner 2002]. Developers can model their own safety properties, and some have used the tool to check for privilege management errors, incorrect construction of `chroot` jails, file access race conditions, and ill-conceived temporary file schemes.

- **Splint** extends the **lint** concept into the security realm [Larochelle and Evans 2001]. By adding annotations, developers can enable splint to find abstraction violations, unannounced modifications to global variables, and possible use-before-initialization errors. Splint can also reason about minimum and maximum array bounds accesses if it is provided with function pre- and postconditions.

Many static analysis approaches hold promise but have yet to be directly applied to security. Some of the more noteworthy ones include **ESP** (a large-scale property verification approach) [Das, Lerner, and Seigle 2002], model checkers such as **SLAM** and **BLAST** (which use predicate abstraction to examine program safety properties) [Ball and Rajamani 2001; Henzinger et al. 2003], and **FindBugs** (a lightweight checker with a good reputation for unearthing common errors in Java programs) [Hovemeyer and Pugh 2004].

Academic work on static analysis continues apace, and research results are published with some regularity at conferences such as USENIX Security, IEEE Security and Privacy (Oakland), ISOC Network and Distributed System Security, and Programming Language Design and Implementation (PLDI). Although it often takes years for results to make a commercial impact, solid technology transfer paths have been established, and the pipeline looks good. Expect great progress in static analysis during the next several years.

Commercial Tool Vendors

In 2004 and 2005, a number of startups formed to address the software security space. Many of these vendors have built and are selling basic source code analysis tools. Major vendors in the space include the following:

- Coverity <http://www.coverity.com>
- Fortify <http://www.fortifysoftware.com>
- Ounce Labs <http://www.ouncelabs.com>
- Secure Software <http://www.securesoftware.com>

The technological approach taken by many of these vendors is very similar, although some are more academically inclined than others. By basing their tools on compiler technology, these vendors have upped the level of sophistication far beyond the early, almost unusable tools like ITS4.[8]

---

[8]Beware of security consultants armed with ITS4 who aren't software people. Consultants with code review tools are rapidly becoming to the software security world what consultants with penetration testing tools are to the network security world. Make sure you carefully vet your vendors.

A critical feature that currently serves as an important differentiator in the static analysis tools market is the kind of knowledge (the ruleset) that a tool enforces. The importance of a good ruleset can't be overestimated.

Commercial Source Code Analyzers

One of the main reasons to use a source code analysis tool is that manual review is costly and time consuming. Manual review is such a pain that reviewers regularly suffer from the "get done, go home" phenomenon—starting strong and ending with a sputter. An automated tool can begin to check every line of code whenever a build is complete, allowing development shops to get on with the business of building software.

Integrating a source code analyzer into your development lifecycle can be painless and easy. As long as your code builds, you should be able to run a modern analysis. Working through the results remains a challenge but is nowhere near as much trouble as painstakingly checking every line of code by hand.

Modern approaches to static analysis can now process on the order of millions of lines of code quickly and efficiently. Though a complete review certainly requires an analyst with a clue, the process of looking through the results of a tool and thinking through potential vulnerabilities beats looking through everything. A time savings of several hundred percent is not out of the question.

Several timesaving mechanisms are built into modern tools. The first is the knowledge encapsulated in a tool. Keeping a burgeoning list of all known security problems found in a language like C (several hundred) in your head while attempting to trace control flow, data flow, and an explosion of states by hand is extremely difficult. Having a tool that remembers security problems (and can easily be expanded to cover new problems) is a huge help. The second timesaving mechanism involves automatically tracking control flow, call chains, and data flow. Though commercial tools make tradeoffs when it comes to soundness (as discussed earlier), they certainly make the laborious process of control and data flow analysis much easier. For example, a decent tool can locate a potential `strcpy()` vulnerability on a given line, present the result in a results browser, and arm the user with an easy and automated way to determine (through control flow, call chains, and data flow structures) whether the possible vulnerability is real. Though tools are getting better at figuring out this kind of thing for themselves, they are not perfect.

The root cause of most security problems can be found in the source code and configuration files of common software applications—especially custom apps that you write yourself. Problems are seeded when vulnerable code is written right into the system, which is undeniably the most efficient and effective time to remove them. The way forward is to use automated tools and processes that systematically and comprehensively target the root cause of security issues in source code. Instead of sorting through millions of lines of code looking for vulnerabilities, a developer using an advanced software security tool that returns a small set of potential vulnerabilities can pinpoint actual vulnerabilities in a matter of seconds—precisely the same vulnerabilities that would take a malicious hacker or manual code reviewer weeks or even months to find. Of course, most bad guys know this and will use these kinds of tools themselves [Hoglund and McGraw 2004].

Key Characteristics of a Tool

To be useful and cost effective, a source code analysis tool must have six key characteristics.

1. **Be designed for security.** Software security may well be a subset of software quality, but software security requires the ability to think like a bad guy. Exploiting software is not an exercise in standard-issue QA. A software defect uncovered during functionality testing might be addressed in such a way that the functional issue is resolved, but security defects may still remain and be reachable via surprising execution paths that are not even considered during functionality testing. It almost goes without saying that software security risks tend to have much more costly business impacts than do standard-issue software risks. Security impact is payable in terms of loss of business data, loss of customer trust and brand loyalty, cost of downtime and inability to perform business transactions, and other intangible costs. Simply put, software quality tools may be of some use when it comes to robustness, but software security tools have more critical security knowledge built into them. The knowledge base built into a tool is an essential deciding factor.[9]

---

[9]While more general quality tools will not pinpoint security issues, they can be used by a seasoned reviewer to identify "smells" in the complexity, cohesion, coupling, and effort/volume relationship of code modules—all good starting points for identifying possible security weak spots. In many cases, security errors arising from sloppy coding don't appear as rare blips among otherwise pristine code. They are usually the consequence of a larger, more pervasive carelessness that can sometimes be seen from high up in terms of quality errors. Don't rely on quality metrics to identify security issues, but keep an eye out for quality weak modules. Vices tend to roll together.

2. **Support multiple tiers.** Modern software applications are rarely written in a single programming language or targeted to a single platform. Most business-critical applications are highly distributed, with multiple tiers each written in a different programming language and executed on a different platform. Automated security analysis software must support each of these languages and platforms, as well as properly negotiate between and among tiers. A tool that can analyze only one or two languages can't meet the needs of modern software.

3. **Be extensible.** Security problems evolve, grow, and mutate, just like species on a continent. No one technique or set of rules will ever perfectly detect all security vulnerabilities. Good tools need a modular architecture that supports multiple kinds of analysis techniques. That way, as new attack and defense techniques are developed, the tool can be expanded to encompass them. Likewise, users must be able to add their own security rules. Every organization has its own set of corporate security policies, meaning that a fixed "one-size-fits-all" approach to security is doomed to fail.

4. **Be useful for security analysts and developers alike.** Security analysis is complicated and hard. Even the best analysis tools cannot automatically fix security problems, just as debuggers can't magically debug your code. The best automated tools make it possible for analysts to focus their attention directly on the most important issues. Good tools support not only analysts but also the poor developers who need to fix the problems uncovered by a tool. Good tools allow users to find *and fix* security problems as efficiently as possible. Used properly, source code analysis tools are excellent teaching tools. Simply by using them, developers can learn about software security (almost by osmosis).

5. **Support existing development processes.** Seamless integration with build processes and IDEs is an essential characteristic of *any* software tool. For a source code analysis tool to become accepted as part of an application development team's toolset, the tool must properly interoperate with existing compilers used on the various platforms and support popular build tools like make and ant. Good tools both integrate into existing build processes and also coexist with and support analysis in familiar development tools.

6. **Make sense to multiple stakeholders.** Software is built for a reason—usually a business reason. Security tools need to support the business. A security-oriented development focus is new to a vast majority of

organizations. Of course, software security is not a product; rather, it is an ongoing process that necessarily involves the contributions of many people across an organization. But good automated tools can help to scale a software security initiative beyond a select few to an entire development shop. Views for release managers, development managers, and even executives allow comparison using relative metrics and can support release decisions, help control rework costs, and provide much-needed data for software governance.

Three Characteristics to Avoid

Source code analysis is not easy, and early approaches (including ITS4) suffered from a number of unfortunate problems. Some of these problems persist in source code analysis tools today. Watch out for these characteristics.

1. **Too many false positives.** One common problem with early approaches to static analysis was their excessive false positive rates. Practitioners seem to feel that tools that provide a false positive rate under 40% are okay. ITS4 would sometimes produce rates in the range of 90% and higher, making it a real pain to use. Glorified `grep` machines have an extremely low signal-to-noise ratio. Modern approaches that include data flow analysis capability dramatically reduce false positives, making source code analysis much more effective.

2. **Spotty integration with IDEs.** Emacs may be great, but it is not for everyone. Developers already have an IDE they like, and they shouldn't have to switch to do a security analysis. Enough said.

3. **Single-minded support for C.** Canonical security bugs are pervasive in C. However, modern software is built with multiple languages and supports multiple platforms. If your system is built of more than C, make sure you don't skip the "non-C" parts when you review code.

The Fortify Source Code Analysis Suite[10]

I think it is important to give you a feel for what a real commercial tool looks like (especially if you read about the use of RATS in *Building Secure Software* [Viega and McGraw 2001]). This section is about one of the

---

[10]*Full disclosure:* I am the chairman of Fortify Software's Technical Advisory Board. Part of Fortify's code analysis technology (in the form of SourceScope) was invented and developed by Cigital.

leading software security tools. Others exist. Make sure that you pick the tool that is right for you.

That said, Fortify Software produces a very successful source code analysis suite that many organizations will find useful. It includes the five components outlined in Table 4–1.

The Source Code Analysis (SCA) Engine searches for violations of security-specific coding rules in source code. An intermediate representation in the form of an AST built using advanced parser technology enables a set of analyzers in the SCA Engine to pinpoint and prioritize violations. This helps to make security code reviews more efficient, consistent, and complete, especially where large code bases are involved.

The SCA Engine determines the location of security vulnerabilities in source code and computes vulnerability relevance based on the relationship of the vulnerability to the surrounding code. The analyzers built into the tool provide multilanguage analysis across multiple tiers, allowing developers to determine which path or paths through a piece of code are actually vulnerable.

The SCA Engine includes four analyzers: semantic, data flow, control flow, and configuration. These analyzers locate security defects across the entire code base, including problems that span multiple tiers. The tool, which supports Java, C, C++, C#, JSP, XML, and PL/SQL, produces an

Table 4–1 The Five Components of the Fortify Source Code Analysis Suite

Component	Description
Source Code Analysis Engine	The Fortify code analysis and vulnerability detection engine performs basic semantic, data flow, control flow, and configuration analysis.
Secure Coding Rulepacks and Rules Builder	Secure Coding Rulepacks provide coverage of 2,000+ base language and third-party functions and over 50,000 vulnerability paths. Rules Builder allows creation of custom rules.
Audit Workbench	Fortify's visual interface enables rapid analysis of software vulnerabilities in order to prioritize the remediation of defects.
Developer Desktop	Fortify integrates critical vulnerability detection directly into popular IDEs (including JBuilder, Visual Studio .NET, Rational Application Developer for WebSphere Software, and Eclipse).
Software Security Manager	Fortify centralizes analysis and reporting of vulnerability trend data across people and projects.

XML results file that is consumed by the results browser. Figure 4–2 shows a basic architecture.

The SCA Engine uses the Secure Coding Rulepacks as the expandable knowledge base for analysis. The prepackaged Secure Coding Rulepacks that come with the tool encapsulate years of security knowledge about anomalous constructs and vulnerable functions in software. The rules can identify dozens of vulnerability categories, including buffer overflows, log forging, cross-site scripting, memory leaks, and SQL injection. The Fortify toolset is extensible and allows automated creation of new application-specific, third-party library, and corporate-standards–based custom rules using the Rules Builder (Figure 4–3).

The Audit Workbench (Figure 4–4) is a visual interface allowing detailed and efficient analysis of potential software vulnerabilities in order to prioritize and fix problems. Human interface concerns are critical in these kinds of tools because the human analyst plays a central role in the process of automated code review. Without a smart human in the loop, the tool is not very useful. The Audit Workbench provides a summary view of security problems with detail related to the defect in focus. The data displayed include information about particular vulnerabilities, the rules that uncovered them, and what to do about them. (This kind of information is extremely useful in context and is available to interested readers at <http://vulncat.fortifysoftware.com>. See Chapter 12 for a taxonomy of vulnerability information.) Potential problems are displayed with surrounding source

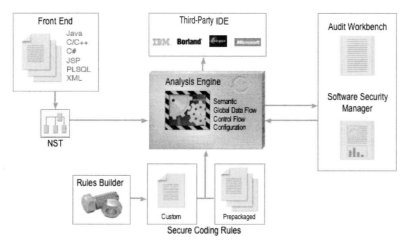

Figure 4–2 Components making up the Fortify Source Code Analysis Suite.

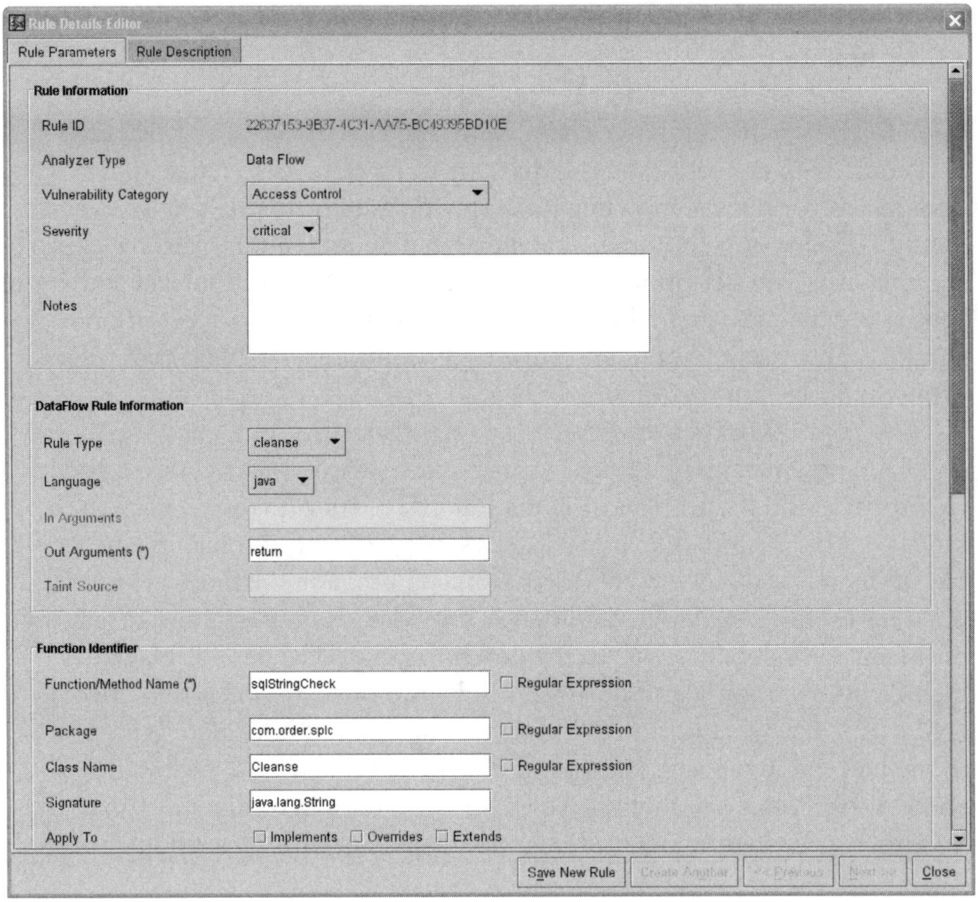

Figure 4–3 The Fortify Rule Details Editor in the Rules Builder allows creation of custom rules.

code and a call tree. Results are categorized into customizable buckets of defects and can be annotated with resolution severity, priority, and status.

The Developer Desktop (Figure 4–5) is a collection of software components for a developer's desktop. It includes the SCA Engine, Secure Coding Rulepacks, and plug-ins for common IDEs. Because it is integrated into standard development tools, adoption is fairly painless. Integration of the toolset enhances a standard IDE with detailed and accurate security vulnerability knowledge. This is an effective way to train developers about secure coding practices as they do their normal thing. Fortify supports Eclipse, Rational Application Developer for WebSphere Software, and Microsoft Visual Studio .NET Add-in.

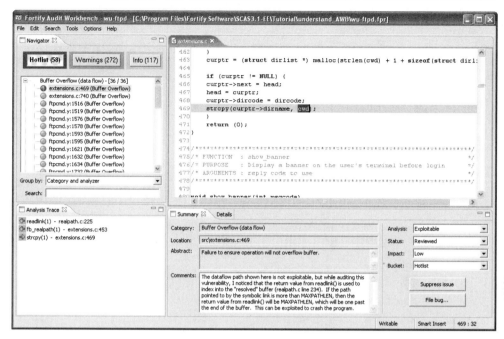

Figure 4–4 The Fortify Audit Workbench window supports in-depth analysis.

Figure 4–5 Developer Desktop components have a familiar look and feel.

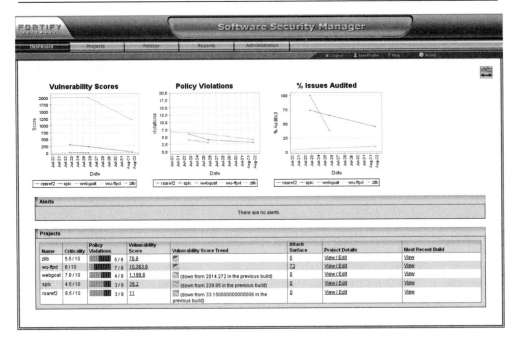

Figure 4–6 The Software Security Manager Dashboard helps bring source code analysis up out of the weeds.

The Software Security Manager is a Web-based security policy and reporting interface that enables development teams to manage and control risk across multiple projects and releases. The Software Security Manager helps to centralize reporting, enable trend analysis, and produce software security reports for management. The Software Security Manager includes a number of predefined metrics that cover the number and type of vulnerabilities, policy violations, and severity. Figure 4–6 shows the Software Security Manager Dashboard.

The Fortify Knowledge Base

The most critical feature of any static analysis tool involves the knowledge built into it. We've come a long way since the early days of RATS and ITS4 when a simple `grep` for a possibly dangerous API might suffice. Today, the software security knowledge expected to drive static analysis tools is much more sophisticated.

A complete taxonomy of software security vulnerabilities that can be uncovered using automated tools is discussed in Chapter 12. Software security rules knowledge has progressed much further than other more subtle knowledge categories such as secure coding patterns and technology-specific guidelines.

The vulnerability descriptions powering the Fortify SCA Engine are far more sophisticated than the early ITS4 database mentioned earlier in this chapter. For the complete taxonomy, see the Fortify Web site at <http://vulncat.fortifysoftware.com>.

Coder's Corner

What follows is an example of one of 78 basic vulnerability descriptions identified and described by Brian Chess and Jacob West. This description shows the kind of knowledge available to developers when they use a sophisticated static analysis tool. Note the similarity between the vulnerability description here and the complete rule shown earlier in the chapter.

Security Functionality: Authentication
(`getlogin`)

Abstract

The `getlogin()` function is easy to spoof. Do not rely on the name it returns.

Explanation

The `getlogin()` function is supposed to return a string containing the name of the user currently logged in at the terminal, but an attacker can cause `getlogin()` to return the name of any user logged in to the machine. Do not rely on the name returned by `getlogin()` when making security decisions.

Example 1: The following code relies on `getlogin()` to determine whether or not a user is trusted. It is easily subverted.

```
pwd = getpwnam(getlogin());
if (isTrustedGroup(pwd->pw_gid)) {
  allow();
} else {
  deny();
}
```

Continued

Recommendations

You should rely on a user's ID, not the username, for identification. The previous example can be rewritten as follows:

```
pwd = getpwuid(getuid());
if (isTrustedGroup(pwd->pw_gid)) {
  allow();
} else {
  deny();
}
```

If multiple users are allowed to share the same user ID (a dubious proposition from a security standpoint), a bit more care is required. The following example checks to see whether the username returned by getlogin() matches the username associated with the user ID; the check ensures that if two users share the same ID, one user cannot act on behalf of the other.

```
pwd = getpwuid(getuid());
pwdName = pwd->pw_name;
/* Bail out if the name associated with the uid does not
  match the name associated with the terminal. */
if (strncmp(pwdName, getlogin(), MAX_NAM_LEN)) {
  printf("shared uid not supported\n");
  deny();
  return;
}
if (isTrustedGroup(pwd->pw_gid)) {
  allow();
} else {
  deny();
}
```

Note: If the process is not being run from a terminal, getlogin() returns NULL.

Using Fortify

A special demonstration version of the Fortify Source Code Analysis product is included with this book. Please note that the demonstration software includes only a subset of the functionality offered by the Source Code

Analysis Suite. For example, this demonstration version scans for buffer overflow and SQL injection vulnerabilities but does not scan for cross-site scripting or access control vulnerabilities.

Appendix A is a tutorial guide reprinted with permission from Fortify Software. If you would like to learn more about how the Fortify Source Code Analysis Suite works in a hands-on way, check out the appendix. The key you will need to unlock the demo on the CD is FSDMOBEBESHIPFSDMO. To prevent any confusion, this key is composed of letters exclusively. There are no numbers.

Touchpoint Process: Code Review

I am not a process person, especially when it comes to software. But there is no denying that complex tools like those described in this chapter can't simply be thrown at the software security problem and expected to solve problems willy-nilly. By wrapping a tool like the Fortify SCA Engine in a process, your organization can benefit much more from tool use than if you buy the tool and stick it on a shelf.

Figure 4–7 shows a very simple process for applying a static analysis. Note that this is only one of many processes that can be wrapped around a source code analysis tool. The process here is very much based on a software assurance perspective and is the kind of process that a software security type or an analyst would use. There are other use cases for developers (e.g., more closely aligned with IDE integration). This process is one of many.

Static code analysis can be carried out by any kind of technical resource. Background in software security and lots of knowledge about software security bugs is very helpful because the tool identifies particular areas of the code for the analyst to check more thoroughly. The tool is really an analyst aid more than anything.

The analyst can choose from any number of security tools (as shown in Figure 4–7), including, in some cases, use of research prototypes. The analyst uses a tool on the code to be analyzed and both refers to external information regarding potential problems and tracks issues that are identified.

Note that raw tool results are not always the most useful form of information that this process can provide. As an analyst pours over results, some possible problems will turn out to be non-issues. Other possible problems will turn out to be exploitable. Figuring this all out is the bulk of the work when using a source code analysis tool.

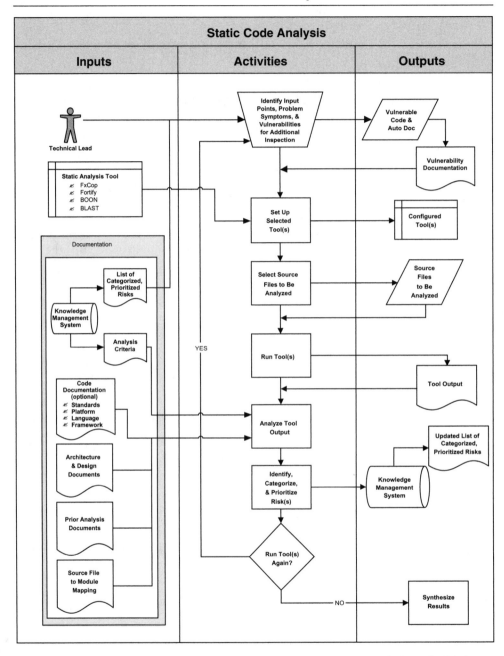

Figure 4–7 A simple process diagram showing the use of a static analysis tool. This is a simplified version of the process used by Cigital.

The simple process shown in Figure 4–7 results in code that has been fully diagnosed and a set of issues that need to be addressed. Fixing the code itself is not part of this process.

A much different approach can be taken by developers who can use a tool to spot potential problems and then fix them as they work. This is probably the most effective use of static analysis technology. Even so, widespread adoption of source code analysis tools by development shops is only now beginning to happen.

Use a Tool to Find Security Bugs

Good static analysis tools must be easy to use, even for non-security people. This means that the results from these tools must be understandable to normal developers who might not know much about security. In the end, source code analysis tools educate their users about good programming practice. Good static checkers can help their users spot and eradicate common security bugs. This is especially important for languages such as C or C++, for which a very large corpus of rules already exists.

Static analysis for security should be applied regularly as part of any modern development process.

5 | Architectural Risk Analysis[1]

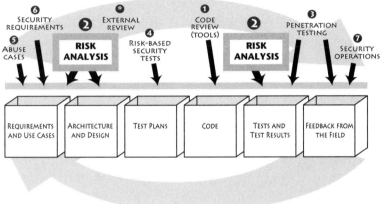

Architecture is the learned game, correct and magnificent, of forms assembled in the light.

LE CORBUSIER

Design flaws account for 50% of security problems. You can't find design defects by staring at code—a higher-level understanding is required. That's why architectural risk analysis plays an essential role in any solid software security program. By explicitly identifying risk, you can create a good general-purpose measure of software security, especially if you track risk over time. Because quantifying impact is a critical step in any risk-based approach, risk analysis is a natural way to tie technology issues and concerns directly to the business. A superior risk analysis explicitly links system-level concerns to probability and impact measures that matter to the organization building the software.

---

[1]Parts of this chapter appeared in original form in *IEEE Security & Privacy* magazine co-authored with Denis Verdon [Verdon and McGraw 2004].

The security community is unanimous in proclaiming the importance of a risk-based approach to security. "Security is risk management" is a mantra oft repeated and yet strangely not well understood. Nomenclature remains a persistent problem in the security community. The term *risk management* is applied to everything from threat modeling and architectural risk analysis to large-scale activities tied up in processes such as RMF (see Chapter 2).

As I describe in Chapter 1, a continuous risk management process is a necessity. This chapter is not about continuous risk management, but it does assume that a base process like the RMF exists and is in place.[2] By teasing apart architectural risk analysis (the critical software security best practice described here) and an overall RMF, we can begin to make better sense of software security risk.

Common Themes among Security Risk Analysis Approaches

Risk management has two distinct flavors in software security. I use the term *risk analysis* to refer to the activity of identifying and ranking risks at some particular stage in the software development lifecycle. Risk analysis is particularly popular when applied to architecture and design-level artifacts. I use the term *risk management* to describe the activity of performing a number of discrete risk analysis exercises, tracking risks throughout development, and strategically mitigating risks. Chapter 2 is about the latter.

A majority of risk analysis process descriptions emphasize that risk identification, ranking, and mitigation is a continuous process and not simply a single step to be completed at one stage of the development lifecycle. Risk analysis results and risk categories thus drive both into requirements (early in the lifecycle) and into testing (where risk results can be used to define and plan particular tests).

Risk analysis, being a specialized subject, is not always best performed solely by the design team without assistance from risk professionals outside the team. Rigorous risk analysis relies heavily on an understanding of business impact, which may require an understanding of laws and regulations as much as the business model supported by the software. Also, human nature dictates that developers and designers will have built up certain assumptions regarding their system and the risks that it faces. Risk and security specialists can at a minimum assist in challenging those assumptions against

---

[2]All of the other touchpoint chapters make this same assumption.

generally accepted best practices and are in a better position to "assume nothing." (For more on this, see Chapter 9.)

A prototypical risk analysis approach involves several major activities that often include a number of basic substeps.

➤ **Learn as much as possible about the target of analysis.**
  • Read and understand the specifications, architecture documents, and other design materials.
  • Discuss and brainstorm about the target with a group.
  • Determine system boundary and data sensitivity/criticality.
  • Play with the software (if it exists in executable form).
  • Study the code and other software artifacts (including the use of code analysis tools).
  • Identify threats and agree on relevant sources of attack (e.g., will insiders be considered?).

➤ **Discuss security issues surrounding the software.**
  • Argue about how the product works and determine areas of disagreement or ambiguity.
  • Identify possible vulnerabilities, sometimes making use of tools or lists of common vulnerabilities.
  • Map out exploits and begin to discuss possible fixes.
  • Gain understanding of current and planned security controls.[3]

➤ **Determine probability of compromise.**
  • Map out attack scenarios for exploits of vulnerabilities.
  • Balance controls against threat capacity to determine likelihood.

➤ **Perform impact analysis.**
  • Determine impacts on assets and business goals.
  • Consider impacts on the security posture.

➤ **Rank risks.**

➤ **Develop a mitigation strategy.**
  • Recommend countermeasures to mitigate risks.

➤ **Report findings.**
  • Carefully describe the major and minor risks, with attention to impacts.
  • Provide basic information regarding where to spend limited mitigation resources.

---

[3]Note that security controls can engender and introduce new security risks themselves (through bugs and flaws) even as they mitigate others.

A number of diverse approaches to risk analysis for security have been devised and practiced over the years. Though many of these approaches were expressly invented for use in the network security space, they still offer valuable risk analysis lessons. The box Risk Analysis in Practice lists a number of historical risk analysis approaches that are worth considering.

My approach to architectural risk analysis fits nicely with the RMF described in Chapter 2. For purposes of completeness, a reintroduction to the RMF is included in the box Risk Analysis Fits in the RMF.

Risk Analysis in Practice

A number of methods calculate a nominal value for an information asset and attempt to determine risk as a function of loss and event probability. Others rely on checklists of threats and vulnerabilities to determine a basic risk measurement.

Examples of risk analysis methodologies for software fall into two basic categories: commercial and standards-based.

Commercial

- STRIDE from Microsoft <http://msdn.microsoft.com/library/default.asp?url=/library/en-us/vbcon/html/vbconOverviewOfWebApplicationSecurityThreats.asp> (also see [Howard and LeBlanc 2003])
- Security Risk Management Guide, also from Microsoft <http://www.microsoft.com/technet/security/topics/policiesandprocedures/secrisk/default.mspx>
- ACSM/SAR (Adaptive Countermeasure Selection Mechanism/Security Adequacy Review) from Sun (see [Graff and van Wyk 2003] for public discussion)
- Cigital's architectural risk analysis process (described later in this chapter), which is designed to fit into the RMF (see Chapter 2)

Standards-Based

- ASSET (Automated Security Self-Evaluation Tool) from the National Institute on Standards and Technology (NIST) <http://csrc.nist.gov/asset/>
- OCTAVE (Operationally Critical Threat, Asset, and Vulnerability Evaluation) from SEI <http://www.sei.cmu.edu/publications/documents/99.reports/99tr017/99tr017abstract.html>
- COBIT (Control Objectives for Information and Related Technology) from Information Systems Audit and Control Association (ISACA) <http://www.isaca.org/Template.cfm?Section=COBIT_Online&Template=/ContentManagement/ContentDisplay.cfm&ContentID=15633>

Risk Analysis Fits in the RMF

Architectural risk analysis fits within a continuous risk management framework (RMF) just as the other touchpoint best practices do. The continuous risk management process we use at Cigital loops constantly and at many levels of description through several stages (Figure 5–1). A simplified version of the RMF shown here is described in gory detail in Chapter 2. In this approach, business goals determine risks, risks drive methods, methods yield measurement, measurement drives decision support, and decision support drives fix/rework and application quality.

During the process of architectural risk analysis, we follow basic steps very similar to those making up the RMF.

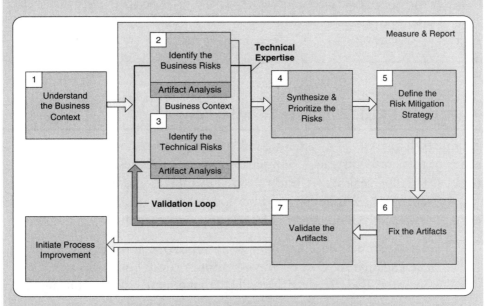

Figure 5–1 Cigital's risk management framework typifies the fractal and continuous nature of risk analysis processes. Many aspects of frameworks like these can be automated—for example, risk storage, business risk to technical risk mapping, and display of status over time.

The RMF shown in Figure 5–1 has a clear loop, called the *validation loop*. This loop is meant to graphically represent the idea that risk management is a continuous process. That is, identifying risks only once in a project is insufficient. The idea of "crossing off a particular stage" once it has been executed and never doing those activities

Continued

again is incorrect. Though the seven stages are shown in a particular serial order in Figure 5–1, they may need to be applied over and over again throughout a software development effort, and their particular ordering may be interleaved in many different ways.

Risk management is in some sense fractal. In other words, the entire continuous, ongoing process can be applied at several different levels. The primary level is the project level. Each stage of the validation loop clearly must have some representation during a complete development effort in order for risk management to be effective. Another level is the software lifecycle artifact level. The validation loop will most likely have a representation given requirements, design, architecture, test plans, and so on. The validation loop will have a representation during both requirements analysis and use case analysis, for example. Fortunately, a generic description of the validation loop as a serial looping process is sufficient to capture critical aspects at all of these levels at once. (See Chapter 2.)

Traditional Risk Analysis Terminology

An in-depth analysis of all existing risk analysis approaches is beyond the scope of this book; instead, I summarize basic approaches, common features, strengths, weaknesses, and relative advantages and disadvantages.

As a corpus, "traditional" methodologies are varied and view risk from different perspectives. Examples of basic approaches include the following:

- Financial loss methodologies that seek to provide a loss figure to be balanced against the cost of implementing various controls
- Mathematically derived "risk ratings" that equate risk to arbitrary ratings for threat, probability, and impact
- Qualitative assessment techniques that base risk assessment on anecdotal or knowledge-driven factors

Each basic approach has its merits, but even when approaches differ in the details, almost all of them share some common concepts that are valuable and should be considered in *any* risk analysis. These commonalities can be captured in a set of basic definitions.

- **Asset:** The object of protection efforts. This may be variously defined as a system component, data, or even a complete system.
- **Risk:** The probability that an asset will suffer an event of a given

negative impact. Various factors determine this calculation: the ease of executing an attack, the motivation and resources of an attacker, the existence of vulnerabilities in a system, and the cost or impact in a particular business context. Risk = probability × impact.

- **Threat**: The actor or agent who is the source of danger. Within information security, this is invariably the danger posed by a malicious agent (e.g., fraudster, attacker, malicious hacker) for a variety of motivations (e.g., financial gain, prestige). Threats carry out attacks on the security of the system (e.g., SQL injection, TCP/IP SYN attacks, buffer overflows, denial of service). Unfortunately, Microsoft has been misusing the term *threat* as a substitute for *risk*. This has led to some confusion in the commercial security space. (See the next box, On Threat Modeling versus Risk Analysis: Microsoft Redefines Terms.)

- **Vulnerability**: For a threat to be effective, it must act against a vulnerability in the system. In general, a vulnerability is a defect or weakness in system security procedures, design, implementation, or internal controls that can be exercised and result in a security breach or a violation of security policy. A vulnerability may exist in one or more of the components making up a system. (Note that the components in question are not necessarily involved with security functionality.) Vulnerability data for a given software system are most often compiled from a combination of OS-level and application-level vulnerability test results (often automated by a "scanner," such as Nessus, Nikto, or Sanctum's Appscan), code reviews, and higher-level architectural reviews. In software, vulnerabilities stem from defects and come in two basic flavors: *flaws* are design-level problems leading to security risk, and *bugs* are implementation-level problems leading to security risk. Automated source code analysis tools tend to focus on bugs. Human expertise is required to uncover flaws.

- **Countermeasures or safeguards**: The management, operational, and technical controls prescribed for an information system which, taken together, adequately protect the confidentiality, integrity, and availability of the system and its information. For every risk, controls may be put in place that either prevent or (at a minimum) detect the risk when it triggers.

- **Impact**: The impact on the organization using the software, were the risk to be realized. This can be monetary or tied to reputation, or may result from the breach of a law, regulation, or contract. Without a quantification of impact, technical vulnerability is hard to deal with—especially when it comes to mitigation activities. (See the discussion of the "techno-gibberish problem" in Chapter 2.)

- **Probability**: The likelihood that a given event will be triggered. This quantity is often expressed as a percentile, though in most cases calculation of probability is extremely rough. I like to use three simple buckets: high (H), medium (M), and low (L). Geeks have an unnatural propensity to use numbers even when they're not all that useful. Watch out for that when it comes to probability and risk. Some organizations have five, seven, or even ten risk categories (instead of three). Others use exact thresholds (70%) and pretend-precision numbers, such as 68.5%, and end up arguing about decimals. Simple categories and buckets seem to work best, and they emerge from the soup of risks almost automatically anyway.

Using these basic definitions, risk analysis approaches diverge on how to arrive at particular values for these attributes. A number of methods calculate a nominal value for an information asset and attempt to determine risk as a function of loss and event probability. Some methods use checklists of risk categories, threats, and attacks to ascertain risk.

On Threat Modeling versus Risk Analysis: Microsoft Redefines Terms

The good news is that Microsoft appears to be taking software security very seriously. The company has its own set of experts (the superstar being Michael Howard) and has even invented its own processes (paramount among these being the STRIDE model). The bad news is that the company also has its own vocabulary, which differs in important ways from standard usage in the security literature.

The biggest problem lies in misuse of the term *threat*. Microsoft describes as *threat modeling* what most others call *risk analysis*. For example, in the book *Threat Modeling*, Swiderski and Snyder explain that:

> *During threat modeling, the application is dissected into its functional components. The development team analyzes the components at every entry point and traces data flow through all functionality to identify security weaknesses.* [Swiderski and Snyder 2004, p. 16]

Clearly they are describing risk analysis. The term *threat modeling* should really refer to the activity of describing and cataloging threats—those actors or agents who want to attack your system. Having an old-style threat model like this is a critical step in thinking about security risk. After all, all the security vulnerabilities and software defects in the world would not matter if nobody were hell-bent on exploiting them.

The Microsoft Approach

Big problems with vocabulary aside, the basic process described in the book *Threat Modeling* is sound and well worth considering. Based on the STRIDE model introduced by Howard and LeBlanc (also from Microsoft), the Microsoft risk analysis process relies a bit too heavily on the notion of cycling through a list of attacks [Howard and LeBlanc 2003]. For example, STRIDE is an acronym for Spoofing, Tampering, Repudiation, Information disclosure, Denial of service, and Elevation of privilege. These are categories of attacks, and like attack patterns, they make useful lists of things to consider when identifying risks. Of course, any list of attacks will be incomplete and is very much unlikely to cover new creative attacks.* In any case, applying the STRIDE model in practice is an exercise in "sliding" known attacks over an existing design and seeing what matches. This is an excellent thing to do.

Risk analysis is the act of creating security-relevant design specifications and later testing that design. This makes it an integral part of building any secure system. The *Threat Modeling* book describes how to build a model of the system using both data flow diagrams and use cases. Then it goes on to describe a simple process for creating attack hypotheses using both lists of vulnerabilities and lists of system assets as starting points. This process results in attack trees similar in nature to the attack trees described in *Building Secure Software* [Viega and McGraw 2001].

Go ahead and make use of Microsoft's process, but please don't call it threat modeling.

---

*You can think of these checklists of attacks as analogous to virus patterns in a virus checker. Virus checkers are darn good at catching known viruses and stopping them cold. But when a new virus comes out and is not in the "definition list," watch out!

Knowledge Requirement

Architectural risk analysis is knowledge intensive. For example, Microsoft's STRIDE model involves the understanding and application of several risk categories during analysis[4] [Howard and LeBlanc 2003]. Similarly, my risk

---

[4]In STRIDE, these are referred to as "threat categories"; however, that term would more correctly be used to refer to groups of attackers, not to groups of risks.

analysis approach involves three basic steps (described more fully later in the chapter):

1. Attack resistance analysis
2. Ambiguity analysis
3. Weakness analysis

Knowledge is most useful in each of these steps: the use of attack patterns [Hoglund and McGraw 2004] and exploit graphs for understanding *attack resistance analysis,* knowledge of design principles for use in *ambiguity analysis* [Viega and McGraw 2001], and knowledge regarding security issues in commonly used frameworks (.NET and J2EE being two examples) and other third-party components to perform *weakness analysis*. These three subprocesses of my approach to risk analysis are discussed in detail in this chapter.

For more on the kinds of knowledge useful to all aspects of software security, including architectural risk analysis, see Chapter 11.

The Necessity of a Forest-Level View

A central activity in design-level risk analysis involves building up a consistent view of the target system at a reasonably high level. The idea is to see the forest and not get lost in the trees. The most appropriate level for this description is the typical whiteboard view of boxes and arrows describing the interaction of various critical components in a design. For one example, see the following box, .NET Security Model Overview.

Commonly, not enough of the many people often involved in a software project can answer the basic question, "What does the software do?" All too often, software people play happily in the weeds, hacking away at various and sundry functions while ignoring the big picture. Maybe, if you're lucky, one person knows how all the moving parts work; or maybe nobody knows. A one-page overview, or "forest-level" view, makes it much easier for everyone involved in the project to understand what's going on.

The actual form that this high-level description takes is unimportant. What is important is that an analyst can comprehend the big picture and use it as a jumping-off place for analysis. Some organizations like to use UML (the Unified Modeling Language) to describe their systems.[5] I believe UML

---

[5]For more on UML, see <http://www.uml.org/>.

is not very useful, mostly because I have seen it too often abused by the high priests of software obfuscation to hide their lack of clue. But UML may be useful for some. Other organizations might like a boxes-and-arrows picture of the sort described here. Formalists might insist on a formal model that can be passed into a theorem prover in a mathematical language like Z. Still others might resort to complex message-passing descriptions—a kind of model that is particularly useful in describing complex cryptosystems. In the end, the particular approach taken must result in a comprehensible high-level overview of the system that is as concise as possible.

The nature of software systems leads many developers and analysts to assume (incorrectly) that code-level description of software is sufficient for spotting design problems. Though this may occasionally be true, it does not generally hold. eXtreme Programming's claim that "the code is the design" represents one radical end of this approach. Because the XP guys all started out as Smalltalk programmers they may be a bit confused about whether the code is the design. A quick look at the results of the obfuscated C contest <http://www.ioccc.org> should disavow them of this belief.[6]

Without a whiteboard level of description, an architectural risk analysis is likely to overlook important risks related to flaws. Build a forest-level overview as the first thing you do in any architectural risk analysis.

.NET Security Model Overview

Figure 5–2 shows a one-page high-level architectural view of the .NET security model prepared while performing a .NET risk analysis. Before this diagram was created, the only high-level description of the .NET security architecture was a book-length description of its (way too many) parts. Putting all the parts together in one picture is an essential aspect of risk analysis.

All risk analyses should begin by understanding and, if necessary, describing and documenting a high-level overview of the system to be analyzed. Sometimes the act of building this picture is a monumental undertaking. Sometimes a one-page overview already exists. In any case, making one is a great idea.

Continued

---

[6]Incidentally, any language whose aficionados purposefully revel in its ability to be incomprehensible (even to the initiated) has serious issues. Perhaps experienced developers should require a license to use C. Newbies would not be permitted until properly licensed.

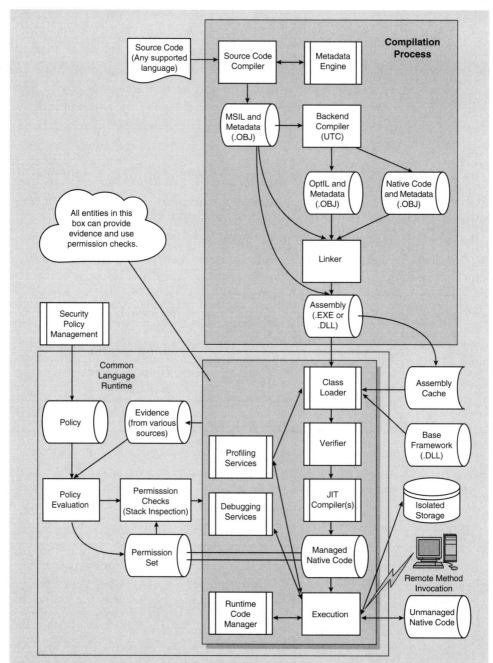

Figure 5–2 A one-page overview of Microsoft's .NET security model. An architectural picture like this, though not in any sense detailed enough to perform a complete analysis, is extremely useful for thinking about components, modules, and possible attacks. Every one-page overview should list all components and show what is connected to what.

By referencing the picture in Figure 5–2, an analyst can hypothesize about possible attacks. This can be driven by a list of known attacks such as the attack patterns described in Chapter 8 (and fleshed out in vivid detail in *Exploiting Software* [Hoglund and McGraw 2004]), or it can be driven by deep technical understanding of the moving parts.

As an example of the latter approach, consider the flow of information in Figure 5–2. In this picture the *Verifier* feeds the just in time (*JIT) compiler*. As noted in *Java Security,* the Verifier exists to ensure that the bytecode (in this case, CLR code) coheres to various critical type-safety constraints [McGraw and Felten 1996]. Type safety is about objects having certain properties that can be guaranteed. If type-safety rules are not followed or the Virtual Machine becomes confused about type safety, very bad things happen.

Anyway, the Verifier does its thing and passes information on to the JIT compiler.

A JIT compiler transforms intermediate CLR code (or Java bytecode) into native code (usually x86 code) "just in time." This is done for reasons of speed. For the security model to retain its potency, the JIT compiler must carry out only transformations that preserve type safety. By thinking through scenarios in which the JIT compiler breaks type safety, we can anticipate attacks and identify future risks. Interestingly, several relevant security issues based on this line of reasoning about attacks and type safety led to the discovery of serious security problems in Java. (For a complete description of the Java attacks, see <http://www.securingjava.com>, where you can find a complete, free, online edition of my book *Securing Java* [McGraw and Felten 1999].)

Unless we built up a sufficient high-level understanding of the .NET security model (probably through the process of creating our one-page picture), we would not likely come across possible attacks like the one described here.

One funny story about forest-level views is worth mentioning. I was once asked to do a security review of an online day-trading application that was extremely complex. The system involved live online attachments to the ATM network and to the stock exchange. Security was pretty important. We had trouble estimating the amount of work to be involved since there was no design specification to go on.[7] We flew down to Texas and got started anyway. Turns out that only one person in the entire hundred-person company knew how the system actually worked and what all the moving parts

---

[7]The dirty little trick of software development is that without a design spec your system can't be wrong, it can only be surprising! Don't let the lack of a spec go by without raising a ruckus. Get a spec.

were. The biggest risk was obvious! If that one person were hit by a bus, the entire enterprise would grind to a spectacular halt. We spent most of the first week of the work interviewing the architect and creating both a forest-level view and more detailed documentation.

A Traditional Example of a Risk Calculation

One classic method of risk analysis expresses risk as a financial loss, or Annualized Loss Expectancy (ALE), based on the following equation:

$$ALE = SLE \times ARO$$

where SLE is the Single Loss Expectancy and ARO is the Annualized Rate of Occurrence (or predicted frequency of a loss event happening).

Consider an Internet-based equities trading application possessing a vulnerability that may result in unauthorized access, with the implication that unauthorized stock trades can be made. Assume that a risk analysis determines that middle- and back-office procedures will catch and negate any malicious transaction such that the loss associated with the event is simply the cost of backing out the trade. We'll assign a cost of $150 for any such event. This yields an SLE = $150. With even an ARO of 100 such events per year, the cost to the company (or ALE) will be $15,000.

The resulting dollar figure provides no more than a rough yardstick, albeit a useful one, for determining whether to invest in fixing the vulnerability. Of course, in the case of our fictional equities trading company, a $15,000 annual loss might not be worth getting out of bed for (typically, a proprietary trading company's intraday market risk would dwarf such an annual loss figure).[8]

Other methods take a more qualitative route. In the case of a Web server providing a company's face to the world, a Web site defacement might be difficult to quantify as a financial loss (although some studies indicate a link simply between security events and negative stock price movements [Cavusoglu, Mishra, and Raghunathan 2002]). In cases where intangible assets are involved (e.g., reputation), qualitative risk assessment may be a more appropriate way to capture loss.

---

[8]There are other quantitative methods that don't use ALE. For example, some organizations use hard numbers such as the actual cost of developing and operating the system, dollar value to paying customers, and so on.

Regardless of the technique used, most practitioners advocate a return-on-investment study to determine whether a given countermeasure is a cost-effective method for achieving the desired security goal. For example, adding applied cryptography to an application server, using native APIs (e.g., MS-CAPI) without the aid of dedicated hardware acceleration, may be cheap in the short term; but if this results in a significant loss in transaction volume throughput, a better ROI may be achieved by investing up front in crypto acceleration hardware. (Make sure to be realistic about just what ROI means if you choose to use the term. See the box The Truth about ROI.)

Interested organizations are advised to adopt the risk calculation methodology that best reflects their needs. The techniques described in this chapter provide a starting point.

The Truth about ROI

ROI sounds great in glossy marketing handouts. But what exactly does ROI mean for security? Other than confirming that getting started with security early in the lifecycle is of critical importance and will save you money, studies of return on security investment (ROSI) have not amounted to much.

Fact is, security is more like insurance than it is like some kind of investment. You can manage risk by identifying and mitigating security issues both technically and at the business level. But you will never hit a "big payoff" if your security holds. You'll only avoid serious negative consequences if it doesn't. We buy car insurance for just that reason: not because we can't wait for the big payoff when we have a crash but just in case we do.

Limitations of Traditional Approaches

Traditional risk analysis output is difficult to apply directly to modern software design. For example, in the quantitative risk analysis equation described in the previous section, even assuming a high level of confidence in the ability to predict the dollar loss for a given event and having performed Monte Carlo distribution analysis of prior events to derive a statistically sound probability distribution for future events, there's still a large gap between the raw dollar figure of an ALE and a detailed software security mitigation definition.

Another, more worrying, concern is that traditional risk analysis techniques do not necessarily provide an easy guide (not to mention an exhaustive list) of all potential vulnerabilities and threats to be concerned about at a component/environment level. This is where a large knowledge base and lots of experience is invaluable. (See Chapter 11 for more on software security knowledge.)

The thorny knowledge problem arises in part because modern applications, including Web Services applications, are designed to span multiple boundaries of trust. Vulnerability of, and risk to, any given component varies with the platform that the component exists on (e.g., C# applications on Windows .NET Server versus J2EE applications on Tomcat/Apache/Linux) and with the environment it exists in (secure production network versus client network versus Internet DMZ). However, few of the traditional approaches adequately address the contextual variability of risk given changes in the core environment. This becomes a fatal flaw when considering highly distributed applications, Service Oriented Architectures, or Web Services.

In modern frameworks, such as .NET and J2EE, security methods exist at almost every layer of the OSI model, yet too many applications today rely on a "reactive protection" infrastructure (e.g., firewalls, SSL) that provides protection below layer four only. This is too often summed up in the claim "We are secure because we use SSL and implement firewalls," leaving open all sorts of questions such as those engendered by port 80 attacks, SQL injection, class spoofing, and method overwriting (to name a handful).

One answer to this problem is to begin to look at software risk analysis on a component-by-component, tier-by-tier, environment-by-environment level and apply the principles of measuring threats, risks, vulnerabilities, and impacts at all of these levels.

Modern Risk Analysis

Given the limitations of traditional approaches, a more holistic risk management methodology involves thinking about risk throughout the lifecycle (as described in Chapter 2). Starting the risk analysis process early is critical. In fact, risk analysis is even effective at the requirements level. Modern approaches emphasize the importance of an architectural view and of architectural risk analysis.

Security Requirements

In the purest sense, risk analysis starts at the requirements stage because design requirements should take into account the risks that you are trying to counter. The box Back to Requirements briefly covers three approaches to interjecting a risk-based philosophy into the requirements phase. (Do note that the requirements systems based around UML tend to focus more attention on security *functionality* than they do on abuse cases, which I discuss at length in Chapter 8.)

Whatever risk analysis method is adopted, the requirements process should be driven by risk.

Back to Requirements

SecureUML* is a methodology for modeling access control policies and their integration into a model-driven software development process. SecureUML is based on Role-Based Access Control and models security requirements for well-behaved applications in predictable environments.

UMLsec [Jurjens 2001] is an extension of UML to include modeling of security-related features, such as confidentiality and access control.

Sindre and Opdahl [2000] attempt to model abuse cases as a way of understanding how an application might respond to threats in a less controllable environment and to describe functions that the system should not allow.

---

*See http://kisogawa.inf.ethz.ch/WebBIB/publications-softech/papers/2002/0_secuml_uml2002.pdf.

As stated earlier, a key variable in the risk equation is *impact*. The business impacts of any risks that we are trying to avoid can be many, but for the most part, they boil down into three broad categories:

1. Legal and/or regulatory risk: These may include federal or state laws and regulations (e.g., the Gramm-Leach-Bliley Act [GLBA], HIPPA, or the now-famous California Senate Bill 1386, also known as SB1386)
2. Financial or commercial considerations (e.g., protection of revenue, control over high-value intellectual property, preservation of brand and reputation)

3. Contractual considerations (e.g., service-level agreements, avoidance of liability)

Even at this early point in the lifecycle, the first risk-based decisions should be made. One approach might be to break down requirements into three simple categories: "must-haves," "important-to-haves," and "nice-but-unnecessary-to-haves."

Unless you are running an illegal operation, laws and regulations should always be classed into the first category, making these requirements instantly mandatory and not subject to further risk analysis (although an ROI study should always be conducted to select the most cost-effective mitigations). For example, if the law requires you to protect private information, this is mandatory and should not be the subject of a risk-based decision. Why? Because the government may have the power to put you out of business, which is the mother of all risks (and if you want to test the government and regulators on this one, then go ahead—just don't say that you weren't warned!).

You are then left with risk impacts that need to be managed in other ways, the ones that have as variables potential impact and probability. At the initial requirements definition stage, you may be able to make some assumptions regarding the controls that are necessary and the ones that may not be.

Even application of these simple ideas will put you ahead of the majority of software developers. Then as we move toward the design and build stages, risk analysis should begin to test those assumptions made at the requirements stage by analyzing the risks and vulnerabilities inherent in the design. Finally, tests and test planning should be driven by risk analysis results as well.

A Basic Risk Analysis Approach

To encompass the design stage, any risk analysis process should be tailored. The object of this tailoring exercise is to determine specific vulnerabilities and risks that exist for the software. A functional decomposition of the application into major components, processes, data stores, and data communication flows, mapped against the environments across which the software will be deployed, allows for a desktop review of threats and potential vulnerabilities. I cannot overemphasize the importance of using a forest-level view of a system during risk analysis. Some sort of high-level model of the system (from a whiteboard boxes-and-arrows picture to a formally

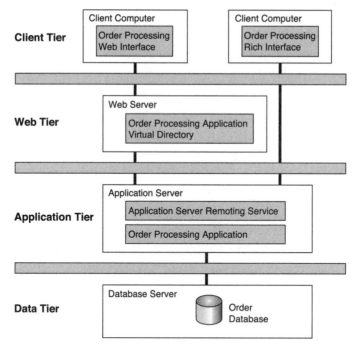

Figure 5–3 A forest-level view of a standard-issue four-tier Web application.

specified mathematical model) makes risk analysis at the architectural level possible.

Although one could contemplate using modeling languages, such as UMLsec, to attempt to model risks, even the most rudimentary analysis approaches can yield meaningful results. Consider Figure 5–3, which shows a simple four-tier deployment design pattern for a standard-issue Web-based application. If we apply risk analysis principles to this level of design, we can immediately draw some useful conclusions about the security design of the application.

During the risk analysis process we should consider the following:

- The threats who are likely to want to attack our system
- The risks present in each tier's environment
- The kinds of vulnerabilities that might exist in each component, as well as the data flow
- The business impact of such technical risks, were they to be realized
- The probability of such a risk being realized

- Any feasible countermeasures that could be implemented at each tier, taking into account the full range of protection mechanisms available (e.g., from base operating system–level security through Virtual Machine security mechanisms, such as use of the Java Cryptography Extensions in J2EE)

This very basic process will sound familiar if you read Chapter 2 on the RMF. In that chapter, I describe in great detail a number of critical risk management steps in an iterative model.

In this simple example, each of the tiers exists in a different security realm or trust zone. This fact immediately provides us with the context of risk faced by each tier. If we go on to superimpose data types (e.g., user logon credentials, records, orders) and their flows (logon requests, record queries, order entries) and, more importantly, their security classifications, we can draw conclusions about the protection of these data elements and their transmission given the current design.

For example, suppose that user logon flows are protected by SSL between the client and the Web server. However, our deployment pattern indicates that though the encrypted tunnel terminates at this tier, because of the threat inherent in the zones occupied by the Web and application tiers, we really need to prevent eavesdropping inside and between these two tiers as well. This might indicate the need to establish yet another encrypted tunnel or, possibly, to consider a different approach to securing these data (e.g., message-level encryption as opposed to tunneling).

Use of a deployment pattern in this analysis is valuable because it allows us to consider both infrastructure (i.e., operating systems and network) security mechanisms as well as application-level mechanisms as risk mitigation measures.

Realize that decomposing software on a component-by-component basis to establish trust zones is a comfortable way for most software developers and auditors to begin adopting a risk management approach to software security. Because most systems, especially those exhibiting the *n*-tier architecture, rely on several third-party components and a variety of programming languages, defining zones of trust and taking an outside→in perspective similar to that normally observed in traditional security has clear benefits. In any case, interaction of different products and languages is an architectural element likely to be a vulnerability hotbed.

At its heart, decomposition is a natural way to partition a system. Given a simple decomposition, security professionals will be able to advise developers and architects about aspects of security that they're familiar with such as network-based component boundaries and authentication (as I highlight in the example). Do not forget, however, that the composition problem (putting the components all back together) is unsolved and very tricky, and that even the most secure components can be assembled into an insecure mess!

As organizations become adept at identifying vulnerability and its business impact consistently using the approach illustrated earlier, the approach should be evolved to include additional assessment of risks found within tiers and encompassing all tiers. This more sophisticated approach uncovers technology-specific vulnerabilities based on failings other than trust issues across tier boundaries. Exploits related to broken transaction management and phishing attacks[9] are examples of some of the more subtle risks one might encounter with an enhanced approach.

Finally, a design-level risk analysis approach can also be augmented with data from code reviews and risk-based testing.

Coder's Corner

Avi Rubin, a professor at Johns Hopkins University, and his graduate students spent much effort performing an architectural risk analysis on Diebold electronic voting machines. Their work is collected here <http://avirubin.com/vote/>.

The abstract of their paper <http://avirubin.com/vote.pdf> on one of their more famous (and controversial) analyses says:

> With significant U.S. federal funds now available to replace outdated punch-card and mechanical voting systems, municipalities and states throughout the U.S. are adopting paperless electronic voting systems from a number of different vendors. We present a security analysis of the source code to one such machine used in a significant share of the market. Our analysis shows that this voting system is far below even the most minimal security standards applicable in other contexts. We identify several problems including unauthorized privilege escalation, incorrect use of cryptography, vulnerabilities to network threats, and poor

Continued

---

[9]For more on phishing, which combines social engineering and technical subterfuge, see <http://www.antiphishing.org/>.

software development processes [emphasis added]. We show that voters, without any insider privileges, can cast unlimited votes without being detected by any mechanisms within the voting terminal software. Furthermore, we show that even the most serious of our outsider attacks could have been discovered and executed without access to the source code. In the face of such attacks, the usual worries about insider threats are not the only concerns; outsiders can do the damage. That said, we demonstrate that the insider threat is also quite considerable, showing that not only can an insider, such as a poll worker, modify the votes, but that insiders can also violate voter privacy and match votes with the voters who cast them. We conclude that this voting system is unsuitable for use in a general election. Any paperless electronic voting system might suffer similar flaws, despite any "certification" it could have otherwise received. We suggest that the best solutions are voting systems having a "voter-verifiable audit trail," where a computerized voting system might print a paper ballot that can be read and verified by the voter.

In the paper, the authors present a number of findings. Before presenting the technical information, a concise overview of the system (a forest-level view) is presented. The overview sets the stage for the technical results, many of which focus on the construction of the system and its architecture. Among the technical results is the following finding:

3.2 Casting multiple votes

In the Diebold system, a voter begins the voting process by inserting a smart card into the voting terminal. Upon checking that the card is "active," the voting terminal collects the user's vote and then deactivates the user's card; the deactivation actually occurs by rewriting the card's type, which is stored as an 8-bit value on the card, from VOTER_CARD *(0x01) to* CANCELED_CARD *(0x08). Since an adversary can make perfectly valid smart cards, the adversary could bring a stack of active cards to the voting booth. Doing so gives the adversary the ability to vote multiple times. More simply, instead of bringing multiple cards to the voting booth, the adversary could program a smart card to ignore the voting terminal's deactivation command. Such an adversary could use one card to vote multiple times. Note here that the adversary could be a regular voter, and not necessarily an election insider.*

Will the adversary's multiple-votes be detected by the voting system?

To answer this question, we must first consider what information is encoded on the voter cards on a per voter basis. The only per voter information is a "voter serial number" (m_VoterSN in the CVoterInfo class). m_VoterSN is only recorded by the voting terminal if the voter decides not to place a vote (as noted in the comments in TSElection/ Results.cpp, this field is recorded for uncounted votes for backward compatibility reasons). It is important to note that if a voter decides to cancel his or her vote, the voter will have the opportunity to vote again using that same card (and, after the vote has been cast, m_VoterSN will no longer be recorded).

If we assume the number of collected votes becomes greater than the number of people who showed up to vote, and if the polling locations keep accurate counts of the number of people who show up to vote, then the back-end system, if designed properly, should be able to detect the existence of counterfeit votes. However, because m_VoterSN is only stored for those who did not vote, there will be no way for the tabulating system to distinguish the real votes from the counterfeit votes. This would cast serious doubt on the validity of the election results. The solution proposed by one election official, to have everyone vote again, does not seem like a viable solution.

Notice how the technical result is presented in terms of impact. The key to a good risk analysis is clearly stated impact statements. The only thing missing in the report is a mitigation strategy that is workable. The Diebold people appear to have their software security work cut out for them!

Touchpoint Process: Architectural Risk Analysis

Architectural risk analysis as practiced today is usually performed by experts in an ad hoc fashion. Such an approach does not scale, nor is it in any way repeatable or consistent. Results are deeply constrained by the expertise and experience of the team doing the analysis. Every team does its own thing. For these reasons, the results of disparate analyses are difficult to compare (if they are comparable at all). That's not so good.

As an alternative to the ad hoc approach, Cigital uses the architectural risk analysis process shown in Figure 5–4. This process complements and extends the RMF of Chapter 2. Though the process described here is certainly not the "be all, end all, one and only" way to carry out architectural risk analysis, the three subprocesses described here are extraordinarily powerful.

A risk analysis should be carried out only once a reasonable, big-picture overview of the system has been established. The idea is to forget about the code-based trees of bugland (temporarily at least) and concentrate on the forest. Thus the first step of the process shown in the figure is to build a one-page overview of the system under analysis. Sometimes a one-page big picture exists, but more often it does not. The one-page overview can be developed through a process of artifact analysis coupled with interviews. Inputs to the process are shown in the leftmost column of Figure 5–4.

Three critical steps (or subprocesses) make up the heart of this architectural risk analysis approach:

1. Attack resistance analysis
2. Ambiguity analysis
3. Weakness analysis

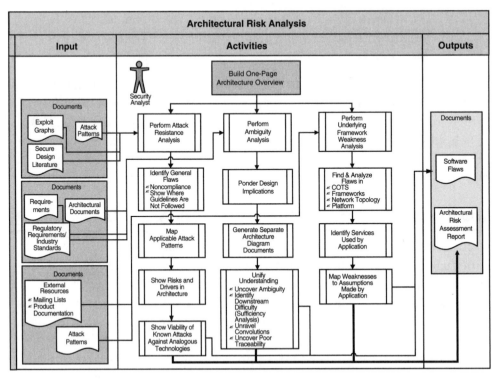

Figure 5–4 A simple process diagram for architectural risk analysis.

Don't forget to refer back to Figure 5–4 as you read about the three subprocesses.

Attack Resistance Analysis

Attack resistance analysis is meant to capture the checklist-like approach to risk analysis taken in Microsoft's STRIDE approach. The gist of the idea is to use information about known attacks, attack patterns, and vulnerabilities during the process of analysis. That is, given the one-page overview, how does the system fare against known attacks? Four steps are involved in this subprocess.

1. Identify general flaws using secure design literature and checklists (e.g., cycling through the Spoofing, Tampering, . . . categories from STRIDE). A knowledge base of historical risks is particularly useful in this activity.
2. Map attack patterns using either the results of abuse case development (see Chapter 8) or a list of attack patterns.
3. Identify risks in the architecture based on the use of checklists.
4. Understand and demonstrate the viability of these known attacks (using something like exploit graphs; see the Exploit Graphs box).

Note that this subprocess is very good at finding *known* problems but is not very good at finding new or otherwise creative attacks.

Example flaws uncovered by the attack resistance subprocess, in my experience, include the following.

- *Transparent authentication token generation/management:* In this flaw, tokens meant to identify a user are easy to guess or otherwise simple to misuse. Web-based programs that use "hidden" variables to preserve user state are a prime example of how not to do this. A number of these flaws are described in detail in *Exploiting Software* [Hoglund and McGraw 2004].
- *Misuse of cryptographic primitives:* This flaw is almost self-explanatory. The best example is the seriously flawed WEP protocol found in 802.11b, which misused cryptography to such an extent that the security was completely compromised [Stubblefield, Ioannides, and Rubin 2004].
- *Easily subverted guard components, broken encapsulation:* Examples here are slightly more subtle, but consider a situation in which an API is subverted and functionality is either misused or used in a surprising new

way. APIs can be thought of as classical "guards" in some cases, as long as they remain a choke point and single point of entry. As soon as they can be avoided, they cease to be useful.

- *Cross-language trust/privilege issues:* Flaws arise when language boundaries are crossed but input filtering and state-preservation mechanisms fail.

Exploit Graphs

An exploit graph helps an analyst understand what kind of access and/or pattern is required to carry out an attack given a software risk. Flowcharts are very useful in describing an exploit and should include some basics such as attack delivery (payloads), gaining access, privilege escalation, subverting protections, descriptions of architectural failure, and discussion of any existing mitigations (and their effectiveness). Charts help. Figure 5–5 shows a simple exploit graph that illustrates a mobile code attack.

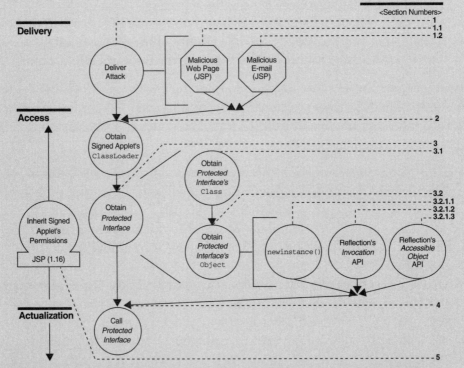

Figure 5–5 An exploit graph showing one of the mobile code attacks described in *Securing Java* [McGraw and Felten 1999]. The section numbers refer to entries in an associated table (in this case, Table 5–1). John Steven of Cigital created this graph.

Table 5–1 A Partial Exploit Graph Table to Accompany Figure 5–5

Step #	Detail: How/What	Conditions	Protection
Delivery 1	Deliver attack: get attack code onto machine with Jewel.	Client must have Internet access.	
Delivery 1.1	Trick user to point browser to JSP.	Browser must have "run JSP" enabled.	Disable JSSP in browser. NOTE: doing so prevents other sites from working.
Delivery 1.2	Send victim e-mail containing malicious JSP.	User's mail reader must interpret JSP.	Disable JSP execution in mail reader.

Note: JSP refers to Java Server Page.

Exploit graphs also require some explanation in text as briefly described earlier. Table 5–1 is a partial view (attack delivery only) of the table meant to accompany Figure 5–5.

Though attack graphs are not yet a mechanism in widespread use, they do help in a risk analysis. Their most important contribution lies in allowing an analyst to estimate the level of effort required to exploit a flaw. When it comes to exploit development, having a set of exploit graphs on hand can help determine which one exploit (usually of many) is the best to develop in the case that some kind of "proof" is required. Sometimes you will find that exploit development is required to convince skeptical observers that there is a serious problem that needs to be fixed.

Ambiguity Analysis

Ambiguity analysis is the subprocess capturing the creative activity required to discover *new* risks. This process, by definition, requires at least two analysts (the more the merrier) and some amount of experience. The idea is for each team member to carry out separate analysis activities in parallel. Only after these separate analyses are complete does the team come together in the "unify understanding" step shown in Figure 5–4.

We all know what happens when two or more software architects are put in a room together . . . catfight—often a catfight of world-bending magnitude. The ambiguity analysis subprocess takes advantage of the multiple points of view afforded by the art that is software architecture to create a critical analysis technique. Where good architects disagree, there lie interesting things (and sometimes new flaws).

In 1998, when performing an architectural risk analysis on early Java Card systems with John Viega and Brad Arkin (their first), my team started with a process very much like STRIDE. The team members each went their solitary analysis ways with their own private list of possible flaws and then came together for a whiteboard brainstorming session. When the team came together, it became apparent that none of the standard-issue attacks considered by the new team members were directly applicable in any obvious fashion. But we could not very well declare the system "secure" and go on to bill the customer (Visa)! What to do?!

As we started to describe together how the system worked (not how it failed, but how it worked), disagreements cropped up. It turns out that these disagreements and misunderstandings were harbingers of security risks. The creative process of describing to others how the system worked (well, at least how we thought it worked) was extremely valuable. Any major points of disagreement or any clear ambiguities became points of further analysis. This evolved into the subprocess of ambiguity analysis.

Ambiguity analysis helps to uncover ambiguity and inconsistency, identify downstream difficulty (through a process of traceability analysis), and unravel convolution. Unfortunately, this subprocess works best when carried out by a team of very experienced analysts. Furthermore, it is best taught in an apprenticeship situation. Perhaps knowledge management collections will make this all a bit less arbitrary (see Chapter 11).

Example flaws uncovered by the ambiguity analysis subprocess in my experience include the following.

- *Protocol, authentication problems:* One example involved key material used to (accidentally) encrypt itself in a complex new crypto system. It turns out that this mistake cut down the possible search space for a key from extremely large to manageably small.[10] This turned out to be a previously unknown attack, but it was fatal.
- *Java Card applet firewall and Java inner class issues:* Two examples. The first was a problematic object-sharing mechanism that suffered from serious transitive trust issues, the gist being that class A shared method foo with class B, and class B could then publish the method to the world (something A did not necessarily condone). The second involved the

---

[10]That is, breakable in some feasible time period with a standard machine.

way that inner classes were actually implemented (and continue to be implemented) in various Java compilers. Turns out that package scoping in this case was somewhat counterintuitive and that inner classes had a privilege scope that was surprisingly large.
- *Type safety and type confusion:* Type-safety problems in Java accounted for a good portion of the serious Java attacks from the mid-1990s. See *Securing Java* [McGraw and Felten 1999].
- *Password retrieval, fitness, and strength:* Why people continue to roll their own password mechanisms is beyond me. They do, though.

Weakness Analysis

Weakness analysis is a subprocess aimed at understanding the impact of external software dependencies. Software is no longer created in giant monolithic a.out globs (as it was in the good old days). Modern software is usually built on top of complex middleware frameworks like .NET and J2EE. Furthermore, almost all code counts on outside libraries like DLLs or common language libraries such as glibc. To make matters worse, distributed code—once the interesting architectural exception—has become the norm. With the rapid evolution of software has come a whole host of problems caused by linking in (or otherwise counting on) broken stuff. Leslie Lamport's definition of a distributed system as "one in which the failure of a computer you didn't even know existed can render your own computer unusable" describes exactly why the weakness problem is hard.

Uncovering weaknesses that arise by counting on outside software requires consideration of:

- COTS (including various outside security feature packages like the RSA libraries or Netegrity's authentication modules)
- Frameworks (J2EE, .NET, and any number of other middleware frameworks)
- Network topology (modern software almost always exists in a networked environment)
- Platform (consider what it's like to be application code on a cell phone or a smart card)[11]
- Physical environment (consider storage devices like USB keys and iPods)
- Build environment (what happens when you rely on a broken or poisoned compiler? what if your build machine is running a rootkit?)

---

[11]Not to mention a smart card living in a cell phone.

In the coming days of Service Oriented Architectures (SOAs), understanding which services your code is counting on and exactly what your code expects those services to deliver is critical. Common components make particularly attractive targets for attack. Common mode failure goes global.

The basic idea here is to understand what kind of assumptions you are making about outside software, and what will happen when those assumptions fail (or are coerced into failing). When assumptions fail, weaknesses are often revealed in stark relief. A large base of experience with third-party software libraries, systems, and platforms is extremely valuable when carrying out weakness analysis. Unfortunately, no perfect clearinghouse of security information for third-party software exists. One good idea is to take advantage of public security discussion forums such as BugTraq <http://www.securityfocus.com/archive/1>, comp.risks <http://catless.ncl.ac.uk/Risks>, and security tracker <http://www.securitytracker.com>.[12]

Example flaws uncovered by the weakness analysis subprocess in my experience include the following.

- *Browser and other VM sandboxing failures*: Browsers are overly complex pieces of software rivaled in complexity only by operating systems. Browsers have so many moving parts that finding unexplored niches and other "between the seams" flaws is easy.
- *Insecure service provision—RMI, COM, and so on*: Protocols and communications systems are often a standard feature of modern software. When Java's RMI was found to fail open <http://www.cs.princeton.edu/~balfanz>, the systems counting on RMI were all subject to the same kind of attack.
- *Debug (or other operational) interfaces*: Debugging code is always as useful to the attacker as it is to the maintainer. Don't send error reports to your (mis)user.
- *Unused (but privileged) product "features"*: If you put overly powerful features into your design, don't be surprised when they are turned against you. See *Building Secure Software* for a good story of what happened when old-fashioned bulletin board systems allowed a user to invoke `emacs` [Viega and McGraw 2001].

---

[12]Have you ever wondered whether the software you're working on (or counting on) has been successfully attacked? Check out the public mailing lists (BugTraq, VulnWatch <http://www.vulnwatch.org/>, comp.risks) to see. You may be surprised.

- *Interposition attacks—DLLs, library paths, client spoofing*: Person-in-the-middle attacks are very popular, mostly because they are very effective. Same goes for PATH hacking, spoofing, and other low-hanging fruit. Carefully consider what happens when an attacker gets between one component and the other components (or between one level of the computing system and the others).

By applying the simple three-step process outlined here, you can greatly improve on a more generic checklist-based approach. There is no substitute for experience and expertise, but as software security knowledge increases, more and more groups should be able to adopt these methods as their own.

Getting Started with Risk Analysis

This whole risk analysis thing seems a bit hard; but risk analysis does not really have to be hard. Sometimes when faced with a seemingly large task like this, it's difficult to get the ball rolling. To counter that problem, Appendix C presents a simple exercise in armchair risk analysis. The idea is to apply some of the ideas you have learned in this chapter to complete a risk analysis exercise on a pretend system (riddled with security flaws). I hope you find the exercise interesting and fun.[13]

Start with something really simple, like the STRIDE model [Howard and LeBlanc 2003]. Develop a simple checklist of attacks and march down the list, thinking about various attack categories (and the related flaws that spawn them) as you go. Checklists are not a complete disaster (as the existence of the attack resistance subprocess shows). In fact, in the hands of an expert, checklists (like the 48 attack patterns in *Exploiting Software* [Hoglund and McGraw 2004]) can be very powerful tools. One problem with checklists is that you are not very likely to find a new, as-yet-to-be-discovered attack if you stick only to the checklist.[14] Another problem is that in the hands of an inexperienced newbie, a checklist is not a very powerful tool. Then again, newbies should not be tasked with architectural risk analysis.

---

[13]Please try this at home! Hint: Try doing the exercise with a group of friends and a bottle of good wine.

[14]This is important because (smart) attackers use checklists too . . . in order to avoid doing something obvious that will get them caught. On the other hand, script kiddies will bumble right into your defenses, like a roach wandering into a roach motel.

Architectural Risk Analysis Is a Necessity

Risk analysis is, at best, a good general-purpose yardstick by which you can judge the effectiveness of your security design. Since around 50% of security problems are the result of design flaws, performing a risk analysis at the design level is an important part of a solid software security program.

Taking the trouble to apply risk analysis methods at the design level of any application often yields valuable, business-relevant results. The process of risk analysis identifies system-level vulnerabilities and their probability and impact on the organization. Based on considering the resulting ranked risks, business stakeholders can determine whether to mitigate a particular risk and which control is the most cost effective.

Software Penetration Testing[1]

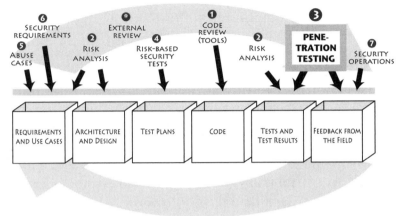

You can't make an omelet without breaking eggs.

ANONYMOUS

Quality assurance and testing organizations are tasked with the broad objective of ensuring that a software application fulfills its functional business requirements. Such testing most often involves running a series of dynamic functional tests late in the lifecycle to ensure that the application's features have been properly implemented. Sometimes use cases and requirements drive this testing. But no matter what does the driving, the result is the same—a strong emphasis on features and functions. Because security is not a feature or even a set of features, security testing (especially penetration testing) does not fit directly into this paradigm.

---

[1]Parts of this chapter appeared in original form in *IEEE Security & Privacy* magazine co-authored with Brad Arkin and Scott Stender [Arkin, Stender, and McGraw 2005].

Security testing poses a unique problem. A majority of security defects and vulnerabilities in software are not directly related to security functionality. Instead, security issues involve often unexpected but intentional misuses of an application discovered by an attacker. If we characterize functional testing as "testing for positives"—as in verifying that a feature properly performs a specific task—then penetration testing is in some sense "testing for negatives." That is, a security tester must probe directly and deeply into security risks (possibly driven by abuse cases and architectural risks) in order to determine how the system behaves under attack. (Chapter 7 discusses how these tests can be driven by attack patterns.)

At its heart, security testing needs to make use of both white hat and black hat concepts and approaches: ensuring that the security features work as advertised (a white hat undertaking) and that intentional attacks can't easily compromise the system (a black hat undertaking). That said, almost all penetration testing relies on black hat methods over white hat methods.[2] In other words, thinking like a bad guy is so essential to good penetration testing that leaving it out leaves penetration testing impotent.

In any case, testing for a negative poses a much greater challenge than verifying a positive. A set of successfully executed, plausible positive tests usually yields a high degree of confidence that a software component will perform functionally as desired. However, enumerating actions with the intention to produce a fault and reporting whether and under which circumstances the fault occurs is not a sound approach to proving the negative outcome does not exist. Got that? What I'm saying is that it's really easy to test whether a feature works or not, but it is very difficult to show whether or not a system is secure enough under malicious attack. How many tests do you do before you give up and declare "secure enough"?

If negative tests do not uncover any faults, this only offers proof that no faults occur under particular test conditions; this by no means proves that no faults exist. When applied to penetration testing where lack of security vulnerability is the negative we're interested in, this means that "passing" a software penetration test provides very little assurance that an application is immune to attack. One of the main problems with today's most common approach to penetration testing is a misunderstanding of this subtle point.

---

[2]One critical exception to this rule occurs when a penetration tester finds out that security functionality does not work as specified and uses this as the basis for attack. The upshot is that a security tester must ensure that the application not only does not do what it is not supposed to do but also does do what it is supposed to do (with regard to security features).

As a result of this problem in testing philosophy, penetration testing often devolves into a feel-good exercise in pretend security. Things go something like this. A set of reformed hackers is hired to carry out a penetration test. We know all is well because they're reformed. (Well, they told us they were reformed, anyway.) The hackers work a while until they discover a problem or two in the software, usually relating to vulnerabilities in base technology such as an application framework or a basic misconfiguration problem. Sometimes this discovery activity is as simple as trawling BugTraq to look up known security issues associated with an essential technology linked into the system.[3]

The hackers report their findings. They look great because they found a "major security problem." The software team looks pretty good because they graciously agreed to have their baby analyzed and broken, and they even know how to fix the problem. The VP of Yadda Yadda looks great because the security box is checked. Everybody wins!

The problem? No clue about security risk. No idea whether the most critical security risks have been uncovered, how much risk remains in the system, and how many bugs are lurking in the zillions of lines of code. Finding a security problem and fixing it is fine. But what about the rest of the system?

Imagine if we did normal software testing like this! The software is declared "code complete" and thrown over the wall to testing. The testers begin work right away, focusing on very basic edge conditions and known failure modes from previous testing on version one. They find one or two problems right off the bat. Then they stop, the problems get fixed, and the testing box gets checked off. Has the software been properly tested? Run this scenario by any professional tester, and once the tester is done laughing, think about whether penetration testing as practiced by most organizations works.

Penetration Testing Today

Penetration testing is the most frequently and commonly applied of all software security best practices. This is not necessarily a good thing. Often penetration testing is foisted on software development teams by overzealous security guys and everyone ends up angry. Plus the focus tends to be too much driven by an outside→in approach. Better to adopt and implement

---

[3]See <http://www.securityfocus.com> for the BugTraq archive.

the first two touchpoints (code review and architectural risk analysis) than to start with number three!

One reason for the prevalence of penetration testing is that it appears to be attractive as a late-lifecycle activity and can be carried out in an outside→in manner. Operations people not involved in the earlier parts of the development lifecycle can impose it on the software (but only when it's done). Once an application is finished, it is subjected to penetration testing as part of the final preoperations acceptance regimen. The testing is carried out by the infosec division. Because of time constraints, most assessments like this are performed in a "time-boxed" manner as a final security checklist item at the end of the lifecycle.

One major limitation of this approach is that it almost always represents a too-little-too-late attempt to tackle security at the end of the development cycle. As we have seen, software security is an emergent property of the system, and attaining it involves applying a series of touchpoints throughout the software lifecycle (see Chapter 3). Organizations that fail to integrate security throughout the development process are often unpleasantly surprised to find that their software suffers from systemic faults both at the design level and in the implementation. In other words, the system has zillions of security flaws and security bugs. In a late-lifecycle penetration testing paradigm, inside-the-code problems are uncovered too late, and options for remedy are severely constrained by both time and budget.

Fixing things at this stage is, more often than not, prohibitively expensive and almost always involves Band-Aids instead of cures. Post-penetration-test security fixes tend to be particularly reactive and defensive in nature—adjusting the firewall ruleset, for example. Though these short-notice kludges may fix up inside problems temporarily, they can be likened to putting a Band-Aid on a laceration. Tracking down the source of the problem and fixing things there is much more effective.

The real value of penetration testing comes from probing a system in its final operating environment. Uncovering environment and configuration problems and concerns is the best result of any penetration test. This is mostly because such problems can actually be fixed late in the lifecycle. Knowing whether or not your WebSphere application server is properly set up and your firewall plays nicely with it is just as important to final security posture as is building solid code. Penetration testing gets to the heart of these environment and configuration issues quickly. (In fact, its weakness lies in not being able to get beyond these kinds of issues very effectively.)

The success of an ad hoc software penetration test is dependent on many factors, few of which lend themselves to metrics and standardization. The first and most obvious variable is the skill, knowledge, and experience of the tester(s). Software security penetration tests (sometimes called application penetration tests) do not currently follow a standard process of any sort and therefore are not particularly amenable to a consistent application of knowledge (think checklists and boilerplate techniques). The upshot is that only skilled and experienced testers can successfully carry out penetration testing. For an example of what happens when not enough attention is paid during a penetration test, see the next box, An Example: Scrubbed to Protect the Guilty.

Use of security requirements, abuse cases, security risk knowledge, and attack patterns in application design, analysis, and testing is rare in current practice. As a result, security findings are not repeatable across different teams and vary widely depending on the skill and experience of the tester(s). Furthermore, any test regimen can be structured in such a way as to influence the findings. If test parameters are determined by individuals motivated (consciously or not) not to find any security issues, it is very likely that penetration testing will result in a self-congratulatory exercise in futility.[4]

Results interpretation is also an issue. Typically, results take the form of a list of flaws, bugs, and vulnerabilities identified during the penetration testing. Software development organizations tend to regard these results as complete bug reports—comprehensive lists of issues to be addressed in order to make the system secure. Unfortunately, this perception does not factor in the time-boxed (or otherwise incomplete) nature of late-lifecycle assessments. In practice, a penetration test can identify only a small representative sample of all of the possible security risks in a system (especially those problems that are environmental or involve operational configuration). If a software development organization focuses solely on a small (and limited) list of issues, it will end up mitigating only a subset of the security risks present (and possibly not even those that present the greatest risk).

All of these issues pale in comparison to the problem that penetration testing is often used as an excuse to declare security victory and "go home." Don't forget, when a penetration test concentrates on finding and removing a handful of issues (and even does so successfully), everyone looks good. Unfortunately, penetration testing done without any basis in security risk analysis leads to the "pretend security" problem with alarming consistency.

---

[4]Put in more basic terms, don't let the fox guard the chicken house. If you do, don't be surprised if the fox finds absolutely no problems with the major hole in the northwest corner of the chicken yard.

An Example: Scrubbed to Protect the Guilty

One major problem with application penetration testing as carried out today is that the testers are often very good, but not very software savvy network security people. If you have the same guys testing your network infrastructure setup (using Nessus) as are testing your applications, you might ask yourself what kind of value you're getting. It's not that network security people are dopes. They're not. It's just that results from a software penetration test need to be described in a coherent fashion so that real software people can act on them. Communicating with software people is difficult enough if you are one! If you're not . . . woe is you.

As a good example of the kind of silly results you get when you have the wrong people do an application penetration test, take a look at the following excerpt of results cut from a real penetration test and carried out by an experienced (network) penetration team. We'll call the company APPSECO to protect the guilty.

Source Code Review of Input Validation Modules

APPSECO conducted a manual security review of a selected set of input validation modules. The modules were provided to CLIENT by the SWVENDOR as an example of their new input validation architecture. APPSECO analyzed the logic flow, input bounds checking, input type and content validation, and error handling. The modules reviewed are listed in the table below:
[*List elided.*]

. . .

Input Validation Modules

The results of the code analysis indicate that input validation is ineffective. Further, the input validation modules introduce potential cross-site scripting vulnerabilities to the application. While some input is validated for type, content, and for authorization, much of the input is not.

Because only a portion of the code base was provided, APPSECO cannot make a definitive and complete statement regarding the effectiveness of the code in controlling user input and restricting user access. As such, conclusions regarding the effectiveness of the code and severity of vulnerabilities identified may change upon review of the code given access to the entire code base. For example, numerous validation functions are called within the validation modules for which no definition was provided. These include: [*functions elided*]. These and all other validation functions must be reviewed.

I find it inexcusable to make claims like those found in the second paragraph given the kind of disclaimers in the third. No non-software person would look at parts of a system and say anything at all about what had been seen (short of identifying local bugs in API usage). Incidentally, later in the same report, a cut-and-paste error in the description of a network access control problem calls out a *different* client. Hmm.

One big benefit of penetration testing that is well worth mentioning is its adherence to a critical (even cynical) black hat stance. By taking on a system in its real production environment, penetration testers can get a better feel for operational and configuration issues often overlooked in software development. That's why penetration testing needs to be adjusted, not abandoned. For more on black box testing and why it is useful as an attacker technique, see Chapter 3 of *Exploiting Software* [Hoglund and McGraw 2004].

Coder's Corner

Here's an interesting little problem published by Professor D. J. Bernstein from the University of Illinois at Chicago and attributed to his student Ariel Berkman. (The original posting can be found at <http://tigger.uic.edu/~jlongs2/holes/changepassword.txt>.)

The posting describes a locally exploitable security hole in ChangePassword, which is a YP/Samba/Squid password-changing utility.

If changepassword.cgi is installed on a multiuser computer, any user with an account on the computer can gain complete control of the computer through the utility. The attacker can read and modify all files, watch all processes, and perform other such nefarious activities.

The bug occurs on line 317 of changepassword.c, which calls

```
system("cd /var/yp && make &> /dev/null");
```

without cleaning its environment in any way first. This is a big no-no.

Unfortunately (or not, depending on your hat color) the Makefile arranges for changepassword.cgi to be setuid root. A malicious user can create an exploit as follows:

Continued

```
set $PATH to point to an evil make program
set $CONTENT_LENGTH to 512
set $REQUEST_METHOD to POST
feed form_user=u&form_pw=p&form_new1=x&form_new2=x&
  to changepassword.cgi, where u is the username and p is the
  password.
```

The attacker's make program then runs with root privileges.

In short, you can use this CGI script to change a password and to root the box, but not through the Web interface. Since this program doesn't clean up its environment properly before running, you can log into the machine, put a malicious command named make early on your path, execute the CGI script, and you're all done.

This bug is interesting for a number of reasons.

- It's a nice example of programmers' assumptions being violated.
- It's a Web application, but you can't find the vulnerability using port 80 nonsense.
- Because the problem is related to the interaction between the program and the environment, exploitability is tied to the configuration of the machine.
- Your QA environment might be okay and your production server might be vulnerable.
- You're unlikely to find it with any sort of black box penetration test since the tester needs to look at the source code to find the problem.

Software Penetration Testing—a Better Approach

All is not lost—security penetration testing can be used effectively. The best approach bases penetration testing activities on security findings discovered and tracked from the beginning of the software lifecycle: during requirements analysis, architectural risk analysis, and so on. To do this, a penetration test must be structured according to perceived risk and offer some kind of metric relating the security posture of the software at the time of the test to risk measurement. Results are less likely to be misconstrued and used to declare pretend security victory if they are related to business impact through proper risk management. (See Chapter 2, which describes a risk management framework amenable to feeding security testing.)

Penetration testing is about testing a system in its final production environment. For this reason, penetration testing is best suited to probing configuration problems and other environmental factors that deeply impact software security. Driving tests that concentrate on these factors with some knowledge of risk analysis results is the most effective approach. Outside→in testing is great as long as it is not the only testing you do. The modern approach that I describe throughout the remainder of this chapter is much more closely aligned with risk-based security testing (see Chapter 7) than it is with application penetration testing as practiced by most consulting shops today. Be careful what you ask for!

Make Use of Tools

Tools (including the static analysis tools discussed in Chapter 4) should definitely be used in penetration testing. Tools are well suited to finding known security vulnerabilities with little effort. Static analysis tools can vet software code, either in source or binary form, in an attempt to identify common implementation-level bugs such as buffer overflows. Dynamic analysis tools can observe a system as it executes. These tools can submit malformed, malicious, and random data to a system's entry points in an attempt to uncover faults—a process commonly referred to as *fuzzing* [Miller et al. 1995]. Faults are then reported to the tester for further analysis. When possible, use of these tools should be guided by risk analysis results and attack patterns. (See the following box, Tools for Penetration Testing.)

Tool use carries two major benefits. First, when used effectively, tools can carry out a majority of the grunt work needed for basic software penetration testing (at the level of a fielded system). Of course, a tool-driven approach can't be used as a replacement for review by a skilled security analyst (especially since today's tools are by their nature not applicable at the design level), but a tool-based approach does help relieve the work burden of a reviewer and can thus drive down cost. Second, tool output lends itself readily to metrics. Software development teams can use these metrics to track progress over time as they move toward a security goal. Simple metrics in common use today do not offer a complete picture of the security posture of a system. Thus it is important to emphasize that a clean bill of health from an analysis tool does not mean that a system is defect free (recall the discussion of badness-ometers from Chapter 1). The value lies in relative comparison: If the current run of the tools reveals fewer defects than a previous run, progress has likely been made.

Tools for Penetration Testing

A number of tools purport utility for application security testing. Beware of those tools that claim to be a "hacker in a box." For a rant about (super-lame) application security testing tools like that, see the box Application Security Testing Tools: Good or Bad in Chapter 1. If we leave aside silly tools that do things like send 50 a's over port 80 in an attempt to cause a buffer overflow, there are a number of very useful tools left.

Fault Injection Tools

Software fault injection has an interesting future as a potential security technology. I coauthored the first book on this technique with Jeff Voas. If you're up for a tedious read, check out *Software Fault Injection* [Voas and McGraw 1998].

One of the most interesting modern fault injection engines for security is the Cenzic tool. This tool uses browser shunts to intercept transactions and allow an analyst to play around with them. Though this kind of testing activity is possible with perl and a command-line interface, results collection and automation make the second-generation tools worth considering. Cenzic began its life as a hacker tool called Hailstorm written by Greg Hoglund. Greg has since abandoned Cenzic, but the company carries on. For more, see <http://www.cenzic.com>.

James Whittaker and his merry band of security grad-students-turned-testers from Florida Tech created a company called Security Innovation. Whittaker takes malicious input to a new level. The Holodeck tool is useful for playback, security fault injection, and a number of other interesting tests. For more, see <http://www.sisecure.com>.

Other Tools

Also worth a look are application attack tools from SPI Dynamics <http://www.spidynamics.com> and Fortify Software <http://www.fortifysoftware.com>.

Dan Geer reports that Dave Aitel and company are having considerable success using Immunity's CANVAS tool <http://www.immunitysec.com/products-canvas.shtml>.

Another fun little tool is a shim that allows you to capture all of the HTTP traffic your browser sees. One such tool is here <http://www.ieinspector.com/httpanalyzer/>. Since these tools run in the browser, you don't have to jump through any hoops to see HTTPS traffic. Nice for messing around with Web interfaces (as a way of "making the client invisible") [Hoglund and McGraw 2004].

The main thing to remember about all of these tools is that they are most valuable in the hands of an expert. Whatever you do, don't set your five-year-old up with a power saw, or if you do, don't be too shocked by the messy results.

Getting Past Fault Injection: The Attacker's Toolkit

In *Exploiting Software,* Greg Hoglund and I go to great lengths to describe the attacker's toolkit. Tools commonly used by bad guys make great fodder for penetration testers. This is where your black hat gets its dark color. Any hacker (malicious or otherwise) worth his or her salt uses these tools.

- *Disassemblers and decompilers:* The notion that source code is required for security attacks is ridiculous. People interested in really understanding the ins and outs of software use disassemblers and decompilers all the time.
- *Control flow and coverage tools:* Though coverage tools were designed to help testers ascertain test effectiveness, they also make excellent attack tools. If you know that there is a vulnerability sitting deep in a target program, the next order of business is getting there. Control flow, data flow, and coverage analysis tools help.
- *APISPY32:* A tool particular to Win32, but well worth a mention. This tool allows an analyst to know when a program uses outside DLLs and/or other libraries. This kind of information is useful for interposition attacks, DLL substitution attacks, and a whole lot of other fun.
- *Breakpoint setters and monitors:* Debuggers are your friend. Breakpoints can even be set on target hardware to look for memory page access, device access, and the like. Understanding a program is much easier if you can watch it and freeze it at will.
- *Buffer overflow:* You know all about this one, right? See *Building Secure Software* if you want to know how a buffer overflow attack really works in painstaking detail [Viega and McGraw 2001]. Advanced attacks are covered in *Exploiting Software* [Hoglund and McGraw 2004]. Also see the new book *The 19 Deadly Sins of Software Security* [Howard, LeBlanc, and Viega 2005].
- *Shell code:* Payload anyone? The attacker's goal is to subvert control and run a program. This is the kind of program that gets run. See *The Shellcoder's Handbook* for more [Koziol et al. 2004].
- *Rootkits:* The ultimate weapon. At the apex of the attacker's toolkit is the rootkit. Rootkits hide away from standard system observers, employing hooks, trampolines, and patches to get their work done. Sophisticated rootkits run in such a way that other programs that usually monitor machine behavior can't easily detect them. A rootkit thus provides insider access only to people who know that it is running and available to accept commands. Kernel rootkits can hide files and running processes

Continued

to provide a back door into the target machine. An excellent book, *Rootkits: Sub-verting the Windows Kernel*—the first book in the world on rootkits—was published in August 2005 [Hoglund and Butler 2005].

Other tools also worth a (much briefer) mention include the following:

- Debuggers (user-mode)
- Kernel debuggers
- SoftIce
- Fuzz
- Boron tagging
- The "depends" tool
- Grammar rewriters

Test More Than Once

As it stands today, automated review is best suited to identifying the most basic of implementation defects. Human review is necessary to reveal flaws in the design or more complicated implementation-level vulnerabilities (of the sort that attackers can and will exploit). However, review by an expert is costly and, for reasons just described, can be ineffective if the "expert" is not. By leveraging the seven software security touchpoints described in this book, software penetration tests can be structured in such a way as to be cost effective *and* give a reasonable estimation of the security posture of the system.

Penetration testing can benefit greatly from knowledge of the security risks built into a system. No design or implementation is perfect, and carrying risk is usually acceptable. Penetration testing can help you find out what this means to your fielded system. In fact, penetration testing in some sense collapses the "risk probability wave" into something much more tangible when testing clarifies ways that a risk can be exploited. That is, if you know what your likely risks are in the design, you can use penetration testing to figure out what impact this has on an actual fielded system.

As noted earlier, static and dynamic analysis tools should be uniformly applied; this holds true at the subsystem level too. In most cases, no customization of basic static analysis tools is necessary for component-level tests. However, dynamic analysis tools will likely need to be written or modified for the target component. Such tools often involve data-driven tests that operate at the API level. Any tool should include data sets known to cause problems, such as long strings, strange encodings, and control characters [Hoglund and McGraw 2004]. Furthermore, the design of the tool should reflect the security test's goal—to misuse the component's assets, to violate intercomponent assumptions, or to probe risks. Customizations are almost always necessary.

Penetration testing should focus at the system level and should be directed at properties of the integrated software system. For efficiency's sake, testing should be structured in such a way as to avoid repeating unit-level testing (as described in Chapter 7), and should therefore be focused on aspects of the system that could not be probed during unit testing.

In order to be defined as penetration tests, system-level tests should analyze the system in its deployed environment. Such analysis may be targeted to ensure that suggested deployment practices are effective and reasonable, and that assumptions external to the system cannot be violated.

Incorporating Findings Back into Development

Perhaps the most common failure of the software penetration testing process is failure to identify lessons learned and propagate them back into the organization. As mentioned, it is tempting to view the results of a penetration test as a complete and final list of issues to be fixed rather than as a representative sample of faults in the system. Of course, even in this case, the existence of such a list does not do anything to actually fix the system. One of the major barriers to software security success is getting organizations to get around to fixing the problems found every day by security consultants. Don't for a minute believe that penetration testing results make you any more secure; only acting on them does.

Mitigation strategy is thus a critical aspect of any penetration test. Rather than simply fixing only those issues identified, developers should carry out a root-cause analysis of the identified vulnerabilities. For example, if a majority of vulnerabilities are buffer overflows, the development organization should determine just how these bugs made it into the code base. In such a scenario, lack of developer training, misapplication (or nonexistence of) standard coding practices, poor choice of languages and libraries, intense schedule pressure, failure to use a source code analysis tool, or any combination thereof may ultimately represent an important cause.

Once a root cause has been identified, mitigation strategies should be devised to address the identified vulnerabilities and any similar vulnerabilities in the software. Furthermore, best practices should be developed and implemented to address such vulnerabilities proactively in the future. (See Chapter 10 for a discussion of how this idea relates to a large-scale software security program.)

Going back to the buffer overflow example, an organization may decide to train its developers and eliminate the use of potentially dangerous functions, such as `strcpy()`, in favor of safer string-handling libraries such as those found in the C++ Standard Templates Library (STL). Perhaps a static analysis tool can be used to enforce this decision.

A good last step involves using test result information to measure progress against a goal. Where possible, tests for a mitigated vulnerability should be added to automated test suites (which can be used in regression testing). If the vulnerability resurfaces in the code base at some point in the future, any measures taken to prevent the vulnerability should be revisited and improved. As time passes, iterative penetration tests should reveal fewer and less severe defects in the system. If a penetration test reveals serious severe problems, the "representative sample" view of the results should give the development organization real reservations about deploying the system.

Using Penetration Tests to Assess the Application Landscape

One of the major problems facing large organizations that have been creating software for years is the unmanageable pile of software they have created. How do you get started when you have over 1000 applications and nobody thought about software security until just recently?

Penetration testing can help. One idea is to run a uniform, fixed-length, standardized penetration test against all of the apps and then rank them according to results. This would best be enhanced by a very basic risk analysis to pin down the business context (see Chapter 5). In this way, a very rough cut at ranking the application pile by security posture is possible. An approach like this results in a plan of attack that makes sense. No reason to work on the most secure application first.

This idea can be expanded to cover sets of common components and libraries and their intersection with the application pile. The move toward Web Services and Service Oriented Architecture (SOA) means that much more attention must be paid to shared services. Put bluntly, shared services are also potential shared vulnerabilities and/or common points of failure. Getting things like state, messaging, and authentication right in the brave new world of SOA is a real challenge.

Proper Penetration Testing Is Good

Penetration testing is the most commonly applied mechanism used to inject security into the SDLC. Unfortunately, it is the most commonly misapplied mechanism as well. By adjusting penetration testing to account for results uncovered during testing at the unit level, driving outside→in test creation from risk analysis, and driving the results back into an organization's SDLC, many common pitfalls can be avoided. Note that the approach described here is extremely useful and important, but also not very common. Ask lots of hard questions about any particular approach to penetration testing before you put too much credence in it, especially if security consultants are involved.

Don't forget that the real value of penetration testing comes from its central role in vetting configuration and other essential environmental factors. Use penetration testing as a "last check" before code goes live instead of as a "first check" of security posture.

As a measurement tool, penetration testing is most powerful when fully integrated into the development process in such a way that early-lifecycle findings are used to inform testing and that results find their way back into development and deployment practices.

7   Risk-Based Security Testing[1]

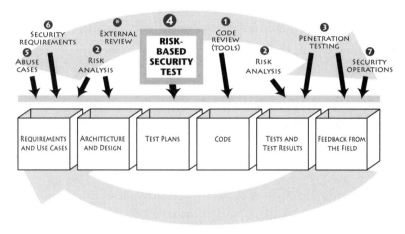

A good threat is worth a thousand tests.

BORIS BEIZER

ecurity testing has recently moved beyond the realm of network port scanning to include probing software behavior as a critical aspect of system behavior (see the box From Outside→In to Inside→Out on page 189). Unfortunately, testing software security is a commonly misunderstood task. Security testing done properly goes much deeper than simple black box probing on the presentation layer (the sort performed by so-called application security tools, which I rant about in Chapter 1)—and even beyond the functional testing of security apparatus.

Testers must carry out a risk-based approach, grounded in both the system's architectural reality and the attacker's mindset, to gauge software

---

[1]Parts of this chapter appeared in original form in *IEEE Security & Privacy* magazine co-authored with Bruce Potter [Potter and McGraw 2004].

security adequately. By identifying risks in the system and creating tests driven by those risks, a software security tester can properly focus on areas of code where an attack is likely to succeed. This approach provides a higher level of software security assurance than is possible with classical black box testing.

Security testing has much in common with (the new approach to) penetration testing as covered in Chapter 6. The main difference between security testing and penetration testing is the level of approach and the timing of the testing itself. Penetration testing is by definition an activity that happens once software is complete and installed in its operational environment. Also, by its nature, penetration testing is focused outside→in and is somewhat cursory. By contrast, security testing can be applied before the software is complete, at the unit level, in a testing environment with stubs and pre-integration.[2] Both approaches work best when they take risk analysis results, abuse cases, and functional security requirements into account.

Security testing should start at the feature or component/unit level, prior to system integration. Risk analysis carried out during the design phase (see Chapter 5) should identify and rank risks and discuss intercomponent assumptions. At the component level, risks to the component's assets must be mitigated within the bounds of contextual assumptions. Tests should be structured in such a way as to attempt both unauthorized misuse of and access to target assets as well as violations of the assumptions the system writ large may be making relative to its components. A security fault may well surface in the complete system if tests like these are not devised and executed.

Security unit testing carries the benefit of breaking system security down into a number of discrete parts. Theoretically, if each component is implemented safely and fulfills intercomponent design criteria, the greater system should be in reasonable shape (though this problem is much harder than it may seem at first blush [Anderson 2001]).[3] By identifying and leveraging security goals during unit testing, the security posture of the entire system can be significantly improved.

Security testing should continue at the system level and should be directed at properties of the integrated software system. This is precisely

---

[2]This distinction is similar to the slippery distinction between unit testing and system testing.

[3]Ross Anderson refers to the idea of component-based distributed software and the composition problem as "programming the devil's computer."

where penetration testing meets security testing, in fact. Assuming that unit testing has successfully achieved its goals, system-level testing should shift the focus toward identifying intracomponent failures and assessing security risk inherent at the design level. If, for example, a component assumes that only another trusted component has access to its assets, a test should be structured to attempt direct access to that component from elsewhere. A successful test can undermine the assumptions of the system and would likely result in a direct, observable security compromise. Data flow diagrams, models, and intercomponent documentation created during the risk analysis stage can be a great help in identifying where component seams exist.

Finally, abuse cases developed earlier in the lifecycle (see Chapter 8) should be used to enhance a test plan with adversarial tests based on plausible abuse scenarios. Security testing involves as much black hat thinking as white hat thinking.

From Outside→In to Inside→Out

Traditional approaches to computer and network security testing focus on network infrastructure, firewalls, and port scanning. This is especially true of network penetration testing (see Chapter 6) and its distant cousin, software penetration testing (sometimes called application penetration testing by vendors). Early approaches to application-level penetration testing were lacking because they attempted to test *all possible* programs with a fixed number of (lame) canned attacks. Better penetration testing approaches take architectural risks, code scanning results, and security requirements into account, but still focus on an outside→in perspective.

The notion behind old-school security testing is to protect vulnerable systems (and software) from attack by identifying and defending a perimeter. In this paradigm, testing focuses on an outside→in approach.

One classic example is the use of port scanning with tools such as Nessus <http://www.nessus.org/> or nmap <http://www.insecure.org/nmap/> to probe network ports and see which service is listening. Figure 7–1 shows a classic outside→in paradigm focusing on firewall placement. In this figure, the LAN is separated from the Internet (or public network) by a firewall. The natural perimeter is the firewall itself, which is supposed to provide a choke point for network traffic and a position from which very basic packet-level enforcement is possible. Firewalls do things like "drop all packets to port 81" or "only allow traffic from specific IP addresses on specific ports through."

Continued

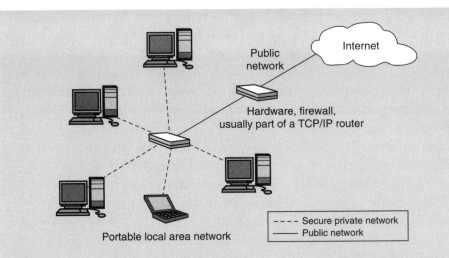

Figure 7–1 The outside→in approach. A firewall protects a LAN by blocking various network traffic on its way in; outside→in security testing (especially penetration testing) involves probing the LAN with a port scanner to see which ports are "open" and which services are listening on those ports. A major security risk associated with this approach is that the services traditionally still available through the firewall are implemented with insecure software.

The problem is that this perimeter is only apparent at the network/packet level. At the level of software applications (especially geographically distributed applications), the perimeter has all but disappeared. That's because firewalls have been configured (or misconfigured, depending on your perspective) to allow advanced applications to tunnel right through them.

A good example of this phenomenon is the SOAP protocol, which is designed (on purpose) to shuttle traffic through port 80 for various different applications. In some sense, SOAP is an anti-security device invented by software people so that they could avoid having to ask hard-nosed security people to open a firewall port for them. Once a tunnel like this is operational, the very idea of a firewall seems quaint.* In the brave new world of Service Oriented Architecture (SOA) for applications, we should not be surprised that the firewall is quickly becoming irrelevant.

By contrast, I advocate an inside→out approach to security, whereby software inside the LAN (and exposed on LAN boundaries) is itself subjected to rigorous risk management and security testing. This is just plain critical for modern distributed applications.

_____

*If you're having trouble getting through the firewall, just aim your messages through port 80, use a little SOAP, and you're back in business.

What's So Different about Security?

Software security is about making software behave in the presence of a malicious attack even though, in the real world, software failures usually happen spontaneously—that is, without intentional mischief [Leveson 1995]. Not surprisingly, standard software testing literature is only concerned with what happens when software fails, regardless of intent. The difference between software safety and software security is therefore the presence of an intelligent adversary bent on breaking the system. Most safety-critical systems (and high-assurance systems) posit a white hat world. Fact is, we live in a world with plenty of black hats as well, and we need to address that (head on).

Security is always relative to the information and services being protected, the skills and resources of adversaries, and the costs of potential assurance remedies; security is an exercise in risk management. Risk analysis, especially at the design level, can help us identify potential design-level security problems and their impact (see Chapter 5). Once identified and ranked, software risks can then help guide software security testing. Using a risk management framework, such as the RMF described in Chapter 2, allows us to track risks over time and thereby construct more relevant and more potent tests.

A *vulnerability* is an error that an attacker can exploit. Many types of vulnerabilities exist, and computer security researchers have created taxonomies of them, one of the first being Carl Landwehr [Landwehr, Bull, and McDermott 1993]. Vulnerabilities arise from defects, which in turn fall into two broad categories—implementation-level bugs and design-level flaws.

Attackers generally don't care whether a vulnerability is due to a flaw or a bug, although bugs tend to be easier to exploit [Koziol et al. 2004]. Because attacks are now becoming more sophisticated, the notion of which vulnerabilities actually matter is changing. Although timing attacks, including the well-known race condition, were considered exotic just a few years ago, they're common now [Bishop and Dilger 1996]. Similarly, two-stage buffer overflow attacks using trampolines were once the domain of software scientists but now appear in zero-day exploits [Hoglund and McGraw 2004]. On the horizon are arc injection attacks and other sophisticated control flow hacks [Pincus and Baker 2004]. I present a taxonomy of software security coding errors in Chapter 12. Thinking carefully about this taxonomy while developing a security test plan is a good tactic.

Design-level vulnerabilities are the hardest defect category to handle, but they're also both prevalent and critical. Unfortunately, ascertaining whether a program has design-level vulnerabilities requires great expertise, which makes finding such flaws not only difficult but also particularly hard to automate. Even though finding flaws is a difficult undertaking, I cover it in some detail in Chapter 5.

Examples of design-level problems include error handling in object-oriented systems, object sharing and trust issues, unprotected data channels (both internal and external), incorrect or missing access control mechanisms, lack of auditing/logging or incorrect logging, and ordering and timing errors (especially in multithreaded systems). These sorts of flaws almost always lead to security risk.

Risk Management and Security Testing

Software security practitioners perform many different tasks to manage software security risks, such as:

- Creating security abuse/misuse cases
- Listing normative security requirements (and security features and functions)
- Performing architectural risk analysis
- Building risk-based security test plans
- Wielding static analysis tools
- Performing security tests
- Performing penetration testing in the final environment
- Cleaning up after security breaches

Three of these practices are particularly closely linked—architectural risk analysis, risk-based security test planning, and security testing—because a critical aspect of security testing relies on directly probing security risks. Chapter 5 explains how to approach a software security risk analysis, the end product being a set of security-related risks ranked by business or mission impact. Chapter 2 explains how to keep track of security risks and properly manage them over time in an RMF.

The pithy aphorism "Software security is not security software" provides an important motivator for security testing. Although security features, such as cryptography, strong authentication, and access control, play a critical role in software security, security itself is an emergent property of the entire system, not just the security mechanisms and features. A buffer overflow is a security problem regardless of whether it exists in a security feature or in the noncritical GUI.

For this reason, security testing must necessarily involve two diverse approaches:

1. **Functional security testing**: testing security mechanisms to ensure that their functionality is properly implemented
2. **Adversarial security testing**: performing risk-based security testing motivated by understanding and simulating the attacker's approach

Together, these two distinct activities are a mix of white hat (security functionality) and black hat (security attack) philosophies. Security testing must mix both approaches or it will fail to cover critical areas.

Many developers erroneously believe that security involves only the liberal application and use of various security features, which leads to the incorrect belief that "adding SSL" is tantamount to securing an application. Software security practitioners bemoan the over-reliance on "magic crypto fairy dust" as a reaction to this problem. Software testers charged with security testing often fall prey to the same thinking.

It's not that we shouldn't test the crypto fairy dust to determine its potency. It's just that most security attacks ignore the security mechanisms in favor of looking for software defects anywhere in the system. Security testing needs to cover the attacker's mindset just as well as it covers security functionality.

How to Approach Security Testing

Like any other form of testing, security testing involves determining who should do the testing and what activities they should undertake.

Who

Because security testing involves two approaches, the question of who should do it has two answers. Standard testing organizations using a traditional approach can perform functional security testing. For example, ensuring that access control mechanisms work as advertised is a classic functional testing exercise. Since we basically know how the software should behave, we can run some tests and make sure that it does.[4]

On the other hand, traditional QA staff will have more difficulty performing risk-based security testing. The problem is one of expertise. First,

---

[4]This is not to trivialize the critical field of software testing. Testing is a difficult and painstaking activity that requires years of experience to do right.

security tests (especially those resulting in complete exploit) are difficult to craft because the designer must think like an attacker. Second, security tests don't often cause direct security exploit and thus present an observability problem. Unlike in the movies, a security compromise does not usually result in a red blinking screen flashing the words "Full Access Granted." A security test could result in an unanticipated outcome that requires the tester to perform further sophisticated analysis. Bottom line: Risk-based security testing relies more on expertise and experience than we would like—and not testing experience, *security* experience.

The software security field is maturing rapidly. I hope we can solve the experience problem by identifying best practices, gathering and categorizing knowledge, and embracing risk management as a critical software philosophy.[5] At the same time, academics are beginning to teach the next generation of builders a bit more about security so that we no longer build broken stuff that surprises us when it is spectacularly exploited.

How

Books, such as *How to Break Software Security* and *Exploiting Software,* help educate testing professionals on how to think like an attacker during testing [Whittaker and Thompson 2003; Hoglund and McGraw 2004]. Nevertheless, software exploits are surprisingly sophisticated these days, and the level of discourse found in books and articles is only now coming into alignment.

White and black box testing and analysis methods both attempt to understand software, but they use different approaches depending on whether the analyst or tester has access to source code. White box analysis involves analyzing and understanding both source code and the design. This kind of testing is typically very effective in finding programming errors (bugs when automatically scanning code and flaws when doing risk analysis); in some cases, this approach amounts to pattern matching and can even be automated with a static analyzer (the subject of Chapter 4). One drawback to this kind of testing is that tools might report a potential vulnerability where none actually exists (a false positive). Nevertheless, using static analysis methods on source code is a good technique for analyzing certain kinds of software. Similarly, risk analysis is a white box approach based on a thorough understanding of software architecture.

---

[5]The three pillars of software security.

Black box analysis refers to analyzing a running program by probing it with various inputs. This kind of testing requires only a running program and doesn't use source code analysis of any kind. In the security paradigm, malicious input can be supplied to the program in an effort to break it: if the program breaks during a particular test, then we might have discovered a security problem. Black box testing is possible even without access to binary code—that is, a program can be tested remotely over a network. If the tester can supply the proper input (and observe the test's effect), then black box testing is possible.

Any testing method can reveal possible software risks and potential exploits. One problem with almost all kinds of security testing (regardless of whether it's black or white box) is the lack of it—most QA organizations focus on features and spend very little time understanding or probing non-functional security risks. Exacerbating the problem, the QA process is often broken in many commercial software houses due to time and budget constraints and the belief that QA is not an essential part of software development.

Case studies can help make sense of the way security testing can be driven by risk analysis results. See the box An Example: Java Card Security Testing.

An Example: Java Card Security Testing

Doing effective security testing requires experience and knowledge. Examples and case studies like the one I present here are thus useful tools for understanding the approach.

In an effort to enhance payment cards with new functionality—such as the ability to provide secure cardholder identification or remember personal preferences—many credit-card companies are turning to multi-application smart cards. These cards use resident software applications to process and store thousands of times more information than traditional magnetic-stripe cards.

Security and fraud issues are critical concerns for the financial institutions and merchants spearheading smart-card adoption. By developing and deploying smart-card technology, credit-card companies provide important new tools in the effort to lower fraud and abuse. For instance, smart cards typically use a sophisticated crypto system to authenticate transactions and verify the identities of the cardholder and issuing bank. However, protecting against fraud and maintaining security and privacy are both very complex problems because of the rapidly evolving nature of smart-card technology.

Continued

The security community has been involved in security risk analysis and mitigation for Open Platform (now known as Global Platform, or GP) and Java Card since early 1997. Because product security is an essential aspect of credit-card companies' brand protection regimen, companies like Visa and MasterCard spend plenty of time and effort on security testing and risk analysis. One central finding emphasizes the importance of testing particular vendor implementations according to our two testing categories: adherence to functional security design and proper behavior under particular attacks motivated by security risks.

The latter category, adversarial security testing (linked directly to risk analysis findings), ensures that cards can perform securely in the field even when under attack. Risk analysis results can be used to guide manual security testing. As an example, consider the risk that, as designed, the object-sharing mechanism in Java Card is complex and thus is likely to suffer from security-critical implementation errors on any given manufacturer's card. Testing for this sort of risk involves creating and manipulating stored objects where sharing is involved. Given a technical description of this risk, building specific probing tests is possible.

Automating Security Testing

Over the years, Cigital has been involved in several projects that have identified architectural risks in the GP/Java Card platform, suggested several design improvements, and designed and built automated security tests for final products (each of which has multiple vendors).

Several years ago, we began developing an automated security test framework for GP cards built on Java Card 2.1.1 and based on extensive risk analysis results. The end result is a sophisticated test framework that runs with minimal human intervention and results in a qualitative security testing analysis of a sample smart card. This automated framework is now in use at MasterCard and the U.S. National Security Agency.

The first test set, the functional security test suite, directly probes low-level card security functionality. It includes automated testing of class codes, available commands, and crypto functionality. This test suite also actively probes for inappropriate card behavior of the sort that can lead to security compromise.

The second test set, the hostile applet test suite, is a sophisticated set of intentionally hostile Java Card applets designed to probe high-risk aspects of the GP on a Java Card implementation.

Results: Nonfunctional Security Testing Is Essential

Most cards tested with the automated test framework (but not all) pass all functional security tests, which we expect because smart-card vendors are diligent with functional testing (including security functionality). Because smart cards are complex embedded devices, vendors realize that exactly meeting functional requirements is an absolute necessity for customers to accept the cards. After all, they must perform properly worldwide.

However, every card submitted to the risk-based testing paradigm exhibited some manner of failure when tested with the hostile applet suite. Some failures pointed directly to critical security vulnerabilities on the card; others were less specific and required further exploration to determine the card's true security posture.

As an example, consider that risk analysis of Java Card's design documents indicates that proper implementation of atomic transaction processing is critical for maintaining a secure card. Java Card has the capability of defining transaction boundaries to ensure that if a transaction fails, data roll back to a pre-transaction state. In the event that transaction processing fails, transactions can go into any number of possible states, depending on what the applet was attempting. In the case of a stored-value card, bad transaction processing could allow an attacker to "print money" by forcing the card to roll back value counters while actually purchasing goods or services. This is called a "torn transaction" attack in credit-card risk lingo.

When creating risk-based tests to probe transaction processing, we directly exercised transaction-processing error handling by simulating an attacker attempting to violate a transaction—specifically, transactions were aborted or never committed, transaction buffers were completely filled, and transactions were nested (a no-no according to the Java Card specification). These tests were not based strictly on the card's functionality—instead, security test engineers intentionally created them, thinking like an attacker given the results of a risk analysis.

Several real-world cards failed subsets of the transaction tests. The vulnerabilities discovered as a result of these tests would allow an attacker to terminate a transaction in a potentially advantageous manner—a critical test failure that wouldn't have been uncovered under normal functional security testing. Fielding cards with these vulnerabilities would allow an attacker to execute successful attacks on live cards issued to the public. Because of proper risk-based security testing, the vendors were notified of the problems and corrected the code responsible before release.

Coder's Corner

Let's take a look at one of the tests that we built for Java Card security testing. This test set as a whole probes whether shareable objects behave properly on a card.

First, the interface specification:

```
package tests.config1.jcre.JcreTest010_1;
import javacard.framework.Shareable;
import ssg.framework.*;

public interface shareableInterface extends Shareable {
    public void shareObject();
}
```

This little glob of code implements the shared interface and sets up the test harness.

```
package tests.config1.jcre.JcreTest010_1;

import javacard.framework.*;
import ssg.framework.*;

public class JcreTest010_1a extends Applet implements shareableInterface
{
    static byte[] shareableObjectBuffer;

    private JcreTest010_1a()
    {
      shareableObjectBuffer = new byte[10];
      for(byte i=0; i < 10; i++)
        shareableObjectBuffer[i] = 0x11;
        register();
    }

    public void shareObject() {
      for(byte i=0; i < 10; i++)
        shareableObjectBuffer[i] = 0x22;
    }

    public void testFunc() {
      for(byte i=0; i < 10; i++)
        shareableObjectBuffer[i] = 0x33;
    }
```

```
      public Shareable getShareableInterfaceObject(AID client_aid, byte parameter)
      {
        /*for(byte i=0; i < 10; i++)
          shareableObjectBuffer[i] = 0x33;*/

          return (this);
      }

      public static void install(byte[] bArray, short bOffset, byte bLength)
      {
        new JcreTest010_1a();
      }

public void process(APDU apdu)
    {
      byte[] apdu_buffer = apdu.getBuffer();
      apdu.setOutgoing();
      apdu.setOutgoingLength((short)10);

      Util.arrayCopy(shareableObjectBuffer, (short)0, apdu_buffer, (short)0,
                  (short)10);

      for(byte i=0; i < 10; i++)
        shareableObjectBuffer[i] = 0x11;

      apdu.sendBytes((short)0, (short)10);
    }
}
```

Then we can run tests like this. (I show you only one of the five tests related to shareable interfaces just to keep things simple.)

```
package tests.config1.jcre.JcreTest010_2;

import javacard.framework.*;
import ssg.framework.*;
import tests.config1.jcre.JcreTest010_1.*;

public class JcreTest010_2a extends Applet
{
    byte [] serverAID = {74,99,114,101,84,101,115,116,48,49,48,49,97};
    byte [] AIDValue;

    private JcreTest010_2a()
    {
```

Continued

```
    AIDValue = new byte[16];
       register();
  }

  public static void install( byte[] bArray, short bOffset, byte bLength )
  {
      new JcreTest010_2a();
  }

  public void process(APDU apdu)
  {
    AID serverAIDObject = JCSystem.lookupAID(serverAID, (short)0,
                        (byte)serverAID.length);

    if(serverAIDObject == null)
    ISOException.throwIt(ISO7816.SW_WRONG_P1P2); // 0x6B00

    if((serverAIDObject.equals(serverAID, (short)0, (byte)serverAID.length)) ==
        false)
    ISOException.throwIt(ISO7816.SW_CORRECT_LENGTH_00); // 0x6C00

    shareableInterface sio = (shareableInterface)
(JCSystem.getAppletShareableInterfaceObject(serverAIDObject, (byte)0));

if(sio == null) {
    byte length = serverAIDObject.getBytes(AIDValue, (short)0);
    byte[] apdu_buffer = apdu.getBuffer();
    apdu.setOutgoing();
    apdu.setOutgoingLength((short)length);
    Util.arrayCopy(AIDValue, (short)0, apdu_buffer, (short)0, (short)length);
    apdu.sendBytes((short)0, (short)length);
    ISOException.throwIt(ISO7816.SW_INS_NOT_SUPPORTED); // 0x6D00
    }

    sio.shareObject();
  }
}
```

What we found in practice on one of the many real cards we tested was that the shareable interface tests all worked fine. What failed was the test teardown procedure that tries to leave the card in the same state as when we started. When this failed, we did some investigation by hand and uncovered some interesting issues.

There is no silver bullet for software security; even a reasonable security testing regimen is just a start. Unfortunately, security continues to be sold as a product, and most defensive mechanisms on the market do little to address the heart of the problem, which is bad software. Instead, they operate in a reactive mode: Don't allow packets to this or that port, watch out for files that include this pattern in them, throw partial packets and oversized packets away without looking at them. Network traffic is not the best way to approach the software security predicament because the software that processes the packets is the problem. By using a risk-based approach to software security testing, testing professionals can help solve security problems while software is still in production.

Of course, any testing approach is deeply impacted by software process issues. Because of eXtreme Programming's (XP) "test first" philosophy, adopting a risk-based approach may be difficult if you are in an XP shop. See the following box, eXtreme Programming and Security Testing.

Thinking about (Malicious) Input

Put simply, the biggest problems in software security exist because software takes input (see the taxonomy of coding errors in Chapter 12). Whether to trust input (including the very format that the input takes) is a critical question that all software builders must ponder.

Exploiting Software is filled with examples of programs that break when malformed or maliciously formed input leads to security compromise [Hoglund and McGraw 2004]. From the much-ballyhooed buffer overflow (which involves putting too much input in too small a place) to the likewise overhyped SQL injection attack and cross-site scripting (XSS) attacks, trusting input turns out to be the common root cause.

Carefully handling input is paramount to software security. Note that input includes things like register settings, environment variables, file contents, and even network configuration. If your program consumes data from "out there," you need to think carefully about who can dink around with the stuff your program eats.

Attacker toolkits (briefly described in Chapter 6) focus plenty of attention on input, with a plethora of fault injection tools, grammar generators, re-players, and the like. By its very nature, penetration testing is obsessed with input as well (mostly because crafting malicious input is the main way to break a system from the outside). If your program accepts input over the network, it needs to be very skeptical of what it is getting.

eXtreme Programming and Security Testing

XP takes an interesting approach to testing, often referred to as "test first" or "test-driven design." Ironically, this approach encourages coding to the tests—an activity that was explicitly discouraged by testing gurus before XP came along. Test-driven design is not a disaster. In fact, coding to the tests may work for standard software "features." I bet you can guess the problem though—security is not a feature.

Tests based too closely on features can fail to probe deeply into more subtle user needs that are nonfunctional in nature. Probing security features only gets us so far. Once again, this is a problem of testing for a negative.

Though unit tests and user stories in XP are supposed to specify the design, they simply don't do this well enough to get to design flaw issues. The code is the design in XP, but finding design flaws by staring at large piles of code is not possible. In fact, refactoring aside, top-down design does not really happen explicitly in some XP shops. That means there is no good time to consider security flaws explicitly.

By using acceptance tests (devised in advance of coding) as release criteria, XP practitioners keep their eyes on the functional ball. However, this myopic focus on functionality causes a propensity to overlook nonfunctional requirements and emergent situations. Security fits there.

One solution to this problem might be to focus more attention on abuse cases early in the lifecycle. This would cohere nicely with XP's user stories. Perhaps some "attacker stories" should be devised as well and used to create security tests.

For more on my opinions about XP and software security, see my talk, "XP and Software Security?! You Gotta Be Kidding," delivered at XP Universe in 2003 <http://www.cigital.com/presentations/xpuniverse/>.

Using a black-list approach (which tries to enumerate all possible bad input) is silly and will not work. Instead, software needs to defend its input space with a white-list approach (and a Draconian white-list approach, for that matter). If your program enforces statements like "Accept only input of 32-bits as an Integer" (something that is easy to do in a modern type-safe language), you're better off right off the bat than with a system that accepts anything but tries to filter out return characters. Make sure that your testing approach delves directly into the black-list/white-list input-filtering issue.

Microsoft pays plenty of attention to malicious input in its approach to software security. You should too. (See *Writing Secure Code* [Howard and LeBlanc 2003].)

Getting Over Input

Don't get too caught up in solving only the input problem. Testing around malicious input is a necessary but not sufficient condition. Security testing needs to get past input myopia by focusing on data structures, components, APIs, program state, and so on.

The forest-level view created during architectural risk analysis (see Chapter 5) is very useful in planning security testing. In addition to building tests around risks that remain in the system, testers should consider things like:

- Sockets
- Pipes
- The Win32 Registry
- Files
- Remote procedure calls (RPCs)
- Command-line arguments
- And so on

Time is a critical issue to think about in modern software systems. There are two major aspects of time to consider. The first has to do with program state and state preservation. Because some modern software protocols in common use (like HTTP) are stateless, a variety of hacks and kludges around the state preservation problem have been devised. Many of these kludges are inherently insecure. Security testers must consider what happens when state is changed by an attacker. This can be as simple as changing a "hidden" variable in a URL or as complex as de-serializing an object, manipulating it, and re-serializing it.

The second aspect of time that is essential to think about is related to state, but only indirectly. When multiple processes interact and share some kind of data structure (either by querying the environment or by using locks and semaphores), a new line of attack is opened up in the form of changing the environment that is being queried or otherwise messing around with locks. Time-of-check–time-of-use (TOCTOU) race conditions are always worth considering when testing a multithreaded system. Even more subtle data races are also an important and often overlooked category of errors to consider.

One problem is that most developers are unfamiliar with the effects of multithreading on their systems. That means they often overlook subtle time-based attacks. I believe that timing attacks (both data races and starvation attacks) are a future attack category that will be much more commonly encountered than they are now. We've begun to see hints of this already (for more, see the taxonomy in Chapter 12).

Leapfrogging the Penetration Test

Getting inside a program and thinking about control flow and data flow is an excellent strategy for devising a solid testing regimen. Penetration testing, because of its outside→in bias, only begins to scratch the surface of an inside-the-software testing approach. Security testing goes beyond penetration testing by adopting a clear inside→out approach focused on software guts.

Books like *The Shellcoder's Handbook, How to Break Software Security,* and *Exploiting Software* help software professionals understand the mind of the attacker and the kinds of program understanding tools commonly used by attackers [Koziol et al. 2004; Whittaker and Thompson 2003; Hoglund and McGraw 2004]. This is a critical undertaking for security testers. Unless a security tester thinks like a bad guy (black hat firmly on head), security testing will not be effective.

Software is so broken today that simple penetration testing usually works. Getting past the obvious is only necessary when the low-hanging fruit discovered during simple penetration testing is taken care of. Then things get tricky fast. Be prepared for things to get tricky. Then plan to adopt risk-based security testing.

8 Abuse Cases[1]

To kill, you must know your enemy, and in this case my enemy is a varmint.
And a varmint will never quit—ever. They're like the Viet Cong—Varmint Cong.
So you have to fall back on superior intelligence and superior firepower.
And that's all she wrote.

BILL MURRAY (AS CARL SPACKLER IN CADDYSHACK)

Software development is all about making software do something. People who build software tend to describe software requirements in terms of what a system will do when everything goes right—when users are cooperative and helpful, when environments are pristine and friendly, and when code is defect free. The focus is on functionality (in a more perfect world). As a result, when software vendors sell products, they talk about what their products do to make customers' lives easier—improving business processes or doing something else positive.

Following the trend of describing the positive, most systems for designing software also tend to describe features and functions. UML, use cases,

---

[1]Parts of this chapter appeared in original form in *IEEE Security & Privacy* magazine co-authored with Paco Hope and Annie Anton [Hope, McGraw, and Anton 2004].

and other modeling and design tools allow software people to formalize what the software will do. This typically results in a description of a system's normative behavior, predicated on assumptions of correct usage. In less fancy language, this means that a completely functional view of a system is usually built on the assumption that the system won't be intentionally abused. But what if it is? By now you should know that if your software is going to be used, it's going to be abused. You can take that to the bank.

Consider a payroll system that allows a human resources department to control salaries and benefits. A use case might say, "The system allows users in the HR management group to view and modify salaries of all employees." It might even go so far as to say, "The system will only allow a basic user to view his or her own salary." These are direct statements of what the system will do.

Savvy software practitioners are beginning to think beyond features, touching on emergent properties of software systems such as reliability, security, and performance. This is mostly due to the fact that more experienced software consumers are beginning to say, "We want the software to be secure" or "We want the software to be reliable." In some cases, these kinds of wants are being formally and legally applied in service-level agreements (SLAs) and acceptance criteria regarding various system properties.[2] (See the box Holding Software Vendors Accountable for an explanation of SLAs and software security.)

The problem is that security, reliability, and other software -ilities are complicated. In order to create secure and reliable software, abnormal behavior must somehow be anticipated. Software types don't normally describe non-normative behavior in use cases, nor do they describe it with UML; but we really need some way to talk about and prepare for abnormal behavior, especially if security is our goal. To make this concrete, think about a potential attacker in the HR example. An attacker is likely to try to gain extra privileges in the payroll system and remove evidence of any fraudulent transaction. Similarly, an attacker might try to delay all the paychecks by a day or two and embezzle the interest that is accrued during the delay. The idea is to get out your black hat and think like a bad guy.

Surprise! You've already been thinking like a bad guy as you worked through previous touchpoints. This chapter is really about making the idea

---

[2]Note that in many of these instances it is still left up to the software developer to define "secure" and "reliable" and then create secure and reliable software.

Holding Software Vendors Accountable

Jack Danahy of Ounce Labs <http://www.ouncelabs.com/> and others have been beating the vendor accountability drum in the software security space for several years. Danahy's approach to accountability centers around the idea of legally binding vendors with SLAs. The good news is that some software consumers have begun to demand security warranties or SLAs from their software vendors. The bad news is that it is not exactly obvious what kinds of things should be covered in an SLA (and how to phrase those things). Ad hoc approaches are the status quo, but when it comes to the law, ad hoc approaches raise serious enforceability questions.

A clear articulation of expectations is the answer, with emphasis on specific, measurable criteria for determining whether expectations have been met. Among the most obvious techniques is to set clear requirements and have a process for confirming (usually through testing) whether the requirements have been properly handled. Positive security requirements fit nicely here (negative ones are a bit trickier).

Danahy suggests that SLA contractual language cover the following:

1. Proper implementation of security features (think crypto and access control)
2. Looking for known security flaws and confirming that they are not present
3. Passing third-party validation and verification security tests agreed on in advance
4. Use of source code analysis tools (see Chapter 4)

In this regime, SLAs must include expectations of security in the acceptance requirements. The idea is that those vendors who do not address security directly will find themselves on the hot seat. When it comes to code development, consumers who outsource development should demand the right to review code. When bugs are found, they should be fixed. If the producer does not meet security obligations, the consumer should be allowed to terminate the business agreement.

explicit. When you were doing source code analysis with a tool, the tool pumped out a bunch of possible problems and suggestions about what might go wrong, and you got to decide which ones were worth pursuing. (You didn't even have to know about possible attacks because the tool took care of that part for you.) Risk analysis is a bigger challenge because you start with a blank page. Not only do you have to invent the system from whole cloth, but you also need to anticipate things that will go wrong. Same goes for testing (especially adversarial testing and penetration testing).

The core of each of these touchpoints is in some sense coming up with a hypothesis of what might go wrong. That's what abuse cases are all about.

Abuse cases (sometimes called misuse cases as well) are a tool that can help you begin to think about your software the same way that attackers do. By thinking beyond the normative features and functions and also contemplating negative or unexpected events, software security professionals come to better understand how to create secure and reliable software. By systematically asking, "What can go wrong here?" or better yet, "What might some bad person cause to go wrong here?" software practitioners are more likely to uncover exceptional cases and frequently overlooked security requirements.

Think about what motivates an attacker. Start here. . . . Pretend you're the bad guy. Get in character. Now ask yourself: "What do I want?" Some ideas: I want to steal all the money. I want to learn the secret ways of the C-level execs. I want to be **root** of my domain. I want to reveal the glory that is the Linux Liberation Front. I want to create general havoc. I want to impress my pierced girlfriend. I want to spy on my spouse. Be creative when you do this! Bad guys want lots of different things. Bring out your inner villain.

Now ask yourself: "How can I accomplish my evil goal given this pathetic pile of software before me? How can I make it cry and beg for mercy? How can I make it bend to my iron will?" There you have it. Abuse cases.

Because thinking like an attacker is something best done with years of experience, this process is an opportune time to involve your network security guys (see Chapter 9). However, there are alternatives to years of experience. One excellent thought experiment (suggested by Dan Geer) runs as follows. I'll call it "engineer gone bad." Imagine taking your most trusted engineer/operator and humiliating her in public—throw her onto the street, and dare her to do anything about it to you or to your customers. If the humiliated street bum can do nothing more than head banging on the nearest wall, you've won. This idea, in some, cases may be even more effective than simply thinking like a bad guy—it's turning a good guy into a bad guy.

The idea of abuse cases has a short history in the academic literature. McDermott and Fox published an early paper on abuse cases at ACSAC in 1999 [McDermott and Fox 1999]. Later, Sindre and Opdahl wrote a paper that explained how to extend use case diagrams with misuse cases [Sindre and Opdahl 2000]. Their basic idea is to represent the actions that systems should prevent in tandem with those that it should support so that security analysis of requirements is easier. Alexander advocates using misuse and use cases together to conduct threat and hazard analysis during requirements analysis [Alexander 2003]. Others have since put more flesh on the idea of abuse cases, but, frankly, abuse cases are not as commonly used as they should be.

Security Is Not a Set of Features

Security is not a feature that can be added to software. There is no convenient "security" pull-down menu where security can be selected and magic things happen. Unfortunately, many software producers mistakenly rely solely on plonking functional security features and mechanisms, such as cryptography, somewhere in their software, and they assume that the security needs are in this way addressed everywhere. Too often product literature makes broad feature-based claims about security such as "Built with SSL" or "128-bit encryption included," and these represent the vendor's entire approach for securing the product. This is a natural and forgivable misconception, but it is still a concerning problem.

Security is an emergent property of a system, not a feature. This is similar to how "being dry" is an emergent property of being inside a tent in the rain. The tent keeps people dry only if the poles are stabilized, vertical, able to support the weight of wet fabric, and so on. Likewise, the tent must have waterproof fabric that has no holes and is large enough to protect all the people who want to stay dry. Lastly, all the people who want to be dry must remain under the tent the entire time it is raining. Whereas it is important to have poles and fabric, it is not enough to say, "The tent has poles and fabric, thus it keeps you dry!" This sort of claim, however, is analogous to the claims software vendors make when they highlight numbers of bits in keys and the use of particular encryption algorithms. It is true that cryptography of one kind or another is usually necessary in order to create a secure system, but security features alone are not sufficient for building secure software.

Because security is not a feature, it can't be "bolted on" after other software features are codified. Nor can it be "patched in" after attacks have occurred in the field. Instead, security must be built in from the ground up—considered a critical part of the design from the very beginning (requirements specification) and included in every subsequent development phase all the way through fielding a complete system.

Sometimes this involves making explicit tradeoffs when specifying system requirements. For example, ease of use may be paramount in a medical system meant to be used by secretaries in a doctor's office. Complex authentication procedures, such as obtaining and using a cryptographic identity, can be hard to use [Gutmann 2004]. But regulatory pressures from HIPPA and California's privacy regulations (SB 1386) force designers to negotiate a reasonable tradeoff.

To extend this example, consider that authentication and authorization can't stop at the "front door" of a program. Technical approaches must go far beyond the obvious features, deep into the many-tiered heart of a software system to be secure enough.

The best, most cost-effective approach to software security incorporates thinking beyond white hat normative features by donning a black hat and thinking like a bad guy, and doing this throughout the development process. Every time a new requirement, feature, or use case is created, someone should spend some time thinking about how that feature might be unintentionally misused or intentionally abused. Professionals who know how features are attacked and how to protect software should play an active role in this kind of analysis (see Chapter 9).

What You Can't Do

Attackers are not standard-issue customers. They are bad people with malicious intent who want your software to act in some unanticipated way—to their benefit. An attacker's goal is to think of something you didn't think of and exploit it in a way you didn't expect—to the gain of the attacker and probably to your detriment. If the development process doesn't address unexpected or abnormal behavior, then an attacker usually has plenty of raw material to work with.

Attackers are creative. Despite this creativity, we can be sure that some well-known locations will always be probed in the course of attacks: boundary conditions, edges, intersystem communication, and system assumptions. Clever attackers always try to undermine the assumptions a system is built on. For example, if a design assumes that connections from the Web server to the database server are always valid, an attacker will try to make the Web server send inappropriate requests in order to access valuable data. If software design assumes that Web browser cookies are never modified by the client before they are sent back to the requesting server (in an attempt to preserve some state), attackers will intentionally cause problems by modifying cookies.

When we are the designers and analyzers of a system, we're in a great position to know our systems better than potential attackers do. We should leverage this knowledge to the benefit of security and reliability. We can do this by asking and answering some critical questions:

- What assumptions are implicit in our system?
- What kinds of things would make our assumptions false?
- What kinds of attack patterns will an attacker bring to bear?

Unfortunately, a system's creators rarely make the best security analysts for their own systems. This is precisely because it is very hard to consciously note and consider all assumptions (especially in light of thinking like an attacker). Fortunately, these professionals, instead, make excellent subject matter experts to be powerfully combined with security professionals. Together this team of system experts and security analysts can ferret out base assumptions in a system under analysis and think through the ways an attacker will approach the software.

Creating Useful Abuse Cases

The simplest, most practical method for creating abuse cases is usually through a process of informed brainstorming. There exist a number of theoretical methods that involve fully specifying a system with rigorous formal models and logics, but such activities are extremely time and resource intensive. The good news is that formal methods are often unnecessary in the real world. A more practical approach that covers a lot of ground more quickly involves forming brainstorming teams that combine security and reliability experts with system designers. This approach relies heavily on experience and expertise.

To guide such brainstorming, software security experts ask many questions that help identify the places where the system is likely to have weaknesses. This activity mirrors the kind of thinking that an attacking adversary performs. Abuse is always possible at the places where legitimate use is possible. Such brainstorming involves a careful look at all user interfaces (including environment factors) as well as functional security requirements and considers what things most developers assume a person can't or won't do. These *can'ts* and *won'ts* take many forms, such as: "Users can't enter more than 50 characters because the JavaScript code won't let them." "The user doesn't understand the format of the cached data. They can't modify it." Attackers, unfortunately, make *can'ts* and *won'ts* happen with some regularity.

All systems have more places that can be attacked than obvious front doors, of course. Where can a bad guy be positioned? On the wire? At a workstation? In the back office? Any communications line between two endpoints or two components is a place where an attacker can try to interpose. What can a bad guy do? Watch communications traffic? Modify and replay such traffic? Read files stored on the workstation? Change registry keys or configuration files? Be the DLL? Be the "chip"? (Note that all of these kinds of attacks are person-in-the-middle attacks, sometimes called PIMs or interposition attacks.) Many of these attacks are elegantly explained in the book *How to Break Software Security* [Whittaker and Thompson 2003].

One of the goals of abuse cases is to decide and document a priori how the software should react to illegitimate use. The process of specifying abuse cases makes a designer differentiate appropriate use from inappropriate use very clearly. Approaching this problem involves asking the right questions. For example, how can the system distinguish between good and bad input? How can the system tell that a request is coming from a legitimate Java applet and not from a rogue application replaying traffic? Trying to answer questions like these helps software designers explicitly question design and architecture assumptions. This puts the designer squarely ahead of the attacker by identifying and fixing a problem before it can even be created!

But No One Would Ever Do That!

System architects and project managers often respond to the very idea of abuse cases by claiming, "But no one would do these things." Interestingly, these claims are correct if the worldview is limited to legitimate users. Virtually any system that has value, however, can be abused. Few systems operate securely in a free-for-all permissions environment, despite how much trust designers may want to place on the users. This problem is exacerbated by the rush to move software into a highly distributed, network-based model. Limiting system activity to legitimate users may be possible on a secure proprietary network, but it is categorically impossible on the Internet. The fact is that malicious users do exist in both kinds of environment, and it is often straightforward to thwart a significant portion of them.

Touchpoint Process: Abuse Case Development

Unfortunately, abuse cases are only rarely used in practice even though the idea seems natural enough. Perhaps a simple process model will help clarify how to build abuse cases and thereby fix the adoption problem. Figure 8–1 shows a simple process model.

Abuse cases are to be built by a team of requirements people and security analysts (called RAs and SAs in the picture). This team starts with a set of requirements, a set of standard use cases (or user stories), and a list of attack patterns.[3] This raw material is combined by the process I describe to create abuse cases.

The first step involves identifying and documenting threats. Note that I am using the term *threat* in the old-school sense. A threat is an actor or agent who carries out an attack. Vulnerabilities and risks are not threats.[4] Understanding who might attack you is really critical. Are you likely to come under attack from organized crime like the Russian mafia? Or are you more likely to be taken down by a university professor and the requisite set of overly smart graduate students all bent on telling the truth? Thinking like your enemy is an important exercise. Knowing who your enemy is likely to be is an obvious prerequisite.

Given an understanding of who might attack you, you're ready to get down to the business of creating abuse cases. In the gray box in the center of Figure 8–1, the two critical activities of abuse case development are shown: creating anti-requirements and creating an attack model.

Creating Anti-Requirements

When developing a software system or a set of software requirements, thinking explicitly about the *things that you don't want your software to do* is just as important as documenting the things that you do want. Naturally,

---

[3]Attack patterns à la *Exploiting Software* [Hoglund and McGraw 2004] are not the only source to use for thinking through possible attacks. A good low-octane substitute might be the STRIDE model list of attack categories: Spoofing, Tampering, Repudiation, Information disclosure, Denial of service, and Elevation of privilege. Cycling through this list of six attack categories one at a time is likely to provide insight into your system. For more on STRIDE, see [Howard and LeBlanc 2003].

[4]Microsoft folks use the term *threat* incorrectly (and also very loudly). When they say "threat modeling," they really mean "risk analysis." This is unfortunate.

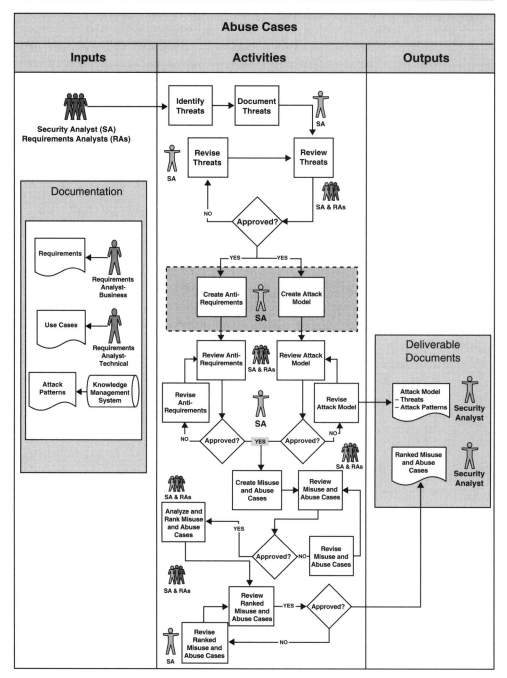

Figure 8–1 A simple process diagram for building abuse cases.

the things that you don't want your system to do are very closely related to the requirements. I call them *anti-requirements*. Anti-requirements are generated by security analysts, in conjunction with requirements analysts (business and technical), through a process of analyzing requirements and use cases with reference to the list of threats in order to identify and document attacks that will cause requirements to fail. The object is explicitly to undermine requirements.

Anti-requirements provide insight into how a malicious user, attacker, thrill seeker, competitor (in other words, a threat) can abuse your system. Just as security requirements result in functionality that is built into a system to establish accepted behavior, anti-requirements are established to determine what happens when this functionality goes away. When created early in the software development lifecycle and revisited throughout, these anti-requirements provide valuable input to developers and testers.

Because security requirements are usually about security functions and/or security features, anti-requirements are often tied up in the lack of or failure of a security function. For example, if your system has a security requirement calling for use of crypto to protect essential movie data written on disk during serialization, an anti-requirement related to this requirement involves determining what happens in the absence of that crypto. Just to flesh things out, assume in this case that the threat in question is a group of academics. Academic security analysts are unusually well positioned to crack crypto relative to thrill-seeking script kiddies. Grad students have a toolset, lots of background knowledge, and way too much time on their hands. If the crypto system fails in this case (or better yet, is made to fail), giving the attacker access to serialized information on disk, what kind of impact will that have on the system's security? How can we test for this condition?

Abuse cases based on anti-requirements lead to stories about what happens in the case of failure, especially security apparatus failure.

Coder's Corner

Here is a systematic approach to anti-requirements suggested by Fabio Arciniegas. This approach formalizes the idea of anti-requirements by focusing on the three key aspects of requirements:

1. Input
2. Output
3. Importance

Continued

Use cases and functional specifications are often presented as shall/given duets. For example: The system *shall* produce a unique identifier valid for N days into the future *given* a present time, a valid authorization token, and N. One way of creating anti-requirements from requirements is to validate the limits of the *given* part against a set of weighted failures in the *shall* part. The game of systematically approaching what can go wrong can be played by defining the goal (distance 0) and a weighted perimeter of failure around it:

Distance 0: Valid response
Distance 1: Denied request
──────────────────────────────── Threshold
Distance 2: Non-unique ID returned
Distance 3: System crash

The combinatory game involves breaking assumptions in the *given* part of the requirement by asking various questions: What if $N < 0$? What if $N < 0$ and authorization is invalid? and so on. Any combination of failed input that results in an output beyond the threshold is a major concern.

This approach not only provides a systematic way to develop anti-requirements from requirements but it also is useful for generating a contractual basis for unacceptable misbehavior; this is something that is fundamental if you are outsourcing development—at least if you want to avoid the retort, "But it does what you said it should, given the input you said it would have!".

Creating an Attack Model

An *attack model* comes about by explicit consideration of known attacks or attack types. Given a set of requirements and a list of threats, the idea here is to cycle through a list of known attacks one at a time and to think about whether the "same" attack applies to your system. Note that this kind of process lies at the heart of Microsoft's STRIDE model [Howard and LeBlanc 2003]. Attack patterns are extremely useful for this activity. An incomplete list of attack patterns can be seen in the box Attack Patterns from *Exploiting Software* [Hoglund and McGraw 2004] on pages 218 through 221. To create an attack model, do the following:

- Select those attack patterns relevant to your system. Build abuse cases around those attack patterns.

- Include anyone who can gain access to the system because threats must encompass *all* potential sources of danger to the system.

Together, the resulting attack model and anti-requirements drive out abuse cases that describe how your system reacts to an attack and which attacks are likely to happen. Abuse cases and stories of possible attacks are very powerful drivers for both architectural risk analysis and security testing.

The simple process shown in Figure 8–1 results in a number of useful artifacts. The simple activities are designed to create a list of threats and their goals (which I might call a "proper threat model"), a list of relevant attack patterns, and a unified attack model. These are all side effects of the anti-requirements and attack model activities. More important, the process creates a set of ranked abuse cases—stories of what your system does under those attacks most likely to be experienced.

As you can see, this is a process that requires extensive use of your black hat. The more experience and knowledge you have about actual software exploit and real computer security attacks, the more effective you will be at building abuse cases (see Chapter 9).

An Abuse Case Example

Cigital reviewed a client-server application that manipulated a financially sensitive database, finding a classic software security problem. In this case, the architecture was set up so that the server counted on a client-side application to manage all of the data access permissions. No permissions were enforced on the server itself. In fact, only the client had any notion of permissions and access control. To make matters worse, a complete copy of the sensitive database (only parts of which were to be viewed by a given user with a particular client) was sent down to the client. The client program ran on a garden-variety desktop PC. This means that a complete copy of sensitive data expressly not to be viewed by the user was available on that user's PC in the clear.

If the user looked in the application's cache on the hard disk and used the unzip utility, the user could see all sorts of sensitive information that should not have been allowed to be seen. It turns out that the client also enforced which messages were sent to the server, and the server honored these messages independent of the user's actual credentials. The server was assuming that any messages coming from the client had properly passed through the client software's access control system (and policy) and were,

Attack Patterns from *Exploiting Software*

Attack patterns are extremely useful in generating valid abuse cases. *Exploiting Software* includes the identification and description of the 48 attack patterns and 1 fragment listed here [Hoglund and McGraw 2004]. This is an incomplete list of attack patterns, which as a catalog of knowledge is in a nascent stage. For examples and stories corresponding to these attack patterns, see *Exploiting Software*. Don't forget that these attack patterns are described from the point of view of the attacker.

Make the Client Invisible

Talk directly with the server, masquerading as the client. Explore the input space.

Target Programs That Write to Privileged OS Resources

Look for programs that write to system directories of registry keys.

Use a User-Supplied Configuration File to Run Commands That Elevate Privilege

Configuration files are excellent targets since they control high-privilege programs. System-wide configuration files are particularly interesting.

Make Use of Configuration File Search Paths

Try to put a malicious config file in the search path ahead of the default config file.

Direct Access to Executable Files

Run programs with privilege. Look for such programs on Web servers especially.

Embedding Scripts within Scripts

Take advantage of the hundreds of languages, compilers, and interpreters (as well as backwards compatibility constraints) to slip through filters. Forgotten nooks and crannies are most interesting.

Leverage Executable Code in Nonexecutable Files

Inject code through a seemingly innocuous route and have a process load and execute the attack.

Argument Injection

When input filtering is poor or nonexistent, spin a shell and use it.

Command Delimiters

Use off-nominal characters (like semicolons) to string commands together.

Multiple Parsers and Double Escapes

Take advantage of several parser pass-throughs with double escapes.

User-Supplied Variable Passed to Filesystem Calls

Filesystem calls are a good attack site since user input is directly consumed. Pass in parameters.

Postfix NULL Terminator

Play with NULL and its various representations to break parsing.

Postfix, Null Terminate, and Backslash

Alternate representations of NULL can be used to bypass filters.

Relative Path Traversal

Take advantage of the current working directory to play relative path games.

Client-Controlled Environment Variables

Supply environment variables before authentication.

User-Supplied Global Variables (DEBUG=1, PHP Globals, and So Forth)

PHP has bad defaults. Try them.

Session ID, Resource ID, and Blind Trust

Change IDs in midstream, or otherwise guess IDs.

Analog In-Band Switching Signals (aka "Blue Boxing")

Play specific control commands across a normal link. When command and data lines are shared, this can be huge fun.

Attack Pattern Fragment: Manipulating Terminal Devices

Use shell commands to aim things at other terminals.

Simple Script Injection

Take advantage of stored data problems to inject scripts and pollute data.

Embedding Scripts in Nonscript Elements

Put scripts into HTML tags that are less obvious.

Continued

XSS in HTTP Headers

Play with HTTP headers.

HTTP Query Strings

Inject scripts into HTTP variables.

User-Controlled Filenames

Put HTML into filenames.

Passing Local Filenames to Functions That Expect a URL

Use local filenames that expect to consume a URL.

Meta-characters in E-mail Headers

E-mail headers are often consumed by client software. Try things.

Filesystem Function Injection, Content Based

Take advantage of headers in media files (and other files) to get elsewhere in the filesystem.

Client-Side Injection, Buffer Overflow

Aim buffer overflow attacks at clients through a malicious server.

Cause Web Server Misclassification

Take advantage of filename extension silliness.

Alternate Encoding of the Leading Ghost Characters

Use multiple encoding attacks to avoid filters.

Using Slashes in Alternate Encoding

Slash characters are interesting because they are related to the filesystem. Use both kinds of slashes.

Using Escaped Slashes in Alternate Encoding

Escape slashes to escape filtering.

Unicode Encoding

Unicode breaks filters.

UTF-8 Encoding

UTF-8 breaks filters.

URL Encoding

HEX breaks filters. URLs can be represented in many ways.

Alternative IP Addresses

Use alternate encodings for IP numbers.

Slashes and URL Encoding Combined

Combine encoding attacks.

Web Logs

Escape characters are translated before being placed in a log. Build fake entries.

Overflow Binary Resource Files

Modify sound, graphics, video, or font files (with a hex editor).

Overflow Variables and Tags

Take advantage of bad tag/variable parsing.

Overflow Symbolic Links

Try links to avoid access restrictions.

MIME Conversion

Play with conversion and translation issues.

HTTP Cookies

Use cookies as an attack vector.

Filter Failure through Buffer Overflow

Make a filter fail open.

Buffer Overflow with Environment Variables

Use environment variables as an attack vector.

Buffer Overflow in an API Call

Use API calls as an attack vector. Buffer overflows in libraries are very valuable.

Buffer Overflow in Local Command-Line Utilities

Use command-line programs as attack vectors.

Parameter Expansion

Parameter expansion can lead to buffer overflow.

String Format Overflow in `syslog()`

The `syslog` function is often misused.

therefore, legitimate. By either intercepting network traffic, corrupting values in the client software's cache, or building a hostile client, a malicious user could inject data into the database that no user was even supposed to read (much less write).

For this simple example, we'll choose to think about a legitimate user (gone bad) as the threat. The *Make the Client Invisible* attack pattern is particularly relevant to this system (as are a number of others). In this case, the server trusts the client to provide correct messages. However, this trust is mostly unfounded since creating a malicious client (either by sniffing traffic and building an attack generator or by reverse-engineering the real client) is so easy. This attack pattern leads to an abuse case describing what happens when a malicious client interacts with the server.

From the anti-requirements side of the story, we consider what happens when an attacker bypasses the access control "security mechanism" built into the client software. In this case, the mechanism is laid bare to attack on a standard PC belonging to the attacker. The resulting abuse case describes why this security mechanism is inadequate and most likely results in a major design change.

Abuse Cases Are Useful

Determining the *can'ts* and *won'ts* is often difficult for those who think only about positive features. Some guidance exists in the form of attack patterns. Attack patterns are like patterns in sewing—a blueprint for creating a kind of attack. Everyone's favorite software security example, the buffer overflow, follows several different standard patterns. Patterns allow for a fair amount of variation on a theme. They can take into account many dimensions, including timing, resources required, techniques, and so forth. Attack patterns can be used to guide abuse case development.

Security requirements specify the security apparatus for software systems. In addition to capturing and describing relevant attacks, abuse cases allow an analyst to think carefully through what happens when these functional security mechanisms fail or are otherwise compromised.

Clearly, generating abuse cases is important. The main benefit of abuse cases is that they provide essential insight into a system's assumptions and how attackers will approach and undermine them. Of course, like all good things, abuse cases can be overused (and generated forever with little impact on actual security). A solid approach to this technique requires a combination of security expertise and subject matter expertise to prioritize abuse cases as they are generated and to strike the right balance between cost and value.

9

Software Security Meets Security Operations[1]

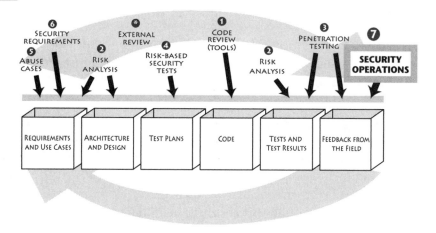

A foolish consistency is the hobgoblin of little minds.
RALPH WALDO EMERSON

Traditionally, software development efforts at large corporations have been about as far removed from information security as they were from HR or any other particular business function. Not only that, but software development also has a tendency to be highly distributed among business units, and for that reason not even practiced in a cohesive, coherent manner. In the worst cases, roving bands of developers are traded like Pokémon cards in a fifth-grade classroom between busy business unit executives trying to get ahead. Suffice it to say, none of this is good.

The disconnect between security and development results in software development efforts that lack any sort of contemporary understanding of

---

[1]Parts of this chapter appeared in original form in *IEEE Security & Privacy* magazine co-authored with Ken van Wyk [van Wyk and McGraw 2005].

technical security risks. Security concerns are myriad for applications in today's complex and highly connected computing environments. By blowing off the idea of security entirely, software builders ensure that software applications end up with way too many security weaknesses that could have and should have been avoided.

This chapter presents various recommendations to solve this problem by bridging the gap between two disparate fields. The approach is born out of experience in two diverse fields—software security and information security.[2] Central among these recommendations is the notion of using the knowledge inherent in information security organizations to enhance secure software development efforts.

Don't Stand So Close to Me

Best practices in software security, such as the touchpoints described in this book, include a manageable number of simple security activities that are to be applied throughout any software development process. These activities are lightweight processes to be initiated at the earliest stages of software development (e.g., requirements and specifications) and then continued throughout the development process and on into deployment and operations.

Although an increasing number of software shops and individual developers are adopting the software security touchpoints as their own, they often lack the requisite security domain knowledge required to do so. This critical knowledge arises from years of observing system intrusions, dealing with malicious hackers, suffering the consequences of software vulnerabilities, and so on. Put in this position, even the best-intended development efforts can fail to take into account real-world attacks previously observed on similar application architectures. Though books, such as *Exploiting Software* and *The Shellcoder's Handbook*, are starting to turn this knowledge gap around, the science of attack is a novel one [Hoglund and McGraw 2004; Koziol et al. 2004].

On the other hand, information security staff—in particular, incident handlers and vulnerability/patch specialists—have spent years responding

---

[2]To be completely honest, it is Ken van Wyk who brings vast experience in information security to this chapter. I'm just a software security guy. Ken cowrote the book *Secure Coding* [Graff and van Wyk 2003], which tackles software security from the point of view of operations-related security people.

to attacks against real systems and thinking about the vulnerabilities that spawned them. In many cases, they've studied application vulnerabilities and their resulting attack profiles in minute detail. However, few information security professionals are software developers, at least on a full-time basis, and their solution sets tend to be limited to reactive techniques such as installing software patches, shoring up firewalls, updating intrusion detection signature databases, and the like. It is very rare indeed to find information security professionals directly involved in major software development projects.

Sadly, these two communities of highly skilled technology experts exist in nearly complete isolation. Their knowledge and experience bases, however, are largely complementary. Finding avenues for interdisciplinary cooperation is very likely to bear fruit in the form of fielded software that is better equipped to resist well-known and easily predicted attacks. A secondary benefit of any interdisciplinary cooperation is having information security personnel who develop a much better understanding of the applications that they are tasked with protecting. This knowledge will no doubt benefit security professionals during their normal job tasks.

Kumbaya (for Software Security)

Software security is a significant and developing topic. The touchpoints described in this book are meant to be carried out by software security specialists in tandem with development teams. The issue at hand is how information security professionals can best participate in the software development process. If you are a CISSP, an operational security professional, or a network administrator, this Bud's for you. After a brief refresher paragraph on each touchpoint, I will introduce some recommendations relevant to both software developers and information security practitioners. The idea is to describe how best to leverage the complementary aspects of the two disciplines.

- *Requirements: Abuse Cases*
  The concept of abuse case development is derived from use case development (see Chapter 8). In an abuse case, an application's deliberate misuse is considered and the corresponding effect is pondered. For example, when addressing user input, a series of abuse cases can be constructed that describe in some detail how malicious users can and will attempt to overflow input buffers, insert malicious data (e.g., using SQL insertion attacks), and basically ride herd over software vulnerability.

An abuse case will describe these scenarios as well as how the application should respond to them. As with their use case counterparts, each abuse case is then used to drive a (non)functional requirement and corresponding test scenario for the software.

Involving information security in abuse case development is such low-hanging fruit that the fruit itself is dirt splattered from the latest hard rain. Simply put, infosec pros come to the table with the (rather unfortunate) benefit of having watched and dissected years of attack data, built forensics tools,[3] created profiles of attackers, and so on. This may make them jaded and surly, but at least they intimately know what we're up against. Many abuse case analysis efforts begin with brainstorming or "whiteboarding" sessions during which an application's use cases and functional requirements are described while a room full of experts pontificate about how an attacker might attempt to abuse the system. Properly participating in these exercises involves carefully and thoroughly considering similar systems and the attacks that have been successful against them. Thorough knowledge of attack patterns and the computer security horror stories of days gone by brings this exercise to life. Getting past your own belly button is important to abuse case success, so consider other domains that may be relevant to the application under review while you're at it. Once again, real battle experience is critical.

Infosec people are likely to find (much to their amusement) that the software developers in the room are blissfully unaware of many of the attack forms seen every day out beyond the network perimeter. Of course, many of the uninformed are also quite naturally skeptical unbelievers. While converting the unbelievers, great care should be taken not to succumb to the tendency toward hyperbole and exaggeration that is unfortunately common among security types. There's really nothing worse than a blustery security weenie on his high horse over some minor skirmish. Do not overstate the attacks that you've seen and studied. Instead, stick to the facts (ma'am) and be prepared to back your statements up with actual examples. Knowledge of actual software technology a plus.

- *Design: Business Risk Analysis*
  Assessing the business impact likely to result from a successful compromise of the software is a critical undertaking (see Chapters 2 and 5).

---

[3]See Dan Farmer and Wietse Venema's excellent new tome on forensics, *Forensic Discovery* [Farmer and Venema 2005].

Without explicitly taking this on, a security analysis will fall short in the "who cares" department. Questions of cost to the parent organization sponsoring the software are considered relative to the project. This cost is understood in terms of both direct cost (think liability, lost productivity, and rework) as well as in terms of indirect cost (think reputation and brand damage).

The most important people to consult when assessing software-induced business risks are the business stakeholders behind the software. In organizations that already practice business-level technology analysis, that fact tends to be quite well understood. The problem is that in a majority of these organizations, technology assessment of the business situation stops well before the level of software. A standard approach can be enhanced with the addition of a few simple questions: What do the people causing the software to be built think about security? What do they expect? What are they trying to accomplish that might be thwarted by successful attack? What worries them about security? The value that information security professionals can bring to answering these questions comes from a wealth of first hand experience seeing security impact when similar business applications were compromised.

That puts them in a good position to answer other security-related questions: What sorts of costs have similar companies incurred from attacks? How much downtime was involved? What was the resulting publicity in each case? In what ways was the organization's reputation tarnished? Infosec people are in a good position to provide input and flesh out a conversation with relevant stories. Here again, great care should be taken to not overstate facts. When citing incidents at other organizations, be prepared to back up your claims with news reports and other third-party documentation.

- *Design: Architectural Risk Analysis*
  Like the business risk analysis just described, architectural risk analysis assesses the technical security exposures in an application's proposed design and links these to business impact. Starting with a high-level depiction of the design, each module, interface, interaction, and so on is considered against known attack methodologies and their likelihood of success (see Chapter 5). Architectural risk analyses are often usefully applied against individual subcomponents of a design as well as on the design as a whole. This provides a forest-level view of a software system's security posture. Attention to holistic aspects of security is paramount as at least 50% of security defects are architectural in nature.

At this point we're beginning to get to the technical heart of the software development process. For architectural risk analysis to be effective, security analysts must possess a great deal of technology knowledge covering both the application and its underlying platform, frameworks, languages, functions, libraries, and so on. The most effective infosec team member in this situation is clearly the one who is a technology expert with solid experience around particular software tools. With this kind of knowledge under her belt, the infosec professional should again be providing *real-world* feedback into the process. For example, the analysis team might be discussing the relative strengths and weaknesses of a particular network encryption protocol.

Information security can help by providing perspective to the conversation. All software has potential weaknesses, but has component X been involved in actual attacks? Are there known vulnerabilities in the protocol that the project is planning to use? Is a COTS component or platform a popular attacker target? Or, on the other hand, does it have a stellar reputation and only a handful of properly handled, published vulnerabilities or known attacks? Feedback of this sort should be extremely useful in prioritizing risk and weaknesses as well as deciding on what, if any, mitigation strategies to pursue.

- *Test Planning: Security Testing*
  Just as testers typically use functional specifications and requirements to create test scenarios and test plans,[4] security-specific functionality should be used to derive tests against the target software's security functions (see Chapter 7). These kinds of investigations generally include tests that verify security features such as encryption, user identification, logging, confidentiality, authentication, and so on. Think of these as the "positive" security features that white hats are concerned with.

  Thinking like a good guy is not enough. Adversarial test scenarios are the natural result of the process of assessing and prioritizing software's architectural risks (see Chapter 7). Each architectural risk and abuse case considered should be described and documented down to a level that clearly explains how an attacker might go about exploiting a weakness and compromising the software. Donning your black hat and thinking like a bad guy is critical. Such descriptions can be used to generate a priority-based list of test scenarios for later adversarial testing.

---

[4]Especially those testers who understand the critical notion of requirements traceability <http://www.sei.cmu.edu/str/descriptions/reqtracing_body.html>.

Although test planning and execution are generally performed by QA and development groups, testing represents another opportunity for infosec to have a positive impact. Testing—especially risk-based testing—not only must cover functionality but also should closely emulate the steps that an attacker will take when breaking a target system. Highly realistic scenarios (e.g., the security analog to real user) are much more useful than arbitrary pretend "attacks." Standard testing organizations, if they are effective at all, are most effective at designing and performing tests based around functional specifications. Designing risk-based test scenarios is a rather substantial departure from the status quo and one that should benefit from the experience base of security incident handlers. In this case, infosec professionals who are good at thinking like bad guys are the most valuable resources. The key to risk-based testing is to understand how bad guys work and what that means for the system under test.

- *Implementation: Code Review*
The design-centric activities described earlier focus on architectural flaws built into software design. They completely overlook, however, implementation bugs that may well be introduced during coding. Implementation bugs are both numerous and common (just like real bugs in the Virginia countryside) and include nasty creatures like the notorious buffer overflow, which owes its existence to the use (or misuse) of vulnerable APIs (e.g., `gets()`, `strcpy()`, and so on in C) (see Chapter 4). Code review processes, both manual and (even more important) automated with a static analysis tool, attempt to identify security bugs prior to the software's release.

By its very nature, code review requires knowledge of code. An infosec practitioner with little experience writing and compiling software is going to be of little use during a code review. If you don't know what it means for a variable to be declared in a header or an argument to a method to be static/final, staring at lines of code all day isn't going to help. Because of this, the code review step is best left in the hands of the members of the development organization, especially if they are armed with a modern source code analysis tool. With the exception of information security people who are highly experienced in programming languages and code-level vulnerability resolution, there is no natural fit for network security expertise during the code review phase. This may come as a great surprise to those organizations currently attempting to impose software security on their enterprises through the infosec division. Even though the idea of security enforcement is solid, making enforcement at the code level successful when it comes to code review requires real hands-on experience with code (see the box Know When Enough Is Too Much).

- *System Testing: Penetration Testing*
  System penetration testing, when used appropriately, focuses on people failures and procedure failures made during the configuration and deployment of software. The best kinds of penetration testing are driven by previously identified risks and are engineered to probe risks directly in order to ascertain their exploitability (see Chapter 6).

  While testing software to functional specifications has traditionally been the domain of QA, penetration testing has traditionally been the domain of information security and incident-handling organizations. As such, the fit here for information security participation is a very natural and intuitive one. Of course, there are a number of subtleties that should not be ignored. As I describe in Chapter 6, a majority of penetration testing today focuses its attention on network topology, firewall placement, communications protocols, and the like. It is therefore very much an outside→in approach that barely begins to scratch the surface of applications. Penetration testing needs to encompass a more inside→out approach that takes into account risk analyses and other software security results as it is carried out. This distinction is sometimes described as the difference between network penetration testing and application penetration testing. Software security is much more interested in the latter. Also worth noting is the use of various black box penetration tools. Network security scanners like Nessus, nmap, and other SATAN derivatives, are extremely useful since there are countless ways to configure (and misconfigure) complex networks and their various services. Application security scanners (which I lambaste in Chapter 1) are nowhere near as useful. If by an "application penetration test" you mean the process of running an application security testing tool and gathering results, you have a long way to go to make your approach hold water.[5]

---

[5]It's worth noting here for non-software people how amusing the idea of a canned set of security tests (hacker in a box, so to speak) for *any possible application* is to software professionals. Software testing is not something that can be handled by a set of canned tests, no matter how large the can. The idea of testing any arbitrary program with, say, a few thousand tests determined in advance before the software was even conceived is ridiculous. I'm afraid that the idea of testing any arbitrary program with a few hundred application security tests is just as silly!

Know When Enough Is Too Much

In one large financial services organization (which shall remain nameless), the infosec people were spinning up an "application security" program. They did many things right. One thing that they got completely wrong, however, was having code review be carried out by infosec people who weren't even sure what a compiler was.

The software guys very quickly determined the level of competence of the security code review people, and they started gaming the system. In some cases they sent code for review that had nothing whatsoever to do with the system they were actually building. This was just plain deceitful and wrong, but the infosec people were too clueless to figure out what was going on.

But even when things weren't taken quite to that extreme, they were bad. Dev was submitting code that would not build for review. This hampered infosec's ability to apply modern analysis techniques (since the code may or may not have actually even compiled). The infosec people had a very hard time comprehending how to push back since they weren't familiar with build processes, nightly builds, and the like. In the end, they had not specified what they needed for a successful review in terms that dev would understand.

There are some big lessons to be learned here. The first is that dev is in a much better position to use code analysis tools than infosec is (though clearly some oversight is required so you don't end up with the fox guarding the chicken house). The second is that real software people need to be attached to and included in modern infosec organizations. The most knowledgeable network security people in the world will sometimes be at a total loss when it comes to software security.

The good news about penetration testing and infosec involvement is that it is most likely already underway. The bad news is that infosec needs to up the level of software clue in order to carry out penetration testing most effectively.

- *Fielded System: Deployment and Operations*
The final steps in fielding secure software are the central activities of deployment and operations. Careful configuration and customization of any software application's deployment environment can greatly enhance its security posture. Designing a smartly tailored deployment environment for a program requires following a process that starts at the network component level, proceeds through the operating system, and ends with the application's own security configuration and setup.

Many software developers would argue that deployment and operations are not even part of the software *development* process. Even if this view was correct, there is no way that operations and deployment concerns can be properly addressed if the software is so poorly constructed as to fall apart no matter what kind of solid ground it is placed on. Put bluntly, operations organizations have put up with some rather stinky software for a long time, and it has made them wary. If we can set that argument aside for a moment and look at the broader picture—that is, safely setting up the application in a secure operational environment and running it accordingly—then the work that needs doing can certainly be positively affected by information security. The best opportunities exist in fine-tuning access controls at the network and operating system levels, as well as in configuring an event-logging and event-monitoring mechanism that will be most effective during incident response operations. Attacks will happen. Be prepared for them to happen, and be prepared to clean up the mess after they have.[6]

Come Together (Right Now)

Let's pretend that the advice given in this chapter is sound. Even if you accept the recommendations wholesale as worthy, the act of aligning information security and software development is a serious undertaking (and not one for the faint of heart). Close cooperation with the development organization is essential to success. If infosec is perceived as the security police or "those people with sticks who show up every once in a while and beat us soundly for reasons we don't understand" by dev, you have a problem that must be addressed (see the box The Infosec Boogey Man).

In many cases, dev is more than willing to accept guidance and advice from information security people who know what they're talking about. One problem is that dev doesn't know who in information security to talk to, who might help them, and who might just be a blowhard security weenie. To fix this problem, the first step for any information security professional who wants to help out with development efforts should be to reach out to the developers, roll up your sleeves, and offer to assist.

Once you have made dev aware of your willingness to help, consider taking small steps toward the goals laid out in this chapter. Rather than

---

[6]This kind of advice is pretty much a "no duh" for information security organizations. That's one reason why their involvement in this step is paramount.

The Infosec Boogey Man

In too many organizations, infosec shows up at the end of a long and strenuous product development march, calls the baby ugly, and stops everything in its tracks. Though shipping ugly babies is not really a good idea, handling things this way engenders hard feelings among developers every time. Imagine busting your hump to get a product completed almost on time and just about kind of on budget (for months or sometimes years), and then having some outsiders come along and impose some kind of mysterious new requirements on your system that you never heard tell of before. To make matters worse, these new requirements are a serious imposition that will take time to address—heck, half of them require architectural-level changes. Does that make you feel all warm and fuzzy? Of course not!

In my work as a software security consultant I have seen the "ugly baby" problem rear its (um) ugly head far too often. Gaining the trust and understanding of the development organization is something that needs to happen early in the lifecycle. Waiting until the end to carry out a penetration test or even a hard-core risk analysis (which is likely to result in the exposure of gigantic security issues that need to be fixed) is just like showing up out of the blue and beating a victim with a stick. Software security is better introduced slowly, methodically, and gradually than with explosions, much trumpet-blaring fanfare, and thumping of chests.

trying to become involved in every phase of a giant world-changing endeavor all at once, try one at a time. Be careful to not overwhelm the overall system by attempting to make too many changes at the same time. (Much more about this and about adopting software security in large organizations can be found in Chapter 10.)

Another positive step is for the information security troops to take the time to learn as much as they can about software development in general and their organization's software development environment in particular. Study and learn about the types of applications that your software people develop; why they are working on them (i.e., what business purpose software is being built for); what languages, platforms, frameworks, and libraries are being used; and so on. Showing up with a clue is much better than showing up willing but clueless. Software people are not the most patient people on the planet, and often you have one and only one shot at getting involved. If you help, that's great. But if you hinder, that'll be the last time they talk to you.

In the end, success or failure is as likely to be driven by the personalities of the people involved as anything else. Success certainly is not guaranteed, even with the best of intentions and the most careful planning. Beer helps.

Coder's Corner

Ken van Wyk tells an interesting story about an enterprise security assessment he performed for a major financial services company. During the assessment, he uncovered a software security problem that could easily have been avoided had there been better coordination between the software developers and the people who deployed and ran the software.

The software that Ken was asked to review was an application that controlled a phone switch system running on a SCO UNIX system connected to the company's internal data network. He began by looking at the virtual environment that the application was running in. (By the way, this approach remains the quickest and easiest way of compromising an application.) In short order, Ken discovered that there were large numbers of OS-level weaknesses that enabled him to get shell access on the UNIX phone switch controller. Once he was "inside," things got worse.

Turns out that the software developers who wrote the controlling application had ported the application from MS-DOS to UNIX. By itself, that's fine, except for the fact that they had evidently taken the path of least resistance—get the application to run and then you're done. MS-DOS, being a single-user, single-tasking operating system, didn't provide much of anything in the way of file access controls, whereas UNIX, being a multiuser, multitasking operating system, did. The software developers apparently failed to spend the time to learn much of anything about the OS that they were porting their application to. This was evident because all of the application's files and directories were left unprotected at the operating system level (all files were mode 666 or 777).

The problem with this approach should be pretty obvious. Once logged into the phone switch controller, any user (or attacker) had complete read/write access to any component of the phone switch system, from its executable files to its configuration data. Ken "owned the farm," as we sometimes say in the security assessment world.

All of this could have been easily avoided. The developers made several flawed assumptions about the operational environment of the phone switch controller. These flawed assumptions would have stood out in stark relief if the developers had spent just a few minutes talking with some IT security people when they were porting the application to UNIX. Further, putting in place even some basic file and directory access controls on the switch controller would have required only a modicum of UNIX filesystem knowledge.

Effective access controls would have made a big difference, adding a very useful additional layer of protection for the application and its data. Of course, other security issues also required attention, but addressing the application's environment was the lowest of low-hanging fruit.

Future's So Bright, I Gotta Wear Shades

The interesting thing about software security is that it appears to be in the earliest stages of development, much as the field of information security itself was ten years or so ago. The security activities I describe in this chapter only touch the tip of the best practice iceberg. The good news is that these best practices are emerging at all! Of course, the software security discipline will evolve and change with time, and best practices and advice will ebb and flow like the tide at the beach. But the advice here is likely to bear fruit for some time.

The recommendations in this chapter are based on years of experience with a large dose of intuition thrown in for good measure. They are presented in the hopes that others will take them, consider them, adjust them, and attempt to apply them in their organizations. I believe that companies' software developers and information security staff can benefit greatly from the respective experiences of the other.

Much work will need to be done before the practical recommendations made here prove themselves to be as useful in practice as I believe that they will be.

PART III

Software Security Grows Up

10 An Enterprise Software Security Program[1]

I have found no greater satisfaction than achieving success through honest dealing and strict adherence to the view that, for you to gain, those you deal with should gain as well.

ALAN GREENSPAN

Adopting software security in a large organization is a challenge that takes careful planning. Cultural change of any variety is difficult in big companies. Minefields surrounding software process (a religious choice),[2] development tools, programming language, platform, and other technical decisions only exacerbate the difficulty.

Corporate politics is also an issue, with real courage required to foment software security change. Two political factors in particular impede progress. The first is momentum. In many cases, lines of business have depended on *applications* and *systems* for five or more years, and the applications have become set in stone. These organizations will *not* jeopardize the support to their top lines without having a huge multiyear program budget and executive sign-off on the risk. The second is territory-related "fear of change." Director and VP (line of business) budget and team size are at stake. It is hard to tell a Director he is losing all five database engineers and his $1.8 million annual maintenance budget when you hook the application up to the more secure (shared services) enterprise reporting interface. Regardless of these issues, leading software shops have been working hard to improve the way they develop software in order to build security in.

In some circles, the term *Secure Development Lifecycle* (SDL) is used to describe the goal state of a software security program. For example,

---

[1]Parts of this chapter appeared in original form in *IEEE Security & Privacy* magazine co-authored with Dan Taylor [Taylor and McGraw 2005].

[2]A number of very large enterprises I have worked with have washed their hands of process and have declared their agnosticism loudly (in many cases turning to the wild west for inspiration). They've all had Big-5s come in and deploy three to six software development processes, but either the processes became immediate shelfware or nobody remembers who is supposed to be using which. Risk management is not practiced.

Microsoft uses this term to describe its adjusted software process. Because of the process-agnostic approach that I prescribe, any SDL is in the end a combination of your already-in-place software development lifecycle (SDLC) and the best practices described in Part II. That is, you already know how to build and ship software (though you may not be perfect), and what you really need to concentrate on is adjusting that existing approach to produce more secure software. This chapter is about how to begin to accomplish the cultural change necessary to put an SDL in place. We start the process by demonstrating the value of software security, showing initial success that will lubricate (fund and motivate) cultural change and building a clear, actionable roadmap for that change.

Software security initiatives are possible and are underway in a growing number of organizations. A number of programs have proven beneficial for those that have implemented them. This chapter describes one approach that works, with an emphasis on business process engineering that may be unfamiliar to technical practitioners. By following a number of common-sense steps, a software security improvement program has a greater chance of achieving its ultimate goal—software security that makes business sense.

The Business Climate

Market forces continue to pressure IT organizations to become as efficient as possible in order to stay competitive. As a cost-cutting maneuver, IT organizations were reorganized during the recent economic downturn and cut to the bone. Since no more obvious costs remain to be cut, more recent efficiency efforts focus on improving productivity instead of cutting costs. Although the situation sounds bleak, software development shops inside IT can take advantage of businesses' drive to improve productivity in order to build better software. By harnessing productivity momentum, efforts to formalize software process improvement programs and achieve productivity goals are flourishing.

The regulatory and compliance environment is aligned with good security too, and in some cases, outweighs the productivity concerns. Many mid-level decision makers are very worried about compliance (or non-compliance, as the case may be). There's lots of bad press out there, and they don't want to be run over by it organizationally.

Any organization can initiate a change, but few have experience in sustaining change over time—the ultimate end state for any software security improvement program. So where to start? How can we define and manage a change program in today's dynamic business environment? How can we prepare for and take advantage of natural change? How can we build a sustainable improvement program and a plan that is flexible enough to adapt over time?

Priority one is aligning software development and operational processes with strategic business objectives. Sometimes technologists forget why they are doing what they are doing. Yet most software today is created to service business. Software security practices and mechanisms will succeed only to the extent that they have clear and explicit connections to the business mission. Recall our discussion of the RMF in Chapter 2. The stakes are high. In terms of pure technology, what is at stake may be some new authentication feature versus avoiding attack 57. But translated into risk-related business terms, when the technologist says the fizzbob-authentificator is broken, mitigation becomes a decision between a $13 million PKI installation and a $10 million Directory service. All the poor, outgunned VP knows is that there is some technical problem with user identity. Making the right decision is essential. Those technologists who understand that security is a risk management process that unfolds over time will have little trouble understanding that business concerns are a fundamental driver in balancing and refining security best practices.

A well-architected vision and plan based on industry standards and best practices is essential to a successful software security program. Throughout this book, I have covered a number of software security touchpoints that are process agnostic and can thus be adopted regardless of an organization's software development methodology. Because every organization is different, a software security improvement program plan that involves the adoption of these best practices must be tailored to the given business and technical situation. For example, organizations that focus more attention on code than on software architecture will likely benefit more quickly from the adoption of static analysis-based code review than they will from architectural analysis. First things first.

A well-defined roadmap lays out the specifics of how best to deploy software security best practices given a particular organization's approach to building (and even buying and integrating) software. Explicit strategic objectives drive prioritization of change to ensure that only those program initiatives that will provide the biggest and/or quickest return are addressed first. Executing such a roadmap is carried out in five basic steps.

1. *Build a plan that is tailored for you:* Recognize the potential dependencies between various initiatives, and plan accordingly. Focus on

developing the building blocks of change. Know how your organization develops software, and determine the best way to gradually adjust what you're doing to fold in security best practices.

2. *Roll out individual best practice initiatives carefully:* Establish champions to drive and take ownership of each initiative. Coach and mentor as needed. Run a successful pilot in part of your company before you attempt to spread best practices far and wide.

3. *Train your people:* Developers and architects remain blithely unaware of security and the critical role that they play in it. Training and mentorship is a necessity.

4. *Establish a metrics program:* Apply a business-driven metrics scorecard to monitor progress and assess success. Metrics and measures (even relative metrics based on risk over time [see Chapter 2] or business metrics such as maintenance budget) are critical to making progress in any large organization.

5. *Establish and sustain a continuous improvement capability:* Create a situation in which continuous improvement can be sustained by measuring results and periodically refocusing attention on the weakest aspects of your software security program.

Building Blocks of Change

Every cultural change program requires buy-in from both management and tactical technical people. Improvement programs will fail if either group is left out or even underemphasized. Every organization, every group within an organization, and every stakeholder will have a different sensitivity toward change. These differences must be understood and accounted for because variances in sensitivity deeply affect expectations. Disconnects in expectation may eventually end up forcing an organization into a least common denominator approach that lacks impact. Some common pitfalls are described in the box Overcoming Common Pitfalls.

Keeping things simple is good because this enables people to understand and support a program—but don't lose track of the big picture. Breaking a major change program down into logical segments of work, with specific deliverables tied to each segment (which we also call an initiative), is a proven tactical approach. In practice, we find that a reasonable time range for any given initiative is three to four months. A stepwise approach minimizes risk while enabling an organization to test the waters as it gauges receptivity to change.

Overcoming Common Pitfalls

Education, accountability, and clear objectives are critical components to any successful software security initiative. Over the years I have observed some initiatives succeed and others fail. A set of common pitfalls is something to familiarize yourself with and keep squarely in mind. Think carefully about avoiding these problems as you initiate a software security program.

Over-reliance on Late-Lifecycle Testing

In many cases, large organizations get a first taste of software security through penetration testing. This can quickly devolve into an inefficient penetrate-and-patch exercise that is too expensive to be workable. Addressing software security exclusively as a testing problem fails because vulnerabilities created during the development phase are uncovered too late. Identifying and eliminating security issues only during the final testing phase fits into the bad habit cycle of "Develop broken stuff and then fix it." Testing for quality is essential, but producing quality is the real goal. How about "Develop pretty good stuff and make sure it's good!"?

A test logically probes some activity (making it observable) and is used to make sure that the activity was successful. As such, a test can only confirm a desired result; it does not by itself *produce* that result. If a development team builds a complex piece of software and does absolutely nothing during the effort to mitigate software security vulnerabilities, what results do you suppose testing will unveil? Imagine giving a high-school calculus test to fourth graders working their way through fractions—of course they will fail. By analogy, the same thing happens when we apply security testing at the end of the lifecycle. There is a good reason that just about every single piece of enterprise software fails today when tested for security vulnerabilities. Frankly, the dev teams didn't know what they were doing.

Of course testing is important—but value will be realized only once you have built something worth testing.

Related to this problem is the obvious fact that test results alone do nothing to fix problems. All too often, risk analysis and security testing results are filed away in the "do one day" drawer and forgotten. When that happens, security problems persist.

Management without Measurement

A basic premise of management theory is: *You can't manage what you don't measure.* This is certainly applicable to building secure software. Unfortunately, I commonly encounter organizations that exhibit a lack of objectives and measures to support their

Continued

software security initiatives. Many companies insist they are creating secure software—and slogans to that affect abound. But when asked how they measure their effectiveness, they are at a loss. Simply demanding that developers create secure code only states a truism without providing any urgency to follow through. No developer sets out in the morning to create insecure code—but they do it anyway. The desire to do it right is naturally present. The missing piece is identifying what is to be done and measuring to ensure that it is.

Training without Assessment

Training not only developers but everyone involved with creating secure software is an essential activity. Unfortunately, a number of companies I have worked with felt that once a training program had been put in place, nothing more needed to be done. Nothing was done to impose objectives, measures, and testing around software security. Training by itself is not very useful unless there is follow-through on the bigger picture.

Lack of High-Level Commitment

Make no mistake; implementing an SDL is a serious undertaking. Getting everyone on board requires a sustained effort. Microsoft is no exception. After the Gates memo in January 2002 (see Chapter 1), Microsoft made a staunch public commitment to improve the security of its operating system.

The company was serious about reaching its goal. Microsoft built metrics to track progress. It hired and empowered some of the world's leading software security authorities. There was a strong management edict to get it right. Any developer at Microsoft who created a security vulnerability after completing the corporate security training program faced "serious consequences." As a result, after an incredible investment of over $300 million, Microsoft has enjoyed considerable success rolling out its own SDL.

At Microsoft, the wealthiest and most powerful software company in the world with its nearly limitless resources and expertise, the effort to adopt an SDL required the involvement and support of the Chairman of the Board, not to mention an incredible amount of effort and diligence on the part of engineers and managers throughout the organization.

Without this commitment from the highest levels, even the most powerful grassroots efforts can hit the wall. I witnessed this myself at a huge Silicon Valley technology producer that is a household name. The managers in the executive suite had lost touch with the builders and did not understand why they needed to put their weight behind software security. The initiative lost steam and was not able to get the budget it needed to succeed.

Ask yourself: Who is the executive champion behind software security in your corporation, and how will they get the job done?

In terms of breaking a program down, my approach recommends a mixed method of planning for dependencies blended with a sequence of initiatives that builds on itself. Dependencies can be used to adjust the general sequence to account for those items likely to require some dependent task prior to being kicked off. For example, building a set of measurement tools will be directly dependent on the software development methodology that is used. If an early segment includes the selection and/or adoption of a given methodology, tool choice issues should be deferred to a later segment because they require an in-place methodology to be effective.

A clear sequence of initiatives allows an organization to achieve a specific level of adoption, test the waters, measure and validate accomplishments, and set the stage for the next level. Cigital follows a change program maturity path sequence with the following six phases:

1. Stop the bleeding.
2. Harvest the low-hanging fruit.
3. Establish a foundation.
4. Craft core competencies.
5. Develop differentiators.
6. Build out nice-to-haves.

Phase 1: Stop the bleeding is targeted at those areas of software development programs that are known to be problem areas. If particular security bugs like buffer overflows are causing the biggest problem, a good phase 1 approach might involve the adoption of a code scanning tool and an associated process for its use. If there are tens of thousands of security-critical applications with unknown risks, a good phase 1 approach might be to carry out a flyover risk analysis process and organize the applications in order of criticality/security exposure so that the plan addresses those applications most at risk first.

Phase 2: Harvest the low-hanging fruit is focused on finding quick wins that are instrumental in getting buy-in from the organization and in helping a change program build momentum. Note that this phase and its predecessor are good barometers for determining the organization's receptivity toward change.

Phase 3: Establish a foundation is about setting in place components that provide building blocks for future initiatives. Typical areas addressed in this phase include creating change control programs, building a root-cause analysis function, and setting up critical feedback loops. One such feedback loop identifies and cycles any security problems discovered through the application of best practices, such as code review, back into training (in order to teach developers how to avoid common security problems in the first place).

Phase 4: Craft core competencies is driven by both current strengths and desired strengths of the organization. If an organization has a strong reputation for creating solid architecture documentation, it will likely be more receptive to architectural risk analysis than it may be to abuse case development. This phase explicitly involves the adoption of software security best practices in a manner tailored to the strengths of the organization.

Phase 5: Develop differentiators in order to emphasize and highlight those capabilities that separate the organization from everyone else in the marketplace. Measurement and metrics systems put in place with a software security improvement program can be used to demonstrate how well things are going from a security perspective. This can serve as an important differentiator in the market.

Phase 6: Build out nice-to-haves involves adopting those capabilities that are not necessarily aligned to a given strategic business objective but bring value by achieving some improvement in productivity. These are left for last for obvious reasons.

Building an Improvement Program

Once a specific and actionable plan is set, a pragmatic approach should drive each initiative. Developing a clear understanding of what will be built during each part of the program; who will own it; and how they will build, deploy, and continue to improve it over time is essential.

The general framework and plan discussed earlier should include a number of factors, including (but not limited to):

- Tools
- Processes
- Decision criteria and associated actions
- Templates
- Examples and blueprints
- Best practices
- Guidelines
- Metrics and measures

All of these concerns should be related and described in terms of *who, what,* and *when,* especially in large organizations. Additionally, there are a number of drivers required that can help align the framework with the strategic business direction. These include current software architectures, security policies and guidelines, and regulatory requirements, to name just a few. An all-encompassing *enterprise information architecture* and associated *enterprise architecture roadmap* (including data sensitivity classifications and user/role/privilege maps across lines of business) is an absolutely essential anchor for framework-based adoption and change.

The most important decision for ensuring success in a cultural change program is the selection of champions—those individuals who will build, deploy, and own each initiative going forward. For example, should an initiative involve the adoption of static analysis tools for code review, a champion well versed in security analysis of implementations, the target language(s), and effective use of source code tools is necessary. Ideally, these individuals are not freshly trained in the area they are meant to own; rather, they should have a hand in developing the initiative and its components (including processes, success measures, and so on). A champion needs to be motivated; driven; and, most important, supported by the management team. Champions must be good communicators and part-time cheerleaders, and they must possess a strong capability to train and mentor others.

For each initiative, the assigned champion will drive the build, pilot, and deployment activities throughout the organization. The champion will also be responsible for monitoring, measuring, and improving the initiative over time. It's important to understand and distinguish a technical champion from a business sponsor. In this case, I mean a technical champion.

Establishing a Metrics Program

The importance of measurement and metrics is hard to overstate. Measurement provides critical insight to management, allowing management to support strategic decision-making processes. Measures are numeric values assigned to a given artifact, software product, or process. A metric is a combination of two or more measures that together provide some business-relevant meaning. For example, when considered separately "lines of code" and "number of security breaches" are two distinct measures that provide very little business meaning because there is no context for their values. A metric made up as "number of breaches / lines of code" provides a more interesting relative value. A comparative metric like this can be used to compare and contrast a given system's "security defect density" against a previous version or similar systems and thus provide management with useful data for decision making.

Ideally, metrics and measures will focus on four primary areas: project, process, product, and organization. The first three are specific to a given artifact or activity in a software development effort, while the purpose of the latter is to determine trends across the three other areas.

Establishing a metrics capability is a challenging undertaking. Early standard software process approaches focused on sequentially building a level of sufficiency in four areas and in a particular order: process, controls, metrics, and improvement. Unfortunately, following these basic steps in the prescribed order implies that metrics are not addressed until late in the program. By then it may be too late. In this case, processes and controls put in place early may not be properly designed to provide the kinds of metrics that are needed later. In those cases, some significant rework may be required to achieve business alignment.

All metrics should render decision criteria based on strategic business objectives. For that reason, business objectives must be articulated first and used to guide the entire program, from process and control development onward.

A Three-Step Enterprise Rollout

Figure 10–1 shows a simple three-step rollout plan for establishing an enterprise-wide, metrics-based software security program. This approach can be adapted for use in rolling out any large initiative. The three fundamental steps are (1) assess and plan, (2) build and pilot, and (3) propagate and improve.

Step 1 involves getting a handle on the current state of the business. This includes understanding the goals of the program writ large, collecting data to assess current state, and then comparing current state to goal state. This is in some sense a gap analysis. As an example, rollout step 1 in a large software security program will include understanding the in-place SDLC and assessing how well it covers the touchpoints discussed in this book. If code review is currently practiced only at the unit level by developers who are not using a static analysis tool, a clear gap has been identified between the goal (state-of-the-art software security) and reality. Since there are likely to be a large number of application development projects underway simultaneously in any large company, developing a rating system to assess each project is an important part of baselining. This leads to a measurement and metrics regimen that can be evenly applied throughout the rollout. Note that some of these measures can be taken from software artifacts as briefly described earlier.

Counterintuitively, it may be best to begin rollout step 2, build and pilot, by identifying a software project that is ahead of the game. That is, because

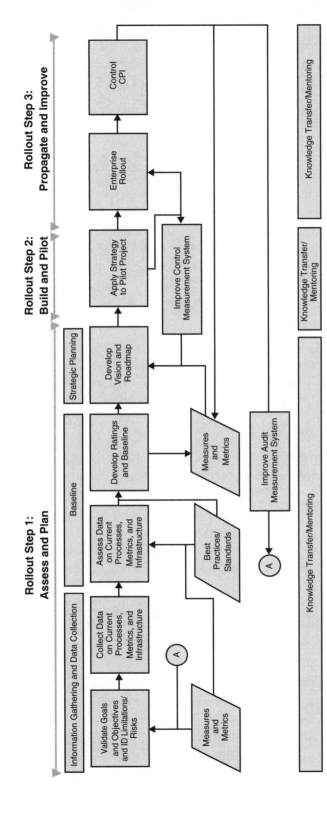

Figure 10–1 A three-step rollout plan for enterprise adoption of software security best practices, based on establishing clear measurements and metrics up front.

you want to maximize the possibility of pilot success, starting with the project with the smallest gap may make things easier. For example, if the software project chosen for pilot is already using static analysis tools for reliability (looking for null pointers and other simple bugs), adopting a security-related source code analysis tool is likely to be fairly straightforward for the project team. Because we have a set of measurements in place, we can assess progress over time in rollout step 2 and refine our measurement system. Note that in almost all cases, training programs will need to be developed that clearly describe both the goals of the improvement program and how to actually carry out the new best practice. The material in Part II of this book should be particularly useful.

A successful pilot program provides an excellent real-world case study of the adoption of a best practice in one part of the enterprise. This success story provides "proof in the pudding" that a best practice, like code review with a source code security scanner, can be successful in the organization. Rollout step 3, propagate and improve, involves taking the best practice wide. By relying on the baseline gap analysis results from step 1, we can logically approach the problem of wide adoption. Our measurement program helps keep tabs on progress and is extremely useful in alerting us of adoption issues as they crop up. The training program developed in step 2 is a critical part of the widespread adoption of a best practice in a company. Also helpful is an information portal for software professionals to use as a resource as they adopt various software security touchpoints.

By following this straightforward rollout plan, a very large organization can transform its existing SDLC (or more likely SDLCs, plural) with the addition of best practices for software security. The idea of an SDL is thereby a combination of *your* SDLC with the software security touchpoints. This key point bears repeating. Presumably your organization already knows how to make software and has already been shipping it for years. There is no reason to throw out everything you're already doing and start from scratch. Instead, your already-in-place SDLC can be adjusted by adding touchpoints. My process-agnostic approach, based around software artifacts, makes this possible.

Continuous Improvement

The targeted end state for any improvement program (security or otherwise) is a sustainable ability to evolve and to change with the business climate. Improvement programs are focused on enabling an organization to develop consistent, effective standards that can be replicated throughout the organization over time.

As any organization carries out its day-to-day software development and maintenance functions, it will execute many processes. A critical foundation for continuous improvement is introspective in nature: Each process must be carefully analyzed, assessed with respect to the need for change, adjusted as appropriate, and reinstantiated after it is refreshed. This feedback cycle is critical for ensuring that any given initiative stays relevant. Process for process' sake is a well-known pitfall that should be avoided. A feedback loop additionally helps to confirm that best practices like the touchpoints are in fact being followed. Unfortunately, many organizations have a tendency to become lazy and slip back into old habits. Control processes help counter this tendency.

A critical feature for the success of continuous improvement involves the periodic auditing and explicit reformulation of the organization's strategic objectives to ensure that they have not changed too much over time. If business needs have moved far enough to push processes and procedures off track, then the entire software security initiative needs to be reevaluated.

All modern businesses are surrounded by change. Any business that does not embrace change will fall victim to the tides of the market. Businesses that successfully manage change become flexible and nimble enough to adjust to rapid market movement; to remain competitive; and, ultimately, to establish sustainable differentiators that improve their strategic position.

What about COTS (and Existing Software Applications)?

In this book, I am primarily interested in discussing how to build secure software by adjusting and updating existing software development processes. The touchpoints are described as simple best practices that can be added to any existing SDLC. That's all fine and good for new projects, but to solve the software security problem, we need to think hard about existing applications, integrated software, and commercial off-the-shelf software (COTS) as well.

Fortunately, the problem of existing applications is very easily addressed. That's because all of the touchpoints, as software security assurance activities, can be carried out against existing software applications as long as you have some artifacts. You'll most certainly have executable binaries, so that's a guaranteed starting place. But you're likely to have other software artifacts, including source code, defect reports, architectural descriptions, and so on. By referring to these artifacts along with the running system itself, you can assess the security posture of an existing application and begin working toward making it more secure.

I am assuming that the existing application will be found lacking in its security. This is not a necessary condition, but it is one so commonly encountered that I treat it as a default. Getting a handle on a large pile of software applications (say, on the order of 1000 or so) is always an essential part of the baselining program described earlier. By measuring all of the applications with the same measuring stick (say, some kind of outside→in penetration testing or application security testing), we can get a rough estimate of which applications need the most help. In my experience, a cursory architectural risk analysis and a quick code review with a tool (the top two touchpoints) provide the most actionable data. Don't forget that business impact is a critical factor here.

Assessing the state of existing software applications is a critical software security practice. The best approach is to perform a very high-level holistic analysis mixing both code review with a tool and architectural risk analysis to determine security posture (see Chapter 5). This can be done as part of routine maintenance schedules in order to be less disruptive in a large organization.

The COTS problem is more of a challenge. Because COTS vendors are often reluctant to provide the necessary software artifacts needed to determine security posture, using the touchpoints against COTS is not as effective.[3] One approach is to attempt to bind the vendor legally (see Chapter 1). The Reagan-esque "trust but verify" idea applies in spades though, so taking a look yourself is almost always a good idea. You'll always have executables, so that starting point exists. The hacker techniques discussed in *Exploiting Software* are also extremely useful when confronted with the COTS analysis problem [Hoglund and McGraw 2004].

A closely related issue involves the kind of modern enterprise software most commonly encountered in large businesses today: software that has both COTS components and middleware glue. In this common situation, it

---

[3]It never hurts to ask, though. Some vendors will provide source code and other artifacts if pressed (especially if the organization asking for artifacts is a key customer). Believe it or not, you can force a "go/no go" decision through your organization by using the "Who cares?" question-answering tactics from Chapter 2.

pays to have a coherent enterprise security framework in place that governs software security policy from development through integration and also covers purchasing.

An Enterprise Information Architecture

Figure 10–2 shows an overview of a generic enterprise information architecture (IA). Please note that any such IA must be adjusted to account for the software situation found in the large company where this architecture is to be applied. The IA is not a one-size-fits-all solution, but rather a large-scale "map" that describes goal state. The IA concept is designed to help large organizations think through what knowledge objects are necessary to apply for each touchpoint.

The IA in Figure 10–2 includes several critical sections. Starting at the bottom, a number of essential documents labeled "Collateral" in the picture describe the security vision, document policy, and point to standards and requirements. For our purposes, the most interesting pieces of collateral are design patterns and code samples. These two essential knowledge categories are extremely useful in constructive software activities. Design patterns provide reference architectures (best tied back into policy and standards) and may address particular platforms such as .NET or J2EE. Code samples are similarly anchored in policy and standards, but they include actual usable code samples, possibly even to the level of class files with standardized APIs. These components allow software professionals to understand what their goal is (not the use of security features, per se, but the use of secure coding design and implementation techniques). Positive examples also make excellent fodder for later assessment and measurement activities.

Moving up the picture, the part labeled "Contractual Artifacts" describes aspects of software projects that allow outsourced development to make sense. By governing a software development project with a clear master services agreement (MSA) and statement of work (SoW), especially if the documents include service-level agreement (SLA) and quality-of-service (QoS) callouts to security, we can hold outsource vendors accountable for software security. Evidence can be provided in terms of risk analysis reviews, test results, code scanning results, and so on.

Moving one set of boxes higher, we encounter activities most useful when buying software. These are loosely analogous to the touchpoints described in this book, but they are more readily applicable to software purchase. Note that the black hat best practices are particularly useful when

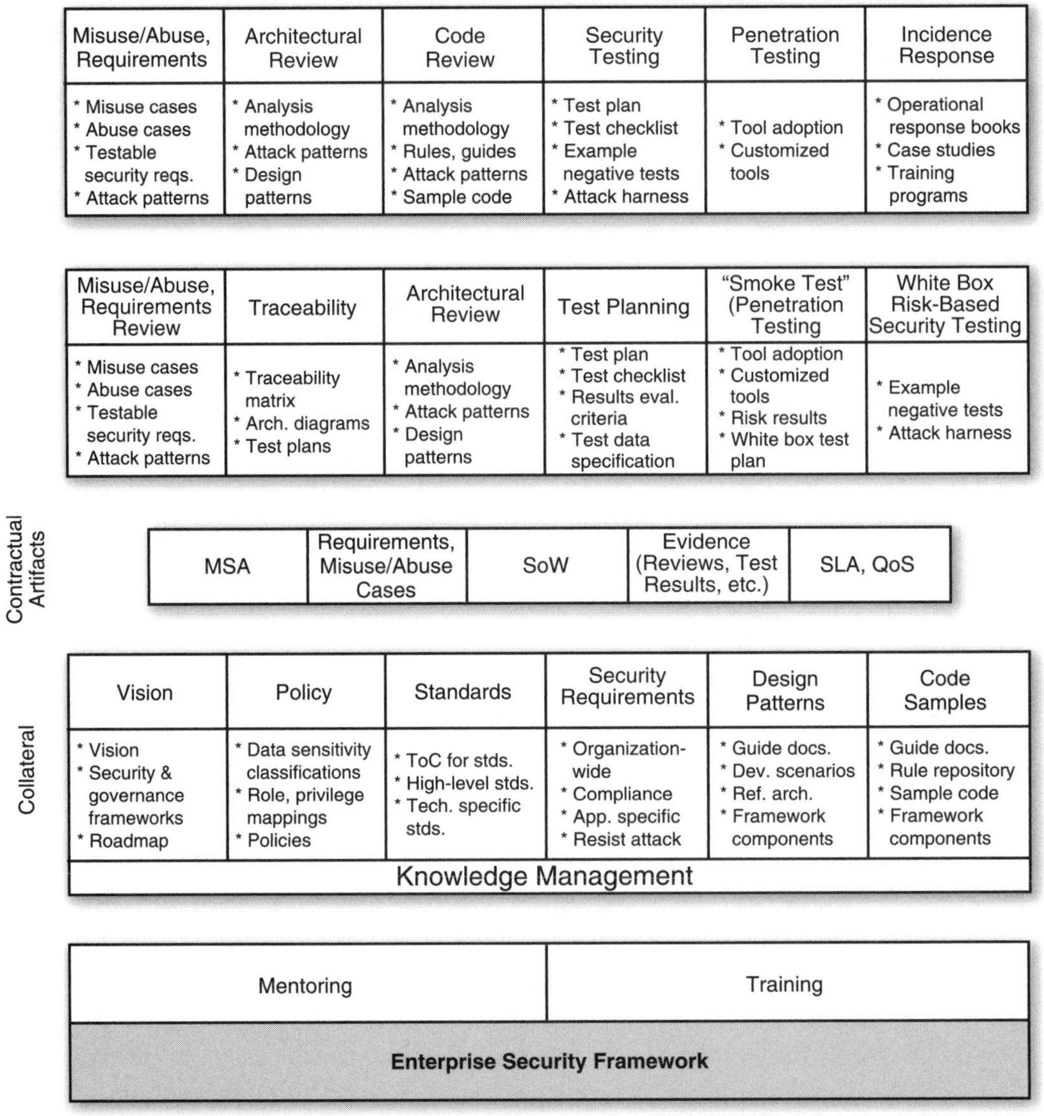

Misuse/Abuse, Requirements	Architectural Review	Code Review	Security Testing	Penetration Testing	Incidence Response
* Misuse cases * Abuse cases * Testable security reqs. * Attack patterns	* Analysis methodology * Attack patterns * Design patterns	* Analysis methodology * Rules, guides * Attack patterns * Sample code	* Test plan * Test checklist * Example negative tests * Attack harness	* Tool adoption * Customized tools	* Operational response books * Case studies * Training programs

Misuse/Abuse, Requirements Review	Traceability	Architectural Review	Test Planning	"Smoke Test" (Penetration Testing)	White Box Risk-Based Security Testing
* Misuse cases * Abuse cases * Testable security reqs. * Attack patterns	* Traceability matrix * Arch. diagrams * Test plans	* Analysis methodology * Attack patterns * Design patterns	* Test plan * Test checklist * Results eval. criteria * Test data specification	* Tool adoption * Customized tools * Risk results * White box test plan	* Example negative tests * Attack harness

Contractual Artifacts

MSA	Requirements, Misuse/Abuse Cases	SoW	Evidence (Reviews, Test Results, etc.)	SLA, QoS

Collateral

Vision	Policy	Standards	Security Requirements	Design Patterns	Code Samples
* Vision * Security & governance frameworks * Roadmap	* Data sensitivity classifications * Role, privilege mappings * Policies	* ToC for stds. * High-level stds. * Tech. specific stds.	* Organization-wide * Compliance * App. specific * Resist attack	* Guide docs. * Dev. scenarios * Ref. arch. * Framework components	* Guide docs. * Rule repository * Sample code * Framework components

Knowledge Management

Mentoring	Training

Enterprise Security Framework

Figure 10–2 An enterprise information architecture, including critical software security documents, processes, and contracts.[4] See the text on previous page for definitions of abbreviations.

---

[4]Thanks to John Steven, who created the IA concept and built this picture.

buying software. Developing threat models, abuse cases, and security requirements while thinking hard about attack patterns is possible even if you are standing outside the "box of code" with little wherewithal to get in the box.

Architectural review is also possible on COTS products, depending on the documentation provided with the code. In the case of open source adoption, you're in better shape. But even when proprietary software is involved, a wealth of information useful to security analysis is often available. In any case, the level of analysis can be dialed in to reflect the information available for the product under review. Penetration testing (see Chapter 6) is almost always useful in assessing a COTS product, especially if it is based on risk analysis results.

Finally, at the top of Figure 10–2 we come to the all-familiar touch-points described in this book. These best practices are best applied when building software (or analyzing existing applications for which you have a nice set of software artifacts). As you can see, the IA as a whole is applicable to a very diverse set of software circumstances, ranging from code you build yourself all the way to off-the-shelf code that you simply integrate into your environment.

Figure 10–3 shows another view of the same IA, this time annotated with various labels. As you can see, the IA labels align with our previous description. The labels help to show how an overall security IA can be used to govern software processes, both for outsourcing situations and for bespoke building situations.

This IA is annotated to indicate the impact that collateral has on defining process and vice versa. It is meant to imply that process (like the famous touchpoints) can't succeed without proper knowledge backup. The good news is that even if you find yourself in an organization with looming process problems, you can still enjoy initial success with the touchpoints. This success comes through building out the knowledge and sneaking the risk management methodology and activities into it.

I have found that those enterprises with more mature corporate governance policies and procedures are better able to comprehend and actualize an IA like this. Those software houses with a smaller handle on policy (and usually a correspondingly larger software clue) are best suited to approach software security through the touchpoints. Those enterprise development shops driven by a top-down governance structure are more likely to see success through clear description and imposition of a corporate IA.

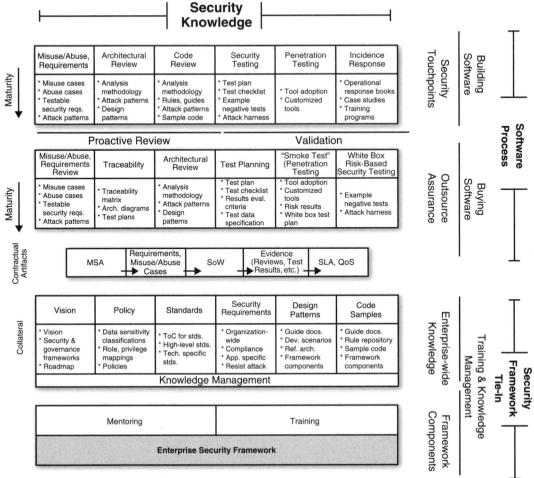

Figure 10–3 An IA annotated to describe different software situations, from buying software to building it. The tie to organizational policy is a key aspect of the IA but necessitates a very mature security organization that has described its vision and policy.[5]

Adopting a Secure Development Lifecycle

An SDL is a combination of your existing SDLC and the best practices described in this book. There is no reason to wipe the software slate clean in order to adopt software security best practices. You know how to build software. The trick to effective software security is to adapt your current approach according to a process-agnostic plan.

---

[5]Thanks to John Steven, who conceived of the IA and built this picture.

A critical challenge facing software security today is the dearth of experienced practitioners. Approaches that rely solely on apprenticeship as a method of propagation are unlikely to scale quickly enough to address the increasingly more serious problem, so as the field evolves and best practices are established, business process engineering can play a central role in encapsulating and spreading the emerging discipline more efficiently.

11 Knowledge for Software Security[1]

Knowledge is power.
FRANCIS BACON

Knowledge management can play a central role in encapsulating and spreading the emerging discipline of software security more efficiently. This chapter is about the kinds of security knowledge that can be used to provide a solid foundation for software security practices.

Knowledge is more than simply a list of things we know or a collection of facts. Simply put, information and knowledge aren't the same thing, and it is important to understand the difference. *Knowledge* is information in context—information put to work using processes and procedures. A checklist of potential security bugs in C and C++ is *information;* the same information built into a static analysis tool is knowledge.

At this nascent stage of the game in software security, a number of early adopters have created various checklists for use when thinking about software security and application security. One of the problems with these lists is that they have a tendency to combine categories of information in hard-to-grok ways. For example, a "Top Ten Things to Know about Application Security" document that treats "Apply the Principle of Least Privilege" the same as "Avoid Buffer Overflows," "Monitor BugTraq," and "Use a Code Scanning Tool" combines lots of good ideas in an incoherent package. It is better to organize software security knowledge into coherent chunks.

The first hurdle along these lines to overcome is the propensity to think of software security as a coding issue. I like to refer to this kind of approach as the "bug parade." Sure, there are hundreds of bugs that can lead to security problems (especially in languages like C and C++). But simply developing a checklist of coding issues to avoid in C and having your developers

---

[1]Parts of this chapter appeared in original form in *IEEE Security & Privacy* magazine as two articles, one coauthored with Sean Barnum [Barnum and McGraw 2005] and one with Nancy Mead [Mead and McGraw 2005].

read it will not solve the software security problem.[2] If instead of making a static list, we build a database of coding issues and create a tool to help us uncover these problems, then we're getting somewhere. This is precisely what is happening with the static analysis space.

Of course, by now we know that we must address bugs (of the sort that a tool can easily find) and flaws (which require a smart human to find). We ignore flaws by declaring them "too hard to deal with at this time" at our peril.

The second hurdle is the incorrect belief that software security is really about adopting various security features and/or conventions. One place where this is going particularly wrong is in the creation of generic classes for filtering input. We all know by now that a black-list solution to the input-filtering problem (trying to identify all possible malicious input) is inferior to a white-list solution (ensuring that only input that plays by certain rules is allowed). The problem is that black lists are potentially infinite every time—there is no way to anticipate future malicious input. Consider for a moment the encoding problem and various Unicode attacks discussed in *Exploiting Software* and you'll see what I mean [Hoglund and McGraw 2004].

Given a thorough understanding of a program (say, when you're building it), you are in a perfect position to create a correct input-filtering approach since you know precisely what kind of input you are expecting. Wrongheaded thinking has led to the idea of "security classes" that you can buy and link into your code. In the case of generic filtering capability, this idea is unlikely to work. Of course, there is nothing wrong with adopting great coding practices and even borrowing solid code to use. In any event, as this book demonstrates, software security is more about assurance than it is about features. Some people call the feature-based approach to software security a "cookbook" approach. Cookbooks can certainly help you with recipes, but just reading cookbooks without ever turning on your stove and actually tasting stuff won't make you a good cook. Experience is the most powerful teacher.

The third and final major hurdle is overuse of the checklist. Checklists are great in the hands of an expert. They serve as reminders of things to think about. However, checklists are by their very definition incomplete. Consider the STRIDE model from *Writing Secure Code* [Howard and LeBlanc 2003]. The activity of thinking carefully about Spoofing, Tampering, Repudiation, Information disclosure, Denial of service, and Elevation of

---

[2]If you want to experience firsthand why reading rules is tedious, check out Appendix B.

privilege while you ponder system security is a great idea. The problem is that there are definitely more than six categories of attack. If you limit your thinking to a checklist, you will likely overlook interesting risks that lead to new attacks. Attackers know this well, and they will go out of their way to game this problem. For example, no virus writer worth his salt will release a new virus without first running every available commercial antivirus checker against it as an acceptance test. (Not to imply that there aren't plenty of really dumb virus writers out there.)

The way around these hurdles is to organize and apply software security knowledge with care.

This chapter may be too academic or research oriented for some. Software security practitioners and software security scientists will certainly want to develop the catalogs we cite (or participate in group exercises to develop a common set of open catalogs for all). But large organizations worried about adopting software security programs (as described in Chapter 10) will be better served with the information architecture covered there. This chapter is more about the intellectual exercise of organizing and cataloging knowledge than it is about making that knowledge actionable in an enterprise.

Experience, Expertise, and Security

Software developers place a high premium on knowledge. Experience is king, and expertise is very valuable. The software field is in a perpetual state of change, and keeping on top of all possible new technologies is very difficult, if not impossible. Developers show great respect for those who master aspects of the expanding field and are able to help bring others along. This is the kind of phenomenon that drives topnotch developer conferences like SD West and SD Best Practices (called SD East by most people)—find both here <http://www.sdexpo.com/>.

Similarly, software security practitioners place a premium on knowledge and experience. In a field where most practitioners are still being exposed to the basics (think checklists and basic coding rules), the value of master craftsmen who have "been there and done that," learned a number of lessons the hard way, and are able to transfer that experience to others is very high.

The bad news is that there aren't enough master craftsmen in software security to apprentice and train all software developers, software architects, and software security newbies effectively. The good news is that critical software security knowledge and expertise can be compiled from those in the know and then shared widely. This possibility yields a potentially higher return than the pervasive one-to-one method of apprenticeship practiced today. Through the aggregation of knowledge from a number of experienced craftsmen, knowledge management can provide a new software security practitioner access to the knowledge and expertise of *all* the masters, not just one or two.

Software security knowledge is multifaceted and can be applied in diverse ways. As the software lifecycle unfolds, security knowledge can be directly and dynamically applied through the use of knowledge-intensive best practices like the touchpoints in this book. During professional training and resource development, security knowledge can be drawn on for pedagogical application, sparking stories and anecdotes. During academic training, security knowledge can inform basic coding and design curricula. All of these activities are beginning to happen in software security. For this reason, a sophisticated knowledge management approach is necessary.

Security Knowledge: A Unified View

Security knowledge can be organized according to the taxonomy introduced in the box Software Security Unified Knowledge Architecture. Seven knowledge catalogs (principles, guidelines, rules, vulnerabilities, exploits, attack patterns, and historical risks) are grouped into three knowledge categories (prescriptive knowledge, diagnostic knowledge, and historical knowledge).

Two of the seven catalogs are likely to be familiar to software developers with only a passing familiarity with software security—vulnerabilities and exploits. These catalogs have been in common use for quite some time and have even resulted in collection and cataloging efforts serving the security community.[3] Similarly, principles—stemming from the seminal work of Saltzer and Schroeder [1975]—and rules—identified and captured in static analysis tools, such as ITS4 (see Appendix B)—are fairly well understood. Knowledge catalogs only more recently identified include guidelines (often built into prescriptive frameworks for technologies such as .NET and J2EE), attack patterns [Hoglund and McGraw 2004], and historical risks. Together, these various knowledge catalogs provide a basic foundation for a unified knowledge architecture supporting software security.

---

[3]Mitre's CVE <http://www.cve.mitre.org/>, the CERIAS database <https://cirdb.cerias.purdue.edu/coopvdb/public/>, and CERT's alert data <http://www.cert.org> are three popular collections.

Software Security Unified Knowledge Architecture

Figure 11–1 shows a basic software security knowledge schema relating the seven catalogs.

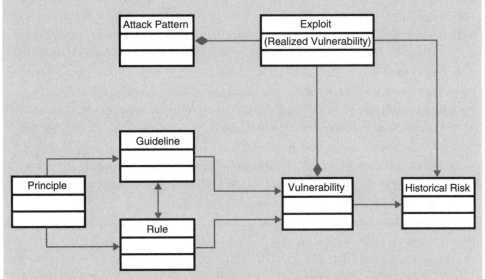

Figure 11–1 The basic schema displayed here shows one way to organize and interrelate software security knowledge. There are seven distinct *knowledge catalogs*, which can be divided into three *knowledge categories*.

The category **prescriptive knowledge** includes three knowledge catalogs: principles, guidelines, and rules. These sets span a continuum of abstraction from high-level architectural principles at the level of philosophy (e.g., the principle of least privilege [Saltzer and Schroeder 1975]) to very specific and tactical code-level rules (e.g., avoid the use of the library function gets() in C). Guidelines fall somewhere in the middle of this continuum (e.g., make all Java objects and classes final(), unless there's a good reason not to [McGraw and Felten 1999]). As a whole, the prescriptive knowledge category offers advice for what to do and what to avoid when building secure software.

The category **diagnostic knowledge** includes three knowledge catalogs: attack patterns, exploits, and vulnerabilities. Rather than prescriptive statements of practice, diagnostic knowledge helps practitioners (including operations people) recognize and deal with common problems that lead to security attack. Vulnerability knowledge

Continued

includes descriptions of software vulnerabilities experienced and reported in real systems (often with a bias toward operations). Exploits describe how instances of vulnerabilities are leveraged into particular security compromise for particular systems. Attack patterns describe common sets of exploits in a more abstract form that can be applied across multiple systems. Such diagnostic knowledge is particularly useful in the hands of a security analyst, though its value as a resource to be applied during development is considerable (e.g., consider the utility of attack patterns to abuse case development).

The category **historical knowledge** includes the knowledge catalog historical risks and, in some cases, vulnerabilities (e.g., the collection in the CVE <http://www.cve.mitre.org/>). Rather than derivations or abstractions, this catalog represents detailed descriptions of specific issues uncovered in real-world software development efforts and must include a statement of impact on the business or mission proposition. As a resource, this knowledge offers tremendous value in helping to identify similar issues in new software efforts without starting from scratch. It also provides a continuing source for identifying new instances of other knowledge catalogs described here: principles, guidelines, rules, vulnerabilities, and attack patterns.

Table 11–1 provides a bird's-eye view of each knowledge catalog. Each entry includes a brief description, a sample schema for tracking instances, and a short list of software artifacts (arising from most software lifecycles) that the knowledge impacts the most. The idea here is to create a number of inter-related catalogs for use throughout the software lifecycle.

Work on fleshing out the knowledge catalogs identified here has been underway for some time by various groups. Makers of static analysis tools have pushed the envelope when it comes to rules, for example, while work sponsored by the Department of Homeland Security (and carried out by Cigital and SEI) has focused on principles and guidelines. The results of these efforts are available on the Web at <http://buildsecurityin.us-cert.gov/portal/> and should prove very useful for software security practitioners. More on the DHS effort can be found later in this chapter.

Table 11–1 A Bird's-Eye View of Software Security Knowledge Catalogs

Knowledge Catalog	Description	Sample High-Level Schema	Relevant SDLC Artifacts
Principles	A principle is a statement of general security wisdom derived from experience. Though principles exist at the level of philosophy, they stem from real-world experience building secure systems. Principles are useful for both diagnosing architectural flaws in software and practicing good security engineering.	• Title • Definition (1..n) 　° Description 　° Examples 　° Reference • Related guidelines • Related rules	• Security requirements • Software architecture • Software design
Guidelines	A guideline is a recommendation for things to *do* or to *avoid* during software development, described at the semantic level. Guidelines exist for a specific technical context (e.g., J2EE, .NET, Linux kernel module, and so on). Guidelines are best enforced and evaluated through human analysis. Guidelines can help uncover both architectural flaws and implementation bugs.	• Context description (platform, OS, language, and so on) • Title • Type • Objective • Development scenario • Description • Related API • Reference • Related principles • Related rules	• Security requirements • Software design • Code

Continued

Table 11–1 A Bird's-Eye View of Software Security Knowledge Catalogs

Knowledge Catalog	Description	Sample High-Level Schema	Relevant SDLC Artifacts
Rules	A rule is a recommendation for things to *do* or to *avoid* during software development, described at the level of syntax. A rule can be verified through lexical scanning or constructive parsing of software (source or binary). Rules exist for specific programming languages (e.g., C, C++, PHP, Java, and so on). Rules can help uncover implementation bugs.	• Context description (platform, OS, language, and so on) • ID • Title • Attack category • Vulnerability kingdom • Location • Description • Method of attack • Solution • Signature • Example (1..n) • Reference (1..n) • Related principles • Related guidelines	• Code
Attack patterns	An attack pattern is a generalized pattern developed by reasoning over large sets of software exploits. Attack patterns are useful for identifying and qualifying the risk that a given exploit will occur in a software system. They are also useful in designing misuse and abuse cases and specific security tests.	• Context description (platform, OS, language, and so on) • Title • Attack category • Description • Example (1..n) • Reference • Related guidelines • Related rules	• Abuse cases • Software design • Security test plan (and tests) • Penetration tests

Table 11–1 *Continued*

Knowledge Catalog	Description	Sample High-Level Schema	Relevant SDLC Artifacts
Historical risks	A historical risk is a risk identified in the course of an actual software development effort. At its core, a risk is a pairing of a condition/event with a quantification of the likelihood that it will occur and a quantification of the impact it will have. Historical risks are good resources for early identification of potential issues in a software development effort, for potential clues to effective mitigations, and for improvements to the consistency and quality of risk management in the software development process.	• Title • Type (business/technical) • Subcategory (taxonometric sorting) • Author • Owner • Project • Risk status • Likelihood • Impact • Severity • Risk context • Risk description • Realization indicators • Impact description • Estimated impact date • Potential cost • Contingency plan/workaround • Related business goals • Related risks • Related mitigations • Diagnostic methods	• Software architecture • Software design • Test plans • Deployed software
Vulnerabilities	A vulnerability is the result of a defect in software that can be used by an attacker to gain access to or negatively affect the security of a computer system.	• Context description (platform, OS, language, application, version, and so on) • Title • Description • Severity • Vulnerability type • Loss type • Reference	• Code • Software architecture • Software design • Penetration tests • Fielded system

Continued

Table 11–1 A Bird's-Eye View of Software Security Knowledge Catalogs

Knowledge Catalog	Description	Sample High-Level Schema	Relevant SDLC Artifacts
Exploits	An exploit is a particular instance of an attack on a computer system that leverages a specific vulnerability or set of vulnerabilities.	• Context description (platform, OS, language, application, version, and so on) • Title • Description • Preconditions • Motivation • Exposure type • Exploit code • Blocking solution • Related vulnerabilities	• Penetration tests • Fielded system

Security Knowledge and the Touchpoints

Software security knowledge can be successfully applied at various stages throughout the entire SDLC. One effective way to apply such knowledge is through the use of software security best practices such as the touchpoints. For example, rules are extremely useful for static analysis and code inspection activities.

Software security best practices and their associated knowledge catalogs can be applied regardless of the base software process being followed. Software development processes as diverse as the waterfall model, RUP, XP, Agile, spiral development, and CMMi (and any number of other processes) involve the creation of a common set of software artifacts (the most common artifact being code). Figure 11–2 shows an enhanced version of the touchpoints diagram that serves as the backbone of this book. In the figure, I identify those activities and artifacts most clearly impacted by the knowledge catalogs described here.

The box Two Example Catalog Entries: A Principle and a Rule (see page 270) and the preceding Table 11–1 provide an overview of each of the knowledge catalogs. Principles, given their philosophical level of abstraction, bring significant value to early-lifecycle activities including the definition of security requirements, performance of software architecture risk

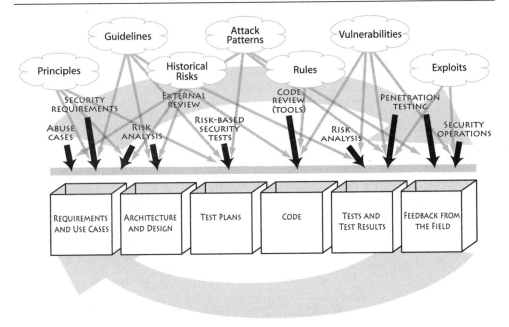

Figure 11–2 Mapping of software security knowledge catalogs to various software artifacts and software security best practices (the touchpoints described in this book).

analysis, and design reviews. Rules, given their tactical, specific, syntactic nature, are primarily applicable during implementation of code review and are particularly well suited for inclusion in a static analysis tool. This opportunity for automation means that rules have an implicit requirement for encapsulation in a deterministic definition language so that they can be consumed by automated code scanning software.

As you can see, this set of software security knowledge catalogs offers an excellent foundation for integrating security knowledge into the full SDLC.

The Department of Homeland Security Build Security In Portal[4]

The U.S. Department of Homeland Security is developing a software security portal (along with the Carnegie Mellon Software Engineering Institute and Cigital). This portal aims to provide a common, accessible, well-organized

---

[4]Known in government acronym speak as the DHS BSI PRTL.

Two Example Catalog Entries: A Principle and a Rule

Knowledge Catalog: Principle
Item: Principle of Least Privilege

Description:

> Every program and every user of the system should operate using the least set of privileges necessary to complete the job. Primarily, this principle limits the damage that can result from an accident or error. It also reduces the number of potential interactions among privileged programs to the minimum for correct operation so that unintentional, unwanted, or improper uses of privilege are less likely to occur. Thus, if a question arises related to misuse of a privilege, the number of programs that must be audited is minimized. Put another way, if a mechanism can provide "firewalls," the principle of least privilege provides a rationale for where to install the firewalls. The military security rule of "need-to-know" is an example of this principle.

Concrete example:

> A good software specific example is a mail server which accepts mail from the Internet, and copies the messages into a spool directory; a local server will complete delivery. It needs rights to access the appropriate network port, to create files in the spool directory, and to alter those files (so it can copy the message into the file, rewrite the delivery address if needed, and add the appropriate "Received" lines). It should surrender the right to access the file as soon as it has completed writing the file into the spool directory, because it does not need to access that file again. The server should not be able to access any user's files, or any files other than its own configuration files.

The excerpts above are from the book *Computer Security: Art and Science* by Matt Bishop [Bishop 2003] and are reprinted with permission from Addison-Wesley Professional.

References: [Bishop 2003; Saltzer and Schroeder 1975; Viega and McGraw 2001]

Knowledge Catalog: Rule
Item: Use of `creat()`

Context: C/C++

Attack Category: TOCTOU—time of check–time of use

Description:

> The `creat(char *pathname,mode_t theMode)` function either creates a new file or prepares to rewrite using `pathname` as the filename. The call

`creat(theName,theMode)` is equivalent to

`open(theName,O_WRONLY | O_CREAT | O_TRUNC, theMode)`

If the file exists, the length is truncated to zero and the mode and owner are unchanged.

This function is a problem because it is possible to unintentionally delete a file or enter a potentially unstable race condition.

`creat()` is vulnerable to TOCTOU attacks. Using automated scanning tools, the existence of a call to this function should be flagged regardless of whether a "check" function precedes it.

Method of Attack:

The `creat()` call is a "use" category call that when preceded by a "check" category call can indicate a TOCTOU vulnerability.

Solution:

Consider using a safer set of steps for opening and creating files as outlined in *Building Secure Software* [Viega and McGraw 2001, p. 220]. If this call must be used, create a directory only accessible by the UID of the running program, and only manipulate files in that directory.

Signature: Presence of the `creat()` function.

Code Example:

```
char filename[] = "rightFile.txt";
strcpy(filename,"wrongfile.txt");
creat(filename,theMode);
```

In this case, the contents of the file passed into the `creat()` function are destroyed. If the results of the function call are used before completion, then the results can also be unstable.

References: [Viega and McGraw 2001] and Microsoft Developer Network Library (MSDN)

set of information for practitioners wishing to practice software security. The portal effort is expressly aimed at the problem of encapsulating, expanding, and spreading software security knowledge.

Like this book, the Build Security In (BSI) Software Assurance Initiative seeks to alter the way that software is developed by building security in from the start so that it's less vulnerable to attack. BSI is a project of the Strategic Initiatives Branch of the Department of Homeland Security's National Cyber Security Division (NCSD). NCSD sponsors development and collection of software assurance and software security information that will help software developers and architects create secure systems.

As part of the initiative, a BSI content catalog will be available on the US-CERT Web site <http://buildsecurityin.us-cert.gov/portal/>. This portal is intended for software developers and software development organizations who want information and practical guidance on how to produce secure and reliable software. The catalog is based on the principle that software security is fundamentally a software engineering problem that we must address systematically throughout the SDLC. The catalog contains and links to a broad range of information about best practices, tools, and knowledge.

Figure 11–3 identifies aspects of software assurance currently covered in the catalog. Material is divided into three major categories: best practices, tools, and foundational knowledge. This is an alternative way of organizing software security content with reference to artifacts.

The categorization is the result of merging an earlier collaboration framework with ideas presented in the lifecycle touchpoints diagram that serves as the skeleton of this book. The National Cyber Security Taskforce's report also identified additional practices to produce secure software—see <http://www.cyberpartnership.org/init-soft.html>. The BSI portal will supplement the taskforce's practices with process models and references to appropriate tools, measurement, and other resources.

Although the team creating the portal won't achieve complete content coverage immediately, DHS has launched the portal with some content in each area shown in Figure 11–3. The BSI team will use feedback received on this content (as well as input from industry) to prioritize further work on the catalog.

The portal includes several types of information, categorized for efficient search and utility as follows.

Best practices: A significant portion of the BSI effort is devoted to best practices that can provide the biggest return considering the current best thinking, available technology, and industry practice. This list will grow as more resources become available, more practices are proven, changes occur in the industry environment, and technology progresses. This book covers a number of critical best practices in some detail.

Knowledge: Software defects with security ramifications—including implementation bugs such as buffer overflows and design flaws such as inconsistent error handling—promise to be with us for years. Recurring patterns of software defects leading to vulnerabilities have been identified by

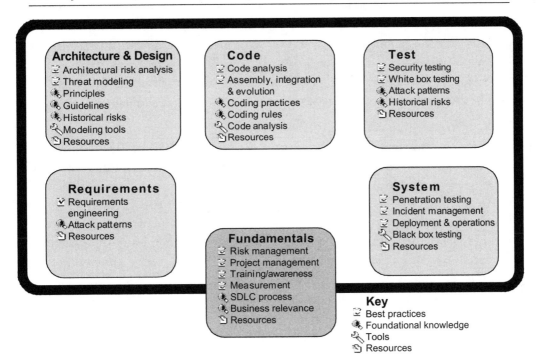

Figure 11–3 The organizing concept for the BSI portal. The alignment of this view shows not only best practices (as Figure 11–2 does) but also knowledge and tools.

long-time software security practitioners, and the BSI team is documenting detailed instructions on how to produce software without these defects. This work shows up in Figure 11–3 as "Guidelines" and "Coding rules."

The BSI team has also identified principles that provide high-level direction for avoiding security problems in design, such as the *principle of least privilege* and the *principle of compartmentalization*. The BSI team is collaborating with the National Institute of Standards and Technology (NIST), the International Organization for Standardization (ISO), and the Institute of Electrical and Electronics Engineers (IEEE) on standards activities focused on developing safe and secure subsets of languages and software assurance style guides.

Tools: The BSI portal includes information about which tools developers and security analysts can use to detect and/or remove common vulnerabilities. Of particular interest are static analysis tools that help developers look for common security-critical problems in source code. The best current commercial tools support languages like Java, CLR, C++, C, and PHP.

Business case: Even with extensive technical content, a business case is required to convince industry to adopt secure software development best practices and educate consumers about the need for software assurance. Therefore, each documented best practice addresses the business case for use of that practice. In addition, we've included an overall business case framework.

Dynamic navigation: The extent to which users will find the content accessible as well as useful will determine how this portal will impact real-world development practices and, thus, overall systems security. The BSI team is making the content approachable in several different ways. For example, a software engineer might use the catalog to determine applicable security guidelines, an architect might use security principles to determine how to design an n-tier application in a secure fashion, and a development team leader might use the information to justify software assurance techniques to management by building a business case. Because the repository will be structured and designed to evolve as well as support usage by a variety of user types, it includes a dynamic navigation interface.

Once practical guidance and reference materials are available for the day-to-day work most development organizations do, the BSI team plans to identify and organize content for practical guidance and reference materials for enterprise-level security concerns.

Although the portal is currently in a nascent stage, the BSI team welcomes feedback on this effort. Information on providing feedback can be found on the portal itself; community involvement and use is crucial to its success.

Knowledge Management Is Ongoing

Efforts to identify and define knowledge constructs for software security are in their infancy. My hope is that a wider population of thought leaders and key practitioners of software security will help to refine and validate this knowledge architecture in an effort to build consensus and move toward standardization. Such discussion and collaboration are critical to the success of software security as a unified practice. As work continues to gain consensus, my colleagues and I will continue to collect real-world examples of content to build out the breadth and depth of catalogs. We will also work to identify further opportunities for directly applying these catalogs in the SDLC.

Software Security Now

There is really no better time to get into software security than now. The field is beginning to explode, mostly due to incredible commercial demand. Turns out that we've built boatloads of pretty bad software over the years, and now that security is being taken more seriously, there's one heck of a cleanup job to do. That's right, we can't solve the problem in "look ahead" mode only. We need to spend some time fixing what we've already built. The cool thing about the touchpoints is that many can be applied just as well to existing software as to new projects. For example, performing an architectural risk analysis on an existing system is well within the realm of possibility.

Getting started in software security is easier than ever. Now there's an entire shelf full of software security books (see Chapter 13), best practices like the touchpoints have been identified, and organizations are looking to build capability. Knowledge managers are creating schemata and taxonomies of software security knowledge, making it much easier than it was just a few short years ago to get started. And the tools don't suck anymore.

If you are a software person interested in security, consider becoming a software security person. We need you!

12 — A Taxonomy of Coding Errors[1]

A horse! A horse! My kingdom for a horse!
KING RICHARD THE THIRD
(WILLIAM SHAKESPEARE)

The purpose of any taxonomy like this one is to help software developers and security practitioners concerned about software understand common coding mistakes that impact security. The goal is to help developers avoid making mistakes and to more readily identify security problems whenever possible. A taxonomy like this one is most usefully applied in an automated tool that can spot problems either in real time (as a developer types into an editor) or at compile time (see Chapter 4). When put to work in a tool, a set of security rules organized according to this taxonomy is a powerful teaching mechanism. Because developers today are by and large unaware of security problems that they can (unknowingly) introduce into code, publication of a taxonomy like this should provide real, tangible benefits to the software security community.

This approach represents a striking alternative to taxonomies of attack patterns (see *Exploiting Software* [Hoglund and McGraw 2004]) or simple-minded collections of specific vulnerabilities (e.g., Mitre's CVE <http://www.cve.mitre.org/>). Attack-based approaches are based on knowing your enemy and assessing the possibility of similar attack. They represent the black hat side of the software security equation. A taxonomy of coding errors is, strangely, more positive in nature. This kind of thing is most useful to the white hat side of the software security world. In the end, both kinds of approaches are valid and necessary.

The goal of this taxonomy is to educate and inform software developers so that they better understand the way their work affects the security of the systems they build. Developers who know this stuff (or at least use a tool

---

[1] Parts of this chapter appeared in original form in *Proceedings of the NIST Workshop on Software Security Assurance Tools, Techniques, and Metrics* coauthored with Katrina Tsipenyuk and Brian Chess [Tsipenyuk, Chess, and McGraw 2005].

that knows this stuff) will be better prepared to build security in than those who don't.

Though this taxonomy is incomplete and imperfect, it provides an important start. One of the problems of all categorization schemes like this is that they don't leave room for new (often surprising) kinds of vulnerabilities. Nor do they take into account higher-level concerns such as the architectural flaws and associated risks described in Chapter 5.[2] Even when it comes to simple security-related coding issues themselves, this taxonomy is not perfect. Coding problems in embedded control software and common bugs in high-assurance software developed using formal methods are poorly represented here, for example.

The bulk of this taxonomy is influenced by the kinds of security coding problems often found in large enterprise software projects. Of course, only coding problems are represented since the purpose of this taxonomy is to feed a static analysis engine with knowledge. The taxonomy as it stands is neither comprehensive nor theoretically complete. Instead it is practical and based on real-world experience. The focus is on collecting common errors and explaining them in such a way that they make sense to programmers.

The taxonomy is expected to evolve and change as time goes by and coding issues (e.g., platform, language of choice, and so on) change. This version of the taxonomy places more emphasis on concrete and specific problems over abstract or theoretical ones. In some sense, the taxonomy may err in favor of omitting "big-picture" errors in favor of covering specific and widespread errors.

The taxonomy is made up of two distinct kinds of sets (which we're stealing from biology). What is called a *phylum* is a type or particular kind of coding error; for example, Illegal Pointer Value is a phylum. What is called a *kingdom* is a collection of phyla that share a common theme. That is, kingdoms are sets of phyla; for example, Input Validation and Representation is a kingdom. Both kingdoms and phyla naturally emerge from a soup of coding rules relevant to enterprise software. For this reason, the taxonomy is likely to be incomplete and may be missing certain coding errors.

In some cases, it is easier and more effective to talk about a category of errors than it is to talk about any particular attack. Though categories are certainly related to attacks, they are not the same as attack patterns.

---

[2]This should really come as no surprise. Static analysis for architectural flaws would require a formal architectural description so that pattern matching could occur. No such architectural description exists. (And before you object, UML doesn't cut it.)

On Simplicity: Seven Plus or Minus Two

I've seen lots of security taxonomies over the years, and they have all shared one unfortunate property—an overabundance of complexity. People are good at keeping track of seven things (plus or minus two).[3] I used this as a hard constraint and attempted to keep the number of kingdoms down to seven (plus one). I present these kingdoms in order of importance to software security.

Without further ado, here are the seven kingdoms (plus one):

1. Input Validation and Representation
2. API Abuse
3. Security Features
4. Time and State
5. Error Handling
6. Code Quality
7. Encapsulation
❖ Environment

A brief explanation of each follows.

Input Validation and Representation

Input validation and representation problems are caused by metacharacters, alternate encodings, and numeric representations. Of course, sometimes people just forget to do any input validation at all. If you do choose to do input validation, use a white list, not a black list [Hoglund and McGraw 2004].

Big problems result from trusting input (too much), including buffer overflows, cross-site scripting attacks, SQL injection, cache poisoning, and basically all of the low-hanging fruit that the script kiddies eat.

API Abuse

An API is a contract between a caller and a callee. The most common forms of API abuse are caused by the caller failing to honor its end of this contract. For example, if a program fails to call `chdir()` after calling `chroot()`, it violates the contract that specifies how to change the active root directory

---

[3]The magic number seven plus or minus two comes from George Miller's classic paper "The Magic Number Seven, Plus or Minus Two," *The Psychological Review,* vol. 63, pp. 81–97, 1956; see <http://www.well.com/user/smalin/miller.html>.

in a secure fashion. Another good example of library abuse is expecting the callee to return trustworthy DNS information to the caller. In this case, the caller abuses the callee API by making certain assumptions about its behavior (that the return value can be used for authentication purposes). Really bad people also violate the caller–callee contract from the other side. For example, if you subclass `SecureRandom` and return a not-so-random value, you're not following the rules.

API abuse categories are very common. Check out Appendix B for a long, boring list of API problems that were built into ITS4 (an early code analysis tool).

Security Features

I've said this before, and I'll say it again: Software security is not security software. All the magic crypto fairy dust in the world won't make you secure. But it's also true that you can drop the ball when it comes to essential security features. Let's say you decide to use SSL to protect traffic across the network, but you really screw things up. Unfortunately, this happens all the time. When I chunk together *security features,* I'm concerned with such topics as authentication, access control, confidentiality, cryptography, privilege management, and all that other stuff on the CISSP exam. This stuff is hard to get right. You in the back, pay attention!

Time and State

Distributed computation is about time and state. That is, in order for more than one component to communicate, state must be shared (somehow), and all that takes time. Playing with time and state is the biggest untapped natural attack resource on the planet right now.

Most programmers anthropomorphize (or, more accurately, only solipsistically ponder) their work. They think about themselves—the single omniscient thread of control manually plodding along, carrying out the entire program in the same way that they themselves would do it if forced to do the job manually. That's really quaint. Modern computers switch between tasks very quickly, and in multi-core, multi-CPU, or distributed systems, two events may take place at *exactly the same time.*[4] Defects rush to fill the gap between the programmer's model of how a program executes and what happens in reality. These defects are related to unexpected

---

[4]Looks like the Police were on to something with that *Synchronicity* album after all.

interactions between threads, processes, time, and information. These interactions happen through shared state: semaphores; variables; the filesystem; the universe; and, basically, anything that can store information.

One day soon, this kingdom will be number one.

Error Handling

Want to break software? Throw some junk at a program and see what errors you cause. Errors are not only a great source of "TMI" from a program, but they are also a source of inconsistent thinking that can be gamed. It gets worse, though. In modern object-oriented systems, the notion of exceptions has reintroduced the banned concept of goto right back on center stage. Alas.

Errors and error handlers represent a class of programming contract. So, in some sense, errors represent the two sides of a special form of API; but security defects related to error handling are so common that they deserve a special kingdom all of their own. As with API Abuse, there are two ways to blow it here: first comes either forgetting to handle errors at all or handling them so roughly that they get all bruised and bloody. The second is producing errors that either give out way too much information (to possible attackers) or are so radioactive that nobody wants to handle them.

Code Quality

Security is a subset of reliability, just as all future TV shows are a subset of monkeys banging on zillions of keyboards. If you are able to completely specify your system and all of its positive and negative security possibilities, then security is a subset of reliability. In the real world, security deserves an entire budget of its own. If you've gotten this far into the book (lucky Chapter 12 plus or minus one), you probably agree that the current state of the art requires some special attention for security. Poor code quality leads to unpredictable behavior. From a user's perspective that often manifests itself as poor usability. For an attacker, bad quality provides an opportunity to stress the system in unexpected ways.

Encapsulation

Encapsulation is about drawing strong boundaries between things and setting up barriers between them. In a Web browser this might mean ensuring that mobile code can't whack your hard drive arbitrarily (bad applet, kennel up). On a Web Services server that might mean differentiating between valid data that have been authenticated and run through the white-list and mystery data that were found sitting on the floor in the men's room under the urinal. Boundaries are critical. Some of the most important boundaries today come between classes with various methods. Trust and trust models require careful and meticulous attention to boundaries. Keep your hands off my stuff!

Environment

Another one of those pesky extra things. Turns out that software runs on a machine with certain bindings and certain connections to the bad, mean universe. Getting outside the software is important (write that down, you heard me say it here). This kingdom is the kingdom of outside→in. It includes all of the stuff that is outside of your code but is still critical to the security of the software you create.

The Phyla

The big list in this section takes the following form:

Kingdom

• Phylum
    <explanatory sentence or two>

   I now introduce the phyla that fit under the seven (plus one) kingdoms. To better understand the relationship between kingdoms and phyla, consider a recently found vulnerability in Adobe Reader 5.0.x for UNIX. The vulnerability is present in a function `UnixAppOpenFilePerform()` that copies user-supplied data into a fixed-size stack buffer using a call to `sprintf()`. If the size of the user-supplied data is greater than the size of the buffer it is being copied into, important information, including the stack pointer, is overwritten. By supplying a malicious PDF document, an attacker can execute arbitrary commands on the target system.

   The attack is possible because of a simple coding error—the absence of a check that makes sure that the size of the user-supplied data is no greater than the size of the destination buffer. Developers will associate this check with a failure to code defensively around the call to `sprintf()`. I classify this coding error according to the attack it enables—"Buffer Overflow." I chose Input Validation and Representation as the name of the kingdom the Buffer Overflow phylum belongs to because the lack of proper input validation is the root cause making the attack possible.

The coding errors represented by phyla can all be detected by static source code analysis tools. Source code analysis offers developers an opportunity to get quick feedback about the code they write. I strongly advocate educating developers about coding errors by having them use a source code analysis tool (see Chapter 4).

1. Input Validation and Representation

- **Buffer Overflow**
  Writing outside the bounds of allocated memory can corrupt data, crash the program, or cause the execution of an attack payload.
- **Command Injection**
  Executing commands from an untrusted source or in an untrusted environment can cause an application to execute malicious commands on behalf of an attacker.
- **Cross-Site Scripting**
  Sending unvalidated data to a Web browser can result in the browser executing malicious code (usually scripts).
- **Format String**
  Allowing an attacker to control a function's format string may result in a buffer overflow.
- **HTTP Response Splitting**
  Writing unvalidated data into an HTTP header allows an attacker to specify the entirety of the HTTP response rendered by the browser.
- **Illegal Pointer Value**
  This function can return a pointer to memory outside of the buffer to be searched. Subsequent operations on the pointer may have unintended consequences.
- **Integer Overflow**
  Not accounting for integer overflow can result in logic errors or buffer overflows.
- **Log Forging**
  Writing unvalidated user input into log files can allow an attacker to forge log entries or inject malicious content into logs.
- **Path Traversal**
  Allowing user input to control paths used by the application may enable an attacker to access otherwise protected files.
- **Process Control**
  Executing commands or loading libraries from an untrusted source or in an untrusted environment can cause an application to execute malicious commands (and payloads) on behalf of an attacker.

- **Resource Injection**
  Allowing user input to control resource identifiers may enable an attacker to access or modify otherwise protected system resources.
- **Setting Manipulation**
  Allowing external control of system settings can disrupt service or cause an application to behave in unexpected ways.
- **SQL Injection**
  Constructing a dynamic SQL statement with user input may allow an attacker to modify the statement's meaning or to execute arbitrary SQL commands.
- **String Termination Error**
  Relying on proper string termination may result in a buffer overflow.
- **Struts: Duplicate Validation Forms**
  Multiple validation forms with the same name indicate that validation logic is not up to date.
- **Struts: Erroneous `validate()` Method**
  The validator form defines a `validate()` method but fails to call `super.validate()`.
- **Struts: Form Bean Does Not Extend Validation Class**
  All Struts forms should extend a Validator class.
- **Struts: Form Field without Validator**
  Every field in a form should be validated in the corresponding validation form.
- **Struts: Plug-in Framework Not in Use**
  Use the Struts Validator to prevent vulnerabilities that result from unchecked input.
- **Struts: Unused Validation Form**
  An unused validation form indicates that validation logic is not up to date.
- **Struts: Unvalidated Action Form**
  Every action form must have a corresponding validation form.
- **Struts: Validator Turned Off**
  This action form mapping disables the form's `validate()` method.
- **Struts: Validator without Form Field**
  Validation fields that do not appear in the forms they are associated with indicate that the validation logic is out of date.
- **Unsafe JNI**
  Improper use of the Java Native Interface (JNI) can render Java applications vulnerable to security flaws in other languages. Language-based encapsulation is broken.

- **Unsafe Reflection**
An attacker may be able to create unexpected control flow paths through the application, potentially bypassing security checks.
- **XML Validation**
Failure to enable validation when parsing XML gives an attacker the opportunity to supply malicious input.

2. API Abuse

- **Dangerous Function**
Functions that cannot be used safely should never be used.
- **Directory Restriction**
Improper use of the `chroot()` system call may allow attackers to escape a `chroot` jail.
- **Heap Inspection**
Do not use `realloc()` to resize buffers that store sensitive information.
- **J2EE Bad Practices: `getConnection()`**
The J2EE standard forbids the direct management of connections.
- **J2EE Bad Practices: Sockets**
Socket-based communication in Web applications is prone to error.
- **Often Misused: Authentication**
(See the complete entry on page 290 in this chapter.)
- **Often Misused: Exception Handling**
A dangerous function can throw an exception, potentially causing the program to crash.
- **Often Misused: Path Manipulation**
Passing an inadequately sized output buffer to a path manipulation function can result in a buffer overflow.
- **Often Misused: Privilege Management**
Failure to adhere to the principle of least privilege amplifies the risk posed by other vulnerabilities.
- **Often Misused: String Manipulation**
Functions that manipulate strings encourage buffer overflows.
- **Unchecked Return Value**
Ignoring a method's return value can cause the program to overlook unexpected states and conditions.

3. Security Features

- **Insecure Randomness**
Standard pseudo-random number generators cannot withstand cryptographic attacks.

- **Least Privilege Violation**
  The elevated privilege level required to perform operations such as `chroot()` should be dropped immediately after the operation is performed.

- **Missing Access Control**
  The program does not perform access control checks in a consistent manner across all potential execution paths.

- **Password Management**
  Storing a password in plaintext may result in a system compromise.

- **Password Management: Empty Password in Configuration File**
  Using an empty string as a password is insecure.

- **Password Management: Hard-Coded Password**
  Hard-coded passwords may compromise system security in a way that cannot be easily remedied.

- **Password Management: Password in Configuration File**
  Storing a password in a configuration file may result in system compromise.

- **Password Management: Weak Cryptography**
  Obscuring a password with trivial encoding does not protect the password.

- **Privacy Violation**
  Mishandling private information, such as customer passwords or social security numbers, can compromise user privacy and is often illegal.

4. Time and State

- **Deadlock**
  Inconsistent locking discipline can lead to deadlock.

- **Failure to Begin a New Session upon Authentication**
  Using the same session identifier across an authentication boundary allows an attacker to hijack authenticated sessions.

- **File Access Race Condition: TOCTOU**
  The window of time between when a file property is checked and when the file is used can be exploited to launch a privilege escalation attack.

- **Insecure Temporary File**
  Creating and using insecure temporary files can leave application and system data vulnerable to attack.

- **J2EE Bad Practices: `System.exit()`**
  A Web application should not attempt to shut down its container.

- **J2EE Bad Practices: Threads**
  Thread management in a Web application is forbidden in some circumstances and is always highly error prone.
- **Signal Handling Race Conditions**
  Signal handlers may change shared state relied on by other signal handlers or application code causing unexpected behavior.

5. Error Handling

- **Catch `NullPointerException`**
  Catching `NullPointerException` should not be used as an alternative to programmatic checks to prevent dereferencing a null pointer.
- **Empty Catch Block**
  Ignoring exceptions and other error conditions may allow an attacker to induce unexpected behavior unnoticed.
- **Overly Broad Catch Block**
  Catching overly broad exceptions promotes complex error-handling code that is more likely to contain security vulnerabilities.
- **Overly Broad Throws Declaration**
  Throwing overly broad exceptions promotes complex error-handling code that is more likely to contain security vulnerabilities.
- **Unchecked Return Value**
  Ignoring a method's return value can cause the program to overlook unexpected states and conditions.

6. Code Quality

- **Double Free**
  Calling `free()` twice on the same memory address can lead to a buffer overflow.
- **Inconsistent Implementations**
  Functions with inconsistent implementations across operating systems and operating system versions cause portability problems.
- **Memory Leak**
  Memory is allocated but never freed, leading to resource exhaustion.
- **Null Dereference**
  The program can potentially dereference a null pointer, thereby raising a `NullPointerException`.
- **Obsolete**
  The use of deprecated or obsolete functions may indicate neglected code.

- **Undefined Behavior**
  The behavior of this function is undefined unless its control parameter is set to a specific value.
- **Uninitialized Variable**
  The program can potentially use a variable before it has been initialized.
- **Unreleased Resource**
  The program can potentially fail to release a system resource.
- **Use After Free**
  Referencing memory after it has been freed can cause a program to crash.

7. Encapsulation

- **Comparing Classes by Name**
  Comparing classes by name can lead a program to treat two classes as the same when they actually differ.
- **Data Leaking Between Users**
  Data can "bleed" from one session to another through member variables of singleton objects, such as servlets, and objects from a shared pool.
- **Leftover Debug Code**
  Debug code can create unintended entry points in an application.
- **Mobile Code: Object Hijack**
  Attackers can use cloneable objects to create new instances of an object without calling its constructor.
- **Mobile Code: Use of Inner Class**
  Inner classes are translated into classes that are accessible at package scope and may expose code that the programmer intended to keep private to attackers.
- **Mobile Code: Non-Final Public Field**
  Non-final public variables can be manipulated by an attacker to inject malicious values.
- **Private Array-Typed Field Returned from a Public Method**
  The contents of a private array may be altered unexpectedly through a reference returned from a public method.
- **Public Data Assigned to Private Array-Typed Field**
  Assigning public data to a private array is equivalent to giving public access to the array.
- **System Information Leak**
  Revealing system data or debugging information helps an adversary learn about the system and form an attack plan.

- **Trust Boundary Violation**
  Commingling trusted and untrusted data in the same data structure encourages programmers to mistakenly trust unvalidated data.

*. Environment

- **ASP .NET Misconfiguration: Creating Debug Binary**
  Debugging messages help attackers learn about the system and plan a form of attack.
- **ASP .NET Misconfiguration: Missing Custom Error Handling**
  An ASP .NET application must enable custom error pages in order to prevent attackers from mining information from the framework's built-in responses.
- **ASP .NET Misconfiguration: Password in Configuration File**
  Do not hardwire passwords into your software.
- **Insecure Compiler Optimization**
  Improperly scrubbing sensitive data from memory can compromise security.
- **J2EE Misconfiguration: Insecure Transport**
  The application configuration should ensure that SSL is used for all access-controlled pages.
- **J2EE Misconfiguration: Insufficient Session-ID Length**
  Session identifiers should be at least 128 bits long to prevent brute-force session guessing.
- **J2EE Misconfiguration: Missing Error Handling**
  A Web application must define a default error page for 404 errors and 500 errors and to catch `java.lang.Throwable` exceptions to prevent attackers from mining information from the application container's built-in error response.
- **J2EE Misconfiguration: Unsafe Bean Declaration**
  Entity beans should not be declared remote.
- **J2EE Misconfiguration: Weak Access Permissions**
  Permission to invoke EJB methods should not be granted to the `ANYONE` role.

More Phyla Needed

This taxonomy includes coding errors that occur in a variety of programming languages. The most important among them are C and C++, Java, and the .NET family (including C# and ASP). Some of the phyla are language-specific because the types of errors they represent apply only to specific languages. One example is the Double Free phylum. This phylum identifies incorrect usage of low-level memory routines and is specific to C and C++ because neither Java nor the managed portions of the .NET languages expose low-level memory APIs.

In addition to being language-specific, some phyla are framework-specific. For example, the Struts phyla apply only to the Struts framework, and the J2EE phyla are only applicable in the context of the J2EE applications. Log Forging, on the other hand, is a more general phylum.

The phylum list as it exists is certainly incomplete, but it is adaptable to changes in trends and discoveries of new defects that are bound to happen over time. The current list reflects a focus on finding and classifying security-related defects rather than more general quality or reliability issues. The Code Quality kingdom could potentially contain many more phyla, but the ones that are currently included are the most likely to affect software security directly. Finally, classifying errors that are most important to real-world enterprise developers is the most important goal of this taxonomy—most of the information here is derived from the literature, various colleagues, and hundreds of customers.

A Complete Example

Each phylum in the taxonomy is associated with a nice number of clear, fleshed-out examples similar in nature to the rules described in Chapter 4. An example of the kingdom API Abuse in the phylum Often Misused: Authentication is included here to give you some idea of the form that a complete entry takes. For more, see <http://vulncat.fortifysoftware.com>.

Often Misused: Authentication

(getlogin)

Abstract
The getlogin() function is easy to spoof. Do not rely on the name it returns.

Explanation
The getlogin() function is supposed to return a string containing the name of the user currently logged in at the terminal, but an attacker can cause getlogin() to return the name of any user who is logged in to the

---

machine. Do not rely on the name returned by `getlogin()` when making security decisions.

Example 1: The following code relies on `getlogin()` to determine whether or not a user is trusted. It is easily subverted.

```
pwd = getpwnam(getlogin());
if (isTrustedGroup(pwd->pw_gid)) {
allow();
} else {
deny();
}
```

Recommendations
You should rely on a user's ID, not the username, for identification. The previous example can be rewritten as:

```
pwd = getpwuid(getuid());
if (isTrustedGroup(pwd->pw_gid)) {
allow();
} else {
deny();
}
```

If multiple users are allowed to share the same user ID (a dubious proposition from a security standpoint), a bit more care is required. The following example checks to see whether the username returned by `getlogin()` matches the username associated with the user ID; the check ensures that if two users share the same ID, one user cannot act on behalf of the other.

```
pwd = getpwuid(getuid());
pwdName = pwd->pw_name;
/* Bail out if the name associated with the uid does not
match the name associated with the terminal. */
if (strncmp(pwdName, getlogin(), MAX_NAM_LEN)) {
printf("shared uid not supported\n");
deny();
return;
}
if (isTrustedGroup(pwd->pw_gid)) {
allow();
```

Continued

```
} else {
deny();
}
```

Note: If the process is not being run from a terminal, `getlogin()` returns `NULL`.

Lists, Piles, and Collections

The idea of collecting and organizing information about computer security vulnerabilities has a long history (see the box Academic Literature). More recently, a number of practitioners have developed "top ten" lists and other related collections based on experience in the field. The taxonomy introduced here negotiates a middle ground between rigorous academic studies and ad hoc collections based on experience.

Two of the most popular and useful lists are the "19 Sins" and the "OWASP top ten." The first list, at one month old as I write this, is carefully described in the new book *19 Deadly Sins of Software Security* [Howard, LeBlanc, and Viega 2005]. The second is the "OWASP Top Ten Most Critical Web Application Security Vulnerabilities" available on the Web at <http://www.owasp.org/documentation/topten.html>. Both of these collections, though extremely useful and applicable, share one unfortunate property—an overabundance of complexity. My hard constraint to stick to seven things helps cut through the complexity.

By discussing the 19 Sins and OWASP top ten lists with respect to the taxonomy here, I hope to illustrate and emphasize why simplicity is essential to any taxonomy. The main limitation of both lists is that they mix specific types of errors and vulnerability classes and talk about them all at the same level of abstraction. The 19 Sins include both "Buffer Overflows" and "Failing to Protect Network Traffic" categories at the same level, even though the first is a very specific coding error, while the second is a class comprised of various kinds of errors. Similarly, OWASP's top ten includes "Cross Site Scripting (XSS) Flaws" and "Insecure Configuration Management" at the same level. This is a serious problem that leads to confusion among practitioners.

My classification scheme consists of two hierarchical levels: kingdoms and phyla. Kingdoms represent classes of errors, while the phyla that

Academic Literature

All scientific disciplines benefit from a method for organizing their topic of study, and software security is no different. The value of a classification scheme is indisputable. A taxonomy is necessary in order to create a common vocabulary and an understanding of the many diverse ways computer security fails. The problem of defining a taxonomy has been of great interest since the mid-1970s. Several classification schemes have been proposed since then [Bishop 2003]. An excellent Web resource at UC Davis can be found at <http://isis.cs.ucdavis.edu/vuln/links.php>.

Vulnerabilities

One of the first studies of computer security and privacy was the RISOS (Research into Secure Operating Systems) project [Abbott et al. 1976]. RISOS proposed and described seven categories of operating system security defects. The purpose of the project was to understand security problems in existing operating systems, including MULTICS, TENEX, TOPS-10, GECOS, OS/MVT, SDS-940, and EXEC-8, and to determine ways to enhance the security of these systems.

The categories proposed in the RISOS project include the following:

- Incomplete Parameter Validation
- Inconsistent Parameter Validation
- Implicit Sharing of Privileges/Confidential Data
- Asynchronous Validation/Inadequate Serialization
- Inadequate Identification/Authentication/Authorization
- Violable Prohibition/Limit
- Exploitable Logic Error

The study shows that a small number of fundamental defects recur in different contexts.

The objective of the Protection Analysis (PA) project was to enable anybody (with or without any knowledge about computer security) to discover security errors in the system by using a pattern-directed approach [Bisbey and Hollingworth 1978]. The idea was to use formalized patterns to search for corresponding errors. The PA project was the first project to explore automation of security defect detection. However, the procedure for reducing defects to abstract patterns was not comprehensive, and the technique could not be properly automated. The database of vulnerabilities collected in the study was never published.

Continued

Landwehr, Bull, and McDermott classified each vulnerability from three perspectives: genesis (how the problem entered the system), time (at which point in the production cycle the problem entered the system), and location (where in the system the problem is manifest) [Landwehr, Bull, and McDermott 1993]. Defects by genesis were broken down into intentional and inadvertent, where the intentional class was further broken down into malicious and non-malicious. Defects by time of introduction were broken down into development, maintenance, and operation, where the development class was further broken down into design, source code, and object code. Defects by location were broken down into software and hardware, where the software class was further broken down into operating system, support, and application.

The advantage of this type of hierarchical classification is the convenience of identifying strategies to remedy security problems. For example, if most security issues are introduced inadvertently, increasing resources devoted to code reviews becomes an effective way of increasing the security of the system. The biggest disadvantage of this scheme is the inability to classify some existing vulnerabilities. For example, if it is not known how the vulnerability entered the system, it cannot be classified by genesis at all.

The schemes discussed here have several limitations in common. One of them is the breadth of the categories, which makes classification ambiguous. In some cases, one issue can be classified in more than one category. The category names, while useful to some groups of researchers, are too generic to be quickly intuitive to a developer in the context of day-to-day work. Additionally, these schemes focus mostly on operating system security problems and do not classify the ones associated with user-level software security. Furthermore, these taxonomies mix implementation-level and design-level defects and are not consistent about defining the categories with respect to the cause or effect of the problem.

Attacks

A good list of attack classes is provided by Cheswick, Bellovin, and Rubin [2003]. The list includes the following:

- Stealing Passwords
- Social Engineering
- Bugs and Back Doors
- Authentication Failures
- Protocol Failures
- Information Leakage

- Exponential Attacks—Viruses and Worms
- Denial-of-Service Attacks
- Botnets
- Active Attacks

A thorough description with examples is provided for each class. These attack classes are applicable to a wide range of software, including user-level enterprise software. This fact distinguishes the list from other classification schemes. The classes are simple and intuitive. However, this list defines attack classes rather than categories of common coding errors that cause these attacks.

A similar but more thorough list of attack patterns is introduced in *Exploiting Software* [Hoglund and McGraw 2004]. Attack-based approaches are based on knowing your enemy and assessing the possibility of similar attack. They represent the black hat side of the software security equation. A taxonomy of coding errors is, strangely, more positive in nature. This kind of thing is most useful to the white hat side of the software security world. In the end, both kinds of approaches are valid and necessary.

Toward a Taxonomy

The classification scheme proposed by Aslam is the only precise scheme discussed here [Aslam 1995]. In this scheme, each vulnerability belongs to exactly one category. The decision procedure for classifying an error consists of a set of questions for each vulnerability category. Aslam's system is well defined and offers a simple way for identifying defects by similarity. Another contribution of Aslam's taxonomy is that it draws on software fault studies to develop its categories. However, it focuses exclusively on implementation issues in the UNIX operating system and offers categories that are still too broad for my purpose.

The most recent classification scheme on the scene is the unpublished PLOVER (Preliminary List of Vulnerability Examples for Researchers) project [Christey 2005]. Twenty-eight main categories that comprise almost three hundred subcategories put Christey's classification scheme at the opposite end of the ambiguity spectrum than mine. Not surprisingly, the vulnerability categories are much more specific than in any of the taxonomies discussed here.

PLOVER is an extension of Christey's earlier work in assigning CVE (Common Vulnerabilities and Exposures) names to publicly known vulnerabilities. An attempt to draw parallels between theoretical attacks and vulnerabilities known in practice is an important contribution and a big step forward from most of the earlier schemes.

comprise the kingdoms represent collections of specific errors. Even though the structure of my classification scheme is different from the structure of the 19 Sins and OWASP top ten lists, the categories that comprise these lists can be easily mapped to the kingdoms (as I show next).

Nineteen Sins Meet Seven Kingdoms

1. Input Validation and Representation
Sin: Buffer Overflows
Sin: Command Injection
Sin: Cross-Site Scripting
Sin: Format String Problems
Sin: Integer Range Errors
Sin: SQL Injection

2. API Abuse
Sin: Trusting Network Address Information

3. Security Features
Sin: Failing to Protect Network Traffic
Sin: Failing to Store and Protect Data
Sin: Failing to Use Cryptographically Strong Random Numbers
Sin: Improper File Access
Sin: Improper Use of SSL
Sin: Use of Weak Password-Based Systems
Sin: Unauthenticated Key Exchange

4. Time and State
Sin: Signal Race Conditions
Sin: Use of "Magic" URLs and Hidden Forms

5. Error Handling
Sin: Failure to Handle Errors

6. Code Quality
Sin: Poor Usability

7. Encapsulation
Sin: Information Leakage

*. Environment

The 19 Sins are an extremely important collection of software security problems at many different levels. By fitting them into the seven kingdoms, a cleaner organization begins to emerge.

Seven Kingdoms and the OWASP Ten

Top ten lists are appealing, especially since the cultural phenomenon that is David Letterman. The OWASP top ten list garners much attention because it is short and also useful. Once again, a level-blending problem is apparent in the OWASP list, but this is easily resolved by appealing to the seven kingdoms.

1. **Input Validation and Representation**
   OWASP A1: Unvalidated Input
   OWASP A4: Cross-Site Scripting (XSS) Flaws
   OWASP A5: Buffer Overflows
   OWASP A6: Injection Flaws

2. **API Abuse**

3. **Security Features**
   OWASP A2: Broken Access Control
   OWASP A8: Insecure Storage

4. **Time and State**
   OWASP A3: Broken Authentication and Session Management

5. **Error Handling**
   OWASP A7: Improper Error Handling

6. **Code Quality**
   OWASP A9: Denial of Service

7. **Encapsulation**

*. **Environment**
   OWASP A10: Insecure Configuration Management

Go Forth (with the Taxonomy) and Prosper

The seven pernicious kingdoms are a simple, effective organizing tool for software security coding errors. With over 60 clearly defined phyla, the taxonomy here is both powerful and useful. Descriptions of the phyla can be found on the Web at <http://vulncat.fortifysoftware.com>.

The classification scheme here is designed to organize security rules and thus be of help to software developers who are concerned with writing secure code and being able to automate detection of security defects. These goals make the taxonomy:

- Simple
- Intuitive to a developer
- Practical (rather than theoretical and comprehensive)
- Amenable to automatic identification of errors with static analysis tools
- Adaptable with respect to changes in trends that happen over time

Taxonomy work is ongoing. Your help is requested.

Taxonomy Work Is Ongoing

The taxonomy presented here results from the good work of Brian Chess and the Security Research Group at Fortify Software. This work was helped along immeasurably by Yekaterina Tsipenyuk and Jacob West. Further refinement and evolution is necessary. Please send feedback regarding this taxonomy to brian@fortifysoftware.com.

13

Annotated Bibliography and References

*Those who cannot remember the past
are condemned to repeat it.*

GEORGE SANTAYANA

Annotated Bibliography: An Emerging Literature

What follows is a noncomprehensive bibliography of software security publications. This list is heavily biased toward recent publications. The references here can serve as a springboard to the wider literature. Below each reference is a brief description of the work and its place in the literature. All opinions are mine.

The bibliography is divided into three sections. First is a very short list of required reading (the top five list for software security). Second is a complete list of all references cited in this book. Third is a list of other important software security references not otherwise mentioned in this book. There are overlaps only between the required reading list and the other two lists.

Required Reading: The Top Five

This is a completely biased list of the top five publications to read in software security (presented in alphabetical order). If you have time to read only a handful of stuff, read everything on this list first.

1. [**Anderson 2001**] Ross Anderson. *Security Engineering: A Guide to Building Dependable Distributed Systems*. John Wiley and Sons, New York, 2001. <http://www.cl.cam.ac.uk/~rja14/book.html>

   This is probably the best security book on the market. If you can buy only one other book relevant to software security, buy this one. *Security Engineering* is about building systems that remain dependable in the face of malicious attack, unintentional error, or accident. Anderson's treatment focuses on the tools, processes, and methods needed to design, implement, and test complete systems and to adapt existing systems as their environment evolves.

2. **[Hoglund and McGraw 2004]** Greg Hoglund and Gary McGraw. *Exploiting Software: How to Break Code*. Addison-Wesley, Boston, MA, 2004. <http://www.exploitingsoftware.com>

   One of my three software security books. *Exploiting Software* goes way beyond the script kiddie hacking basics by describing the software attacker's toolkit and how it is commonly used by bad guys. This book includes hard-core information on real attacks against real software. It also introduces the notion of attack patterns.

3. **[Howard and LeBlanc 2003]** Michael Howard and David LeBlanc. *Writing Secure Code*, 2nd edition. Microsoft Press, Redmond, WA, 2003. Mike Howard's blog serves as the de facto site for this book <http://blogs.msdn.com/michael_howard/>.

   Writing Secure Code is a very good treatment of software security with an emphasis on code and implementation problems (bugs). The introduction of the STRIDE model is particularly noteworthy. If you're serious about software security, you need to read this book.

4. **[Saltzer and Schroeder 1975]** Jerome Saltzer and Michael Schroeder. "The Protection of Information in Computer Systems," *Proceedings of the IEEE* 9(63), September 1975, pp. 1278–1308. <http://web.mit.edu/Saltzer/www/publications/protection/>

   An absolutely classic paper that everyone cites but few actually read. This paper introduces and discusses a number of central security principles. The paper itself is a pithy, short, essential read. (By the way, a treatment of the principles idea related to software security can be found in *Building Secure Software*.)

5. **[Viega and McGraw 2001]** John Viega and Gary McGraw. *Building Secure Software: How to Avoid Security Problems the Right Way*. Addison-Wesley, Boston, MA, 2001. <http://www.buildingsecuresoftware.com/>

   One of my three software security books. *Building Secure Software* launched the field of software security. Though there is plenty of code in *BSS,* the book itself is really a philosophical treatment introducing the idea of building security in.

References Cited in *Software Security: Building Security In*

A complete alphabetical listing of all references in this book, including those references mentioned in footnotes.

[Abbott et al. 1976] Robert Abbott, Janet Chin, James Donnelley, William Konigsford, Shigeru Tokubo, and Douglas Webb. "Security Analysis and Enhancements of Computer Operating Systems," NBSIR 76-1041, National Bureau of Standards, ICST, Washington, DC, 1976.

> Abbott introduces the RISOS taxonomy of computer security problems related to operating systems. Very early work in understanding security vulnerabilities.

[Alexander 2003] Ian Alexander. "Misuse Cases: Use Cases with Hostile Intent," *IEEE Software* 20(1), January/February 2003, pp. 58–66.

> Alexander advocates using misuse and use cases together to conduct threat and hazard analysis during requirements analysis.

[Anderson 2001] Ross Anderson. *Security Engineering: A Guide to Building Dependable Distributed Systems.* John Wiley and Sons, New York, 2001.

> See entry in *Required Reading.*

[Arkin, Stender, and McGraw 2005] Brad Arkin, Scott Stender, and Gary McGraw. "Software Penetration Testing," *IEEE Security & Privacy* 3(1), 2005, pp. 84–87.

> One of the original BSI articles from *IEEE Security & Privacy* magazine that sparked this book. See <http://www.computer.org/security> for subscription information.

[Ashcraft and Engler 2002] Ken Ashcraft and Dawson Engler. "Using Programmer-Written Compiler Extensions to Catch Security Holes," *Proceedings of the IEEE Symposium on Security and Privacy,* Oakland, CA, IEEE Computer Society Press, 2002, pp. 131–147.

> Engler's work on static analysis is now being commercialized by Coverity. This academic paper describes the bug-finding technology developed at UC Berkeley.

[Aslam 1995] Taimur Aslam. "A Taxonomy of Security Faults in the UNIX Operating System." Master's Thesis, Purdue University, 1995.

> An early taxonomy focused on UNIX security problems.

[Ball and Rajamani 2001] Tom Ball and Sriram Rajamani. "Automatically Validating Temporal Safety Properties of Interfaces," *Proceedings of the 8th International SPIN Workshop on Model Checking of Software,* Springer Lecture Notes in Computer Science, vol. 2057, 2001, pp. 103–122.

> The SLAM model checker uses predicate abstraction to examine program safety properties. Tom Ball now runs a research group at Microsoft.

[Barnum and McGraw 2005] Sean Barnum and Gary McGraw. "Knowledge for Software Security," *IEEE Security & Privacy* 3(2), 2005, pp. 74–78.

> One of the original BSI articles from *IEEE Security & Privacy* magazine that sparked this book. See <http://www.computer.org/security> for subscription information.

[Bisbey and Hollingworth 1978] Richard Bisbey and Dennis Hollingworth. "Protection Analysis Project Final Report," ISI/RR-78-13, DTIC AD A056816, USC/Information Sciences Institute, 1978.

> A description of the Protection Analysis (PA) project meant to enable anybody (with or without any knowledge about computer security) to discover security errors in a system by using a pattern-directed approach. Formalized patterns were used to search for corresponding errors. The PA project was the first project to explore automation of security defect detection.

[Bishop 2003] Matt Bishop. *Computer Security: Art and Science.* Addison-Wesley, Boston, MA, 2003.

> A decent though overly formal textbook on computer security. Matt Bishop is one of the pioneers of software security. Echoes of his philosophy of building security in are evident in this book.

[Bishop and Dilger 1996] Matt Bishop and Mike Dilger. "Checking for Race Conditions in File Accesses," *Computing Systems* 9(2), 1996, pp. 131–152.

> Matt Bishop's seminal paper explains a simple static analysis tool for detecting time-of-check–time-of-use (TOCTOU) defects.

[Bush, Pincus, and Sielaff 2000] William Bush, Jonathan Pincus, and David Sielaff. "A Static Analyzer for Finding Dynamic Programming Errors," *Software Practice and Experience,* 30(7), June 2000, pp. 775–802.

> The only paper published about Prefix, the complicated precursor to Prefast invented by Jon Pincus and used internally at Microsoft for many years.

[Cavusoglu, Mishra, and Raghunathan 2002] Huseyin Cavusoglu, Birendra Mishra, and Srinivasan Raghunathan. "The Effect of Internet Security Breach Announcements on Market Value of Breached Firms and Internet Security Developers," Technical Report from the University of Texas at Dallas School of Management, February 2002.

> A minor academic study indicating a link between security events and negative stock price movements.

[**Chen and Wagner 2002**] Hao Chen and David Wagner. "MOPS: An Infrastructure for Examining Security Properties of Software," *Proceedings of the 9th ACM Conference on Computer and Communications Security (CCS2002)*, Washington, DC, ACM Press, 2002, pp. 235–244.

> MOPS takes a model-checking approach to look for violations of temporal safety properties. Developers can model their own safety properties, and some have used the tool to check for privilege management errors, incorrect construction of chroot jails, file access race conditions, and ill-conceived temporary file schemes.

[**Chess 2002**] Brian Chess. "Improving Computer Security Using Extended Static Checking," *Proceedings of the IEEE Symposium on Security and Privacy*, Oakland, CA, IEEE Computer Society Press, 2002, pp. 118–130.

> The Eau Claire tool uses a theorem prover to create a general specification-checking framework for C programs. It can help find common security problems like buffer overflows, file access race conditions, and format string bugs. Developers can use specifications to ensure that function implementations behave as expected.

[**Chess and McGraw 2004**] Brian Chess and Gary McGraw. "Static Analysis for Security," *IEEE Security & Privacy* 2(6), 2004, pp. 76–79.

> One of the original BSI articles from *IEEE Security & Privacy* magazine that sparked this book. See <http://www.computer.org/security> for subscription information.

[**Cheswick and Bellovin 1994**] Bill Cheswick and Steve Bellovin. *Firewalls and Internet Security*, 1st edition. Addison-Wesley, Reading, MA, 1994.

> The very first edition of a classic security tome. See the next entry for up-to-date information; especially note that the new edition is coauthored with Avi Rubin.

[**Cheswick, Bellovin, and Rubin 2003**] Bill Cheswick, Steve Bellovin, and Avi Rubin. *Firewalls and Internet Security*, 3rd edition. Addison-Wesley, Boston, MA, 2003.

> A classic computer security book, now available in a revised and updated edition featuring Avi Rubin as coauthor.

[**Christey 2005**] Steven Christey. "PLOVER—Preliminary List of Vulnerability Examples for Researchers," NIST Draft, August 2005 (unpublished).

> An unpublished attempt to categorize the CVE vulnerabilities into some kind of bottom-up taxonomy.

[Das, Lerner, and Seigle 2002] Manuvir Das, Sorin Lerner, and Mark Seigle. "ESP: Path-Sensitive Program Verification in Polynomial Time," *Proceedings of the ACM Conference on Programming Language Design and Implementation (PLDI2002),* Berlin, Germany, ACM Press, 2002, pp. 57–68.

> The static analysis tool ESP is a large-scale property verification approach.

[Davis et al. 2004] Noopur Davis, Samual Redwine, Gerlinde Zibuski, Gary McGraw, and Watts Humphrey. "Summary of National Cyber Security Summit Subgroup Report: Processes for Producing Secure Software." April 2004.

> A committee-produced paper describing the software security problem used to set national policy. The touchpoints were prominently included in this paper. The complete report can be found here: <http://www.cyberpartnership.org>.

[Engler et al. 2000] Dawson Engler, Benjamin Chelf, Andy Chou, and Seth Hallem. "Checking System Rules Using System-Specific, Programmer-Written Compiler Extensions," *Proceedings of the Symposium on Operating System Design and Implementation (OSDI),* San Diego, CA, USENIX Association, October 2000.

> This paper introduces a set of small extensions that were used to find roughly 500 bugs in Linux, OpenBSD, and Xok. The engine behind Coverity is described in this paper.

[Evans et al. 1994] David Evans, John Guttag, Jim Horning, and Yang Meng Tan. "LCLint: A Tool for Using Specifications to Check Code," *Proceedings of the SIGSOFT Symposium on the Foundations of Software Engineering,* New Orleans, LA, ACM Press, December 1994, pp. 87–96.

> LCLint is introduced, a simple tool that accepts ANSI C programs and some annotations to find and report inconsistencies.

[Fagan 1976] Michael Fagan. "Design and Code Inspections to Reduce Errors in Program Development," *IBM Systems Journal* 15(3), 1976, pp. 182–211.

> The seminal work on manual code inspection.

[Farmer and Venema 2005] Dan Farmer and Wietse Venema. *Forensic Discovery.* Addison-Wesley, Boston, MA, 2005.

> Dan Farmer and Wietse Venema (purveyors of SATAN and other great security stuff) recently released this long-awaited, excellent new tome on forensics.

[Foster, Terauchi, and Aiken 2002] Jeffrey Foster, Tachio Terauchi, and Alex Aiken. "Flow-Sensitive Type Qualifiers," *Proceedings of the ACM Conference on Programming Language Design and Implementation (PLDI2002)*, Berlin, Germany, ACM Press, 2002, pp. 1–12.

> One of the many papers on CQual. Inspired by Perl's taint mode, CQual uses type qualifiers to perform a taint analysis, which detects format string vulnerabilities in C programs. CQual requires a programmer to annotate a few variables as either tainted or untainted and then uses type inference rules (along with pre-annotated system libraries) to propagate the qualifiers. Once the qualifiers are propagated, the system can detect format string vulnerabilities by type checking.

[Geer 1998] Dan Geer. "Risk Management Is Where the Money Is," The Digital Commerce Society of Boston, Boston, MA, November 1998. This paper has been widely reprinted, including RISKS 20.06 <http://catless.ncl. ac.uk/Risks/20.06.html>.

> An early discussion of the criticality of risk management to security. This paper provides a reasonable overview and history.

[Geer et al. 2003] Dan Geer, Rebecca Bace, Peter Gutmann, Perry Metzger, Charles Pfleeger, John Quarterman, and Bruce Schneier. "Cyber*In*security: The Cost of Monopoly, How the Dominance of Microsoft's Products Poses a Risk to Security." Published on the Web by the Computer & Communications Industry Association (CCIA), September 2003. <http://www.ccianet. org/papers/cyberinsecurity.pdf>

> The famous "monoculture" paper that caused Dan Geer to be fired from @stake. Computer security is so important that it is becoming political. This paper argues that by dominating the software market so completely, Microsoft is putting security at risk.

[Ghosh, O'Connor, and McGraw 1998] Anup Ghosh, Tom O'Connor, and Gary McGraw. "An Automated Approach for Identifying Potential Vulnerabilities in Software," *Proceedings of the IEEE Symposium on Security and Privacy*, Oakland, CA, IEEE Computer Society Press, May 1998, pp. 104–114.

> FIST is a tool for software fault injection for security. This work inspired a number of commercial dynamic testing tools.

[Gilb and Graham 1993] Tom Gilb and Dorothy Graham. *Software Inspection*. Addison-Wesley, Reading, MA, 1993.

> After Fagan [1976], this book is the classic text on code review.

[Graff and van Wyk 2003] Mark Graff and Kenneth van Wyk. *Secure Coding: Principles and Practices*. O'Reilly and Associates, Sebastopol, CA, 2003.

One of the key books in software security, aimed at network and operations security types. This book explains the importance of software security to computer security people.

[Gutmann 2004] Peter Gutmann. "Simplifying Public Key Management," *IEEE Computer* 37(2), February 2004, pp. 101–103.

A paper explaining why many security errors exist because of user problems caused by overly complicated technology (ever try to use early versions of pgp?). Simplicity for users and consumers of software and software security technology is essential.

[Henzinger et al. 2003] Thomas Henzinger, Ranjit Jhala, Rupak Majumdar, and Gregoire Sutre. "Software Verification with BLAST," *Proceedings of the 10th International Workshop on Model Checking of Software,* Springer Lecture Notes in Computer Science, vol. 2648, 2003, pp. 235–239.

A paper explaining the BLAST model checker, which uses predicate abstraction to examine program safety properties.

[Hoglund and Butler 2005] Greg Hoglund and James Butler. *Rootkits: Subverting the Windows Kernel.* Addison-Wesley, Boston, MA, 2005.

The first complete book on the important topic of rootkits. Rootkits are the apex of the attacker's toolkit, and understanding how they really work is essential for today's software security professionals. Better get this book.

[Hoglund and McGraw 2004] Greg Hoglund and Gary McGraw. *Exploiting Software: How to Break Code.* Addison-Wesley, Boston, MA, 2004. <http://www.exploitingsoftware.com>

See entry in *Required Reading.*

[Hope, McGraw, and Anton 2004] Paco Hope, Gary McGraw, and Annie Anton. "Misuse and Abuse Cases: Getting Past the Positive," *IEEE Security & Privacy* 2(3), 2004, pp. 32–34.

One of the original BSI articles from *IEEE Security & Privacy* magazine that sparked this book. See <http://www.computer.org/security> for subscription information.

[Hovemeyer and Pugh 2004] Dave Hovemeyer and William Pugh. "Finding Bugs Is Easy," *Companion of the 19th Annual ACM Conference on Object-Oriented Programming, Systems, Languages, and Applications (OOPSLA),* Vancouver, Canada, ACM Press, 2004.

Bill Pugh's FindBugs program is a very popular open source code analysis system for Java bytecode.

[Howard and LeBlanc 2002] Michael Howard and David LeBlanc. *Writing Secure Code,* 1st edition. Microsoft Press, Redmond, WA, 2002.

See entry in *Required Reading.*

[**Howard and LeBlanc 2003**] Michael Howard and David LeBlanc. *Writing Secure Code,* 2nd edition. Microsoft Press, Redmond, WA, 2003.

> See entry in *Required Reading.*

[**Howard, LeBlanc, and Viega 2005**] Michael Howard, David LeBlanc, and John Viega. *19 Deadly Sins of Software Security.* McGraw-Hill Osborne Media, New York, 2005.

> This book discusses in detail 19 serious software security problems. The 19 sins are not presented in a hierarchy.

[**Howard and Lipner 2003**] Michael Howard and Steve Lipner. "Inside the Windows Security Push," *IEEE Security & Privacy* 1(1), 2003, pp. 57–61.

> A description of Microsoft's Trustworthy Computing Initiative one year after the effort began. Microsoft's work provides a critical case study for the adoption of software security best practices in a large enterprise.

[**Jurjens 2001**] Jan Jurjens. "Towards Secure Systems Development with UMLsec," *Proceedings of FASE'01.* Springer Lecture Notes in Computer Science, 2001.

> UMLsec is one way of thinking about security at the design level. This work is overly focused on security features.

[**Kernighan and Ritchie 1988**] Brian Kernighan and Dennis Ritchie. *The C Programming Language,* 2nd edition. Prentice Hall, New York, 1988.

> The C bible. Unfortunately, this language has serious security problems. The string functions are particularly notorious for introducing buffer overflow conditions. And `gets()`? Ouch. The best software security advice about C is "don't use it."

[**Koziol et al. 2004**] Jack Koziol, David Litchfield, Dave Aitel, Chris Anley, Sinan "noir" Eren, Neel Mehta, and Riley Hassell. *The Shellcoder's Handbook: Discovering and Exploiting Security Holes.* John Wiley & Sons, New York, 2004.

> One of the books helping to describe (in great technical detail) how software attacks work. This book makes an excellent companion to *Exploiting Software.* This is a black hat must-read.

[**Landwehr, Bull, and McDermott 1993**] Carl Landwehr, Alan Bull, and John McDermott. "A Taxonomy of Computer Program Security Flaws, with Examples," Technical Report NRL/FR/5542—93/9591, United States Navy, Naval Research Laboratory, November 1993.

> An important early taxonomy of computer security problems. This work set the stage for an escalation of excellent computer security research in the mid-1990s.

[**Larochelle and Evans 2001**] David Larochelle and David Evans. "Statically Detecting Likely Buffer Overflow Vulnerabilities," *Proceedings of the 10th*

Usenix Security Symposium (USENIX'01), Washington, DC, USENIX Association, 2001.

> Splint extends the lint concept into the security realm. By adding code annotations, developers can enable splint to find abstraction violations, unannounced modifications to global variables, and possible use-before-initialization errors. Splint can also reason about minimum and maximum array bounds accesses if it is provided with function pre- and postconditions.

[Leveson 1995] Nancy Leveson. *Safeware: System Safety and Computers.* Addison-Wesley, Reading, MA, 1995.

> The classic book on software safety. Safety has a number of critical lessons to teach software security, only a few of which have been absorbed so far.

[McDermott and Fox 1999] John McDermott and Chris Fox. "Using Abuse Case Models for Security Requirements Analysis," *Proceedings of the 15th Annual Computer Security Applications Conference,* Scottsdale, AZ, IEEE Computer Society Press, 1999, p. 55.

> The first paper on record about abuse cases.

[McGraw 1998] Gary McGraw. "Testing for Security During Development: Why We Should Scrap Penetrate-and-Patch," *IEEE Aerospace and Electronic Systems* 13(4), 1998, pp. 13–15.

> A paper describing why penetrate-and-patch is a failed approach. This paper represents some of my earliest thinking about software security. Note that it was published in a journal devoted to very high assurance systems (those that control aircraft).

[McGraw 2003] Gary McGraw. "From the Ground Up: The DIMACS Software Security Workshop," *IEEE Security & Privacy* 1(2), 2003, pp. 59–66.

> The results of the first conference devoted entirely to software security. This intimate workshop of around 50 people helped to crystallize and define the emerging field of software security. Presentations and notes from the workshop are here <http://www.cigital.com/ssw/>.

[McGraw 2004] Gary McGraw. "Software Security," *IEEE Security & Privacy* 2(2), 2004, pp. 80–83.

> The first of the BSI articles from *IEEE Security & Privacy* magazine that sparked this book. See <http://www.computer.org/security> for subscription information.

[McGraw 2005] Gary McGraw. "The 7 Touchpoints of Secure Software," *Software Development,* September 2005, pp. 42–43.

> A popular press treatment of the touchpoints that appeared in *Software Development* magazine.

[**McGraw and Felten 1996**] Gary McGraw and Edward Felten. *Java Security: Hostile Applets, Holes, and Antidotes.* John Wiley & Sons, New York, 1996.

The first book on Java security, written with Ed Felten, leader of the Princeton Team. This book made quite a splash when it appeared. See the next entry for *Securing Java,* the second edition.

[**McGraw and Felten 1999**] Gary McGraw and Edward Felten. *Securing Java: Getting Down to Business with Mobile Code.* John Wiley & Sons, New York, 1999. <http://www.securingjava.com/>

The second edition of my book *Java Security,* updated with new attacks and advice. The complete book is available for free on the Web. Ed Felten ran the Princeton team of security researchers who consistently challenged assumptions about Java.

[**McGraw and Morrisett 2000**] Gary McGraw and Greg Morrisett. "Attacking Malicious Code: A Report to the Infosec Research Council," *IEEE Software* 17(5), September/October 2000, pp. 33–41.

Malicious code is a side effect of bad software. This paper introduced the *trinity of trouble.* This paper describes a U.S. government-sponsored set of workshops (which I set up and chaired) meant to dig deeply into the root causes of viruses, worms, and other nasty beasties.

[**Mead and McGraw 2005**] Nancy R. Mead and Gary McGraw. "A Portal for Software Security," *IEEE Security & Privacy* 3(4), 2005, pp. 75–79.

One of the original BSI articles from *IEEE Security & Privacy* magazine that sparked this book. See <http://www.computer.org/security> for subscription information.

[**Miller et al. 1995**] Barton Miller, David Koski, Cjin Lee, Vivekananda Maganty, Ravi Murphy, Ajitkumar Natarajan, and Jeff Steidl. "Fuzz Revisited: A Re-examination of the Reliability of UNIX Utilities and Services," Technical Report CS-TR-95-1268, University of Wisconsin, April 1995.

An excellent description of the fuzz tool, five years after it was first introduced (by the same authors). The simple idea of sending random input to UNIX commands and seeing what happens helped to spark dynamic testing approaches offered on the commercial market today.

[**Pincus and Baker 2004**] Jon Pincus and Brandon Baker. "Beyond Stack Smashing: Recent Advances in Exploiting Buffer Overruns," *IEEE Security & Privacy* 2(4), 2004, pp. 20–27.

An in-depth description of new buffer overflow attacks not yet commonly encountered in the wild. You know what that means—coming soon to software near you. This was the best paper in a special issue of

IEEE Security & Privacy magazine, which I edited with Ivan Arce, devoted to attacking systems.

[Potter and McGraw 2004] Bruce Potter and Gary McGraw. "Software Security Testing," *IEEE Security & Privacy* 2(5), 2004, pp. 81–85.

> One of the original BSI articles from *IEEE Security & Privacy* magazine that sparked this book. See <http://www.computer.org/security> for subscription information.

[Saltzer and Schroeder 1975] Jerome Saltzer and Michael Schroeder. "The Protection of Information in Computer Systems," *Proceedings of the IEEE* 9(63), September 1975, pp. 1278–1308.

> See entry in *Required Reading.*

[Sindre and Opdahl 2000] Guttorm Sindre and Andreas Opdahl. "Eliciting Security Requirements by Misuse Cases," *Proceedings of the 37th International Conference on Technology of Object-Oriented Languages and Systems (TOOLS-37'00),* Sydney, Australia, IEEE Press, 2000, pp. 120–131.

> Sindre and Opdahl explain how to extend use case diagrams with misuse cases. Their basic idea is to represent the actions that systems should prevent in tandem with those that systems should support so that security analysis of requirements is easier.

[Stubblefield, Ioannides, and Rubin 2004] Adam Stubblefield, John Ioannides, and Avi Rubin. "A Key Recovery Attack on the 802.11b Wired Equivalent Privacy Protocol (WEP)," *ACM Transactions on Information and System Security,* May 2004, pp. 319–332.

> WEP is a prime example of the widespread security risk brought about by architectural security flaws.

[Swiderski and Snyder 2004] Frank Swiderski and Window Snyder. *Threat Modeling.* Microsoft Press, Redmond, WA, 2004.

> The unfortunately titled book explaining how Microsoft approaches security risk analysis. This book is worth a quick glance.

[Taylor and McGraw 2005] Dan Taylor and Gary McGraw. "Adopting a Software Security Improvement Program," *IEEE Security & Privacy* 3(3), 2005, pp. 88–91.

> One of the original BSI articles from *IEEE Security & Privacy* magazine that sparked this book. See <http://www.computer.org/security> for subscription information.

[Tsipenyuk, Chess, and McGraw 2005] Katrina Tsipenyuk, Brian Chess, and Gary McGraw. "Seven Pernicious Kingdoms: A Taxonomy of Software Security Errors," *Proceedings of the NIST Workshop on Software Security*

Assurance Tools, Techniques, and Metrics (SSATTM), Los Angeles, CA, 2005.

> A paper introducing the seven pernicious kingdoms and associated phyla expounded in this book. A related BSI article from *IEEE Security & Privacy* magazine is also in the works but was not published at the time of this writing. See <http://www.computer.org/security> for subscription information.

[van Wyk and McGraw 2005] Kenneth R. van Wyk and Gary McGraw. "Bridging the Gap between Software Development and Information Security," *IEEE Security & Privacy* 3(4), 2005, pp. 64–68.

> One of the original BSI articles from *IEEE Security & Privacy* magazine that sparked this book. See <http://www.computer.org/security> for subscription information.

[Verdon and McGraw 2004] Denis Verdon and Gary McGraw. "Risk Analysis in Software Design," *IEEE Security & Privacy* 2(4), 2004, pp. 79–84.

> One of the original BSI articles from *IEEE Security & Privacy* magazine that sparked this book. See <http://www.computer.org/security> for subscription information.

[Viega et al. 2000a] John Viega, J. T. Bloch, Tadyoshi Kohno, and Gary McGraw. "ITS4: A Static Vulnerability Scanner for C and C++ Code," *Proceedings of Annual Computer Security Applications Conference*, New Orleans, LA, December 2000, pp. 257–267.

> An early ITS4 publication describing a simple source code security analysis tool. The paper includes a couple of case studies showcasing how to use ITS4. This paper won the best paper award at ACSAC in 2000 even though it is not really all that good.

[Viega et al. 2000b] John Viega, Gary McGraw, Tom Mutdosch, and Ed Felten. "Statically Scanning Java Code: Finding Security Vulnerabilities," *IEEE Software* 17(5), September/October 2000, pp. 68–74.

> A paper describing a very simple static analysis tool written by Tom during a summer internship at Cigital. The Jscan prototype captured the guidelines from *Securing Java* [McGraw and Felten 1999] in a simple tool.

[Viega and McGraw 2001] John Viega and Gary McGraw. *Building Secure Software: How to Avoid Security Problems the Right Way*. Addison-Wesley, Boston, MA, 2001. <http://www.buildingsecuresoftware.com/>

> See entry in *Required Reading*.

[Voas and McGraw 1998] Jeff Voas and Gary McGraw. *Software Fault Injection: Inoculating Programs against Errors.* John Wiley & Sons, New York, 1998.

> The first book in the world on software fault injection, a technology pioneered by Jeff Voas, cofounder of Cigital.

[Wagner et al. 2000] David Wagner, Jeffrey Foster, Eric Brewer, and Alexander Aiken. "A First Step Towards Automated Detection of Buffer Over-run Vulnerabilities," *Proceedings of the Year 2000 Network and Distributed System Security Symposium* (NDSS), San Diego, CA, 2000, pp. 3–17.

> Wagner describes a tool that uses constraints to scan for buffer over-flows in C code. The paper has an excellent analysis of the buffer over-flow problem itself. This paper won the best paper award at ISOC NDSS in 2000 and most certainly deserved it.

[Walsh 2003] Larry Walsh. "Trustworthy Yet?" *Information Security Magazine,* February 2003. <http://infosecuritymag.techtarget.com/2003/feb/cover.shtml>

> A skeptical look at Microsoft's Trustworthy Computing Initiative, one year into the program.

[Whittaker and Thompson 2003] James Whittaker and Herbert Thompson. *How to Break Software Security.* Addison-Wesley, Boston, MA, 2003.

> A good, simple, black-hat-related book about probing software security through input. Whittaker is a master of compelling tools that are easy to understand and useful at the same time.

[Wing 2003] Jeannette Wing. "A Call to Action: Look Beyond the Horizon," *IEEE Security & Privacy* 1(6), 2003, pp. 62–67.

> Jeannette wrote this interesting paper after a summer at Microsoft being exposed to software security in a large corporate software environment. Software security is listed among the top three major issues to work on in computer security.

Government and Standards Publications Cited

[IEC 61508] International Standards Organization, "IEC 61508"; Version 4.0 (1997). <http://www.iee.org>

[NIST 800-30] U.S. Federal Government, NIST Special Publication 800-30, "Risk Management Guide for Information Technology Systems." <http://csrc.nist.gov/publications/nistpubs/>

[NIST 800-37] U.S. Federal Government, NIST Special Publication 800-37,

"Guide for the Security Certification and Accreditation of Federal Information Systems." <http://csrc.nist.gov/publications/nistpubs/>

[NIST 800-53] U.S. Federal Government, NIST Special Publication 800-53, "Recommended Security Controls for Federal Information Systems." <http://csrc.nist.gov/publications/nistpubs/>

Other Important References

There are plenty of other references not directly cited in this book that are worth a look. Though this list is by no means complete, it can serve as a springboard into the wider software security literature.

[Aleph1 1996] Aleph One. "Smashing the Stack for Fun and Profit," *Phrack* 49, November 1996.

A comprehensive study of classic stack-smashing attacks. This is among the earliest papers dedicated to software security. *Phrack* is an excellent black hat resource that is well worth checking out.

[Amoroso 1994] Ed Amoroso. *Fundamentals of Computer Security Technology*. Prentice Hall, Englewood Cliffs, NJ, 1994.

Introduction of threat trees, the Bell-LaPadula model, Biba integrity, and other basic models. An oldie, but a goodie.

[Anderson and Kuhn 1996] Ross Anderson and Marcus Kuhn. "Tamper Resistance—A Cautionary Note," *Proceedings of the Second Usenix Workshop on Electronic Commerce,* Oakland, CA, USENIX Association, November 1996, pp. 1–11. <http://www.cl.cam.ac.uk/users/rja14/tamper.html>

Attacking smart cards with interesting, surprising attacks. This great article shows how to think like an attacker (with your black hat on).

[Anderson and Needham 1995] Ross Anderson and Roger Needham. "Programming Satan's Computer," *Computer Science Today,* Springer Lecture Notes in Computer Science, vol. 1000, 1995, pp. 426–441. <http://www.cl.cam.ac.uk/ftp/users/rja14/satan.ps.gz>

Why programming distributed systems is really hard.

[Arbaugh, Fithen, and McHugh 2000] Bill Arbaugh, Bill Fithen, and John McHugh. "Windows of Vulnerability: A Case Study Analysis," *IEEE Computer* 33(12), December 2000, pp. 52–59.

Ever wonder whether patching works? This paper shows conclusively that it doesn't work very well at all. The most surprising result describes how attack scripts appear to be developed well after patches are released.

[Bell and LaPadula 1974] David Bell and Len LaPadula. "Secure Computer Systems," ESD-TR-73-278, Mitre Corporation; vols. I and II (November 1973), vol. III (April 1974).

> A classic paper describing principals (actors) and objects in a matrix of permissions. This is the seminal work behind access control lists and role-based access control.

[Brooks 1995] Frederick Brooks, Jr. *The Mythical Man-Month: Essays on Software Engineering,* 2nd edition. Addison-Wesley, Reading, MA, 1995.

> Ever wonder why throwing more programmers at a software project only makes things take longer? Read this great book and find out why.

[Brown 2000] Keith Brown. *Programming Windows Security.* Addison-Wesley, Boston, MA, 2000.

> Windows security APIs. Security features are important, too.

[Cowan et al. 1998] Crispin Cowan, Calton Pu, David Maier, Heather Hinton, Peat Bakke, Steve Beattie, Aaron Grier, Perry Wagle, and Qian Zhang. "Automatic Detection and Prevention of Buffer-Overflow Attacks," *Proceedings of the 7th USENIX Security Symposium,* San Antonio, TX, USENIX Association, January 1998, pp. 63–78.

> Stackguard was the clear inspiration for Microsoft's maligned /GS flag. Though I am not a fan of detecting or stopping buffer overflows dynamically, this is a great paper.

[Denning 1998] Dorothy Denning. *Information Warfare and Security,* Addison-Wesley, Reading, MA, 1998.

> Possibly the ultimate black hat technique—war. This is a scary and relevant book well worth comprehending.

[DOD 1985] *Trusted Computer System Evaluation Criteria* ("The Orange Book"). U.S. Department of Defense, 1985.

> A failed attempt, but a valiant attempt to codify security assurance. The problem with this approach to security is that computer systems are extensible, networked, and way more complicated than ever.

[Ford 1994] Warwick Ford. *Computer Communications Security: Principles, Standard Protocols, and Techniques.* Prentice Hall, Englewood Cliffs, NJ, 1994.

> Network and communications security. Basic coverage of crypto, CIA, and some aspects of privacy. The Open Systems Interconnection (OSI) security architecture explained.

[Forrest, Hofmeyr, and Somayaji 1997] Stephanie Forrest, Steven Hofmeyr, and Anil Somayaji. "Computer Immunology," *Communications of the ACM* 40(10), October 1997, pp. 88–96.

Why computer security might benefit by analogy with biology.

[**Gamma et al. 1995**] Erich Gamma, Richard Helm, Ralph Johnson, and John Vlissides. *Design Patterns*. Addison-Wesley, Reading, MA, 1995.

This is an instrumental software architecture book. This book led to the idea of attack patterns.

[**Garfinkel and Spafford 1996**] Simson Garfinkel and Gene Spafford. *Practical UNIX and Internet Security*, 2nd edition. O'Reilly, Sebastopol, CA, 1996.

A classic tome on UNIX security. UNIX root must-read, but applicable widely to other operating systems.

[**Gasser 1988**] Morrie Gasser. *Building a Secure Computer System*. Van Nostrand Reinhold, New York, 1988.

A very old but interesting read that anticipates the philosophy of building security in some twenty years earlier.

[**Goldberg and Wagner 1996**] Ian Goldberg and Dave Wagner. "Randomness and the Netscape Browser," *Dr. Dobbs Journal*, no. 243, January 1996, pp. 66–70.

A great case study in broken software and the resulting attacks.

[**Gollmann 1999**] Dieter Gollmann. *Computer Security*. John Wiley & Sons, New York, 1999.

Probably the best basic security book (textbook style) out there. Use this to enhance Amoroso [1994]. By the way, we need a better basic computer security book.

[**Kahn 1996**] David Kahn. *The Code-Breakers* (revised edition). Scribner, New York, 1996.

A historically accurate treatment of cryptography. Long, interesting, and worth slogging through.

[**Kaner and Pels 1998**] Cem Kaner and David Pels. *Bad Software: What to Do When Software Fails*. John Wiley & Sons, New York, 1998.

Ever wonder whether those software licenses that you click on stand up in court? This lawyer tells why they don't.

[**Knuth 1997**] Donald Knuth. *The Art of Computer Programming: Seminumerical Algorithms*, 3rd Edition. Addison-Wesley, Reading, MA 1997.

Knuth; alpha geek. What, you don't own this book and its two companions? For shame.

[**Kocher 1999**] Paul Kocher. "Differential Power Analysis," *Advances in Cryptology—Crypto 99*, Springer Lecture Notes in Computer Science, vol. 1666, 1999, pp. 388–397.

How smart cards leak critical security information through their power consumption. This is a great study in thinking outside the box to break a system.

[Krusl 1998] Ivan Krsul. *Software Vulnerability Analysis*. Ph.D. Thesis, COAST TR 98-09, Department of Computer Sciences, Purdue University, 1998.

This thesis is one of the first modern attempts at a computer security vulnerability taxonomy.

[LaMacchia et al. 2002] Brian LaMacchia, Sebastian Lang, Matther Lyons, Rui Martin, and Kevin Price. *.NET Framework Security*. Addison-Wesley, Boston, MA, 2002.

From the guy who brought you .NET security. Good, but not very clear.

[Maguire 1993] Steve Maguire. *Writing Solid Code*. Microsoft Press, Redmond, WA, 1993.

Too bad the Microsoft guys didn't eat their own dog food in 1993! Get this book. Internalize.

[McClure, Scambray, and Kurtz 1999] Stuart McClure, Joel Scambray, and George Kurtz. *Hacking Exposed: Network Security Secrets and Solutions*. Osborne, New York, 1999.

The now-classic script kiddie book explaining black hat computer security to the masses. Not much software security in here, but an important book nonetheless.

[McGraw 1999] Gary McGraw. "Software Assurance for Security," *IEEE Computer* 32(4), April 1999, pp. 103–105.

My first real paper on software security. This short article introduces the idea of software risk management for security.

[Menezes, van Oorschot, and Vanstone 1997] Alfred Menezes, Paul van Oorschot, and Scott Vanstone. *Handbook of Applied Cryptography*. CRC Press, 1997. <http://www.cacr.math.uwaterloo.ca/hac/>

The best applied cryptography book. Written by hard-core crypto guys.

[Miller, Fredricksen, and So 1990] Barton Miller, Lars Fredricksen, and Bryan So. "An Empirical Study of the Reliability of UNIX Utilities," *Communications of the ACM* 33(12), December 1990, pp. 32–44.

The first fuzz paper. See the second entry in the references cited for *Software Security* earlier in this chapter.

[Necula and Lee 1998] George Necula and Peter Lee. "Safe, Untrusted Agents Using Proof-Carrying Code," *Mobile Agents and Security,* Springer Lecture Notes in Computer Science, vol. 1419, 1998, pp. 61–91.

The seminal paper on proof-carrying code (also known as certified code). This paper describes a system very much likely to be fielded in the future.

[Neumann 1995] Peter Neumann. *Computer-Related Risks*. Addison-Wesley, Reading, MA, 1995.

From the comp.risks mailing list. This book explains (through a huge number of examples) just how dependent we are on computer technology and what can happen when it fails.

[Rivest, Shamir, and Adleman 1978] Ron Rivest, Adi Shamir, and Leonard Adleman. "A Method for Obtaining Digital Signatures and Public-Key Cryptosystems," *Communications of the ACM* 21(2), February 1978, pp. 120–126.

RSA.

[Rubin 1999] Avi Rubin. *The Whitehat Security Arsenal: Tackling the Threats*. Addison-Wesley, Reading, MA, 1999.

A good-guy book describing computer security basics. This book even has white hats on its cover.

[Schmid and Ghosh 1999] Matt Schmid and Anup Ghosh. "An Approach to Testing COTS Software for Robustness to Operating System Exceptions and Errors," *1999 International Symposium on Software Reliability Engineering,* Boca Raton, FL, IEEE Reliability Society, November 1–4, 1999.

Software fault injection for COTS software.

[Schneider 1998] Fred Schneider, ed. *Trust in Cyberspace*. National Academy Press, Washington, DC, 1998.

Why computer security is essential.

[Schneier 1996] Bruce Schneier. *Applied Cryptography*. John Wiley & Sons, New York, 1996.

Applied cryptography explained in layman's terms.

[Schneier 2000] Bruce Schneier. *Secrets and Lies*. John Wiley & Sons, New York, 2000.

A great read, this book is pithy and fun. Need some stories to scare the pants off of upper management? Try this book.

[Thompson 1984] Ken Thompson. "Reflections on Trusting Trust," *Communications of the ACM* 27(8), August 1984, pp. 761–763. <http://www.acm.org/classics/sep95/>

This classic paper goes well with Saltzer and Schroeder's work on security principles. Once again, a paper that everyone cites and all too few read. Should you trust your C compiler? Probably not.

[Whittaker 2002] James Whittaker. *How to Break Software: A Practical Guide to Testing*. Addison-Wesley, Boston, MA, 2002.

Whittaker's first simple book on software testing. A good short read filled with compelling ideas.

[Whitten 1999] Alma Whitten. "Why Johnny Can't Encrypt: A Usability Evaluation of PGP 5.0," *Eighth USENIX Security Symposium*, Washington, DC, USENIX Association, 1999, pp. 169–183.

A great paper on usability (and un-usability) in computer security technology.

[**Winkler 1997**] Ira Winkler. *Corporate Espionage*. Prima Publishing, 1997.
    Winkler's excellent treatment of the insider problem makes this book worth a read.

[**Zuse 1991**] Horst Zuse. *Software Complexity: Measures and Methods* (Programming Complex Systems, No. 4). Walter de Gruyter, Inc., Berlin, 1991.
    The ultimate software metrics tome. Also useful as a doorstopper for the heaviest of doors.

Software Security Puzzle Pieces

As you can see by perusing the annotated references, software security exists at the intersection of several disciplines. The following areas of interest are focal points in the field of software security, both among practitioners and among scientists.

- Reconciling security goals and software goals: software quality management in commercial practice
- Security requirements engineering
- Design for security, software architecture, architectural analysis
- Security analysis, security testing, use of the Common Criteria
- Guiding principles for software security, case studies in design and analysis, pedagogical approaches to teaching security architecture
- Software security education: educating students and commercial developers
- Auditing software: implementation risks, architectural risks, automated tools, technology developments (code scanning, information flow, and so on)
- Common implementation risks: buffer overflows, race conditions, randomness, authentication systems, access control, applied cryptography, trust management
- Application security: protecting code postproduction, commercial technologies
- Survivability and penetration resistance, type safety, dynamic policy enforcement
- Denial-of-service protection for concurrent software
- Penetrate-and-patch as an approach to securing software

- Code obfuscation and digital content protection
- Malicious code detection and analysis

Much work remains to be done in each of these areas, but some basic practical solutions are becoming available in the market.

Basic Science: Open Research Areas

Most security researchers agree that we have a pressing problem. In "A Call to Action: Look Beyond the Horizon," Jeannette Wing includes "software design and security" as one of three critical areas to tackle if security research is to make progress [Wing 2003]. In "From the Ground Up: The DIMACS Software Security Workshop," I introduce the software security problem, discuss trends that demonstrate the problem's growth, and introduce the philosophy of proactively attacking the problem at the architectural level [McGraw 2003].

Much work remains to be done in software security, some of it basic and practical (e.g., working software security into the standard software development lifecycle as described by the touchpoints) and some of it far beyond current capabilities (e.g., automated analysis of software architecture for security flaws). Scientists and researchers from academic and commercial labs are working on some of the more difficult problems.

The National Science Foundation suggests that the following eleven open questions be used as drivers for research.

1. How to avoid building security flaws and security bugs into programs
2. How to know when a system has been compromised
3. How to design systems that can tolerate attack and carry out the intended mission
4. How to design systems with security that can be reasonably managed
5. How to provide reasonable protection of intellectual property
6. How to support privacy enforcement technically
7. How to get trustworthy computations from untrusted platforms
8. How to prevent/withstand denial-of-service attacks
9. How to quantify security tradeoffs
10. How to reveal and minimize assumptions in security system designs
11. How to build programs and systems and know exactly what they will do and what they are doing

There is clearly overlap among these problems, but the number of interesting subquestions raised by this list is large.

Careful consideration must be given to design for security. Given a set of principles and properties that we wish a system to have, we must identify guidelines for design and rules for enforcement. Open questions along this line of thinking include: Can principles be refined to guidelines? How can guidelines be reduced to rules that can be enforced statically? What technologies are suited for automated analysis?

Some concrete open research problems include the following:

- Explain why the software security problem is growing.
- Quantify, analyze, and explain bug/flaw categories.
- Do cost/benefit analysis proving that early is good.
- Untangle security software from software security at the requirements stage.
- Explore how to teach software security most effectively both to students and to professionals.
- Invent and apply measures and metrics.

The field is young and there is much to do. Please help!

APPENDICES

Appendix A
Fortify Source Code
Analysis Suite Tutorial[1]

A special demonstration version of the Fortify Source Code Analysis product is included with this book. Please note that the demonstration software includes only a subset of the functionality offered by the Source Code Analysis Suite. For example, this demonstration version scans for buffer overflow and SQL injection vulnerabilities but does not scan for cross-site scripting or access control vulnerabilities.

The key you will need to unlock the demo on the CD is FSDMOBEBESHIPFSDMO. To prevent any confusion, this key is composed of letters exclusively. There are no numbers.

This tutorial presents a set of lessons that cover a number of different source code analysis topics. Each lesson builds on the knowledge gained in the previous lessons, so the lessons should be taken on in the order they are presented. The final lesson allows you to practice what you have learned using a set of open source code bases.

The tutorial provides an introduction to the Fortify Source Code Analysis Suite for Java, C/C++ (using gcc), and .NET projects (using Visual Studio). Specifically, we include information about how to use the Fortify Source Code Analysis Engine and the Fortify Audit Workbench (see Chapter 4).

There are nine lessons in this tutorial:

1. Introducing the Audit Workbench
2. Auditing Source Code Manually

---

[1]This appendix was created and is maintained by Fortify Software and is reprinted here with permission.

3. Ensuring a Working Build Environment
4. Running the Source Code Analysis Engine
5. Exploring the Basic SCA Engine Command Line Arguments
6. Understanding Raw Analysis Results
7. Integrating with an Automated Build Process
8. Using the Audit Workbench
9. Auditing Open Source Applications

By using this tutorial, you will learn how to audit programs for security in order to ferret out the kinds of vulnerabilities that cause real security problems. The kinds of problems that you can find are exactly like those uncovered and publicized by experienced security researchers and malicious hackers—sometimes becoming major news events. Who knows, you may even find yourself discovering previously unknown vulnerabilities in open source code that has been fielded for years!

The directories containing the files used in this tutorial are located in the *Install_Directory*/Tutorial directory, where *Install_Directory* is the directory in which the Fortify Source Code Analysis Suite is installed. See the CD accompanying this book.

1. Introducing the Audit Workbench

This exercise examines the results of a successful source code security audit of the Washington University FTP daemon wu-ftpd version 2.6.0 that was performed using the Enterprise version of Fortify Software. In this exercise, you use the Audit Workbench to explore a results file that was generated by the Source Code Analysis Engine and annotated by a code auditor.

The files for this lesson are located in the following directory: *Install_Directory*/Tutorial/understand_AWB

1. Start Audit Workbench and load the audit.
   - Start Audit Workbench:
     - On Windows, navigate from the Start menu as follows: Start → All Programs → Fortify Software → Fortify SCA Suite 3.1.1— Demonstration Edition → Audit Workbench.
     - On UNIX, enter auditworkbench at a command prompt.
   - Choose the **Continue Audit** option.
   - Select the wu-ftpd.fpr file.
2. Examine the information displayed in the Project Summary dialog. Click **Skip AuditGuide** to close the Project Summary.

3. Examine the information displayed in the navigation tree in the Navigator panel.
   - Expand the items in the tree to see the individual issues.
   - Click on the issues to see how the panels are populated for each issue. For example, notice that the Analyzer Trace panel shows data flow information when the issue is related to issues identified by the Data Flow Analyzer.
   - Examine the Summary and Detail panels for information about the issues.
   - Click the **Hotlist, Warnings,** and **Info** buttons to see how the issues are grouped by severity level.
   - Select different options in the "Group by" drop-down list to see the issues in the navigation tree grouped by file name, sink, source, taint flag, or category and analyzer (the default).
   - Locate and select the following issue: `ftpd.c:5290 (Format String)`.

4. Examine an issue.
   - Read the auditor's comments concerning the issue in the Summary panel and note the settings for the analysis, status, impact, and severity buckets that the auditor has selected for the issue. In this case, the auditor considers the issue to be a remotely exploitable problem that could lead to a root compromise.
   - Click on the four code lines displayed in the Analysis Trace panel to see how the SCA Engine traced the malicious data through the program.
   - Examine the Details panel to read more about auditing format string problems.

5. Explore other issues.
   - Click the **Hotlist, Warning,** and **Info** buttons to explore some of the other buckets.
   - Explore some of the other categories and the issues they contain for an overview of the types of problems that Fortify Software finds in C and C++ programs.

6. Generate an audit report.
   - Select Generate Report from the Tools menu to generate a report.
   - Select Formatted Text from the "Export As" drop-down list.
   - Read the summary sections at the top of the report and some of the detailed findings that follow.
   - Click **Cancel** to return to the main audit view.

Exercises for the Reader

Beginner

1. How many categories of security vulnerabilities are listed for this application?
2. Starting with buffer overflow, how many vulnerability categories can you name?
3. In your company, what categories of security vulnerabilities are most critical?
4. Can you think of (or write) a line of code that would be acceptable in one program but would cause a serious security problem in another program?

Advanced

1. Describe a scenario in which a security issue that is not currently exploitable can become a critical security issue in the future.
2. What are some common reasons that developers introduce security vulnerabilities?
3. What makes one security issue more important than another? How do you determine the importance of a security issue?
4. Once you have identified and corrected all exploitable security issues, what are the arguments for and against addressing nonexploitable security issues?

2. Auditing Source Code Manually

This exercise introduces the goals of auditing source code for security and spells out the steps involved in performing a basic audit.

Any kind of manual source code review requires patience, an eye for detail, and extensive knowledge about the types of problems that can cause a program to fail. A security audit is no different, but instead of thinking "what could go wrong?" the auditor must consider "what could an attacker *force* to go wrong?" The auditor's role is to pare down this infinite search space and identify the most dangerous problems and weaknesses in a program. Experience is invaluable but can only be gained through practice.

This exercise demonstrates a simple manual audit process for a small Web application. The files for this lesson are located under two subdirectories in the following directory: *Install_Directory*/Tutorial/ do_manual_audit. The webapp subdirectory contains a sample Web application for this lesson. The `Answers` subdirectory contains responses to the questions posed below.

1. Examine the `webapp` application. Do not look for specific issues yet, just become familiar with the application by asking the same types of questions that an auditor starting a code audit would ask, such as:
   - How large is the application?
   - What are the technologies involved?
   - What is the basic design of the application?
   - Who are the likely attackers?
   - What would an attacker hope to achieve?
   - How are the developers trying to protect the application?
   - What sorts of techniques might an attacker use to subvert the application?
   - What risks would a successful attack pose to the company (e.g., customer confidence, public image, etc.)?

   Some vulnerabilities are easier to spot than others. Generally speaking, when the scope of an issue is limited to a single screen of source code, it is much easier to find than an issue that requires understanding the interaction between pieces of code from multiple (far-flung) locations.

2. Examine the source code of the following Servlet: `webapp/src/java/ com/simpleco/CountServlet.java`.
   - How and when is this code executed?
   - What can an attacker control?
   - Can an attacker violate the programmer's assumptions?
   - What is vulnerable about this Servlet?
3. Examine each of the application files, consider the interaction between the various modules, and identify issues that render the application vulnerable.

Exercises for the Reader

Beginner

1. How many vulnerability patterns can you consciously look for as you are manually auditing the code—5, 10, 100, 1,000?
2. What techniques would you use to keep track of paths across files?
3. How often should a security audit be performed? If you performed an audit today and fixed the problems, what would your confidence be

in the code 90, 120, or 180 days later? How much new code would your developers write in 90, 120, or 180 days?

Advanced

1. If you had to set up a process for manually auditing code in your company, how would you estimate the amount of effort and time required to do it effectively? How do the requirements scale as the size of the code base grows?
2. What are the ideal skills for a security code auditor? How many people in your organization are well qualified? What jobs do they do today?
3. Why do people perform security code audits rather than simply testing the software?
4. If you cannot audit all of the code, how should you choose which section of code to audit? How confident are you about the results of the audit?
5. Enumerate five programming styles or techniques that make auditing easier or harder.

3. Ensuring a Working Build Environment

To make it easy to integrate the Source Code Analysis Engine into your environment, the SCA Engine uses the same conventions as the tools you use to compile and build the application. The purpose of this exercise is to ensure that you are comfortable within your existing build environment before you attempt to integrate source analysis.

For analyzing C and C++ programs, ensure that there is a compiler supported by Fortify Software installed on your computer. (See the README.txt on the CD for a list of supported compilers.)

This exercise assumes that you are using gcc to compile C and C++. If you are using Windows and have not yet installed a supported compiler (such as Microsoft cl), you can install gcc as part of Cygwin <http://www.cygwin.com/>.

Depending on how you typically build your project, it is likely that you will also need a build tool, such as make or ant, installed on your computer.

Typical compilers and linkers search for and resolve certain symbols when building a working program. The SCA Engine is similar to a "security compiler" that operates on the source code base. As such, the SCA Engine functions optimally when it can resolve all of the symbols found in the program.

The more code you analyze, the more comprehensive the results will be. C, C++, and .NET projects must compile completely in order for the SCA Engine to analyze them successfully. However, the architecture of the SCA Engine does make it capable of analyzing individual or incomplete Java files if you choose to do so—albeit at the cost of reduced accuracy due to the unresolved symbols.

1. Verify that you can compile a simple program without any errors.
   - For C and C++ source code:
     - Change to the following directory:
       Install_Directory/Samples/basic/stackbuffer
     - Enter the following command:
       gcc stackbuffer.c
   - For Java source code:
     - Change to the following directory:
       Install_Directory/Samples/basic/eightball
     - Enter the following command:
       javac EightBall.java
   - For .NET projects:
     - Open the following file in Visual Studio .NET:
       Install_Directory\Samples\advanced\csharp\Sample1\
       Sample1.sln
     - Verify that the project is configured to build in debug mode.
     - Choose Rebuild Solution from the Build menu.
2. Ensure that you can successfully build the project that you plan to use for source code analysis.
   - For C and C++ projects, you typically run the make or nmake utility.
   - For Java projects, you typically use ant.
   - For .NET projects, you typically use Visual Studio.

4. Running the Source Code Analysis Engine

This exercise introduces the Source Code Analysis Engine. You will verify that the SCA Engine is properly installed and analyze a few small programs.

1. Run an analysis on a single source file:
   - For C and C++ source code:
     - Change to the following directory:
       Install_Directory/Samples/basic/stackbuffer

- ○ Enter the following command:
  ```
  sourceanalyzer gcc stackbuffer.c
  ```
- ○ Compare the output with the expected results given at the end of this exercise.
  - For Java source code:
    - ○ Change to the following directory:
      Install_Directory/Samples/basic/eightball
    - ○ Enter the following command:
      ```
      sourceanalyzer EightBall.java
      ```
    - ○ Compare the output with the expected results given at the end of this exercise.
  - For .NET code:
    - ○ Change to the following directory:
      Install_Directory\Samples\advanced\csharp\Sample1
    - ○ Enter the following command:
      ```
      sourceanalyzer Sample1.exe
      ```
    - ○ Compare the output with the expected results given at the end of this exercise.

Analysis Results of `stackbuffer.c`

The following output shows the results of an analysis of `stackbuffer.c`:

```
[Install_Directory\Samples\basic\stackbuffer]

[BB73F23E46159FBE5ED3C1968C046828 : low : Unchecked Return Value : semantic ]
stackbuffer.c(13) : read()

[EDACF5BD763B329C8EE8AA50F8C53D08 : high : Buffer Overflow : data flow ]
stackbuffer.c(4) : -> memcpy(2)
    stackbuffer.c(17) : -> doMemCpy(2)
    stackbuffer.c(15) : <- scanf(1)
```

Analysis Results of `EightBall.java`

The following output shows the results of an analysis of `EightBall.java`:

```
[Install_Directory\Samples\basic\eightball]

[F7A138CDE5235351F6A4405BA4AD7C53 : low : Unchecked Return Value : semantic ]
EightBall.java(12) : Reader.read()

[EFE997D3683DC384056FA40F6C7BD0E8 : medium : Resource Injection : data flow ]
EightBall.java(12) : -> new FileReader(0)
```

```
EightBall.java(8) : <=> (filename)
EightBall.java(8) : <-> Integer.parseInt(0->return)
EightBall.java(6) : <=> (filename)
EightBall.java(4) : -> EightBall.main(0)


[397D4B4A4FF20A0C13369B1D47844C53 : medium : Unreleased Resource : control flow ]
    EightBall.java(12) : start -> loaded : <inline expression>.new FileReader(...)
    EightBall.java(14) : loaded -> end_of_scope : #end_scope(<inline expression>)
```

Analysis Results of `Sample1.exe`

The following output shows the results of an analysis of `Sample1.exe`. *Note:* `Sample1.exe` was generated in the "Ensuring a Working Build Environment" section.

```
[Install_Directory\Samples\advanced\csharp\Sample1]


[C0EB5C44F4E926C3748984B3C4B869A5 : high : SQL Injection : data flow ]
Sample1/Class1.cs(29) : -> new SqlDataAdapter(0)
    Sample1/Class1.cs(19) : -> Sample1.Main(0)


[3CC21A4EF4179833409BEC57C9420379 : high : SQL Injection : data flow ]
Sample1/Class1.cs(31) : -> new SqlDataAdapter(0)
    Sample1/Class1.cs(20) : <=> (tainted_query)
    Sample1/Class1.cs(20) : <-> String.Concat(1->return)
    Sample1/Class1.cs(20) : <-> String.Clone(this->return)
    Sample1/Class1.cs(19) : -> Sample1.Main(0)


[8A25799D696115E0FD031CB294454B84 : medium : Unreleased Resource : control flow ]
    Sample1/Class1.cs(24) : start -> loaded : conn.Open(. . .)
    Sample1/Class1.cs(39) : loaded -> end_of_scope : #end_scope(conn)
```

Exercises for the Reader

Beginner

1. What are the benefits of integrating the SCA Engine into your environment as a compiler?
2. Why must you specify a compiler for C/C++ code but not for Java or .NET code?
3. Where is the log file used by the SCA Engine?

Advanced

1. If the SCA Engine cannot find some of the files for the software being built, what information is missing? Consider header files and source files. How will the missing information affect the results?

2. How do you know whether or not the SCA Engine was able to find and read all of the required files?

5. Exploring the Basic SCA Engine Command Line Arguments

This exercise continues the introduction of the Source Code Analysis Engine. In this exercise, you will experiment with the basic command line arguments accepted by the SCA Engine.

1. Consider the command line syntax:
   - For C and C++ source code, the syntax is:
     ```
     sourceanalyzer [options] compiler [compiler-flags]
     files
     ```
   - For Java source code, the syntax is:
     ```
     sourceanalyzer -cp classpath [options] files
     ```
   - For a .NET executable, the syntax is:
     ```
     sourceanalyzer [options] -libdirs dirs executable
     ```
2. Experiment with the following basic command line arguments using the sample programs from the previous exercise.
   - Compiler:
     For C and C++ code, the `sourceanalyzer` command is included in the compile line as a prefix to the actual build command, such as `gcc` or `cl`. For complex builds, the `sourceanalyzer` command is also used to intercept archiving commands, such as `ar`, and linking commands, such as `link` and `ld`. The SCA Engine interprets the flags passed in to the build command and adjusts its own operation accordingly, without affecting the actual build.
     For Java code, the compiler is implicitly `javac`.
   - Output Format: -format *format*
     This option specifies the output format. The default format is text. To select the Fortify Vulnerability Description Language (FVDL) format, which is the Fortify Software XML-based vulnerability description language, specify –format fvdl. You can also specify fvdl-zip, which produces a zipped FVDL file. FVDL is more verbose than text and is used by the Fortify Audit Workbench and other tools.
   - Output Location: -f *filename*
     This option specifies a file location to which the output will be

written. By default, if a file location is not specified, the output is written to the console.

For a detailed description of the command line syntax and options supported by the SCA Engine, see the following topics in the *Source Code Analysis Engine User's Guide:*

- "Using Source Code Analysis Engine from the Command Line"
- "Using Source Code Analysis Engine Command Line Options"

The *Source Code Analysis Engine User's Guide* is located at: `Install_Directory/Documentation/SCA/index.htm`

The next lesson, "Understanding Raw Analysis Results," explains how to interpret the results produced by the SCA Engine.

Exercises for the Reader

Beginner

1. If a single source code base is used to build multiple executable programs, how can you use the SCA Engine to evaluate the programs independently?

6. Understanding Raw Analysis Results

This exercise describes the Source Code Analysis Engine output. You will examine the different output formats and contents generated by the various analyzers.

The SCA Engine produces two primary output formats: text and FVDL. The text format is human-readable and is designed for quick scans and easy verification of results. FVDL is an XML format that is consumed by Audit Workbench and other tools.

- The Java source file for this lesson is:
  `Tutorial/understand_results/StringSearch.java`
- The expected output from the SCA Engine is located in:
  `Install_Directory/Tutorial/understand_results/Answers`

1. Examine the text output format. Run the SCA Engine on `StringSearch.java` as follows:
   `sourceanalyzer StringSearch.java`
   The output shows three issues.

Issue 1

```
[C9FE6AF8A29314E2DC22F0E9191802F8 : low : Unchecked Return Value : semantic ]
    StringSearch.java(18) : FileInputStream.read(0)
```

Issue 2

```
[2AE729678F97328125F563C53BEB1524 : medium : Resource Injection : data flow ]
    StringSearch.java(16) :  -> new FileInputStream(0)
    StringSearch.java(14) : <=> (searchIn)
    StringSearch.java(6)  :  -> StringSearch.main(0)
```

Issue 3

```
[3A8FE7972DB6C28956AC54DF8E63424D : medium : Unreleased Resource : control
flow ]
    StringSearch.java(16) : start -> loaded : fos.new FileInputStream(...)
    StringSearch.java(21) : loaded -> end_of_scope : #end_scope(fos)
```

The first line of the text output is the common root directory of all the files that have reported vulnerabilities, such as:

```
[/opt/FortifySoftware/SCAS3.1-EE/Tutorial/understand_results]
```

The first line of each issue has the following format:

```
[Instance ID : severity : category : analyzer ]
```

For example, **Issue 1** reports that on line 18 in the `StringSearch.java` file, the return value of `FileInputStream.read()` is not checked. The issue details also indicate that this was detected by the Semantic Analyzer and that, by default, it was assigned the severity `low`.

If the SCA Engine has more information about a particular issue, it includes the information on subsequent lines.

For example, **Issue 2** reports that line 16 in `StringSearch.java` contains a potential resource injection vulnerability that could allow an attacker to control a resource used by the application. The subsequent lines of output show that the value, potentially controlled by an attacker, enters the program at line 6 as the first argument to `StringSearch.main()`. This issue is identified by the Data Flow Analyzer and assigned a medium risk.

Values that cause data flow issues can pass through several hops between where they enter the program and the point at which the program uses the data as part of a sensitive operation.

The Control Flow Analyzer can also provide additional information about an issue. **Issue 3** reports that the resource created on line 16 was not properly released before it went out of scope. In other words, the code fails to call `close()` on the resource.

2. Rerun the analysis engine, this time producing FVDL output. Use the
   -format option to create the FVDL and the -f option to send the output to an XML results file, as follows:
   ```
   sourceanalyzer -format fvdl -f results.fvdl
   StringSearch.java
   ```
3. Open and inspect results.fvdl in a text editor. Note that it contains
   all of the information found in the text output, plus the following
   information in the preamble:
   • Date and time of the analysis.
   • Number of lines of code analyzed.
     Note also that the first issue corresponds to the first issue in the
     text output. It has the same information regarding location and
     category, plus it shows the unique identifier for the vulnerability
     class. The vulnerability class identifier references a description of
     the vulnerability class, located at the end of the FVDL file. The
     unique instance ID unambiguously refers to this vulnerability.

Exercises for the Reader

Beginner

1. How many of the Fortify vulnerability categories can you describe in
   detail?

Advanced

1. Write a piece of code containing an issue that is identified by each of
   the different analyzers.
2. Give an example in which a single issue will be found more than once.
3. Give an example in which a single issue will be found by more than
   one analyzer.
4. What is the cost of being wrong about an issue (that is, calling a finding a vulnerability when it is not, and calling a finding benign when it
   is a vulnerability)?

7. Integrating with an Automated Build Process

This exercise demonstrates how to integrate the Source Code Analysis
Engine with an existing build process.

• For C and C++ code, build processes typically use some form of the
  make utility, such as gmake or nmake, and a project-specific Makefile to
  build the project.

- For Java code, projects are typically built using the `ant` utility and a `build.xml` file.

The SCA Engine mirrors the way the compiler processes the source code of an application. This means that source code that is excluded due to conditional compilation (`#ifdef`) and code that is not included in the build is automatically excluded by the SCA Engine. Thus, extraneous and misleading results that are not part of the actual application are avoided.[2]

Integrating with a `Makefile`

1. Edit a `Makefile` to invoke the SCA Engine during the build process. An easy way to cause a `Makefile` to invoke the SCA Engine is to locate the `CC` variable in the `Makefile` and insert the `sourceanalyzer` command and any options before the actual compiler name. Consider the following `Makefile` segment:

```
 6:  #### Tools
 7:
 8:  CC = gcc
 9:  AR = ar sr
10: LINK = ld
11:
12: #### Options
```

The following shows the addition of the SCA Engine to the `Makefile`:

```
 5:  #### Tools: introduced sourceanalyzer command and
 6:  #### buildid/projectid=345
 7:
 8:  CC = sourceanalyzer -b 345 -c gcc
 9:  AR = sourceanalyzer -b 345 -c ar sr
10: LINK = sourceanalyzer -b 345 -c ld
11:
12: #### Options
```

The command line options specify the following:

- −b specifies the build ID, in this case 345.
- −c specifies that the SCA Engine runs the compiler as well as performs the translation.

---

[2]And problems not found in one build path but found in another can slip by auditors.

This modified `Makefile` causes the SCA Engine to generate an intermediate security representation of the source files and the dependencies of the build process. It also invokes the compiler and build commands so that there is no interference with the regular build output. However, actual security analysis is performed as a separate step.

2. Run the build as you normally would, but follow it with a command to perform the security analysis with a reference to the build ID:

```
make; sourceanalyzer -scan -b 345 -f /bld/results.fvdl -format fvdl
```

The command line options specify the following:

- `-scan` specifies that the SCA Engine should perform an analysis on the provided build ID.
- `-b` specifies the build ID, in this case 345.
- `-f` specifies the file to which the results are written.
- `-format` controls the output format (`fvdl`, `fvld-zip`, or `text`).

The output file is specified as an absolute path because most `make` projects enter and exit various directories during the build, and compilations that occur in each directory create their own output files. If you specify an absolute path for the output file, all results for the `make` are generated in one FVDL file.

If an output file with the same name already exists and the `-append` option is specified, the output is appended to the existing file. If the `-append` option is not included, the existing results are overwritten. To keep data from different analysis runs separately identifiable, rename or delete the output file before running each `make`.

3. To see the details, including resolution suggestions, open the `results.fvdl` file in Audit Workbench.

Integrating with an ant Build File

1. Ensure that the `Install_Directory` is included in the PATH environment variable.
2. Add the following to either `ant`'s `lib` directory or to your CLASSPATH:

```
Install_Directory/Core/lib/sourceanalyzer.jar
```

Note: In ant 1.6 and above, it is also possible to pass the path to `sourceanalyzer.jar` on the command line through the `-lib` parameter.

- Set the `build.compiler` property using either the command line or the property tag.

  The command line syntax is:

  ```
  >$ant -Dbuild.compiler="com.fortify.dev.ant.SCACompiler"
  -Dsourceanalyzer.buildid=Build_ID
  ```

  The property tag syntax is:

  ```
  <property name="build.compiler" value="com.fortify.dev.ant.SCACompiler"/>
  <property name="sourceanalyzer.buildid" value="Build_ID"/>
  ```

  Tip: When build files are used on systems without the SCA Engine, use the `ant <available>` task to define `build.compiler`:

  ```
  <available classname="com.fortify.dev.ant.SCACompiler"
  property="build.compiler" value="com.fortify.dev.ant.SCACompiler"/>
  ```

3. Perform the following steps to use the `sourceanalyzer` task to select files to be scanned or to run analysis. Include a `typedef` for the task in the build file as follows:

   ```
   <typedef name="sourceanalyzer"
   classname="com.fortify.dev.ant.SourceanalyzerTask"/>
   ```

   You can now include the `sourceanalyzer` task in any target.

4. Specify parameters, or define attributes in nested elements for the `sourceanalyzer` task. Valid parameters are listed in the *Source Code Analysis Engine User's Guide.*

   The following is an example of running `ant` from the command line:

   ```
   >$ ant -Dcom.fortify.dev.ant.SCACompiler.args=" \ -f resultsFile.fvdl
         -format fvdl"
   ```

   The following is an example of modifying the `build.xml` `sourceanalyzer` task:

   ```
   <sourceanalyzer buildid="${sourceanalyzer.buildid}"
              scan="true"
              resultsfile="results_file.fvdl"
              format="fvdl"
   ```

```
rules="rules_file.xml"
filter="filter_file.xml" />
```

Advanced Command Line Syntax for Java

Using the command line syntax for Java makes it easy to scan Java and J2EE code bases. In many cases, a J2EE project can be accurately analyzed without integrating with the build process. The syntax is:

```
sourceanalyzer –cp classpath [options] srcfile-specifier1 srcfile-specifier2 . . .
```

For example, the following command invokes the analysis of the source code of a typical Web-based J2EE application:

```
sourceanalyzer –cp "app_directory\WEB-INF\lib\*.jar;app_directory\WEB-INF\classes"
               -f results.fvdl -format fvdl .
```

Note: The dot at the end of the statement specifies the current directory.

Run the preceding command from the directory where the `build.xml` file is located. In this case it is assumed that the source files are located in a directory that is below the current directory. If the source files are located in a different location, use that as the *srcfile-specifier* instead of the current directory.

If there are multiple `jar` file directories under `WEB-INF`, you can also specify the following as part of the classpath: `"app_directory\WEB-INF\ **\*.jar"`

Exercises for the Reader

1. How often do you do a build? How often do you perform system tests? What are the benefits of doing a security analysis with every build?
2. Assuming you cannot review the results from `sourceanalyzer` every time you build, how can you use the information that comes from `sourceanalyzer` in each build?

8. Using the Audit Workbench

This exercise describes how to use the Audit Workbench to review results obtained from the Source Code Analysis Engine and generate audit reports based on those results.

The J2EE application for this lesson is located at `Tutorial/use_AWB/webapp`.

The SCA Engine has already analyzed the source code, and the FVDL output is located at `Tutorial/use_AWB/webapp.fvdl` file.

1. Start the Audit Workbench.
   - For Window systems, select Start → All Programs → Fortify Software → Fortify SCA Suite 3.1.1—Demonstration Edition → Audit Workbench.
   - For UNIX systems, if your installation directory is on the path, enter `auditworkbench` on the command line; otherwise enter the fully qualified path to Audit Workbench.
2. Select the **New Audit** option.
3. Select and load the following file: `Tutorial/use_AWB/webapp.fvdl`
4. Name the new project "SimpleCo Web Application."
5. Examine the information in the Project Summary dialog box.
6. Click **Continue to AuditGuide >>** and answer the questions that follow. When you are finished, AuditGuide limits the issues that Audit Workbench displays to the ones that are relevant to the application being audited.
7. Examine the information in the Navigator panel.
   - The three severity buttons, **Hotlist**, **Warnings**, and **Info**, display the number of detected issues for each severity type and control the contents of the navigation tree.
   - The items that appear in the navigation tree vary according to which "Group by" option is selected.
   - When expanded, the navigation tree lists the files in which issues were detected and the vulnerability categories.
   - The pair of numbers in square brackets shown next to each item in the expanded tree indicates how many of the issues have been audited (the number on the left) and how many issues there are total (the number on the right).
   - The "group by" feature allows you to group and display issues by category and analyzer (the default), file name, sink function, source function, and taint flag.
   - The Search field allows you to limit the displayed issues to those containing the search string.

8. Audit the first issue.
   - Expand the first element in the `LoginPkg.sql:26` navigation tree, and examine the information that populates the other panels.
     - The Source Code Viewer panel displays the section of code in `LoginPkg.sql` containing the issue.
     - The Analysis Trace panel in the lower left corner displays the flow of tainted data through the program.
     - The Summary panel displays the issue's vulnerability category and location (file name and line number) and an abstract summary of the issue. It also allows you to enter comments, change status, move it to another issue bucket, specify its impact, suppress the issue, and (if integrated with a bug tracking system) file a bug.
   - Click the **Details** tab to examine the following information about the issue: vulnerability category, description, auditing tips, and reference.
9. Audit the remaining issues following the same steps.
10. Save your work. On the File menu, select **Save Project**.
11. Generate and export an audit report as follows:
    - Select **Generate report** in the Tools menu.
    - Select **Raw XML** from the "Export as" drop-down menu and click **OK**.
    - Open the report that you exported in an XML viewer or text editor and verify that your comments and settings are present.

Exercises for the Reader

Beginner

1. Assuming that an attacker does not have your source code, what advantages do you have in finding vulnerabilities?
2. How do you envision feeding back vulnerabilities found in Audit Workbench to the developers who will fix them?
3. If you only had the text output for a large project, how would you go through it without Audit Workbench?
4. If the Source Code Analysis Engine runs on a build server but you run Audit Workbench on your local machine, will you run into problems? How will you solve them?

Advanced

1. How many Source Code Analysis vulnerability categories can you describe in detail along with example exploitable code?
2. What kind of comments do you tend to use most often when you are auditing?
3. In the last 30 days, how many of these vulnerability categories have appeared on BugTraq?
4. Name some vulnerability categories that have appeared on BugTraq that are not Fortify Source Code Analysis vulnerability categories.
5. Do you think an external attacker viewing the program as a black box would name vulnerability categories in the same manner as an internal auditor who is analyzing the source code (white box) from the inside, or would they be different? Why?

9. Auditing Open Source Applications

Now you know how to use the Fortify Source Code Analysis Suite, and you are ready to embark on your own independent security audits, equipped with analysis capabilities that would have typically taken a source code auditor many years to learn. This final exercise allows you to practice using the Source Code Analysis Engine and Audit Workbench by auditing open source projects.

The following subdirectories are located at *Install_Directory/* Tutorial/do_open_source_audit:

- splc—A small J2EE application that provides a Web interface for managing inventory.
- webgoat—A set of Java servlets developed by the Open Web Application Security Project (OWASP) to illustrate various Web security issues.
- wu-ftpd-2.6.0—The Washington University FTP daemon (also used in "Introducing the Audit Workbench").
- Answers—Contains subdirectories for each of the four projects listed above with notes, output, and security findings.

Note: These projects can be evaluated independently and in any order.

splc

1. Use ant to build splc.
2. When you are certain that the project is building correctly, add the

sourceanalyzer command to the build process, perform an "ant clean," and rebuild.

   Note: For help, see the "Integrating with an Automated Build Process" exercise.

3. Analyze the resulting FVDL with Audit Workbench. Note that the application contains suspicious use of sockets.

4. Compare your results to those in the *Install_Directory/* Tutorial/do_open_source_audit/Answers/splc directory.

webgoat

1. Use ant to build webgoat.

2. Once you are satisfied that the project is building correctly, add the sourceanalyzer command to the build process, perform an "ant clean," and build again.

   Note: For help, see the "Integrating with an Automated Build Process" exercise.

3. Analyze the resulting FVDL with Audit Workbench.

4. Compare your results to those in the *Install_Directory/* Tutorial/do_open_source_audit/Answers/webgoat directory.

wu-ftpd-2.6.0

1. Use the configure command to create a makefile for wu-ftpd. You may need to add options to the configure command, as in the following example:

```
./configure -host localhost --disable-dns
```

2. Build wu-ftpd using the make utility.

3. When you are certain that the project is building correctly, add the sourceanalyzer command to the build process.

   Note: For help, see the "Integrating with an Automated Build Process" exercise.

   Rerun the configure command, as follows:

```
rm config.cache config.h  config.log config.status
CC="sourceanalyzer -b wu-ftpd -c gcc"
./configure -host localhost --disable-dns
```

4. Run the SCA Engine:

```
make clean
make
sourceanalyzer -scan -b wu-ftpd -format fvdl -f wu-ftpd.fvdl
```

5. Analyze the results using Audit Workbench.
6. Compare your results to those located at *Install_Directory/*
   Tutorial/do_open_source_audit/Answers/wu-ftpd-2.6.0.
   Note: This demo does not utilize the full set of rules, therefore your
   output will contain only summary results in some cases.

Exercises for the Reader

Advanced

1. Return to the first lesson, "Introducing the Audit Workbench," and
   locate the Buffer Overflow in the `wu-ftpd-2.6.0` file using the SCA
   Engine and Audit Workbench.
2. What other methods for identifying security vulnerabilities can you
   name? How do they overlap or complement source code analysis?

Answers

For answers to the questions in this tutorial, see this book's Web site at <http://
www.swsec.com>.

Appendix B
ITS4 Rules

ITS4 <http://www.cigital.com/its4/> and its counterparts RATS and Flawfinder provided an early set of software security rules built into very basic static analysis tools. See Chapter 4 for more on static analysis tools and their use.

The rules shown here are enforced in ITS4 by essentially greping through source code looking for simple patterns—an approach filled with potential false positives. Not surprisingly, most of these rules are about APIs in UNIX- or Windows-based systems. What follows is a complete list of the kinds of rules that were built into ITS4. RATS added several hundred more rules of a very similar nature.[1]

The rules shown here were taken from Cigital's extensive knowledge base of software security rules. Only three (of many more) fields are shown. Every basic security scanner should include these rules. Any scanner that doesn't is not worth its salt. Consider this the tiniest *minimum set of security rules* that every static analysis tool should cover. A better minimum set would include all rules from ITS4, RATS, and SourceScope (see Chapter 4).

This is not an endorsement of ITS4, which is ancient technology that should no longer be used. Instead, the idea is to give you an idea of the kinds of rules that static analysis tools enforce.

Surgeon General's Warning

Use of ITS4 by clueless security people in the name of imposing software security on unsuspecting developers may cause a severe allergic reaction.

---

[1]A Venn diagram of rules overlap for early tools can be seen in Figure 4–1 (of Chapter 4).

API	Kingdom	Description
access	Time and State	The access() function should not be used to attempt to eliminate the need to change to a less privileged mode. The access() function allows one to check the permissions of a file. access() is vulnerable to TOCTOU attacks. It's commonly accepted that one should never use access() as a way of avoiding changing to a less privileged mode. Because this is the typical usage, this function should be avoided. On Windows platforms the APIs _access and _waccess are synonymous with access.
acct	Time and State	acct can be abused if an arbitrary path is passed as an argument, specifically if NULL is passed in.
au_to_path	Time and State	Vulnerable to malicious changes to path passed as a parameter.
basename	Time and State	*Note:* dirname and basename functions should be analyzed together. The basename() function returns the last component from the pathname pointed to by path, deleting any trailing "/" characters. If path consists entirely of "/" characters, a pointer to the string "/" is returned. If path is a null pointer or the empty string, a pointer to the string "." is returned.
bcopy	Input Validation and Representation	Many functions are susceptible to off-by-one and bounds-checking errors. There are many generic types of errors that can apply to usage of a wide variety of functions. These include: * Using a function that does not permit one to specify the size of a buffer to prevent overflows. * Mis-specifying the size of a buffer or the amount of data to be written. Off-by-one errors are common. * Failing to plan for correct behavior when input is larger than expected. * Failing to allow space for a terminating null character.

API	Kingdom	Description
		* Failing to ensure that a terminating null character is present; many standard functions consistently experience this failure. * Specifying the size of a buffer or the amount of data to be transferred using incorrect units. This is particularly a problem with multibyte strings. On the Windows platform, these functions tend to include a "W" in the name. * Assuming the wrong semantics for a parameter that controls data transfer and prevents buffer overflows. Because various functions use the buffer size, buffer size minus one, the remaining space in the buffer, etc., it is important to understand the bounding semantics for each function. Note that while some functions, such as `strcpy()`, are intrinsically dangerous, even the "safe" functions like `strncpy()` are still susceptible to subtle errors if bounds checks are not done properly.
`bind`	Time and State	Potential race condition with access, according to CERT/CC. Also, `bind(s, INADDR_ANY, )` followed by `setsockopt(s, SOL_SOCKET, SO_REUSEADDR)` leads to potential packet-stealing vulnerability.
`catopen`	Input Validation and Representation	The `catopen()` function is vulnerable to manipulations that will substitute a different catalog file than the expected one. The `catopen(char *name, int oflag)` function is used to open a message catalog and returns a catalog descriptor. The first argument is the name of the message catalog to be opened. If it contains a /, then the name is a pathname, otherwise it is a basename. The second input is used to specify locale differences. The function implicitly uses the values of environment variables, even when the name argument contains a /. It can do vaguely `printf()`-like substitutions on the filename. It does things like replacing %L with the value of the LANG environment variable.

API	Kingdom	Description
chdir	API Abuse	Call chdir("/") after using the chroot() function.
		The chroot() function establishes a virtual root directory for the owning process. This may be used to limit the amount of filesystem access a potential hacker could use if he or she gained control of the process. Programs like ftp and httpd commonly make use of this function.
		One weakness of the chroot() function is that it does not work as advertised unless a chdir("/") call is issued after the chroot(). Otherwise, the current working directory could be outside the isolated hierarchy and provide the attacker with access via relative paths.
		Use of chroot is desirable but should also be a flag to indicate that one needs to carefully check to ensure that related security issues are addressed.
chgrp	Time and State	The chown() function sets the owner ID and group ID of the file specified by path or referenced by the open file descriptor fildes to owner and group, respectively. If owner or group is specified as -1, chown() does not change the corresponding ID of the file.
		The lchown() function sets the owner ID and group ID of the named file in the same manner as chown(), unless the named file is a symbolic link. In this case, lchown() changes the ownership of the symbolic link file itself, while chown() changes the ownership of the file or directory to which the symbolic link refers.
		The fchownat() function sets the owner ID and group ID of the named file in the same manner as chown(). If, however, the path argument is relative, the path is resolved relative to the fildes argument rather than the current working directory. If the fildes argument has the special value FDCWD, the path resolution reverts back to the current working directory relative. If the flag argument is set to SYMLNK, the function behaves like lchown() with respect to symbolic links. If the path argument is absolute, the fildes argument is ignored. If

API	Kingdom	Description
		the path argument is a null pointer, the function behaves like fchown().
		If chown(), lchown(), fchown(), or fchownat() is invoked by a process other than super-user, the set-user-ID and set-group-ID bits of the file mode, S_ISUID and S_ISGID, respectively, are cleared.
		chown() is vulnerable to TOCTOU attacks. The existence of a call to this function should be flagged regardless of whether a "check" function precedes it.
chmod	Time and State	The chmod() and fchmod() functions set the access permission portion of the mode of the file whose name is given by path or referenced by the open file descriptor files to the bit pattern contained in mode. This function is used to change the read/write permissions of a file.
		Note: The functions of the chmod class have significantly differing functionality and warrant individual description.
		lchmod(), while having the same function signature as chmod, differs from chmod in that it does not follow symbolic links.
		fchmod(), while performing the same function as chmod, operates on a file descriptor, and not a filename.
		chmod() is vulnerable to TOCTOU attacks. The existence of a call to this function should be flagged regardless of whether a "check" function precedes it.
chown	Time and State	The chown() function sets the owner ID and group ID of the file specified by path or referenced by the open file descriptor fildes to owner and group, respectively. If owner or group is specified as -1, chown() does not change the corresponding ID of the file.
		The lchown() function sets the owner ID and group ID of the named file in the same manner as chown(), unless the named file is a symbolic link. In this case, lchown() changes the ownership of the symbolic link file itself, while chown() changes the ownership of the file or directory to which the symbolic link refers.

API	Kingdom	Description
chown *continued*		The fchownat() function sets the owner ID and group ID of the named file in the same manner as chown(). If, however, the path argument is relative, the path is resolved relative to the fildes argument rather than the current working directory. If the fildes argument has the special value FDCWD, the path resolution reverts back to current working directory relative. If the flag argument is set to SYMLNK, the function behaves like lchown() with respect to symbolic links. If the path argument is absolute, the fildes argument is ignored. If the path argument is a null pointer, the function behaves like fchown(). If chown(), lchown(), fchown(), or fchownat() is invoked by a process other than super-user, the set-user-ID and set-group-ID bits of the file mode, S_ISUID and S_ISGID, respectively, are cleared. chown() is vulnerable to TOCTOU attacks. The existence of a call to this function should be flagged regardless of whether a "check" function precedes it.
chroot	Time and State	Unset root SUID after calling chroot(). The chroot() function establishes a virtual root directory for the owning process. This may be used to limit the amount of filesystem access a potential hacker could use if he or she gained control of the process. Programs like ftp and httpd commonly make use of this function. The chroot() function requires root (super-user) access to call. If the programmer continues to run as root after the chroot() call, he or she opens up a potential vulnerability window for an attacker to use elevated privilege. Use of chroot is desirable, but should also be a flag to indicate that one needs to carefully check to ensure that related security issues are addressed.
copylist	Time and State	Care must be taken when accessing files from passed-in filenames.

API	Kingdom	Description
creat	Time and State	The creat function creates a new ordinary file or prepares to rewrite an existing file named by the pathname pointed to by path.
		If the file exists, the length is truncated to 0 and the mode and owner are unchanged.
		If the file does not exist, the file's owner ID is set to the effective user ID of the process. The group ID of the file is set to the effective group ID of the process, or if the S_ISGID bit is set in the parent directory, then the group ID of the file is inherited from the parent directory. The access permission bits of the file mode are set to the value of mode modified as follows:
		If the group ID of the new file does not match the effective group ID or one of the supplementary group IDs, the S_ISGID bit is cleared.
		All bits set in the process's file mode creation mask (see umask(2)) are correspondingly cleared in the file's permission mask.
		The "save text image after execution bit" of the mode is cleared (see chmod(2) for the values of mode).
		Upon successful completion, a write-only file descriptor is returned and the file is open for writing, even if the mode does not permit writing. The file pointer is set to the beginning of the file. The file descriptor is set to remain open across exec functions (see fcntl(2)). A new file may be created with a mode that forbids writing.
		The call creat(path, mode) is equivalent to:
		open(path, O_WRONLY | O_CREAT | O_TRUNC, mode)
		This function is a problem because it is possible to unintentionally delete a file or enter a potentially unstable race condition.
		creat() is vulnerable to TOCTOU attacks. The existence of a call to this function should be flagged regardless of whether a "check" function precedes it.

API	Kingdom	Description
cuserid	API Abuse	cuserid() generates a character-string representation of the username corresponding to the effective user ID of the process. If s is a NULL pointer, this representation is generated in an internal static area, the address of which is returned. Otherwise, s is assumed to point to an array of at least L_cuserid characters; the representation is left in this array. The constant L_cuserid is defined in the <stdio.h> header file. cuserid() should be considered obsolete. This function has been or will be deprecated in several systems (e.g., HPUnix, ISO POSIX-1). Additionally this function has changed capability within a given OS (HP). Therefore, in all cases, convert to getpwuid (getuid()), getpwuid (geteuid()), or getlogin(), depending on which username is desired.
db_initialize	Time and State	Watch out when files are passed in as pathnames.
dbm_open	Time and State	Can be involved in a race condition if you open things after a poor check. For example, don't check to see if something is not a symbolic link before opening it. Open it, then check by querying the resulting object. Don't run tests on symbolic filenames.
dbminit	Time and State	TOCTOU problems when opening a file.
dirname	Time and State	*Note*: dirname, basename functions should be analyzed together. The dirname() function takes a pointer to a character string that contains a pathname, and returns a pointer to a string that is a pathname of the parent directory of that file. Trailing '/' characters in the path are not counted as part of the path. If path does not contain a '/', then dirname() returns a pointer to the string ".". If path is a null pointer or points to an empty string, dirname() returns a pointer to the "." string. A call to dirname() should be flagged if the argument (the directory name) is used previously in a "check" category call.

API	Kingdom	Description
dlopen	Time and State	Take care when accessing files from passed-in pathnames; they are vulnerable to symbolic linking.
drand48 erand48	Security Feature	The random function is a Linear Congruential Generator (LCG) used to create pseudorandom integers. That by itself is not a security issue. However, how the numbers are used can be a problem. The algorithm that generates the numbers is well known, the range of numbers generated is very small (in a cryptographic context), and the generated numbers can be guessed with reasonable ease. Hence, if the pseudorandom numbers are used as the basis for encryption computations, then it becomes a security problem. There is simply not enough randomness or entropy in the pseudorandom numbers generated by the LCGs for them to be used in high-security encryption.
execl execle execlp	API Abuse	The exec() class of functions is used for executing a file as a process image. The exec() family of calls is vulnerable to TOCTOU attacks. A call to an exec() family function should be flagged if the first argument (the directory or filename) is used earlier in a "check" category call. Path-searching exec functions are susceptible to malicious programs inserted into the search path. The APIs execlp, execvp, popen, and system are usually implemented through a shell or exhibit shell-like characteristics. If user input can affect the arguments to the function, a malicious user could change or add commands to be run. These functions search the path if a full path to the program is not specified. When using these functions, always specify the full path to the program. The Windows _exec and system family of functions is also vulnerable in the same manner. Also be sure to include the file extension (.exe, .com, .bat) to prevent unwanted matches.

API	Kingdom	Description
execv execve execvp	API Abuse	The exec() class of functions is used for executing a file as a process image. The exec() family of calls is vulnerable to TOCTOU attacks. A call to an exec() family function should be flagged if the first argument (the directory or filename) is used earlier in a "check" category call. Path-searching exec functions are susceptible to malicious programs inserted into the search path. The APIs execlp, execvp, popen, and system are usually implemented through a shell or exhibit shell-like characteristics. If user input can affect the arguments to the function, a malicious user could change or add commands to be run. These functions search the path if a full path to the program is not specified. When using these functions, always specify the full path to the program. The Windows _exec and system family of functions is also vulnerable in the same manner. Also be sure to include the file extension (.exe, .com, .bat) to prevent unwanted matches.
fattach fchmod fchown fdetatch	Time and State	Care must be taken when accessing files passed in pathnames. ACL-based race conditions are possible.
fdopen	Time and State	Can be involved in a race condition if you open things after a poor check. For example, you don't check to see if something is not a symbolic link before opening it. Open it, then check by querying the resulting object. Don't run tests on symbolic filenames.
fgetc	Input Validation and Representation	Be careful not to introduce a buffer overflow when using a loop.
fgets	Input Validation and Representation	Low risk of buffer overflows.

API	Kingdom	Description
fopen	Time and State	The fopen() function, used to open files, is vulnerable to several attacks. First, if proper checks are not made, an attacker could replace an important file, such as a password file, causing the program to read and process incorrect data. The function is also vulnerable to TOCTOU attacks, where an attacker can modify a file between execution of a check function and a use function. *Note:* On Windows platforms, the APIs _tfopen and _wfopen are synonymous with fopen.
fprintf	Input Validation and Representation	The printf family of functions is susceptible to a variety of format string and buffer overflow attacks. Flag any instance of the printf() family of functions in the code. Determine whether or not the format string is being provided through some input channel. If it is using a single argument, this is a definite vulnerability. Replace the code with the "fix" section. If the first argument is a string literal constant, this rule does not apply. If the first argument is a variable string, try to determine if it is user supplied. If so, it will be more difficult to determine whether it is vulnerable to the threat or not. If it is influenced by any data that comes into the current function, it should be flagged as a (potentially false positive) vulnerability. All of these functions have potential format string problems. Some (as marked) also have potential BO problems when they write their output to strings.
fread	Input Validation and Representation	Check to make sure malicious input can have no ill effect.
freopen	Time and State	The freopen() function first attempts to flush the stream and close any file descriptor associated with stream. Failure to flush or close the file successfully is ignored. The error and end-of-file indicators for the stream are cleared.

API	Kingdom	Description
freopen *continued*		The freopen() function opens the file whose pathname is the string pointed to by filename and associates the stream pointed to by stream with it. The mode argument is used just as in fopen().
		freopen() is vulnerable to TOCTOU attacks. A call to freopen() should be flagged if the first argument (the directory or filename) is used earlier in a "check" category call.
		On Windows platforms the APIs _freopen, _tfreopen, and _wfreopen are synonymous with freopen.
fscanf	Input Validation and Representation	The scanf family of functions scans input according to a format as described below. This format may contain conversion specifiers; the results from such conversions, if any, are stored through the pointer arguments. The scanf function reads input from the standard input stream stdin, fscanf reads input from the stream pointer stream, and sscanf reads its input from the character string pointed to by str.
		The vulnerability of the scanf() function resides in the fact that it has no bounds-checking capability. If the string that is being accepted is longer than the buffer size, the characters will overflow into the adjoining memory space. This is a classic buffer overflow security vulnerability problem.
		scanf() function is susceptible to buffer overflow.
fstat ftok ftw	Time and State	Verify file states before file operations; they are susceptible to races. (Also make sure that buffers are large enough.)
fwprintf	Input Validation and Representation	The printf family of functions is susceptible to a variety of format string and buffer overflow attacks. Flag any instance of the printf() family of functions in the code. Determine whether or not the format string is being provided through some input channel. If it is using a single argument, this is a definite vulnerability. Replace the code with the "fix" section.

API	Kingdom	Description
		If the first argument is a string literal constant, this rule does not apply.
		If the first argument is a variable string, try to determine if it is user supplied. If so, it will be more difficult to determine whether it is vulnerable to the threat or not. If it is influenced by any data that comes into the current function, it should be flagged as a (potentially false positive) vulnerability.
		All of these functions have potential format string problems. Some (as marked) also have potential BO problems when they write their output to strings.
getattr	Time and State	Subject to race on reference to device by name.
getc	Input Validation and Representation	The getc() function is used to get the next character from the standard input stream. (The function returns the character read as an unsigned char cast to an int or EOF on end of file or error.) Other similar functions get the next character from other input streams (e.g., from files).
		The getc() function, in isolation, is not a security risk. However, the function is often misused when filling buffers. Often, programmers will repeatedly call getc() and copy the characters into a buffer until a certain character is encountered, without checking the current position in the buffer. This can easily cause a buffer overflow.
		Also, it is easy to forget to include the null terminator at the end of the string in the buffer. Otherwise, the unterminated string can cause problems such as access violations.
getchar	Input Validation and Representation	The getc() function is used to get the next character from the standard input stream. (The function returns the character read as an unsigned char cast to an int or EOF on end of file or error.) Other similar functions get the next character from other input streams (e.g., from files).
		The getc() function, in isolation, is not a security risk. However, the function is often misused when filling buffers. Often,

API	Kingdom	Description
getchar *continued*		programmers will repeatedly call getc() and copy the characters into a buffer until a certain character is encountered, without checking the current position in the buffer. This can easily cause a buffer overflow. Also, it is easy to forget to include the null terminator at the end of the string in the buffer. Otherwise, the unterminated string can cause problems such as access violations.
getenv	Input Validation and Representation	Value of variables stored in character array, return value size unknown.
getlogin		The results of getlogin() should not be trusted. The getlogin() function returns a pointer to a string that contains the name of the user associated with the calling process. The function is not reentrant, meaning that if it is called from another process, the contents are not locked out and the value of the string can be changed by another process. This makes it very risky to use because the username can be changed by other processes, so the results of the function cannot be trusted. Also, according to the Linux man page: "Unfortunately, it is often rather easy to fool getlogin(). Sometimes it does not work at all, because some program messed up the utmp file. Often, it gives only the first 8 characters of the login name. The user currently logged in on the controlling tty of our program need not be the user who started it. Avoid getlogin() for security-related purposes." *Guidance:* Using names for security purposes is not advised. Names are easy to forge and can have overlapping user IDs, potentially causing confusion or impersonation.
getopt getopt_long getopt_long _only	Input Validation and Representation	Some implementations of getopt() are vulnerable to internal buffer overflows. The getopt(int argc, char *const argv[], const char *optstring) function is used to parse the command line parameters. The level of security risk is implementation dependent, in

API	Kingdom	Description
		that for some C packages, it is possible for a buffer overflow to occur. The third argument of the function is a list of option characters. If the option character is followed by a colon, then the option requires an argument; two consecutive colons means the argument is optional. This is used to specify options, such as `-w`, in the command line.
		Flag instances of `getopt()`, and `getopt_long()`. Look for nearby bounds checks.
		There is a portability issue for old platforms. Check documentation for your particular platform.
getpass	Input Validation and Representation	Some versions of `getpass()` allow overflow of an internal buffer.
		The `getpass` function is designed to accept a password from the console, which is a null-terminated string. The echo is off, so it will not appear on the screen. It can lead to a buffer overflow problem, but that is very implementation dependent. In some implementations of the function, there is a maximum length defined for the password, and in other implementations, the password can be of arbitrary length.
gets	Input Validation and Representation	The `gets()` function is intrinsically unsafe and should not be used.
		The `gets()` function reads characters from `stdin` and stores them in a buffer until a newline or EOF character is encountered. There is no way to specify the size of the buffer, so this function is very vulnerable to buffer overflows.
jrand48	Security Feature	The random function is a Linear Congruential Generator (LCG) used to create pseudorandom integers. That by itself is not a security issue. However, how the numbers are used can be a problem. The algorithm that generates the numbers is well known, the range of numbers generated is very small (in a cryptographic context), and the generated numbers can be guessed with reasonable ease. Hence, if the pseudorandom numbers are used as the basis for encryption computations, then it becomes a security problem. There is simply not enough randomness or entropy in the pseudorandom numbers generated by the LCGs for them to be used in high-security encryption.

API	Kingdom	Description
`krb_recvauth` `krb_set_tkt` `_string`	Time and State	Kerberos functions related to keys and all are susceptible to races.
`kvm_open`	Encapsulation	Susceptible to races.
`lchown`	Time and State	The chown() function sets the owner ID and group ID of the file specified by path or referenced by the open file descriptor `fildes` to owner and group, respectively. If owner or group is specified as -1, chown() does not change the corresponding ID of the file.
		The lchown() function sets the owner ID and group ID of the named file in the same manner as chown(), unless the named file is a symbolic link. In this case, lchown() changes the ownership of the symbolic link file itself, while chown() changes the ownership of the file or directory to which the symbolic link refers.
		The fchownat() function sets the owner ID and group ID of the named file in the same manner as chown(). If, however, the path argument is relative, the path is resolved relative to the `fildes` argument rather than the current working directory. If the `fildes` argument has the special value FDCWD, the path resolution reverts back to current working directory relative. If the `flag` argument is set to SYMLNK, the function behaves like lchown() with respect to symbolic links. If the `path` argument is absolute, the `fildes` argument is ignored. If the `path` argument is a null pointer, the function behaves like fchown().
		If chown(), lchown(), fchown(), or fchownat() is invoked by a process other than super-user, the set-user-ID and set-group-ID bits of the file mode, S_ISUID and S_ISGID, respectively, are cleared.
		chown() is vulnerable to TOCTOU attacks. The existence of a call to this function should be flagged regardless of whether a "check" function precedes it.
`link`	Time and State	Can lead to Process/File interaction race conditions (TOCTOU).

API	Kingdom	Description
lrand48	Security Feature	The random function is a Linear Congruential Generator (LCG) used to create pseudorandom integers. That by itself is not a security issue. However, how the numbers are used can be a problem. The algorithm that generates the numbers is well known, the range of numbers generated is very small (in a cryptographic context), and the generated numbers can be guessed with reasonable ease. Hence, if the pseudorandom numbers are used as the basis for encryption computations, then it becomes a security problem. There is simply not enough randomness or entropy in the pseudorandom numbers generated by the LCGs for them to be used in high-security encryption.
lstat	Time and State	The stat() function obtains information about the file pointed to by path. Read, write, or execute permission of the named file is not required, but all directories listed in the pathname leading to the file must be searchable. lstat() is like stat() except in the case where the named file is a symbolic link, in which case lstat() returns information about the link, while stat() returns information about the file the link references. fstat() obtains the same information about an open file known by the file descriptor fd. stat() is used in combination with other functions that manipulate the file being queried (e.g., mkdir is vulnerable to TOCTOU attacks). A call to stat() should be flagged if the first argument (the directory name) is used later in a use category call.
mbstowcs	Input Validation and Representation	Internal stack allocated buffer can be overflowed on some versions. Also watch for the NULL terminator.
memcpy	Input Validation and Representation	Many functions are susceptible to off-by-one and bounds-checking errors. There are many generic types of errors that can apply to usage of a wide variety of functions.

API	Kingdom	Description
memcpy *continued*		These include:
		* Using a function that does not permit one to specify the size of a buffer to prevent overflows.
		* Mis-specifying the size of a buffer or the amount of data to be written. Off-by-one errors are common.
		* Failing to plan for correct behavior when input is larger than expected.
		* Failing to allow space for a terminating null character.
		* Failing to ensure that a terminating null character is present; many standard functions consistently experience this failure.
		* Specifying the size of a buffer or the amount of data to be transferred using incorrect units. This is particularly a problem with multibyte strings. On the Windows platform, these functions tend to include a "W" in the name.
		* Assuming the wrong semantics for a parameter that controls data transfer and prevents buffer overflows. Because various functions use the buffer size, buffer size minus one, the remaining space in the buffer, etc., it is important to understand the bounding semantics for each function.
		Note that while some functions, such as strcpy(), are intrinsically dangerous, even the "safe" functions like strncpy() are still susceptible to subtle errors if bounds checks are not done properly.
mkdir mkdirp	Time and State	The mkdir() function attempts to create a new empty directory. It is generally vulnerable to classic TOCTOU attacks. A call to mkdir() should be flagged if the first argument (the directory) is used earlier in a "check" category call.
mknod	Time and State	The mknod function creates a new file (or directory or special file) called pathname with theMode as the mode. The file type and permissions of the new file are initialized from

API	Kingdom	Description
		the mode. `mknod()` is often used to create device files. `mknod()` is vulnerable to TOCTOU attacks. A call to `mknod()` should be flagged if the first argument (the filename) is used previously in a "check" category call.
`mkstemp`	Time and State	Unique temporary filenames may not have correct file modes. Use with care.
`mktemp`	Time and State	The `mktemp(char *template)` creates a unique temporary file using the input template. The last six characters of the template must be XXXXXX, and these are replaced with a string that will make the filename unique. THIS FUNCTION SHOULD NOT BE USED. Some implementations replace the XXXXXX combination with the current process ID followed by a single letter. With only 26 possible values, it is relatively easy for an attacker to guess the filename and access the contents. It is also possible for a race condition to exist between testing whether the name exists and opening the file. `mktemp()` is vulnerable to TOCTOU attacks. A call to `mktemp()` should be unilaterally flagged. If this call must be used and if a "check present" is done, then a race condition is possible. This function creates a file; as such there is a vulnerability (based on the above description) that the filename can be "guessed."
`mount`	Time and State	Can lead to Process/File interaction race conditions (and runs as root).
`mrand48`	Security Feature	The random function is a Linear Congruential Generator (LCG) used to create pseudorandom integers. That by itself is not a security issue. However, how the numbers are used can be a problem. The algorithm that generates the numbers is well known, the range of numbers generated is very small (in a cryptographic context), and the generated numbers can be guessed with reasonable ease. Hence, if the pseudorandom numbers are used as the basis

API	Kingdom	Description
mrand48 *continued*		for encryption computations, then it becomes a security problem. There is simply not enough randomness or entropy in the pseudorandom numbers generated by the LCGs for them to be used in high-security encryption.
nftw nis_getserv list nis_mkdir nis_ping nis_rmdir nlist	Time and State	Susceptible to race conditions. Watch for file substitution.
nrand48	Security Feature	The random function is a Linear Congruential Generator (LCG) used to create pseudorandom integers. That by itself is not a security issue. However, how the numbers are used can be a problem. The algorithm that generates the numbers is well known, the range of numbers generated is very small (in a cryptographic context), and the generated numbers can be guessed with reasonable ease. Hence, if the pseudorandom numbers are used as the basis for encryption computations, then it becomes a security problem. There is simply not enough randomness or entropy in the pseudorandom numbers generated by the LCGs for them to be used in high-security encryption.
open	Time and State	The open function establishes a connection between a file and a file descriptor. Pathname is the name of the file to open, and fileFlags is the bitwise OR of a series of constants used to specify the file access modes. An optional additional input is used to specify the permissions, such as read-only. open() is vulnerable to TOCTOU attacks. A call to open() should be flagged if the first argument (the directory or filename) is used earlier in a "check" category call.
opendir	Time and State	The opendir() function opens a directory stream corresponding to the directory name and returns a pointer to the directory stream. The stream is positioned at the first entry in the directory.

API	Kingdom	Description
		opendir() is vulnerable to TOCTOU attacks.
		A call to opendir() should be flagged if the argument (the directory name) is used previously in a "check" category call.
openlog	Time and State	Can lead to Process/File interaction race conditions (TOCTOU category B).
pathconf	Time and State	The pathconf function is used to provide methods for the application to determine the current value of a configurable limit or option that is associated with a file or directory. The first input is the name of a file or directory, and the second input is a constant that represents the configurable system limit or option to be returned.
		pathconf() is vulnerable to TOCTOU attacks. The existence of a call to this function should unilaterally be flagged.
pathfind	Time and State	Can lead to Process/File interaction race conditions (TOCTOU problems).
popen	Encapsulation	Path-searching exec functions are susceptible to malicious programs inserted into the search path.
		The APIs execlp, execvp, popen, and system are usually implemented through a shell or exhibit shell-like characteristics. If user input can affect the arguments to the function, a malicious user could change or add commands to be run.
		These functions search the path if a full path to the program is not specified. When using these functions, always specify the full path to the program. The Windows _exec and system family of functions is also vulnerable in the same manner. Also be sure to include the file extension (.exe, .com, .bat) to prevent unwanted matches.
printf	Input Validation and Representation	The printf family of functions is susceptible to a variety of format string and buffer overflow attacks. Flag any instance of the printf() family of functions in the code. Determine whether or not the format string is being provided through some input channel. If it is using a single argument, this is a definite vulnerability. Replace the code with the "fix" section.

API	Kingdom	Description
printf *continued*		If the first argument is a string literal constant, this rule does not apply.
		If the first argument is a variable string, try to determine if it is user supplied. If so, it will be more difficult to determine whether it is vulnerable to the threat or not. If it is influenced by any data that comes into the current function, it should be flagged as a (potentially false positive) vulnerability.
		All of these functions have potential format string problems. Some (as marked) also have potential BO problems when they write their output to strings.
rand random	Security Feature	The random function is a Linear Congruential Generator (LCG) used to create pseudorandom integers. That by itself is not a security issue. However, how the numbers are used can be a problem. The algorithm that generates the numbers is well known, the range of numbers generated is very small (in a cryptographic context), and the generated numbers can be guessed with reasonable ease. Hence, if the pseudorandom numbers are used as the basis for encryption computations, then it becomes a security problem. There is simply not enough randomness or entropy in pseudorandom numbers generated by LCGs for them to be used in high-security encryption.
read	Input Validation and Representation	The read function attempts to read nbyte bytes from the file associated with the open file descriptor, fildes, into the buffer pointed to by buf.
		If nbyte is 0, read will return 0 and have no other results.
		On files that support seeking (e.g., a regular file), the read starts at a position in the file given by the file offset associated with fildes. The file offset is incremented by the number of bytes actually read.
		Files that do not support seeking (e.g., terminals) always read from the current position. The value of a file offset associated with such a file is undefined.

API	Kingdom	Description
		If `fildes` refers to a socket, `read` is equivalent to `recv` (3SOCKET) with no flags set.
		No data transfer will occur past the current end-of-file. If the starting position is at or after the end-of-file, 0 will be returned. If the file refers to a device special file, the result of subsequent read requests is implementation-dependent.
		If the value of `nbyte` is greater than SSIZE_MAX, the result is implementation-dependent.
		The developer must ensure that the buffer is large enough to hold the number of bytes read. This is most commonly a problem when an input file stream contains a "count" for number of bytes to follow. If the attacker can corrupt this and specify a number of bytes significantly larger than the amount of buffer space available, the attacker could overrun a buffer.
`readlink`	Time and State	Can lead to Process/File interaction race conditions (TOCTOU category A).
`realpath`	Input Validation and Representation *plus* Time and State	`realpath` expands all symbolic links and resolves references to `'/./'`, `'/../'`, and extra `'/'` characters in the null-terminated string named by path and stores the canonicalized absolute pathname in the buffer of size PATH_MAX named by `resolved_path`. The resulting path will have no symbolic link, `'/./'`, or `'/../'` components.
		Never use this function (or do so at very high potential risk). It is broken by design since it is impossible to determine a suitable size for the output buffer. According to POSIX a buffer of size PATH_MAX suffices, but PATH_MAX need not be a defined constant and may have to be obtained using `pathconf()`. And asking `pathconf()` does not really help, since on the one hand, POSIX warns that the result of `pathconf()` may be huge and unsuitable for mallocing memory. And on the other hand, `pathconf()` may return -1 to signify that PATH_MAX is not bounded.
		The libc4 and libc5 implementation contains a buffer overflow (fixed in libc-5.4.13). Thus, suid programs like mount need a private version.

API	Kingdom	Description
recv recvfrom recvmsg	Input Validation and Representation	May receive input from untrusted source. May cause buffer overflow.
remove	Time and State	The remove() function makes a file/directory inaccessible by that name. An attempt to open that file/directory using that name does not work unless you recreate it. If the file is open, the subroutine does not remove it. If the file has multiple links, the link count of files linked to the removed file is reduced by 1. For files, remove() is identical to unlink(). For directories, remove() is identical to rmdir(). remove() is vulnerable to TOCTOU attacks. A call to remove() should be flagged if the first argument (the directory or filename) is used earlier in a "check" category call.
rename	Time and State	The rename() function changes the name of a file. The old argument points to the pathname of the file to be renamed. The new argument points to the new pathname of the file. If old and new both refer to the same existing file, the rename() function returns successfully and performs no other action. If old points to the pathname of a file that is not a directory, new must not point to the pathname of a directory. If the link named by new exists, it will be removed and old will be renamed to new. In this case, a link named new must remain visible to other processes throughout the renaming operation and will refer to either the file referred to by new or the file referred to as old before the operation began. If old points to the pathname of a directory, new must not point to the pathname of a file that is not a directory. If the directory named by new exists, it will be removed and old will be renamed to new. In this case, a link named new will exist throughout the renaming operation and will refer to either the file referred to by new or the file referred to as old before the operation began. Thus, if new names an existing directory, it must be an empty directory.

API	Kingdom	Description
		The new pathname must not contain a path prefix that names old. Write access permission is required for both the directory containing old and the directory containing new. If old points to the pathname of a directory, write access permission is required for the directory named by old, and, if it exists, the directory named by new. If the directory containing old has the sticky bit set, at least one of the following conditions must be true: * The user must own old. * The user must own the directory containing old. * Old must be writable by the user. A call to rename() should be flagged if either argument is referenced earlier in a "check" category call.
rmdir rmdirp	Time and State	The rmdir function attempts to remove a directory. It is generally vulnerable to classic TOCTOU attacks. A call to rmdir() should be flagged if the first argument (the directory) is used earlier in a "check" category call.
scandir	Time and State	The scandir() function scans the directory dir, calling filter() on each directory entry. Entries for which filter() returns non-zero are stored in strings allocated via malloc(); sorted using qsort() with the comparison function compar(); and collected in array namelist, which is allocated via malloc(). If filter is NULL, all entries are selected. The alphasort() and versionsort() functions can be used as the comparison function compar(). The former sorts directory entries using strcoll(3); the latter using strverscmp(3) on the strings (*a)->d_name and (*b)->d_name. This function is in essence a TOCTOU security vulnerability. It can be used to return information about the directory structure of a system. If an attacker can select the value of dirname (due to the classic "check"/"use" scenario), then it is possible for the attacker to determine what directories exist on a system.

API	Kingdom	Description
scandir *continued*		A call to scandir() should be flagged if the argument (the directory name) is used previously in a "check" category call.
scanf	Input Validation and Representation	The scanf family of functions scans input according to a format as described below. This format may contain conversion specifiers; the results from such conversions, if any, are stored through the pointer arguments. The scanf function reads input from the standard input stream stdin, fscanf reads input from the stream pointer stream, and sscanf reads its input from the character string pointed to by str. The vulnerability of the scanf() function resides in the fact that it has no bounds-checking capability. If the string that is being accepted is longer than the buffer size, the characters will overflow into the adjoining memory space. This is a classic buffer overflow security vulnerability problem. The scanf() function is susceptible to buffer overflow.
select	Input Validation and Representation	Adding a +1 to MAX_FDS can cause a 1-bit heap overflow.
snprintf	Input Validation and Representation	Many functions are susceptible to off-by-one and bounds-checking errors. There are many generic types of errors that can apply to usage of a wide variety of functions. These include: * Using a function that does not permit one to specify the size of a buffer to prevent overflows. * Mis-specifying the size of a buffer or the amount of data to be written. Off-by-one errors are common. * Failing to plan for correct behavior when input is larger than expected. * Failing to allow space for a terminating null character. * Failing to ensure that a terminating null character is present; many standard functions consistently experience this failure. * Specifying the size of a buffer or the amount of data to be transferred using incorrect units.

API	Kingdom	Description
		This is particularly a problem with multibyte strings. On the Windows platform, these functions tend to include a "W" in the name. * Assuming the wrong semantics for a parameter that controls data transfer and prevents buffer overflows. Because various functions use the buffer size, buffer size minus one, the remaining space in the buffer, etc., it is important to understand the bounding semantics for each function. Note that while some functions, such as strcpy(), are intrinsically dangerous, even the "safe" functions like strncpy() are still susceptible to subtle errors if bounds checks are not done properly.
socket	API Abuse	Watch for cases when root process allows its children to inherit privilege. An inherited socket could enable privileged connections from untrusted machines.
sprintf	Input Validation and Representation	The sprintf function is used to build strings by embedding format field specifiers in a string and having the data converted into the equivalent string form and then substituted for the specifier. {v}sprintf() is susceptible to buffer overflow if used improperly. Mark any instance of vsprintf() and sprintf() as vulnerabilities. Replace calls with {v}snprintf() or change the format string. Check the format string to see if it includes "%.111s" formatting limit. The return result of sprintf() tells how many characters were actually written. If the number of chars is larger than the original buffer, that means memory has been overwritten and the program state is invalid.
srand srand48	Security Feature	The random function is a Linear Congruential Generator (LCG) used to create pseudorandom integers. That by itself is not a security issue. However, how the numbers are used can be a problem. The algorithm that generates the numbers is well known, the range of numbers generated is very small (in a cryptographic context), and the generated numbers can be guessed with reasonable ease. Hence, if the pseudorandom numbers are used as the basis

API	Kingdom	Description
srand srand48 *continued*		for encryption computations, then it becomes a security problem. There is simply not enough randomness or entropy in pseudorandom numbers generated by LCGs for them to be used in high-security encryption.
sscanf	Input Validation and Representation	The scanf family of functions scans input according to a format as described below. This format may contain conversion specifiers; the results from such conversions, if any, are stored through the pointer arguments. The scanf function reads input from the standard input stream stdin, fscanf reads input from the stream pointer stream, and sscanf reads its input from the character string pointed to by str. The vulnerability of the scanf() function resides in the fact that it has no bounds-checking capability. If the string that is being accepted is longer than the buffer size, the characters will overflow into the adjoining memory space. This is a classic buffer overflow security vulnerability problem. The scanf() function is susceptible to buffer overflow.
stat	Time and State	The stat() function obtains information about the file pointed to by path. Read, write, or execute permission of the named file is not required, but all of the directories listed in the pathname leading to the file must be searchable. lstat() is like stat() except in the case where the named file is a symbolic link, in which case lstat() returns information about the link, while stat() returns information about the file the link references. fstat() obtains the same information about an open file known by the file descriptor fd. stat() is used in combination with other functions that manipulate the file being queried (e.g., mkdir is vulnerable to TOCTOU attacks). A call to stat() should be flagged if the first argument (the directory name) is used later in a use category call.

API	Kingdom	Description
statvfs	Time and State	Can lead to Process/File interaction race conditions (TOCTOU).
strcadd	Input Validation and Representation	Low risk of buffer overflows.
strcat	Input Validation and Representation	The strcat() function is unsafe and should not be used. The strcat() function will concatenate two strings by placing the second input on the end of the first. If the space in the first buffer is not capable of storing both strings, the data of the second string will overflow into the adjacent memory space.
strccpy	Input Validation and Representation	Many functions are susceptible to off-by-one and bounds-checking errors. There are many generic types of errors that can apply to usage of a wide variety of functions. These include: * Using a function that does not permit one to specify the size of a buffer to prevent overflows. * Mis-specifying the size of a buffer or the amount of data to be written. Off-by-one errors are common. * Failing to plan for correct behavior when input is larger than expected. * Failing to allow space for a terminating null character. * Failing to ensure that a terminating null character is present; many standard functions consistently experience this failure. * Specifying the size of a buffer or the amount of data to be transferred using incorrect units. This is particularly a problem with multibyte strings. On the Windows platform, these functions tend to include a "W" in the name. * Assuming the wrong semantics for a parameter that controls data transfer and prevents buffer overflows. Because various functions use the buffer size, buffer size minus one, the remaining space in the buffer, etc., it is important to understand the bounding semantics for each function.

API	Kingdom	Description
strccpy *continued*		Note that while some functions, such as `strcpy()`, are intrinsically dangerous, even the "safe" functions like `strncpy()` are still susceptible to subtle errors if bounds checks are not done properly.
strcpy	Input Validation and Representation	The string copy library functions are vulnerable to buffer overflow attack. `strcpy()` is the classic buffer overflow attack. Any variant of `strcpy` or any routine that behaves like it, copying a C-string from one buffer to another, is vulnerable to the same misuse and attack patterns. The destination buffer must be big enough to hold the source string plus the null (\0) terminating character. Even if the destination buffer is large enough, there is a chance that the source buffer might not be null terminated and thus might overrun. Many of the string copy functions do not check buffer sizes and simply look for a null character to determine end of input. This gives an attacker an opportunity to send input larger than the buffer size, overflowing the buffer. The attacker can exploit this to implement a denial-of-service (DoS) or buffer overflow attack.
streadd strecpy	Input Validation and Representation	The `strecpy()` and `streadd()` functions are dangerous unless care is taken to allocate a large enough output buffer. The `strecpy(char *theTarget, const char *theSource, const char *exceptions)` function is used to copy an input string into a target, expanding nongraphic characters to their escape sequence representations. The string is copied until a null byte is encountered. The third argument is a list of characters that are not to be expanded. A pointer to the first byte of the target buffer is returned. This function is a security risk because there is the potential to overflow the target buffer. The risk for this function is greater than that for the functions that compress because a simple test of the size of the source string is not enough to guarantee that the target is large enough.

API	Kingdom	Description
strncpy	Input Validation and Representation	Many functions are susceptible to off-by-one and bounds-checking errors. There are many generic types of errors that can apply to usage of a wide variety of functions. These include: * Using a function that does not permit one to specify the size of a buffer to prevent overflows. * Mis-specifying the size of a buffer or the amount of data to be written. Off-by-one errors are common. * Failing to plan for correct behavior when input is larger than expected. * Failing to allow space for a terminating null character. * Failing to ensure that a terminating null character is present; many standard functions consistently experience this failure. * Specifying the size of a buffer or the amount of data to be transferred using incorrect units. This is particularly a problem with multibyte strings. On the Windows platform, these functions tend to include a "W" in the name. * Assuming the wrong semantics for a parameter that controls data transfer and prevents buffer overflows. Because various functions use the buffer size, buffer size minus one, the remaining space in the buffer, etc., it is important to understand the bounding semantics for each function. Note that while some functions, such as strcpy(), are intrinsically dangerous, even the "safe" functions like strncpy() are still susceptible to subtle errors if bounds checks are not done properly.
strtrns	Input Validation and Representation	The strtrns function will take currentString and replace every instance of oldsegment with newsegment. The constructed string will be placed in newString. This function is a security risk because it is possible to overflow the newString buffer. If the currentString buffer is larger than the newString buffer, then an overflow will occur.

API	Kingdom	Description
`strtrns` *continued*	Input Validation and Representation	Flag all instances of `strtrns()` as a potential vulnerability. Identify bounds checks for the function.
`swprintf`	Input Validation and Representation	The `printf` family of functions is susceptible to a variety of format string and buffer overflow attacks. Flag any instance of the `printf()` family of functions in the code. Determine whether or not the format string is being provided through some input channel. If it is using a single argument, this is a definite vulnerability. Replace the code with the "fix" section. If the first argument is a string literal constant, this rule does not apply. If the first argument is a variable string, try to determine if it is user supplied. If so, it will be more difficult to determine whether it is vulnerable to the threat or not. If it is influenced by any data that comes into the current function, it should be flagged as a (potentially false positive) vulnerability. All of these functions have potential format string problems. Some (as marked) also have potential BO problems when they write their output to strings.
`symlink`	Time and State	Can lead to Process/File interaction race conditions (TOCTOU Category A).
`syslog`	Input Validation and Representation	`syslog()` has internal buffer limitations, so size of input should be bounded. `syslog()` is used to log system messages. It has internal buffer limitations that are implementation dependent.
`system`	Encapsulation	Path-searching exec functions are susceptible to malicious programs inserted into the search path. The APIs `execlp`, `execvp`, `popen`, and `system` are usually implemented through a shell or exhibit shell-like characteristics. If user input can affect the arguments to the function, a malicious user could change or add commands to be run.

API	Kingdom	Description
		These functions search the path if a full path to the program is not specified. When using these functions, always specify the full path to the program. The Windows _exec and system family of functions is also vulnerable in the same manner. Also be sure to include the file extension (.exe, .com, .bat) to prevent unwanted matches.
t_open	Time and State	The first step in initializing a transport endpoint. Watch for sensitive data going to untrusted parties.
tempnam	Time and State	Incorrect temporary file usage can lead to TOCTOU and accessibility vulnerabilities. A call to tmpfile should be flagged.
		Temporary filenames created by the tmpnam family of functions can be easily guessed by an attacker.
tmpfile	Time and State	Incorrect temporary file usage can lead to TOCTOU and accessibility vulnerabilities. A call to tmpfile should be flagged.
tmpnam	Time and State	Incorrect temporary file usage can lead to TOCTOU and accessibility vulnerabilities. A call to tmpfile should be flagged.
		Temporary filenames created by the tmpnam family of functions can be easily guessed by an attacker.
tmpnam_r	Time and State	Temporary filenames created by the tmpnam family of functions can be easily guessed by an attacker.
truncate	Time and State	Can lead to Process/File interaction race conditions (TOCTOU problems).
ttyname	API Abuse	It is possible to return a nonterminated string.
umask	Encapsulation	Setting a liberal umask can be bad when you exec an untrusted process.
umount	Time and State	Can lead to Process/File interaction race conditions (TOCTOU CATEGORY A).

API	Kingdom	Description
unlink	Time and State	The unlink() function removes a link to a file. If path names a symbolic link, unlink() removes the symbolic link named by path and does not affect any file or directory named by the contents of the symbolic link. Otherwise, unlink() removes the link named by the pathname pointed to by path and decrements the link count of the file referenced by the link.
		The unlinkat() function also removes a link to a file. See fsattr(5). If the flag argument is 0, the behavior of unlinkat() is the same as unlink() except in the processing of its path argument. If path is absolute, unlinkat() behaves the same as unlink() and the dirfd argument is unused. If path is relative and dirfd has the value AT_FDCWD, defined in <fcntl.h>, unlinkat() also behaves the same as unlink(). Otherwise, path is resolved relative to the directory referenced by the dirfd argument.
		If the flag argument is set to the value AT_REMOVEDIR, defined in <fcntl.h>, unlinkat() behaves the same as rmdir(2) except in the processing of the path argument as described above.
		When the file's link count becomes 0 and no process has the file open, the space occupied by the file will be freed and the file is no longer accessible. If one or more processes have the file open when the last link is removed, the link is removed before unlink() or unlinkat() returns, but the removal of the file contents is postponed until all references to the file are closed.
		The path argument must not name a directory unless the process has appropriate privileges and the implementation supports using unlink() and unlinkat() on directories.
		Upon successful completion, unlink() and unlinkat() will mark for update the st_ctime and st_mtime fields of the parent directory. If the file's link count is not 0, the st_ctime field of the file will be marked for update.

API	Kingdom	Description
`utime` `utimes`	Time and State	Changes timestamps. Watch use by `setuid` or `setgid` programs.
`utmpname` `utmpxname`	Time and State	Any `setuid` program that runs as root or other authorized user can modify location of the files.
`vfscanf`	Input Validation and Representation	The `scanf` family of functions scans input according to a format as described below. This format may contain conversion specifiers; the results from such conversions, if any, are stored through the pointer arguments. The `scanf` function reads input from the standard input stream `stdin`, `fscanf` reads input from the stream pointer stream, and `sscanf` reads its input from the character string pointed to by `str`. The vulnerability of the `scanf()` function resides in the fact that it has no bounds-checking capability. If the string that is being accepted is longer than the buffer size, the characters will overflow into the adjoining memory space. This is a classic buffer overflow security vulnerability problem. The `scanf()` function is susceptible to buffer overflow.
`vfwprintf`	Input Validation and Representation	The `printf` family of functions is susceptible to a variety of format string and buffer overflow attacks. Flag any instance of the `printf()` family of functions in the code. Determine whether or not the format string is being provided through some input channel. If it is using a single argument, this is a definite vulnerability. Replace the code with the "fix" section. If the first argument is a string literal constant, this rule does not apply. If the first argument is a variable string, try to determine if it is user supplied. If so, it will be more difficult to determine whether it is vulnerable to the threat or not. If it is influenced by any data that comes into the current function, it should be flagged as a (potentially false positive) vulnerability. All of these functions have potential format string problems. Some (as marked) also have potential BO problems when they write their output to strings.

API	Kingdom	Description
vscanf	Input Validation and Representation	The scanf family of functions scans input according to a format as described below. This format may contain conversion specifiers; the results from such conversions, if any, are stored through the pointer arguments. The scanf function reads input from the standard input stream stdin, fscanf reads input from the stream pointer stream, and sscanf reads its input from the character string pointed to by str. The vulnerability of the scanf() function resides in the fact that it has no bounds-checking capability. If the string that is being accepted is longer than the buffer size, the characters will overflow into the adjoining memory space. This is a classic buffer overflow security vulnerability problem. The scanf() function is susceptible to buffer overflow.
vsnprintf	Input Validation and Representation	Many functions are susceptible to off-by-one and bounds-checking errors. There are many generic types of errors that can apply to usage of a wide variety of functions. These include: * Using a function that does not permit one to specify the size of a buffer to prevent overflows. * Mis-specifying the size of a buffer or the amount of data to be written. Off-by-one errors are common. * Failing to plan for correct behavior when input is larger than expected. * Failing to allow space for a terminating null character. * Failing to ensure that a terminating null character is present; many standard functions consistently experience this failure. * Specifying the size of a buffer or the amount of data to be transferred using incorrect units. This is particularly a problem with multibyte strings. On the Windows platform, these functions tend to include a "W" in the name. * Assuming the wrong semantics for a parameter that controls data transfer and prevents buffer overflows. Because various

API	Kingdom	Description
		functions use the buffer size, buffer size minus one, the remaining space in the buffer, etc., it is important to understand the bounding semantics for each function.
		Note that while some functions, such as `strcpy()`, are intrinsically dangerous, even the "safe" functions like `strncpy()` are still susceptible to subtle errors if bounds checks are not done properly.
`vsprintf`	Input Validation and Representation	The `sprintf` function is used to build strings by embedding format field specifiers in a string and having the data converted into the equivalent string form and then substituted for the specifier.
		`{v}sprintf()` is susceptible to buffer overflow if used improperly. Mark any instance of `vsprintf()` and `sprintf()` as vulnerabilities. Replace calls with `{v}snprintf()` or change the format string.
		Check the format string to see if it includes `"%.111s"` formatting limit.
`vsscanf`	Input Validation and Representation	The return result of `sprintf()` tells how many characters were actually written. If the number of chars is larger than the original buffer, that means memory has been overwritten and the program state is invalid.
		The `scanf` family of functions scans input according to a format as described below. This format may contain conversion specifiers; the results from such conversions, if any, are stored through the pointer arguments. The `scanf` function reads input from the standard input stream `stdin`, `fscanf` reads input from the stream pointer stream, and `sscanf` reads its input from the character string pointed to by `str`.
		The vulnerability of the `scanf()` function resides in the fact that it has no bounds-checking capability. If the string that is being accepted is longer than the buffer size, the characters will overflow into the adjoining memory space. This is a classic buffer overflow security vulnerability problem.
		The `scanf()` function is susceptible to buffer overflow.

API	Kingdom	Description
vswprintf	Input Validation and Representation	The printf family of functions is susceptible to a variety of format string and buffer overflow attacks. Flag any instance of the printf() family of functions in the code. Determine whether or not the format string is being provided through some input channel. If it is using a single argument, this is a definite vulnerability. Replace the code with the "fix" section.
		If the first argument is a string literal constant, this rule does not apply.
		If the first argument is a variable string, try to determine if it is user supplied. If so, it will be more difficult to determine whether it is vulnerable to the threat or not. If it is influenced by any data that comes into the current function, it should be flagged as a (potentially false positive) vulnerability.
		All of these functions have potential format string problems. Some (as marked) also have potential BO problems when they write their output to strings.
vwprintf	Input Validation and Representation	NON-CONSTANT FORMAT STRINGS can often be attacked.
wprintf	Input Validation and Representation	The printf family of functions is susceptible to a variety of format string and buffer overflow attacks. Flag any instance of the printf() family of functions in the code. Determine whether or not the format string is being provided through some input channel. If it is using a single argument, this is a definite vulnerability. Replace the code with the "fix" section.
		If the first argument is a string literal constant, this rule does not apply.
		If the first argument is a variable string, try to determine if it is user supplied. If so, it will be more difficult to determine whether it is vulnerable to the threat or not. If it is influenced by any data that comes into the current function, it should be flagged as a (potentially false positive) vulnerability.

API	Kingdom	Description
		All of these functions have potential format string problems. Some (as marked) also have potential BO problems when they write their output to strings.

As you can see by perusing this list, the kind of information that a simple tool gives back is valuable but not very useful as a large list. Using a tool to look for the myriad possible problems is really the only way to go.

Modern static analysis tools use much better techniques and much more thorough analyses than yesteryear's `grep`-based scanners like ITS4 and RATS. Nevertheless, the ruleset that was included in ITS4 is still applicable. The knowledge itself ages well. All static analysis tools should provide coverage on this basic ruleset. If your static analysis tool doesn't, you should get a new one.

Many more static analysis rules are available on the Building Security In portal from the U.S. Department of Homeland Security <http://buildsecurityin.us-cert.gov/portal/>.

Appendix C
An Exercise in Risk Analysis: Smurfware[1]

The following simple study can give you a flavor of what it is like to do an architectural risk analysis (see Chapter 5). Even though this example is beyond contrived, working through it (especially if you follow the process described in this book) is an excellent pedagogical tool. Try doing this exercise with a group. Drink some wine. And don't cheat!

SmurfWare SmurfScanner Risk Assessment Case Study

Instructions

This case study presents a real-world architecture and description of a software system. Please read through the description, look at the architecture diagram, and then answer the questions given. Thinking about how the system works (and how your understanding differs from someone else's) will frequently result in finding ways to break it.

SmurfWare SmurfScanner Architecture and Implementation Description

The Smurfs are developing a new biometric authentication device to keep non-Smurfs out of the Smurfland network. The biometric device is being dubbed the SmurfScanner by Papa Smurf. The SmurfScanner is a hardware device that scans a user's skin color for blueness. Since only Smurfs have that unique Saturday morning cartoon blue color, if the device can successfully identify the unique blue, then this will do for making a determination

---

[1]This exercise was developed by Michal Propieszalski and has been used at Cigital to teach architectural risk analysis for several years.

as to whether or not a person really is a Smurf (or at least we make this assumption for the purpose of this exercise, be it based in actual fact or not).

The SmurfScanner is attached to a PC running MicroSmurf Windoze XP via serial port. Along with an all-blue user manual and a blue SmurfWare coffee mug, the SmurfScanner comes with software that allows it to act as the login screen manager in Windoze. To even get to the login screen, a user's Smurfness has to be established by the SmurfScanner. Once calibrated by the manager application, the SmurfScanner returns whether or not a user is sufficiently blue. The software architecture of this system is represented by the diagram in Figure C–1. Each box represents a separate process running on either the PC or the hardware of the SmurfScanner device.

SmurfScanner Architecture Component Description

SmurfScanner Crypto Helper: Since actual authentication traffic between the scanner and the software has to be encrypted and integrity has to be ensured, the software package provides an API for making encrypted calls, such as `IsUserASmurf()`, to the SmurfScanner. The caller gets to decide whether to use the proprietary but extensively tested (by two Smurf crypto experts) Smurfcrypto library or the equally solid Microsmurf Windoze implementation of crypto. The Helper exists in both the PC and the SmurfScanner hardware to facilitate two-way integrity and privacy.

SmurfScanner Common Command Layer: The SmurfScanner formats higher-level API calls into a format that the serial driver can understand, be they encrypted or not.

SmurfScanner Manager: Since this application is rarely used, crypto was deemed unnecessary. Instead, the Smurfs hard-coded a hash of Smurfette's body weight in milligrams in both the SmurfScanner and the Embedded I/O Manager so that the SmurfScanner's Embedded I/O Manager would recognize that the privileged commands were coming from only the SmurfScanner Manager application. The Manager application appends this hash to every command sent to the scanner. The Smurfs chose this secret method because Smurfette's body weight is a well-known fact within the entire Smurf community but not known at all outside of it. The Manager application is used to set up the scanner's calibration and to run diagnostics in case it is malfunctioning. The scanner must be calibrated for local light conditions with a sample Smurf before use. The Manager is also used to ini-tialize the Helper apps on both the PC and the scanner with secrets to allow

SmurfWare SmurfScanner Architecture

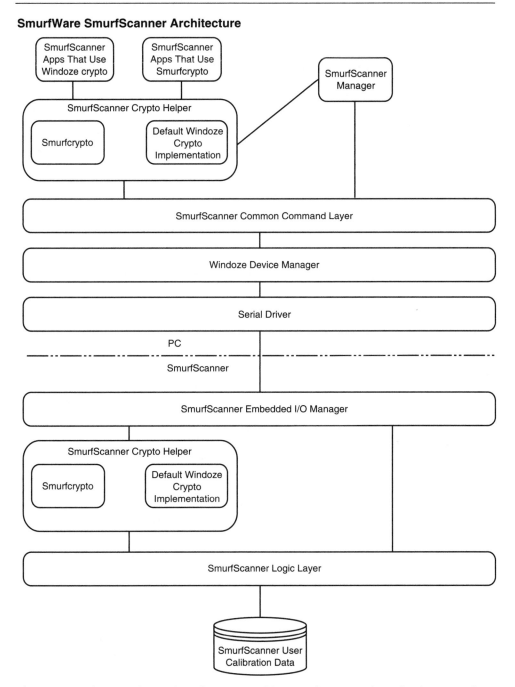

Figure C–1 The SmurfWare SmurfScanner architecture has a number of serious security flaws. Can you identify some?

the integrity and privacy functionality to work. The secrets are a hash of the system clock.

SmurfScanner Embedded I/O Manager: This app sorts encrypted versus unencrypted commands and forwards them to either the Helper or directly to the Logic Layer. Commands are sent directly to the Logic Layer when the I/O Manager recognizes the Smurfette body weight shared secret hash.

SmurfScanner Logic Layer: This layer takes the hardware measurement of a user's blueness and compares it to the calibrated value and returns a *yes* or *no,* thus performing authentication on a Smurf. The Logic Layer also does other things like calibrate the scanner based on data received from the Manager app, track usage, and run diagnostics.

SmurfScanner Business Application: It is critical to understand the business context in order to estimate impact (in such a way as to answer the "Who cares?" question). In this case, the SmurfScanner is being used to protect SmurfTunes from use by non-Smurfs. SmurfTunes is set up to deliver Saturday morning cartoon theme songs to SmurfPod personal digital listening devices.

Questions

1. What are the business goals and associated risks for the SmurfTunes system?
2. What goals could an attacker have in mind when thinking about attacking this system?
3. What are the implementation bugs and architectural flaws in this system that could be used for attack?
4. How can these technical problems be stated as risks (and then ranked)?
5. What ways could an attacker exploit technical weaknesses to achieve attack goals?
6. Given your answers to the preceding questions, list at least three risks posed by this software system and rank them starting with the greatest first.

Tons of extra credit for performing this exercise by following the risk analysis process from Chapter 5.

DO NOT CHEAT. Work out answers before you look at the ones I provide.

Answers

Some of the questions have more correct answers than the ones listed here.

1. What are the business goals and associated risks for the SmurfTunes system?

    Provide digital Saturday morning cartoon music with Smurfs only.
    Loss of digital IP (value).
    Provide music on demand.
    Store and retrieve essential Smurf theme song data.

2. What goals could an attacker have in mind when thinking about attacking this system?

    Theft of Saturday morning cartoon music.
    Determine what others are listening to.
    Cause a certain song to become a "hit."
    Substitute theme song from the *Brady Bunch* for the Smurf theme song.
    Deny service to all SmurfTunes.

3. What are the implementation bugs and architectural flaws in this system that could be used for attack?

    SmurfScanner Manager and the I/O Manager use a hard-coded shared secret that has low entropy and could be reverse-engineered. SmurfScanner Manager commands are not protected from tampering since they use no encryption. The Manager seeds the helper apps with low-entropy system clock output.
    The software components in the system don't authenticate with each other, hence it would be easy for an attacker to substitute a malicious component on the PC side.
    The Smurfcrypto is roll-your-own crypto, which is weak, and an attacker app can choose which crypto to use.
    The SmurfScanner Common Command Layer does not authenticate calls made to it, hence it provides an effective and easy means to a denial-of-service attack.

4. How can these technical problems be stated as risks (and then ranked)?

    Left as an exercise for the reader. Think about the business goals and risks you already identified.

5. What ways could an attacker exploit technical weaknesses to achieve attack goals?

    Denial of service using Common Command Layer functionality.

Recalibration of the scanner to allow the evil "Red Smurfs" onto the network through reverse-engineering the Manager's secret and recalibrating the scanner on the fly.

Substitution of a software component and sniffing to steal usage data. Guessing of the secret seed input to facilitate theft of encrypted data. One could also use this method to make the device return the wrong outputs and hence cause problems for legit Smurf users.

6. Given your answers to the preceding questions, list at least three risks posed by this software system and rank them starting with the greatest first.

Again, left as an exercise for the reader. This answer depends on your ranking.

SmurfWare SmurfScanner Design for Security

Instructions

Given your answers from the SmurfScanner Risk Assessment, draw a new software architecture diagram for the SmurfScanner system that mitigates the risk. Also, list the other things you could do to secure the application.

Answers (Incomplete)

The various processes should only accept commands from the other processes explicitly shown in the diagram. Each piece of software should be signed by SmurfWare, and this signature should be used to verify the caller.

- SmurfScanner Manager communications should be encrypted.
- There should be only one solid crypto implementation in the solution.
- The first time the device is used, the password for the Manager-level functions should be set by the Manager app. The password should be used from that point on. The hard-coded shared secret should be eliminated.
- The Crypto Helper should be seeded with something more entropic, such as mouse movements, not the system clock.
- A sample fixed architecture is depicted in Figure C–2.

SmurfWare SmurfScanner Architecture Fixed

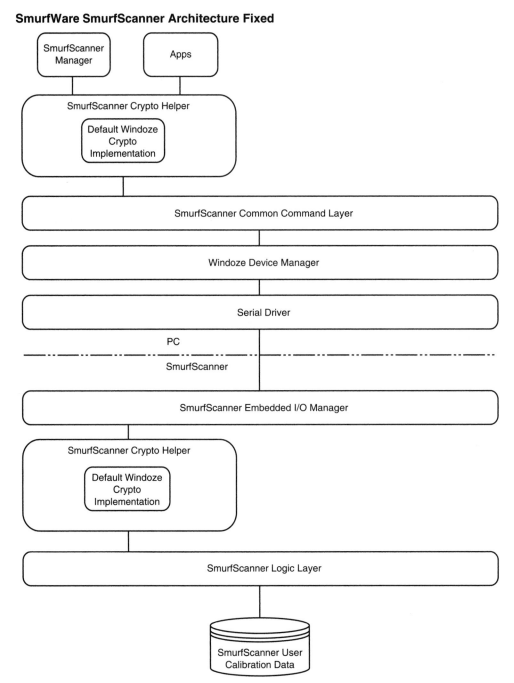

Figure C–2 The SmurfWare SmurfScanner architecture with some adjustments for security. Not all possible fixes are shown in this picture, but many of the most critical ones are.

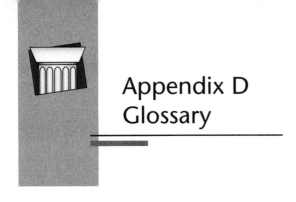

Appendix D
Glossary

A number of terms in this book are used very loosely out there in the world. I provide this small glossary to pin things down a bit more.

Artifact (*especially*, software artifact)—Those documents and objects created in the course of building software. The touchpoints in this book are software security best practices meant to be applied to common software artifacts including requirements, use cases, design documents, architecture documents, test plans, test results, code, executables, and feedback from the field.

Attack pattern—Like a design pattern, only applicable to attacks. A high-level description of a set of software attacks. See Chapter 8.

Bug—A bug is an implementation-level software problem. Bugs may exist in code but never be executed. Though the term *bug* is applied quite generally by many software practitioners, I reserve use of the term to encompass fairly simple implementation errors. Bugs are implementation-level problems that can be easily discovered and remedied. See Chapter 1.

COTS—Commercial off-the-shelf software.

Defect—Both implementation vulnerabilities and design vulnerabilities are defects. A defect is a problem that may lie dormant in software for years only to surface in a fielded system with major consequence.

Exploit—A script or plan that executes against a vulnerability, leading to security compromise.

Flaw—A design-level or architectural software defect. High-level defects cause 50% of software security problems. See Chapter 1.

Risk—Flaws and bugs lead to risk. Risks are not failures. Risks capture the probability that a flaw or a bug will impact the purpose of the software (i.e., risk = probability × impact). Risk measures must also take into account the potential damage that can occur. A very high risk is not only likely to happen but also likely to cause great harm. Risks can be managed by technical and non-technical means. See Chapter 1.

Software security—The idea of engineering software so that it continues to function correctly under malicious attack.

SDL—Secure Development Lifecycle.

SDLC—Software development lifecycle.

Threat—The actor or agent who is the source of danger. Within information security, this is invariably the danger posed by a malicious agent (e.g., fraudster, attacker, malicious hacker) for a variety of motivations (e.g., financial gain, prestige). Threats carry out attacks on the security of the system (e.g., SQL injection, TCP/IP SYN attacks, buffer overflows, denial of service). Unfortunately, Microsoft has been misusing the term *threat* as a substitute for *risk*. This has led to some confusion in the commercial security space. See Chapter 5.

Touchpoint—Process-agnostic software security best practice applied on a software artifact.

Vulnerability—A defect or weakness in system security procedures, design, implementation, or internal controls that can be exercised and result in a security breach or a violation of security policy. A vulnerability may exist in one or more of the components making up a system. See Chapter 5.

Index

Additional Software Security Titles
from Addison-Wesley

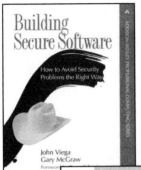

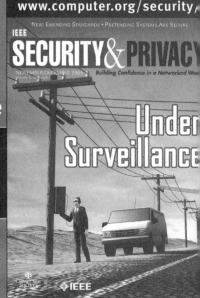

BOOKS ONLINE

ENABLED

THIS BOOK IS SAFARI ENABLED

INCLUDES FREE 45-DAY ACCESS TO THE ONLINE EDITION

The Safari® Enabled icon on the cover of your favorite technology book means the book is available through Safari Bookshelf. When you buy this book, you get free access to the online edition for 45 days.

Safari Bookshelf is an electronic reference library that lets you easily search thousands of technical books, find code samples, download chapters, and access technical information whenever and wherever you need it.

TO GAIN 45-DAY SAFARI ENABLED ACCESS TO THIS BOOK:

● Go to **http://www.awprofessional.com/safarienabled**

● Complete the brief registration form

● Enter the coupon code found in the front of this book on the "Copyright" page

If you have difficulty registering on Safari Bookshelf or accessing the online edition, please e-mail customer-service@safaribooksonline.com.

More information and updates are available at:
http://www.awprofessional.com/

System requirements:
Web/internet connection

Memory Requirement
Fortify recommends using a high-end Pentium processor or equivalent with at least 1 GB of RAM.

Operating Systems
The following operating systems are supported.

Windows:	Windows 2000, Pro, Server, Advanced Server, and Datacenter
	Windows XP, Home and Pro Editions
	Windows 2003, Standard, Web, and Enterprise Editions
Linux:	Red Hat Linux 9
	Red Hat Enterprise Linux ES 2.1 and 3.0
Solaris:	Solaris 8
Macintosh:	MacOSX 10.3
IBM AIX:	AIX 5.3

Supported Browsers
The following browsers are supported:
Mozilla 1.5 or later
Firefox 0.9 or later
Internet Explorer 6 (Windows only)
Internet Explorer 5 for Macintosh (Macintosh only)

Note: On Unix operating systems a Web browser must be specified in the path in order for the installation to complete succesfully.

Version: Fortify Source Code Analysis Suite 3.1.1—Demonstration Edition
Date: 09/23/2005